Manchester Medieval Sources Series

series advisers Rosemary Horrox and Simon MacLean

This series aims to meet a growing need amongst students and teachers of medieval history for translations of key sources that are directly usable in students' own work. It provides texts central to medieval studies courses and focuses upon the diverse cultural and social as well as political conditions that affected the functioning of all levels of medieval society. The basic premise of the new series is that translations must be accompanied by sufficient introductory and explanatory material and each volume therefore includes a comprehensive guide to the sources' interpretation, including discussion of critical linguistic problems and an assessment of the most recent research on the topics being covered.

also available in the series

THE REIGN OF RICHARD II

Manchester University Press

MedievalSources*online*

Complementing the printed editions of the Medieval Sources series, Manchester University Press has developed a web-based learning resource which is now available on a yearly subscription basis.

Medieval Sources*online* brings quality history source material to the desktops of students and teachers and allows them open and unrestricted access throughout the entire college or university campus. Designed to be fully integrated with academic courses, this is a one-stop answer for many medieval history students, academics and researchers keeping thousands of pages of source material 'in print' over the Internet for research and teaching.

titles available now at MedievalSources*online include*

Trevor Dean *The towns of Italy in the later Middle Ages*

John Edwards *The Jews in Western Europe, 1400–1600*

Paul Fouracre and Richard A. Gerberding *Late Merovingian France: History and hagiography 640–720*

Chris Given-Wilson *Chronicles of the Revolution 1397–1400: The reign of Richard II*

P. J. P. Goldberg *Women in England, c. 1275–1525*

Janet Hamilton and Bernard Hamilton *Christian dualist heresies in the Byzantine world, c. 650–c. 1450*

Rosemary Horrox *The Black Death*

David Jones *Friars' Tales: Thirteenth-century exempla from the British Isles*

Graham A. Loud and Thomas Wiedemann *The history of the tyrants of Sicily by 'Hugo Falcandus', 1153–69*

Simon MacLean *History and politics in late Carolingian and Ottonian Europe: The* Chronicle *of Regino of Prüm and Adalbert of Magdeburg*

Anthony Musson with Edward Powell *Crime, law and society in the later Middle Ages*

Janet L. Nelson *The Annals of St-Bertin: Ninth-century histories, volume I*

Timothy Reuter *The Annals of Fulda: Ninth-century histories, volume II*

R. N. Swanson *Catholic England: Faith, religion and observance before the Reformation*

Elisabeth van Houts *The Normans in Europe*

Jennifer Ward *Women of the English nobility and gentry 1066–1500*

Visit the site at *www.medievalsources.co.uk* for further information and subscription prices.

THE REIGN OF RICHARD II

From minority to tyranny 1377–97

selected sources translated and annotated
by Alison K. McHardy

Manchester University Press
Manchester and New York

distributed exclusively in the USA by Palgrave Macmillan

Published by Manchester University Press
Oxford Road, Manchester M13 9NR, UK
and Room 400, 175 Fifth Avenue, New York, NY 10010, USA
www.manchesteruniversitypress.co.uk

Distributed exclusively in the USA by
Palgrave Macmillan, 175 Fifth Avenue, New York, NY 10010, USA

Distributed exclusively in Canada by
UBC Press, University of British Columbia, 2029 West Mall,
Vancouver, BC, Canada V6T 1Z2

British Library Cataloguing-in-Publication Data
A catalogue record for this book is available from the British Library

Library of Congress Cataloging-in-Publication Data applied for

ISBN   978 0 7190 3852 5 *hardback*
        978 0 7190 3853 2 *paperback*

First published 2012

Typeset in Monotype Bell
by Koinonia, Manchester
Printed in Great Britain
by Bell & Bain Ltd, Glasgow

For Bob Leeming

For loving support during more than thirty years

CONTENTS

91. The questions to the judges 177
    (a) The Statute of Treason, 1352 177
    (b) The questions to the judges, Nottingham, August 1387 178
92. Rising political tension 181
    (a) According to Walsingham 181
    (b) Reported by the *Eulogium* 183
93. Unrest in London: an illegal fraternity 184
94. Richard seeks papal excommunication of those challenging his
    authority, c. August 185
95. The appeals of treason 186
    (a) The first appeal, 14 November 1387 187
    (b) Both sides seek support 188
    (c) Another account of events of November 1387 190
    (d) The second appeal, 17 November 1387 191
96. The growing crisis, from London records 192
    (a) Proclamation made in the city by the king's command 192
    (b) The king orders investigation of disloyalty in London 192

The Radcot Bridge campaign
97. Two views of the crisis from the west midlands 193
    (a) By a monastic observer 193
    (b) By a clerk of the bishop of Worcester 194
98. Four further accounts of the fighting 197
    (a) Walsingham: a preliminary encounter 197
    (b) *Westminster*: probably from a follower of Arundel 198
    (c) Knighton: the fight at Radcot Bridge 200
    (d) The victors' summary of the campaign 201
99. Brembre tries to hold London for the king 202
100. After the battle 203
101. An attempt at mediation 205
102. An alleged deposition of Richard during the winter of 1387–8 206
103. Robert de Vere in exile 207

III: The rule and fall of the Appellants, 1388–89 208
104. Power passes from the king 208

The 'merciless' parliament, 1388
105. Two short accounts of the parliament: 210
    (a) According to Walsingham 210
    (b) According to the *Eulogium* 211

The first session of parliament, 3 February–20 March
106. The opening, and protestations of loyalty, 3 February 212
    (a) According to *Westminster* 212
    (b) According to Favent 212
107. Proceedings against the five accused 213
    (a) Legal arguments and protestations, 4 February 214
    (b) Selected charges against the accused 216

MAPS

ABBREVIATIONS

Anon. Chron.	*The Anonimalle Chronicle 1331 to 1381*, ed. V. H. Galbraith (Manchester, 1927)
BIHR	*Bulletin of the Institute of Historical Research*
CCR	*Calendar of Close Rolls, 1385–9, 1389–92* (HMSO, 1921, 1922)
CPR	*Calendar of Patent Rolls, 1374–76, 1377–81, 1385–9, 1391–6* (HMSO, 1916, 1895–1909)
CR	*Chronicles of the Revolution 1397–1400*, trans. C. Given-Wilson (Manchester, 1993)
EHR	*English Historical Review*
Eulogium	*Eulogium Historiarum sive Temporis: Continuatio Eulogii*, ed. F. S. Haydon, vol. III (RS, 9, 1863)
Favent, *Wonderful Parliament*	Thomas Favent, *Historia sive Narracio de modo et forma mirabilis Parliamenti*, ed. May McKisack (Camden Society 3rd series, xxxvii, 1926: Camden Miscellany xiv)
Froissart, *Chronicles*	Jean Froissart, *Chronicles of England, France, Spain and the Adjoining Countries*, trans. Thomas Johnes, 2 vols. (London, 1839)
HBC	E. B. Fryde, D. E. Greenway, S. Porter and I. Roy, *Handbook of British Chronology*, 3rd edn (London, 1986)
KC	*Knighton's Chronicle 1337–1396*, ed. and trans. G. H. Martin (Oxford, 1995)
ODNB	*Oxford Dictionary of National Biography* (online edition)
PROME	*The Parliament Rolls of Medieval England*, ed. C. Given-Wilson *et al.* (Leicester, 2005), CD-ROM version: cited by date, with the parliament indicated when necessary, and by section number
Riley, *Memorials of London*	H. T. Riley, *Memorials of London and London Life in the XIII, XIV and XV Centuries* (London, 1868)
RP	*Rotuli Parliamentorum*, ed. J. Strachey *et al.*, 6 vols. (London, 1767–77)
RS	Rolls Series
Rymer, *Foedera*	*Feodera, Conventiones, Litterae*, ed. Thomas Rymer

SAC I   *The St. Albans Chronicle, volume I,1376–1394: The Chronica*
               Maiora of Thomas Walsingham, ed. and trans. J. Taylor,
               W. R. Childs and L. Watkiss (Oxford, 2003)

SAC II   *The St. Albans Chronicle, volume II, 1394–1422: The*
               Chronica Maiora of Thomas Walsingham, ed. and trans. J.
               Taylor, W. R. Childs and L. Watkiss (Oxford, 2011)

Saul   Nigel Saul, *Richard II* (New Haven CT and London,
               1997)

SR   *Statutes of the Realm*, 11 vols. (Record Commission,
               1810–28)

TNA   The National Archives, Kew

TRHS   *Transactions of the Royal Historical Society*

VR   *Historia Vitae et Regni Ricardi Secundi*, ed. G. B. Stow jr
               (Pennsylvania, 1977)

WC   *The Westminster Chronicle 1381–1394*, ed. and trans.
               L. C. Hector and B. F. Harvey (Oxford, 1982)

NOTES ON THE TRANSLATIONS

All the translations from French, Anglo-Norman, Latin and Middle English are my own, except where otherwise stated. In the case of the Oxford Medieval Text editions, this fact is indicated by reference to the Latin texts, which are printed on the even-numbered pages. 'You are asked, then, to read with sympathetic attention, and to make allowances wherever you think that, in spite of all the devoted work that has been put into the translation, some of the expressions I have used are inadequate'.[1] The use of [*square*] brackets indicates editorial additions. I have used words in *italics* within round brackets *(parentheses)* to give words in the original language where these are especially significant, or where the original words posed particular problems.

Money

The English currency was based on the pound (£), divided into twenty shillings (s.), each containing twelve pennies (d.). Other amounts, used in accounting, were the groat, worth 4d., the mark, which was worth 13s. 4d. (two-thirds of a £), and the half mark, 6s. 8d.

Dates

The dates indicated in brackets are the days on which the action named in the document was to take place. For example 'twelve days from the Nativity of the Blessed Virgin Mary' is shown as [*19 September*], because the feast occurs on 8 September, and the twelve days were calculated as being on that day and the eleven following. Years are taken to begin on 1 January, though the year then officially began on 25 March.

---

1 Preface to *Ecclesiasticus*, The Revised English Bible.

PREFACE

This is the long-awaited prequel to Chris Given-Wilson's *Chronicles of the Revolution, 1397–1400*. Richard II's reign has rightly been called 'the perfect special subject' and it is hoped that this volume will join that book in providing students with the guidance they need in approaching this fascinating period, and its rich documentation, for the first time. I am very conscious that this collection is focused narrowly on the politics of the reign, and is not a complete portrait of the period. In particular, I am painfully aware of the almost total exclusion of any reference to church history. In crown–church relations there was important anti-papal legislation, while this was an exciting time for religious controversy and popular religion. The lack of coverage of the lollard movement is something I much regret, and can only plead a shortage of space, in mitigation.

A. K. McHardy

ACKNOWLEDGEMENTS

My most pleasant task is to acknowledge the many debts I have incurred during this book's long gestation. Caroline Barron gave me useful practical help as I embarked on the teaching of my Richard II Special Subject, and the enthusiastic recruitment by Gwilym Dodd, my successor at Nottingham, reassures me of the enduring appeal which this reign has for students. The support and approval of Jinty Nelson was invaluable at points when my courage was failing, as was Mark Ormrod's encouragement.

Help and information on specific matters were kindly provided by David Green, Anne Hudson, Maureen Jurkowski, Helen Phillips, John Post, Nigel Saul, George Stow, Rob Wheeler and James Willoughby. Wendy Childs has been exceedingly generous. Dorothy Johnston, a friend and colleague for thirty-five years in two universities, has most generously shared with me her unrivalled knowledge of Richard II's dealings with Ireland; her sessions on this subject with my classes were always the high point of the course. Michael Jones, whom I have known for even longer, has always put his unique knowledge of fourteenth-century Brittany at my disposal. At a late stage in the work he kindly cast his learned eye over some tricky passages of Anglo-Norman. Hilary Walter has nobly helped me with passages of Latin which I *knew* I could not unravel; I *thought* I could do the rest; and Alan Wilson, the Rolls-Royce of computer consultants, rescued me from many a tricky technical situation. As I was finishing this book news came of the death of Barbara M. Wilson, my 'A' level history teacher, who prepared me so well for university learning, and whose own lifelong devotion to historical research was such a fine example. My greatest debt, however, is to Mr Duncan Harriss FRCS, whose swift and skilful ministrations ensured that I survived to complete this project.

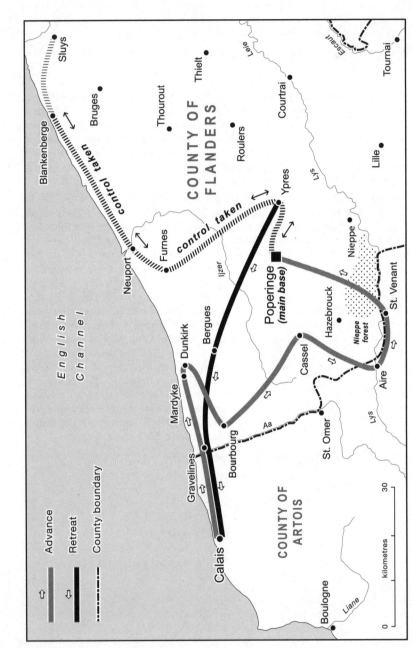

Map 1 The Norwich 'crusade', 1383

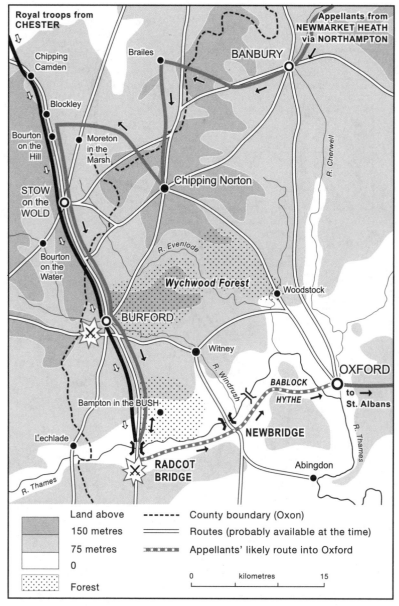

Map 2 The Radcot Bridge campaign, 1387

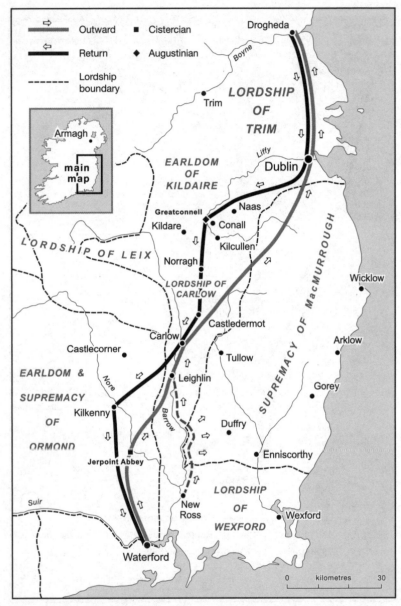

Map 3 Richard II and Ireland, 1394–5

INTRODUCTION

As Edward III lay dying in the summer of 1377, the nation's mood was anxious and sombre; Edward had ascended the throne early in 1327, so very few of his subjects could remember a time when he was not their king. During his fifty-year reign Edward had restored the prestige and glamour of crown and court at home and abroad, defeated the Scots and humiliated the French. Though his later years had been less successful, people were sad at his passing and fearful for the future.[1] The feeling that a golden age came to an end in 1377 was to haunt Richard for years [62, 82a, 84].[2]

Sorrow at the king's death was compounded by the fact that his eldest son, Edward of Woodstock, the prince of Wales, had predeceased him [1]. This successful soldier, known to posterity as the Black Prince, won a series of battles in France and Spain, married for love his kinswoman the beautiful widow Joan of Kent, went to learn the art of government by acting as his father's representative in Gascony,[3] and fathered two sons. Richard, the younger, was born at Bordeaux on Wednesday 6 January 1367. Four days later his father led an army from Bordeaux towards Spain.[4] Then everything started to go wrong: the prince returned from this Spanish campaign in poor health, and in 1371 his own firstborn, the seven-year-old Edward of Angoulême, died. Later that year the sick prince, his widow and their surviving son returned to England and settled at the royal manor of Langley in Hertfordshire, though Prince Edward actually died at Westminster on 8 June 1376.[5] Richard II was thus unusual in being the first king since Henry II (1154–89) who was not himself the son of a king of England, nor was brought up at court. Richard, therefore, had no male role model to show him how a king, or even a king's heir, should conduct himself.

---

1 The mood was captured in poetry, Dobson (1983): 88–91.

2 Numbers in **bold** type [within brackets] refer throughout to the translated sources in this book.

3 The names Gascony, Aquitaine and Guyenne will be treated as interchangeable in this volume.

4 Froissart, *Chronicles*, Book 1, chap. 236.

5 On his illness, see Green (2009): 34–51.

At his grandfather's death Richard was ten years old. To sadness at the old king's passing was added the anxiety of the political community as it pondered three questions: who would succeed Edward III [2, 3], who would govern during Richard's minority [11, 13] and what would happen if Richard himself did not survive to father an heir? [5] The precedents for solving these problems were distant: over the succession, it was the contest between the adult Prince John and his nephew Arthur in 1199; the last royal minority was that of Henry III (acceded 1216); and since Henry I's death in 1135 every king except Richard I (died 1199) had left a legitimate son to succeed him.[6]

Edward III's second son to survive to adulthood was Lionel of Antwerp (born 1338), who was married in childhood to Elizabeth de Burgh, heiress to the earldom of Ulster. Lionel died in 1368, leaving a daughter, Philippa, who married the earl of March. Some thought that the earl of March, who was a popular figure in the late 1370s, had a claim to the throne in right of his wife, while their son, Roger Mortimer, fourth earl of March, was to be widely regarded as Richard's heir [3, 89].

Edward III's next surviving son was John of Gaunt, born 1340, styled duke of Lancaster from 1361.[7] Gaunt had many assets: he was a healthy adult, already twice married and the father of four legitimate children; he had considerable experience in war, home politics and international affairs; and, through his first marriage to Blanche, heiress of Henry of Lancaster, he had become the king's wealthiest subject. Finally, and most importantly, all the evidence suggested that Gaunt had enormous respect for, and loyalty to, the English crown, whoever was king.

Against these advantages Gaunt had a number of failings which made him unpopular during the last years of his father's reign and which would prevent him from being regent – a position for which he was the obvious choice – during his nephew's minority. He was seen as a supporter of corrupt and greedy courtiers, and an enemy of patriotic critics of those mismanaging the war effort and domestic administration in his father's last years. His haughty manner was also a handicap, along with his inability to envisage the effect of this, and of his actions, upon others. His military record was undistinguished. Towards the end of his father's reign he became embroiled with leading Londoners because of his perceived threat to the rights and independence of the city, which explains the city's anxiety to curry favour with the new king [6, 7, 8].

6 Richard I was succeeded by his brother John.

7 Goodman (1994).

Gaunt was also the patron of John Wycliffe whom he supported very publicly when this controversial and finally heretical Oxford scholar was summoned before the archbishop of Canterbury and the bishop of London in 1377 [7]. Another cause of scandal was his private life; in 1368 the duchess Blanche died and in 1371 Gaunt married Constance of Castile and assumed the title 'king of Castile' thereafter. The new duchess of Lancaster suffered the humiliation of her husband's public liaison with Katherine Swynford, a lady of the ducal household, which provoked critical comment [16]. In the new reign he proved quarrelsome [43, 45]. Gaunt was not without admirers [44] but all these circumstances combined to disqualify him from becoming regent at a time when a unifying figure was needed.

Two further sons of Edward III were still alive in 1377. Edmund of Langley (born 1341) took part in several campaigns in the years 1369–74, became duke of York in 1385 and was the chief commissioner to negotiate Richard's first marriage, but he played no significant role in the politics of the reign. Despite his eminent social position, Langley seems rarely to have held an opinion recorded by contemporaries and showed little military skill; his expedition to Portugal in 1381–2 achieved nothing.[8] His wife Isabel, younger sister of Constance of Castile, was perhaps selected by his father or elder brother. In 1399 he proved ineffective as a defender of the realm, though by then he was elderly and perhaps crippled by arthritis. Like his younger brother, Edmund lacked any landed endowment and had to make do with exchequer annuities, which were not always promptly paid [133a] but, unlike Thomas, he seems to have borne no grudge against Richard for the failure to grant him a landed income appropriate to his status. He was loyal and conscientious during our period [154b]. His nature may have been easy-going, even lazy; his wife certainly found him dull.[9]

Thomas of Woodstock, Edward III's youngest son, was very different. Born in 1355, he was too young to have shared in his brothers' chances of military glory; when he came to choosing a wife, his father was too senile to help him. Though Thomas married Eleanor, a daughter and co-heiress of the Bohun family, he was unable to prevent Gaunt's heir Henry Bolingbroke from marrying her sister Mary and thus sharing the Bohun inheritance. Thomas of Woodstock was created earl of

8 See Russell (1955): chap. xiv; Lopes (1989): 63–4, 69–70, 75–6; Froissart I, chaps. 72, 80, 84–5, 100–102.

9 Cockayne, *Complete Peerage* XII pt 2, 895–9. Cf. Biggs (1994): 253–72, for a more favourable assessment.

Buckingham in 1377 and duke of Gloucester – the title by which he is
best known – in 1385. Like Edmund, Thomas was forced to rely heavily
upon exchequer annuities to support his status [**24**] but, unlike him,
he became embittered and combative. It could be argued that Richard's
failure to provide a suitably substantial landed endowment for his
youngest uncle lay at the root of Gloucester's aggressive attitude, both
in domestic policy and in foreign affairs.[10]

The new king's mother – Princess Joan, Edward of Woodstock's widow
– was of royal blood, being, like Edward III, a grandchild of Edward I.
She had previously been married to Sir Thomas Holand and was also
the mother of Richard's two much older half-brothers, Thomas and
John, and two daughters. Once a girl of great beauty and allure [**150**],
she acquired a reputation for stylish and extravagant living while in
France with Prince Edward. On their return to England it is possible
that his illness gave her extra importance in public affairs, but there is
no evidence to prove that she wielded political power except a petition
from the prior of Coventry addressed to 'the council and the king's
mother', sometime between 1377 and her death in 1385.[11]

The problems facing the government in 1377

The government of the young king had immediately to find a way of
running the country while Richard was too young to act for himself.
Gaunt, the obvious choice as regent, was considered unsuitable [**8,
11**], so the fiction was adopted that the king was actually governing.
In practice the daily work of administration was done by a continual
council [**12, 13**] whose composition reflected the bitterness caused by
the political disputes of the previous eighteen months.[12]

The domestic political situation would not have been so tense and bitter
had it not been for the problems which had arisen from the conduct
of foreign warfare. In 1377 England was fighting a number of wars,
and their course was strongly to influence politics at home. First
in importance was the war with France. Begun in 1337, it brought
England military glory for over twenty years. In 1360, by a peace treaty
concluded at Bretigny, the English king agreed to give up his claim to

10 McHardy (1989): 284–6.
11 TNA, Ancient Petitions, SC 8/209/10448.
12 Lewis (1926): 246–51.

the French crown, and France would renounce sovereignty over the English-held duchy of Aquitaine and other territories. But neither side ratified these terms, so Edward III and Richard II continued to style themselves kings of France, while the French retained the lands they had agreed to cede.

When fighting was resumed in 1369 the English were not nearly so successful as they had been in the 1340s and 1350s; the king was failing in health and judgement, and their great commanders were either incapacitated or dead. The French, by contrast, were now led by Charles V (1364–80), a politically astute king with a talent for picking able generals. The cross-Channel reasons for the French resurgence were not apparent to the English, who were quick to blame failure in war entirely on the incompetence, corruption or even treachery of their own military leaders and courtiers [**16, 62c, 78, 80c, 82a–b**]. But there was another element also; for over forty years the English had been petitioning God for success in war, in prayers which stressed the link between moral virtue and military victory, and their prayers had mostly been answered. Now, after 1369, divine favour appeared to be withdrawn. We cannot understand the politics of Richard's reign unless we recognise the bitterness, puzzlement and hurt with which the political nation viewed English failures in the French war, and a natural wish to find scapegoats for this decline.[13] Neither Richard nor any of those exercising power on his behalf were ever able to resolve the French problem; they could neither win outright victory nor negotiate an honourable peace. Richard's failure to prosecute a successful continental war underlay much of the political friction of his reign. The amount of space devoted to foreign wars by chroniclers in this reign is relatively modest, but feelings were freely expressed by all the political nation [**16**]; this was a subject on which everyone had an opinion, but few had accurate information.

France was not the only enemy. By 1377 the Anglo-French conflict had become linked to several other wars; these added further complications to attempts to end the Anglo-French conflict through diplomacy. The oldest of these wars was with Scotland. By 1377 Scots had been fighting the English for eighty years in order to gain and keep their independence, and since 1295 they had been allied with France. The danger of England having to fight a war on two fronts was shown during Edward III's reign, and became very evident during Richard's too [**31, 69a–c**].

13 McHardy (2001b): 181–2.

Full-scale invasions were only part of the problem; the nature of the terrain meant that the border – whose very position was uncertain – was impossible to defend, and northern society had evolved its own ways of dealing with cross-border contacts, both peaceful and violent.[14] The pattern of warfare before 1377 was that the English won most major battles (except Bannockburn, 1314) but the Scots were better at gradual wars of attrition. This was especially so from 1369 when the Scots began to recover the lands which Edward III had previously conquered. This pattern of success was continued for the next two decades. Edward III's death, shortly before the Anglo-Scottish truce was due to expire, prompted a rise in Scots' aggression [11].

The king of Scots at Richard's accession was Robert II (r. 1371–90). The first Stewart king was fifty-five when he came to the throne and was in poor health throughout his reign; his successor Robert III (r. 1390–1406)[15] was fifty-three at his accession and was also physically infirm and politically weak. Yet the Scots were more militarily successful than the English throughout Richard's reign, and Scottish border magnates like the earls of Douglas, who were allied to Robert II's heir, pursued an aggressive and successful path in the 1370s and 1380s.[16]

Edward III and Richard had two handicaps in dealing with Scotland: Scottish warfare was less attractive than fighting in France, offering less prestige and lower financial rewards in worse weather; and the great distance from Westminster to the northern marches posed logistical problems. These two circumstances meant that English kings had to rely greatly upon leading northern families to organise defence. Edward III's relations with marcher magnates were good; his grandson was less sensitive [128a–b], with ultimately fatal consequences.

England had also become embroiled in two dynastic struggles in continental Europe: in Brittany and Castile. The independent duchy of Brittany was a state which neither England nor France could ignore. It lay adjacent to the political heartland of the French kingdom and was crucially situated for control of shipping between Gascony and England. The Breton problem had complicated Anglo-French relations since 1341 when Duke John III died leaving no legitimate children.[17]

---

14 Nevill (1998).
15 Formerly John, earl of Carrick.
16 Boardman (1997); Macdonald (2000).
17 Jones (1970) is indispensable.

Two of his relatives then claimed the duchy, his half-brother John de Montfort and his niece Joan de Penthièvre. In the ensuing civil war both sides appealed for, and received, outside help: John turned to Edward III, while Joan was supported by Philip VI of France whose nephew, Charles de Blois, she had married. In 1345 Montfort died leaving his wife and young son as refugees in England, and Edward III, as the boy's guardian, carried on the war on his ward's behalf. John IV, duke of Brittany 1364–99, grew up in England and married Joan Holand, Richard II's half-sister in 1366. Some years later he recovered the extensive lands of the earldom of Richmond which had been held by the counts and dukes of Brittany since the twelfth century.[18]

Brittany remained a running sore, though at times it looked as though the English side would be victorious. In 1347 an English force captured Charles de Blois in battle; in 1353 Edward III recognised Blois as duke and appeared to abandon Montfort; in 1358 Edward was able to insist that the duchy's sovereignty would remain with England whichever side in the ducal contest eventually triumphed. The English had established a military and administrative presence in western Brittany where control of ports, especially Brest, was crucial to their interests [14]. Any duke of Brittany had to balance competing considerations. If French influence was too strong, the Breton nationalist element in his duchy, mainly in the west, turned against him, he risked attacks from England and he was deprived of the lucrative English lands he held as earl of Richmond [133b]. If English influence grew strong, the pro-French among his subjects became restive and he risked full-scale invasion from France. Caught between two great powers the duke's situation was difficult, though he was sometimes able to mediate between them [56, 58].

A further area of conflict lay in the Iberian peninsula, where England had a long-standing interest because of its strategic importance to Gascony. Here too, dynastic disputes became enmeshed with the Anglo-French conflict. The largest Spanish kingdom was Castile. The story of the Castilian royal family in the fourteenth century was colourful and dramatic;[19] when Alfonso XI died in 1350, his legitimate son Pedro was challenged by his illegitimate son Henry (Enrique) of Trastamara. Both sides received support from abroad, for, apart from strategic considerations, Castile was an attractive ally because of her naval power, the

---

18 He held the lands and title 1372–84, 1398–9, *HBC*: 479.

19 Russell (1955): genealogy, 12.

greatest in Europe. France backed Henry, while England sided with
Pedro. Henry of Trastamara was cunning (it was his propaganda which
branded his half-brother Pedro 'the Cruel'), ruthless and determined in
his pursuit of the throne. Even the great English-led victory of Nájera
in 1367 could not save Pedro; the English later deserted him and he
was murdered by Henry in 1369. Pedro's interests descended to his
surviving children, his daughters Constance (Constanza) and Isabel(la),
who married sons of Edward III. From 1371 the head of the 'legiti-
mist' party in Castile was Constance's husband 'John king of Castile
and Leon' [4]: John of Gaunt, duke of Lancaster. Gaunt's Castilian
ambitions, not least his absences from England, had profound consequences for his nephew's reign.

A complication in Iberian affairs was the continuing tension between
Portugal and Castile. Considerable intermarriage between their
two ruling families[20] did not prevent Portuguese fears of a Castilian
takeover. The Portuguese royal family had also a colourful history at
this time – featuring murders and bastards – and by 1377 the court
of Fernando I (r. 1367–83) was awash with faction and intrigue. As
'patriotic' elements in Portuguese political society cast around for allies
against the Castilian threat, England (and Gaunt especially) was glad
to make an agreement which promised access to the second-best navy
in Europe, and offered support in his contest for the Castilian throne
[79].

Thus by the mid-1370s England was embroiled in wars from Scotland
to Spain and was losing all of them, as the territorial gains of the
1340s and 1350s were gradually lost. Dismay at England's recent
poor showing in the French war was closely linked to criticism of the
conduct of some courtiers who were seen as incompetent war leaders
and domestic profiteers. Among the unpopular courtiers was Alice
Perrers. This champion gold-digger had been the king's mistress since
1364, but it was only after Queen Philippa's death in 1369, after several
years of illness, that Alice came to public notice. Public anger against
those running the realm on behalf of the increasingly infirm king boiled
over in the summer of 1376; the 'good parliament', as it was soon called,
was a focus for many problems and was notable on several counts.[21]
This heroic, yet non-violent confrontation between rulers and ruled
lasted from 28 April until (probably) 10 July.

20 *Ibid*: 356.
21 Holmes (1975).

The chancellor's opening demand for a tax grant outraged the commons, and in their separate deliberations, held in the chapter house of Westminster Abbey, they resolved to press charges against individuals whom they held responsible for the country's ills, especially William, Lord Latimer (the king's chamberlain), Alice Perrers and four leading London merchants, of whom Richard Lyons was regarded as the worst. Latimer and Lyons had conspired together to defraud the king by such devices as selling licences to evade the regulations for exporting wool; Latimer was also alleged to have relinquished two foreign fortresses for money.[22] Perrers was accused of receiving grants worth £2,000 or £3,000 a year from the crown and of taking bribes to pervert the course of justice, while all the Londoners, but especially Lyons, had used their financial power to fleece the crown by such methods as advancing loans at injurious rates of interest, and by buying up its old debts very cheaply.

Two important constitutional developments resulted from this parliament. One was that, when the commons were asked who accused Latimer and the others, they replied, 'We all do'. This procedure, known as impeachment, was thus established as the way to bring unsatisfactory crown servants to account; the commons as a group made the accusation and the lords conducted the trial. The second important development occurred during the commons' separate deliberations. At the end of the first day the speeches were summarised so clearly by the MP for Herefordshire that the commons appointed him as their spokesman in future meetings with the lords and with Gaunt, who was deputising for the infirm Edward III. So Sir Peter de la Mare became the first known speaker of the commons. Sir Peter, who was the steward of the earl of March, proved a doughty fighter, who stood up against attempts to intimidate him by both the lords and John of Gaunt. Several of those accused were imprisoned, while Alice Perrers was driven from court. Some court officials were ousted and nine new councillors were appointed. And the king did not get the tax grant he wanted.

Yet much of the 'good' parliament's work was reversed during the next parliament, in January 1377, which annulled all its acts. This was mainly due to Gaunt, who was outraged at the commons' boldness, but there was probably a feeling that the 1376 parliament had gone too far in pursuing certain individuals upon insufficient evidence, especially Lord Latimer. So the imprisoned men were released, Alice

22 They were Bécherel (Brittany) and St Sauveur (Normandy).

Perrers returned to court, Sir Peter de la Mare was gaoled and the bishop of Winchester, William of Wykeham, who was seen by Gaunt as the hidden force behind the commons' demands, was accused of misconduct while chancellor (1367–71) and stripped of his temporalities. Yet Gaunt, in his turn, was felt to have overplayed his hand, and when Richard became king on 22 June 1377 political tensions were still strong, and the most senior member of the royal family was compromised by his leadership of one faction.

The story of the next twenty years has traditionally been told mainly through chronicles written in religious houses mostly in the south of England or the midlands: St Albans, Westminster, Canterbury, Leicester and Evesham. Whole scholar-lifetimes have been spent studying these texts, and controversy still surrounds some of them. But these are not the only sources of information at the historian's disposal. In casting a net widely over a variety of evidence I have been trying not only to avoid duplicating excessively material already available in translation, but to offer students the opportunity to create a new narrative by using a wider variety of sources, including administrative documents generated by government and other institutions, legal records, petitions, letters and wills. I have also used chronicles written both outside England and – within England – outside the main centres of history-writing, to offer different perspectives on the traditional accounts. Nevertheless, some chronicles are so useful that they demand at least brief introductory comments.

The written sources: a very brief introduction

Students of Richard II's reign are blessed with numerous written sources. This reign saw the last great flowering of medieval chronicle-writing; these interesting times gave authors plenty to write about! Most of the chronicles will be introduced on their first appearance in the book, but a brief word must be said here about some of the most important. Thomas Walsingham (c.1340–c.1422) was a monk of St Albans, a large and wealthy Benedictine abbey in Hertfordshire where he spent all but two adult years of his long life.[23]

Walsingham is immensely useful to later historians because he had

---

23 From 1394 to 1396 he was prior of the abbey's daughter-house of Wymondham, Norfolk; J. Taylor, 'Walsingham, Thomas' in *ODNB*. See also the introductions to *SAC* I and II on which these paragraphs rely heavily.

some knowledge of almost everything that happened, and laced events with his forthright opinions, thus providing future generations with an outline chronology and interpretation.[24] But he has two drawbacks. One is that he was not always well informed. Exceptions to this were the 'good' parliament – on which he was briefed by Sir Thomas Hoo, MP for Bedfordshire, who had strong links with the abbey – and the towns-men's revolt against St Albans Abbey in 1381, of which Walsingham himself was a horrified front-row spectator. Indeed, his account of the Peasants' Revolt takes up more space in his chronicle than any other subject. On the other hand, his account of the 'merciless' parliament (1388) is slight, and he knew little of attempts at peacemaking in the 1390s.

Walsingham's other drawback is that he changed his mind and revised his opinions as the reign progressed. He began by viewing John of Gaunt as a villain, epitomising all that was wrong with all aspects of government in Edward III's last years. Richard, thought Thomas Walsingham, would put everything right upon reaching manhood. Disillusionment and disappointment with the king grew stronger as the reign progressed, and Gaunt consequently went up in Walsing-ham's estimation. During the 1380s his opinions of Richard and Gaunt changed; in the 1390s either Walsingham, or his monastic colleagues at St Albans, removed the 'scandalous' opinions of Gaunt from the chron-icle. Walsingham's direct composition of the chronicle ceased in 1394, and the passages covering 1394–6 [148, 156, 165] were written by others and show no knowledge of events after 1397. From July 1397 the chronicle changes again, and Walsingham's hand is once more evident.

The charge of hindsight cannot be made against Henry Knighton, who died about 1396, the year when his chronicle finally petered out.[25] Knighton was a canon of the Augustinian abbey of St Mary in the Meadows, Leicester, from at least 1363. In his later years he went blind and his chronicle effectively ends in 1392. Leicester was dominated by the house of Lancaster, whose castle was an important centre for its administration, and, though the abbey itself was in crown patronage, Knighton's loyalty to the Lancastrians coloured his outlook. His first hero was Henry of Grosmont (c.1310–61), Gaunt's father-in-law and first duke of Lancaster (1351), and he remained an admirer of the next duke of Lancaster and his heir: John of Gaunt and Henry Boling-

24 For example, McKisack (1959): chaps. XIII–XV.
25 G. H. Martin's introduction to KC. He also wrote the Knighton entry in ODNB.

broke. He evidently had links with the Lancastrian administrators in
Leicester, which he put to use in his chronicle. An important aspect of
Knighton's methods was his use of documentary sources. Knighton's
latest editor identified 110 passages which were heavily dependent
on written sources, especially newsletters, or were documents copied
verbatim into the text. Thus, although Knighton was far removed from
the seat of government at Westminster, he combined the knowledge he
acquired through local contacts with information which was dissemi-
nated nationally.

By contrast, the authors of the Westminster Chronicle were very close
to the heart of government. It was originally written as a continuation
of the *Polychronicon* of Ranulph Higden and was published in 1886 as the
ninth volume of that work;[26] in the early twentieth century it was established that the chronicle was written at Westminster Abbey. Anthony
Steel used 'The Monk of Westminster' in his biography of Richard;[27]
Anthony Tuck, who wrote an account of Richard's relations with his
higher nobility,[28] cautiously described this chronicle as 'probably by a
monk of Westminster'. The publication of a free-standing edition – a
translation with detailed notes and an extensive introduction – in 1982
removed the work from the shadow of the *Polychronicon* and its continu-
ations, and transformed the standing of this source. Nigel Saul's life of
Richard made full use of this edition and established Westminster as the
best-informed narrative source of the reign.[29]

The author was certainly a monk of Westminster – or, more likely, there
were two monks of Westminster.[30] The first monk began with the story
of 1381 and continued until November 1383. The second author took
up the tale and continued until 1394. If the first writer was moved to
composition by the Peasants' Revolt, the second was prompted by the
'merciless' parliament of 1388, to which he devoted a large proportion
of his work. The Westminster authors were uniquely placed to learn
of events at the heart of government; the abbey was adjacent to the
king's palace of Westminster and to the hall where the central courts
sat, and when parliament met in London the abbey chapter house was
used as the commons' meeting-chamber. The abbey also had strong

26 *Polychronicon Ranulphi Higden* vol. IX, ed. J. R. Lumby (RS, 41, 1866).
27 Steel (1941, repr. 1962).
28 Tuck (1973).
29 Saul (1997), *passim.*
30 *WC*: xxii–xxxi, on which this paragraph is based.

links with some members of the king's administration, especially clerks of his chancery. Like many large abbeys, they retained as 'legal counsel' men with appropriate expertise and contacts to advise them on particular matters and keep a watching brief on their interests.[31] Thanks to Westminster Abbey's detailed archives we know who some of these men were, though there must have been many informal contacts which have left no written record but which furnished information not available to other chroniclers. This close relationship with the crown administration enabled the monastic author to gather extensive material covering the turbulent years from 1386 to 1388, which he wrote up some time after the event, perhaps in the early 1390s and certainly before Richard's 'revenge' parliament of September 1397.

Historians, therefore, have abundant material for the early years of the reign, but from 1394 the position is problematic: much of Walsingham's account was written after Richard's deposition, and the chronicles by Henry Knighton and the Monk of Westminster finish about then. Two other chronicles should be considered. The *Historia Vitae et Regni Ricardi Secundi* was written at Evesham Abbey.[32] This was also the work of two authors, one writing from 1377 to 1390, another from 1390 to 1402. The first Monk of Evesham was often heavily dependent on Walsingham, incorporating many passages from Walsingham's work into his own narrative. The second author was much more independent but has the disadvantages of being very brief, having a much greater local focus than his predecessor and being prone to glaring errors. Yet this second monk, who was much more hostile to Richard than the first, had important information to impart and was especially well informed about ecclesiastical politics.

Another important source which becomes less useful in the 1390s goes by the cumbersome title of 'The Continuation of the *Eulogium Historiarum*'. The *Eulogium*, as we may conveniently call it, has been linked to Canterbury, and especially the Franciscan house there. Useful though it often is in earlier years, the *Eulogium* becomes very confused from 1390, and is probably for these years a fifteenth-century compilation. It is the *Eulogium* which described, under the latter part of 1397, the king sitting alone on his throne for hours on end, forcing those on whom his eye fell to bend their knee in submission.[33] We now know that this

31 Ramsay (1985): 95–112; Smith (1987): 176–91.
32 For the rest of this paragraph, see *VR*: 1–7.
33 Printed *CR*: 68.

passage was written long after the reign, probably in the 1420s when the Lancastrian regime was shaky and its supporters were anxious to denigrate the king whom Henry IV had supplanted.[34] Failure to recognise the problems posed by the lack of contemporary chronicles for the years from 1394 is exemplified by the interpretation offered by Steel's biography. Steel considered that Richard was already unbalanced by the time Queen Anne died in spring 1394, and he believed the chronicle stories of Richard's immediate destructive frenzy against the manor house where Anne died. As we shall see [146a, 158] the truth was much more subtle. Steel concluded that 'the course of Richard's mental disease was certainly accelerated from 1394.'[35] This is open to discussion, but what is certain is that the chronicle sources from 1394 onwards were nearly all written after Richard II's deposition in 1399, and therefore reflect the reality of the Lancastrian *fait accompli*.

Nevertheless, some aspects of his court and style were recorded by commentators and certain rituals, especially funerals, were noted by chroniclers as elaborate and novel [146b]. Written information can be supplemented by works of art and architecture,[36] and in the inventory of his treasure.[37] The evidence about some of the elaborate food he ate affords opportunities for 'hands-on history'; actually cooking some of the recipes gives a unique insight into the labour-intensive nature of his dishes.[38] Many kitchen-boys [82a] were certainly required! The king's extravagant tastes are evident from his rising expenditure in this decade, as shown in financial records.[39]

Visual evidence of Richard's self-image can be seen in the Wilton Diptych, which was probably commissioned for the king's private devotions.[40] An almost blasphemous work, it depicts Richard being recommended by his patron saints (John the Baptist, Edward the Confessor and Edmund king and martyr) and eleven angels, which are already wearing his 'team badge' of the white hart and chaplets of white and red roses, the

---

34 Stow (2004): 667–81, regards the passage describing Richard's character and crown-wearing ceremonies as 'suspicious' and 'examples of textual manipulation', 677–8 and nn. 50–1.

35 Steel (1941, repr. 1962): 204.

36 Including the 'unusual imperial shrine', which he had erected in St Paul's after the death of his mother-in-law in 1391, *WC*: 516.

37 The 23m-long inventory of his treasure is being edited by Dr Jenny Stratford.

38 Mathew (1968); Scattergood and Sherborne (1983); Sass (1976).

39 Gordon *et al.* (1997); Given-Wilson (1986).

40 Gordon *et al.* (1997): esp. 95–114 (by Campbell).

king's colours.[41] Other visual evidence is Richard's use from c.1395 of
the spurious coat-of-arms of Edward the Confessor, which he impaled
with the arms of England. He allowed some of his close associates to
do the same. The use of these arms indicates Richard's devotion to the
Confessor and something of his sense of history. Further, it shows the
creation of an inner family circle, a group even more exclusive than the
Garter knights.

But there is also plenty of written evidence on which to base a judgement of Richard's character. He was quick-tempered [**62c, 67, 82a,
141b, 169a**]. He was very sensitive to criticism [**125, 135, 169a**], but
those governing in his minority also refused to tolerate criticism of the
king [**21**]; and, though the laws of war show what seems an excessive
deference to the monarch [**68**], they were agreed by all the leaders of
the Scottish expedition. His strong sense of lineage and status is shown
in attempts to have his great-grandfather canonised [**159**], the sense
of history reported after his capture in 1399,[42] and the commissioning
of thirteen statues of kings for Westminster Hall.

Richard's self-image in words can be observed in the provisions of his
will [**171**] and in the epitaph to be inscribed on his tomb [**160**], and
his most precious documents are listed in the contents of his personal
'safe deposit-box' which was placed under the Confessor's protection
while Richard was in Ireland [**150**]. These documents, which mostly
derived from Joan of Kent's colourful marital career, might be taken
to show insecurity, while some personally authorised instructions to
envoys negotiating with France show a lack of political realism [**161**].
Though we can sympathise with any king trying to deal with someone
as awkward as the earl of Arundel [**62c, 145a–c, 146b**] it is true that
Richard showed little skill at 'public relations'. Perhaps he thought that
in life, as in a game of hazard, the dice would always roll his way [**6**].

---

41 The red of the roses has now faded to a creamy-yellow.
42 Usk: 63–5.

PROLOGUE:
THE END OF EDWARD III'S REIGN, 1376–77

1. Death of the Black Prince, 1376

As he was dying, the Black Prince commended his wife and son to Edward III and Gaunt.

Life of the Black Prince by the Herald of Sir John Chandos, ed. M. K. Pope and E. C. Lodge (Oxford, 1910), 129.

Then he called the king his father
And the duke of Lancaster his brother.
He commended his wife unto them,
And the son he loved so dearly,
And he begged them at that moment
That each would swear to help them.
Each one swore it on the book
And promised to deliver this:
They would give comfort to the child
And would maintain his rights.
All the princes, all the barons
Standing round them swore this too.
And in return for this the noble prince
Gave them a hundred thousand thanks.
Never, so help me the true God,
Was there such deep sadness ever come
As there was at his departure.
The noble, lovely princess
Felt such sorrow in her breast
That she could not bear its burden.
Now the moaning and the sighing
With loud mourning and the crying
Made a noise so great
That in the world was no man yet
But if he saw such heavy sorrow
Pity would lodge within his heart.

2. Richard recognised as heir apparent, June 1376

Richard was the first king since Henry II (acceded 1154) who was not himself a king's son. This explains the occasion recorded here.

RP II.330; *PROME* (1376), section 50.

The commons humbly begged the lord king in parliament that he would be pleased, for the great comfort of the whole realm, to cause to come into parliament the noble child Richard of Bordeaux, son and heir of the lord Edward, formerly eldest son of our lord king and prince of Wales, whom God absolve, so that the lords and commons of the realm could there view and honour the said Richard as true heir apparent of the kingdom. This request was granted, and so Richard came before all the prelates, lords and commons in parliament on the morrow of St John's Day *[25 June]*, by the king's command and desire. The archbishop of Canterbury there spoke the words expressing the king's will which had been made known to him, and said that since the most noble and puissant prince the lord Edward, formerly prince of Wales, had died ... yet it was as though he was present and not absent, by leaving behind him so noble and so handsome a son who was his very image and true likeness ... and the archbishop said to all present that the same Richard should be the true heir apparent to the kingdom in the same way as his noble father the prince had been, and should be held by them and by all the king's other subjects in great honour and reverence. To this the whole commons called with one voice for their noble liege lord to be pleased to grant to Richard the name and honour of prince of Wales, just as the lord Edward his father had been while he was alive. To this came the response that it was not appropriate for the prelates or lords to do in parliament, or elsewhere, what clearly belonged to the king himself to do with great solemnity and celebration. But the prelates and lords promised to make diligent representations on this matter to the king.

3. Discussion about the succession, summer 1376

Walsingham is the only chronicler who mentions this discussion of the succession. His account carries weight in the light of **5**.

SAC I.38–40.

The death of Prince Edward while parliament[1] was still in session raised despair among the knights of the commons, and a swelling of pride among the duke [Lancaster] and evildoers. The duke entered the assembly of the knights,[2] and constantly asked that while parliament was still in session at which the kingdom's affairs were being debated, the knights themselves and the lords and barons associated with them should discuss who ought to inherit the kingdom of England after the death of the king and the prince his [eldest] son. He sought, furthermore, that, following the French example, they should enact that no woman should become the king's heir. For he considered both the age of the king, who was now at death's door, and the youth of the prince's son, whom, it was said, he planned to poison if he was not otherwise able to attain the throne; because if these two who intervened were removed, and this law was ratified in full parliament, he would be the next heir to the kingdom; for no male was closer to the throne. At the time discussion of these matters was on everyone's lips. But Lord Edmund Mortimer, earl of March, had married the daughter of Lord Lionel, his [Lancaster's] elder brother; the right of succession to the kingdom would belong to him, because of his wife, if the prince's only son were to die without an heir. The duke feared March above all, knowing that he was a good and just man, and so worked hard to make sure that inheritance of the kingdom should not devolve on him. When the duke broached this in council the response was that it was useless to bother with such matters when they had other more serious business still on their hands which merited fuller discussion. 'And especially,' they said, 'since our lord the king is still hale and hearty, despite his age, and could outlive us all. And on the day when the king dies we shall still not lack an heir while the son of our lord the prince, now ten years old, is still alive. During their lifetimes it is not fitting for us to meddle in such matters'. When he heard these words the discomfited duke was silenced.

4. Edward III puts his private affairs in order

Early in his reign, Richard II's government overrode the provisions of the will and trust; see **28, 85biii**.

---

1 The 'Good Parliament', 28 April to c.10 July 1376. The prince died on 8 June.
2 The commons met in the Chapter House of Westminster Abbey, separately from the lords.

(a) The king establishes a charitable trust, 5 and 6 October 1376

This was intended to benefit several houses, principally St Mary Graces by the Tower, for the good of Edward's soul.

CPR 1374–7, 347, adapted.

Grant in fee to the king's son John duke of Lancaster, Simon *[Sudbury]* archbishop of Canterbury, John *[Buckingham]* bishop of Lincoln, Henry *[Wakefield]* bishop of Worcester, William Lord Latimer, John Knyvet chancellor, Robert Ashton treasurer, Roger Beauchamp chamberlain, John de Ipre steward of the household and Nicholas Carew keeper of the privy seal, of the castle and manor of Leybourne, Kent, and all other property which the king has acquired in fee or in reversion from Juliana de Leybourne, late countess of Huntingdon; and the castle and town of Queenborough and manor of Gravesend, Kent, and the castle and manor of Moorend *[in Potterspury]*, Northamptonshire, the manors of Worplesdon, Surrey, Brockenhurst, Hampshire, and Easthampstead, Berkshire, a messuage[3] in London formerly belonging to John Beauchamp of Warwick, in which the king's wardrobe[4] now is, and all other tenements and rents in London which the king has in any manner acquired in fee; and also of all other manors, lordships and lands, with reversions, which the king has acquired in fee from any persons, to hold with knights' fees, advowsons[5] of churches, royalties, liberties, reversions, parks, woods, warrens, chases, fisheries, rents, services of tenants and all other appurtenances.

Grant to them on the same terms of all castles, manors, lordships and lands in Kent or elsewhere which the king has acquired in fee from any persons and which any persons hold for life or terms of years of his grant, so that they take the rents and farms of all these until the reversions fall in.

(b) Edward III's will, 7 October 1376

A Collection of all the Wills now known to be extant of the Kings and Queens of England, ed. John Nichols (London, 1780), 59–64.

[After an elaborate preamble, omitted here:] First of all, being in purity and sincerity of the Catholic faith, we leave to Almighty God the Creator, our soul which he redeemed by his precious blood, and we commend it to

3 A house with outbuildings and land.

4 The financial department of the royal household.

5 Rights of presentation.

him with the most intense devotion of which we are capable; and for our body, we desire that it be buried in the church of St Peter at Westminster among our distinguished progenitors the kings of England, and we wish our funeral rites to be celebrated in the royal manner …. We also wish, and specially direct, that the monastery of St Mary Graces by our Tower of London, previously founded by us, should be enriched with a sufficient endowment and with other support, according to our original intention …

We also wish, and expressly direct, that in the convent of the Friars Preachers of Langley, of our foundation, there should be constructed and made both a house and buildings, at our expense, as had been ordered by us previously. We wish also that the convent of the said friars should be increased by the number of twenty persons of that order, and that new rents be acquired from our goods sufficient to pay ten marks a year, every year, to each of those twenty friars, who shall all be specially bound to intercede perpetually for the good state of our health while we live, and for our soul when we die, and for the soul of Philippa queen of England of glorious memory, our dearest consort, and for the good estate of all our living children, and for the souls of those who are dead, before God, in Masses and in their other prayers and devotions.

Next we give and leave to our future heir, on whom may God confer his saving grace, Richard, namely the son of Edward of honoured memory lately prince of Wales our firstborn son, one bed complete with all its fittings with our complete arms of England and France which is in our palace of Westminster. Also we give and leave to him four other beds which used to be erected in four lesser chambers of that same palace, also with their complete fittings. Also we give and leave to him two sets of furnishings for his hall, of which one is large and noble, but the other is chosen to be light and delicate for portability. Also we give and leave to him two complete [sets of] furnishings for the chapel.

To Joan, lately the wife of our said firstborn son Edward of famous memory 1,000 marks in which he was bound to us as a loan, wishing that his jewels, which are for that reason mortgaged to us, should be freely returned to her.

To our dearest daughter Isabel countess of Bedford for her financial assistance and the maintenance of her daughter[6] 300 marks a year

6 Philippa, who married Robert de Vere, the ninth earl, on or before 5 Oct. 1376, Cockayne, *Complete Peerage*, X, 231.

arising from the lands and rents of the son and heir of the earl of Oxford, deceased, of good memory ... as long as the heir to the same shall be under age.[7] ....

[The king granted the rest of his moveable goods to his executors to pay his debts, and for the good of his soul.]

We name, make, and depute as executors of this our royal testament our illustrious son John king of Castile and Leon and duke of Lancaster, and the venerable fathers John bishop of Lincoln, Henry bishop of Worcester, John [Gilbert] bishop of Hereford, and our dear and faithful men William Lord Latimer, John Knyvet chancellor, Robert Ashton treasurer, Roger Beauchamp chamberlain, John de Ipre steward, our knights, and Nicholas Carew keeper of the privy seal .... As supervisors of this testament we create, make, ordain and constitute the reverend fathers in Christ Simon archbishop of Canterbury and Alexander [Neville] archbishop of York ...

The present testament was given, written and ordained in our royal manor of Havering atte Bower, in our lower chamber, 7 October 1376.

[The will was proved before Archbishop Sudbury, Lambeth 25 June 1377.]

5. Edward III's entail of the crown, autumn 1376

This document presents many difficulties, not least because, through fire damage, parts are illegible. The use of French suggests the king's personal involvement, and it may have been a draft which was not translated into Latin, the language of formal chancery business for, despite being a letter patent, it was not enrolled as a 'file copy' in the chancery records: the Patent Rolls. It survives only in a fifteenth-century copy, perhaps made in 1460 in connection with the Yorkist claim to the throne. No apology is made for including this damaged but important document, which presents considerable difficulties of translation, for it shows the problems that historical researchers sometimes encounter.

British Library, Cotton Charter XVI 63. Printed: Michael Bennett, 'Edward III's entail and the succession to the crown, 1376–1471', *EHR* 103 (1998), 580–609; text: 607–9.

1. ...   land
2. ...   his faithful people in God also dwelling within our realm of
3. ...   moral sign and the arguments as well of the law of God as

---

7 Thomas de Vere, eighth earl of Oxford, died mid-Sept. 1371; his son and heir Robert had been born Jan. 1362, *ibid.*, 227.

4. ...   policy and sound government of the realms ought to be before
5. ...   greater perils, which according to the rules of one
6. ...   these things formed in general words purporting that he [or it]
7. ...   to the king of heaven, as we would wish. Edward of good
         [memory]
8. ...   of our old age among other occupations incumbent on
9. ...   sound government in our realm of England and to ordain
10. ... to keep between the subjects of the said realm. And
11. ... the purport and passing [?] of the years of our age and
12. ... [good] memory our eldest son, to whom may God grant grace
         and holy
13. ... repugnant to the creation [?] of children, all he will have
         contracted [?]
14. ... inasmuch as we are of sound courage and of suitable health
15. ... and good conscience have ordained to declare our will and
16. ... the aforesaid Richard should succeed us loyally in all and every
         right of
17. ... lawfully begotten without impediment or hindrance whatsoever
18. ... as is said above, begotten, we wish and our conscience
19. ... [honour]able son John king of Castile and of Leon, duke of
         Lancaster
20. ... of his body lawfully begotten. And if the said John without heir
21. ... is said, should be withdrawn from this life, then our very dear
         son
22. ... his heirs male of his body lawfully begotten. And if the said
23. ... begotten we wish that there should succeed him Thomas our
         dear son and
24. ... begotten. And if the aforesaid Thomas our youngest son should
         die without
25. ... and of our certain knowledge we ordain that thenceforth the
         succession of
26. ... of our lineage and blood. This is the firm declaration of our will
27. ... ordained with good counsel and the most extensive deliberation
28. ... desired in those same realms of ours after our decease, God
29. ... manor of Havering atte Bower, in the presence of the reverend
         father [in God ...]
30. ... of Latimer, John Knyvet our chancellor, Robert Ashton
31. ... John Burley, Richard Sturry and Philip La Vache, knights,[8]
         Nicholas

---

8 These were chamber knights, Given-Wilson (1986): 144.

32. ... Bridgecourt, John Salisbury,[9] Walter Walsh esquire of our
    [chamber]
33. ... to attest such declaration especially called by us
34. ... to these our letters patent we have put our great seal. Given in
35. ... *[13]*76 and of our realm of England the 50th and of our
36. ...

6. Londoners curry favour with Prince Richard

John Stow (1524/5–1605), was a London antiquary especially interested in
local pageantry; he consulted many sources which have since disappeared.

John Stow, *A Survey of London*, ed. Charles Lethbridge Kingsford (corr. repr.
Oxford, 1971), I.96–7 (spelling and punctuation modernised).

On the Sunday before Candlemas *[26 Jan. 1377]* in the evening, 130
citizens disguised, and well horsed in a mummery[10] with sound of
trumpets, sackbuts, cornets, shawms[11] and other instruments, and
innumerable torch-lights of wax, rode from Newgate through Cheap[12]
over *[London]* bridge, through Southwark and so to Kennington beside
Lambeth, where the young prince remained with his mother and the
duke of Lancaster his uncle ... with divers other lords. In the first
rank did ride 48 in the likeness and habit of esquires ... After them
came riding 48 knights ... There followed one richly arrayed like an
emperor, and some distance after him, one stately attired like a pope,
whom followed 24 cardinals .... These maskers, after they had entered
the Manor of Kennington, alighted from their horses, and after they
had entered the hall on foot ... the prince, his mother and the lords
came out of the chamber into the hall, whom the said mummers did
salute: showing by a pair of dice upon the table their desire to play
with the prince, which they so handled that the prince did always win
when he threw them. Then the mummers set to the prince three jewels,
one after another, which were a bowl of gold, a cup of gold and a ring
of gold, which the prince won at three throws. Then they set to the
prince's mother, the duke, the earls and other lords, to everyone a ring
of gold, which they did also win. After which they were feasted, and the

---

9 Later one of Richard's household knights; knighted in 1385.

10 Traditional form of dumb show.

11 These were all wind instruments.

12 A ward in the centre of the city, north-east of St Paul's Cathedral.

music sounded, the prince and lords danced on the one part with the mummers, who did also dance. Which jollity being ended they were again made to drink, and then departed in order as they came.

7. John of Gaunt's unpopularity: the 'trial' of John Wycliffe, early 1377

Exemplifying the behaviour that made Gaunt unpopular, this episode took place between 27 January and 2 March 1377. Walsingham, SAC I.80–92, placed the incident on Thursday 20 February. The two accounts are so similar that they probably used a common source.

Anon. Chron., 103–4.

At the same time as parliament met there began a great dispute between the duke of Lancaster and the citizens of London about a master of divinity called Master John Wycliffe, who had preached in London and elsewhere against the clergy on various subjects, like a man possessed. For these reasons Master John was summoned by the pope's authority to appear before the archbishop of Canterbury and the bishop of London in St Paul's cathedral. On the appointed day, the duke of Lancaster, who had no business with the men of Holy Church, came with several others, as Master John's maintainers.[13] The duke began contemptuously to scold and harangue the bishop of London because Master John was being brought as though before judges to answer those charges, saying that Wycliffe was more worthy to sit in judgment than any of them. The bishop replied that, in that case, no judgment would be passed upon him and that no man ought to maintain him in this quarrel with Holy Church. Whereupon the duke grew very irate and extremely angry with the bishop; he ordered Lord Percy, at that time marshal of England, who was carrying his tipstaff,[14] to arrest those who were against Master John. The bishop wisely replied that no one ought to carry the staff of such office inside a church, nor arrest anyone, because this would be contrary to the law and the constitutions of Holy Church; and those who did would be publicly excommunicated. The duke answered that if he spoke like that he personally would drag the bishop to the ground by his hair; and so they all departed in heaviness of heart.

13 Maintenance: lending assistance to a party in a legal dispute, without having a personal interest in the case; a crime in England until 1967.

14 A staff with a badge or cap of metal carried as a sign of office.

Afterwards the citizens of London, on hearing that the duke had threatened or beheaded their bishop, immediately erupted and assembled, and
they came from Cheapside and St Paul's cathedral to the Savoy,[15] where
the duke had gone, to behead him or put him to death. When the bishop
heard of this he hurried after them as far as Fleet Street and there he
begged them, on his knees and for the love of God, to desist from their
plan and to disperse, because he was unharmed. Seeing their bishop in
good health, and because of his entreaty, they returned to London and
considered how to proceed. At the same time the duke, fearful of the
citizens, went by barge to Kennington, where the prince was staying.

---

15 Gaunt's palace on the Strand (site of the present Savoy Hotel and theatre), which was
   destroyed in 1381; see **40**.

I: THE MINORITY, 1377–81

1377

Despite forebodings, Richard's accession was domestically peaceful, and the political community attempted to compose old enmities. Though Gaunt soon retired from court, his interests were represented in government. A parliament was held, and a succession of councils chosen to run the country.[1] But warfare continued, with attacks by both Scots and French, the latter inflicting serious damage along the south coast and on the Isle of Wight.

8. The accession

SAC I.124–8.[2]

When it was learnt that the illustrious King Edward III after the Conquest ... had ended his life on 21 June, the Londoners sent some of the more powerful citizens to Kennington where both the Prince and his mother the Princess *[Joan]* were then living, in order to commend the city and citizens of London to them. John Philpot, citizen of London, began his speech on behalf of his fellow-citizens like this:

'We have heard the news, most excellent Lord, which we cannot report without great sorrow, concerning the undoubted imminent death of the most victorious King Edward. He, as I say, has guarded and governed us and this kingdom for many years in tranquil peace, and now – the signs of death being manifest upon him – is ceasing to be our ruler. Wherefore, on behalf of the citizens and city of London, we beseech that you, who very soon will be our king, whom we acknowledge as sole king, should show graciousness to your city, which is almost your chamber;[3] to your rule only shall we be subject, to your will we shall bend, obedient to your supreme authority, whom we shall serve in deed and word. And this embassy also announces that your reverence should know that your city is indescribably perturbed because you have long

---

1 Lewis (1926): 246–51, describes these in detail.

2 Nightingale (1995), chap. 10 has essential background.

3 Meaning 'treasure house'.

remained absent from it, which is known to be so devoted to you that it is prepared to expend, for you, not only its temporal goods but even, if need be, its life. Therefore we have come to your presence to beg that you will wish to live there, as much for the consolation of the citizens as for your own safety and solace. Moreover, we entreat you, most illustrious prince, that you should deign to make an end – fruitful both to the duke himself and to our citizens – of the discord which by the dissensions of certain people has recently arisen between our citizens and our lord the duke of Lancaster, which is to the advantage of no one but at the expense of many'. To these and similar words spoken by him, the reply from the prince and his council was that he would make satisfaction in everything in which they wished to be satisfied. Dismissed in this way, they carried back the glad news to their citizens.

Next day, St Alban's day [22 June], there were sent to London on the king's behalf Lord Latimer, Sir Nicholas Bonde, Sir Simon Burley and Sir Richard Adderbury, who greeted the citizens in the new king's name (for, as we said, King Edward had died on the previous day) and carried to them the sad tidings of the old king's death, and the happy news of the intention of the new king, who promised that he would be gracious to them and their city, and that he was about to come to their city, and to reside there, as they had asked. And, executing the new king's other orders, they said that the lord king had spoken to the duke on their behalf, and that the duke submitted himself entirely to the king's will in this business. So it was the king's wish that they would likewise submit themselves to him, and he would labour so that peace would be strengthened between them, to the honour of the citizens and the profit of the city. But the citizens, afraid of such a form of peacemaking, replied that no way would they do this; especially because they knew that the king was a boy and too weak to defend them in so great a business, and because their case would be discussed, not by him, but by their rivals and deadly enemies; and that they would be punished for their opinion if they consented to the king's order in this matter. Finally, after discussing this business among themselves for six hours and more, they agreed on this: that if those knights would swear to the citizens that their submission would result in no material damage to them, nor corporate expense, or prejudice to their city, they would gladly accede to the royal commands.

9. Richard's triumphal entry into London

Elaborate ceremonial, a characteristic of the reign, was not new in London,
but civic triumphs, both English and continental, were a feature of this period.[4]
Compare SAC I.136–40.

Anon. Chron., 107–9.

The Wednesday before the coronation, after the hour of nones,[5] all the
great lords who were present in the city, and the mayor, aldermen and
the commons of London, rode to the Tower of London where the prince
was, and waited there for his arrival. At last the prince left the Tower
well and honourably arrayed in a garment of white cloth, as befits such
a lord, all his knights likewise, and they rode towards London. At the
head of their procession rode the commons of London, clothed in white,
then the lords' and knights' esquires, then the knights and after them
the aldermen followed by the mayor and the two sheriffs, all dressed
in white; and after, the duke of Lancaster and the earls of Cambridge
and Hereford, then the prince by himself, a long way back, all alone;
and after the prince came the earls, barons and other lords. They rode
through London and through Cheap to the palace of Westminster. In
Cheap there was a tower of painted canvas, subtly made with a timber
framework, on which were constructed four turrets; in them were four
very beautiful damsels, finely-dressed, who threw gold bezants[6] before
the prince. In the same tower was a small bell, and on top of the bell was
an angel carrying a golden crown, and showing this to the prince to
encourage him. At the same time the conduits of Cheap were painted in
various colours and ran from this time with red and white wine, which
everyone who wanted could, in the heat, drink at will. The wine was
collected in great vats, into which the wine ran without loss. The prince
rode *via* Fleet Street to the palace of Westminster to rest and recover.
The other lords returned to London and elsewhere to their lodgings.

That night the prince was bathed, as is customary, and next day,
Thursday, after he rose, was suitably clothed in a new garment and
shod only with slippers (*chaunces*). At this time the archbishop and the
other bishops, abbots and priors, and the monks of the abbey, fittingly
robed, came in procession from Westminster Abbey to the hall of the
palace. Then the lords led the young prince from the palace to the

---

4 Stow, *Survey of London*: I.95–6; Kipling (1998): 12, 273–4.

5 The ninth hour: mid-afternoon.

6 A coin originally minted at Byzantium.

White Chamber in that hall near the king's bench[7] and there delivered the prince to the archbishop and other bishops and clergy. On that
occasion the duke of Lancaster carried the first sword[8] before him, the
earl of March the second and the earl of Warwick the third; the earl
of Cambridge[9] carried the gold sceptre, and Sir Thomas Woodstock[10]
the royal staff. The archbishop and the other bishops and others of the
clergy led him in procession to Westminster Abbey; and the earls of
Stafford, Arundel, Suffolk and others carried him on their shoulders,
and the *[representatives of]* the Cinque Ports carried a baldaquin[11] of
cloth of gold on four poles above him, towards the abbey. And when they
were come into the church a platform had been made before the choir,
above the choir and the high altar, onto which he was carried and placed
in a seat, one degree higher than the others, so that he could be seen.
[A detailed description of the coronation liturgy follows.]

10. An unfortunate incident at the coronation, 16 July 1377

The renewal of his coronation oath in 1388 [116 a, b] apparently prompted
Richard to make good the loss of this part of the coronation regalia. He sent
a new pair of shoes to the curia for papal blessing, and their reception back at
Westminster Abbey stirred the chronicler's memory. Although this chronicle
begins in 1381, the entry under 1390 gives a vivid picture of the coronation
ceremonies of 1377. The unfavourable impression made by Burley is notable,
but the nave of Westminster Abbey was being rebuilt then, and there may have
been considerable confusion.[12]

WC, 414–16.

On 10 March *[1390]* the king sent to Westminster a pair of shoes,
which had been blessed by Pope Urban VI before his death,[13] of red
velvet embroidered with pearls in a pattern of fleur-de-lis, there to be
placed with the other royal regalia belonging to the king's coronation,
which are kept in the monastery. For it is agreed that the king, immediately after his crowning, should enter the vestry where he should put

7 The court of king's bench sat in Westminster Hall.
8 It was named 'Curtana', *CCR 1377–81*, 1.
9 Edmund of Langley, the king's middle uncle, later duke of York.
10 The king's youngest uncle, later duke of Gloucester.
11 Or 'baldachin', a rich, ritual canopy.
12 This incident was also mentioned by Usk: 90, and Flete, ed. Robinson (1909): 19.
13 Died 15 Oct. 1389.

off his regalia and should put on other clothes placed there for him by his attendants, and from there he should go back to his palace by the nearest way. But the reverse was done at the coronation of this *[present]* king, and it was badly done, for a certain knight called Sir Simon Burley, after the coronation had been performed, gathered up the king, who was still clothed with his regalia, into his arms while going into the palace through the royal gate. There the crowds pressed and jostled him, and in so going he lost one of the consecrated royal shoes, through carelessness.[14] In future, therefore, our people must be on their guard lest they allow the king to go anywhere outside the church with his regalia on; but, as is traditional, once the coronation is complete, he should turn aside into the vestry, as is advised, and there should suitably take off his regal adornments.

11. Events of summer 1377

SAC I.156–8.

A few days later – because the duke *[of Lancaster]* saw, now that his father was dead and the new king installed, that everything in the kingdom would be different in future, and that his standing would be totally diminished among the new men; and also afraid that if anything unfortunate happened to the king or kingdom it would be blamed on him, but that for his good services he would receive no or few thanks – he received the king's permission to depart to his own lands. He promised the king that, if his help was needed, he would come with greater forces than any lord of England to assist him, or do anything which would contribute to his profit or honour .... He withdrew from court to his castle of Kenilworth; but before his withdrawal there were chosen, by his influence, those who would be on the king's Council, and who would be like guardians. There were, however, chosen for the Council good men, prudent and famous: the lord William Courtenay bishop of London, Lord Edmund Mortimer, earl of March, and several others of whom the common people thought very well. But because the bishop of Salisbury and Lord Latimer[15] were among them, a murmuring arose

---

14 The shoes (or slippers) had originally belonged to Alfred the Great and were worn by him at his consecration in Rome in 853, and were subsequently owned by Edward the Confessor.

15 Ralph Erghum, bishop of Salisbury, was Gaunt's chancellor 1372–5; Latimer was one of the courtiers attacked in the 'good' parliament.

among the common people. At the same time the Marshal of England, Lord Henry Percy, earl of Northumberland, resigned his staff of office and withdrew to his estates; in his place there was appointed Lord John Arundel, brother of the earl of Arundel, who strenuously resisted the French when they attacked the town of Southampton, manfully thwarted their entry into the town and drove them back to the sea.

About the same time, disturbances arose from some trivial cause on market days at Roxburgh between the English and Scots; members of each race were killed, the Scots coming off worse. This drove them to fury, and shortly after, led by the earl of Dunbar, they returned to the town and occupied it by night; they killed the citizens, seized their goods rapaciously and consigned the town to devouring flames. When these events became known, the new earl of Northumberland was touched to the heart with sorrow, especially for the deaths of the citizens of this town, and he set out to wreak vengeance on their enemies, and to wipe out the disgrace of the people of the land. So, entering Scotland with 10,000 men, he plundered the lands of the earl of Dunbar, who was the originator of all this evil, setting fire to everything in his path. When he had more than taken vengeance, he returned with all his men to his own country.

12. The first parliament of the reign, 13 October–28 November 1377

The implication of this account is that there was a reaction against the temper of the January 1377 parliament, and a swing back to the personnel and mood of the 1376 'good parliament'.

SAC I.168–170.

A parliament was held at London which lasted from Michaelmas *[29 September]* until the feast of St Andrew the Apostle *[20 November]*. In that parliament there were present nearly all the knights, along with Sir Peter de la Mare, who so nobly stood firm in that parliament which was rightly called 'good', for the improvement of the country and the welfare of the kingdom. These men, therefore, resuming their petitioning in the place where they had first gone apart,[16] pressed for the banishment of that Alice Perrers who scorned parliamentary statute and the oath by which she was bound, and dared to attend the royal

16 The chapter house of Westminster Abbey.

court to beg and beseech from him [*the king*] whatever she wanted. This woman had completely corrupted with money several of the lords and all the lawyers of England, who aided her not only secretly but publicly. But by the diligence and wisdom of these said knights she was publicly convicted by her own mouth, and all her goods, moveable and non-moveable, were confiscated to the royal treasury. In addition, there were granted for the king's use by church and clergy, two tenths, payable that year, on condition that the king should not burden the people with other demands for his subjects' money, but should live of his own and should continue his war. Because, in any case it was alleged, his own royal resources were sufficient both to maintain the king's household and to sustain the war, if suitable ministers managed them. There were deputed as custodians of this money two citizens of London, William Walworth and John Philpot.[17]

13. Appointment of the Council of Nine during the meeting of parliament

Despite Richard's youth no formal minority was established. Instead, the pretence was made that the king was ruling in person, and a series of councils was established to administer the realm.[18] The first 'continual council' of government, chosen in July 1377 at a meeting of the great council, had twelve members. This second version was chosen during Richard's first parliament. A third council, selected partly in the Gloucester parliament (October 1378), partly after the court's return to Westminster, remained in office until disbanded after representations in parliament, January 1380. For the members of each version see Lewis (1926): 246–51.

RP III.6; *PROME* 1377 (2), sections 18, 22–3.

The commons request that the king's council be enlarged by eight sufficient persons of differing ranks and status, to be continually in attendance as members of the council, with the officers … on the business of the king and realm while our lord is of such tender years, in such a way that no major or costly business shall be done or discussed without the assent and advice of them all, and other lesser business by the assent and advice of at least four of them, as the case requires; so that four of them shall continually remain in the king's council; humbly beseeching

17 Philpot was mayor in 1379–80, Walworth in 1380–1. They were appointed to receive the lay tax of two fifteenths and tenths voted in this parliament, Jurkowski, Smith and Crook (1998): 57.

18 Dodd (2008b): 103–59.

that ... now in this parliament the eight councillors be elected from the most suitable persons of the realm and those who are best informed and who can, and will, work hardest and take pains to amend the evils and perils which were mentioned. They also request that these councillors should not in future be chosen, created or elected except in parliament, and, except any die, none should be removed unless for a reasonable cause between one parliament and another; in which case the king, on the advice of his council, should create and appoint at his pleasure other suitable men in their places.

Understanding that this request would be honourable and profitable both to himself and his realm, the lord king authorised this, provided always that the chancellor, treasurer, keeper of the privy seal, the justices of both Benches[19] and all the king's other officers could do and transact the business of their offices without the presence of those councillors. The king, for certain reasons which influenced him at present, by the advice of the lords of parliament, who wished to have, during this present year, only nine of such councillors, caused them to be chosen in that parliament, namely: the bishops of London, Carlisle and Salisbury; the earls of March and Stafford; Sirs Richard de Stafford and Henry Lescrope bannerets;[20] Sirs John Devereux and Hugh Segrave, bachelors.[21] And it was decided that those said nine councillors who should be chosen, and also the eight councillors in future, should not remain in office longer than one year. At the end of the year the same persons would not be re-elected to this office for the two years following.

Additionally, it was decided that no gift of escheat, wardship, marriage, rent or anything else belonging to the king should be given to any of those same councillors during that year, except with the common assent of all those same councillors, or the greater part of them; that they take nothing from any person for a favour, except food and drink of small value, or any other thing which could be reasonably called a bribe, for any business which would be discussed or dealt with before them, on pain of paying to that party double of anything so taken, along with sufficient damages and expenses, and to our lord king six times more than they had taken. Also it was decided that none of those councillors should become tainted with, or sustain, any quarrel by maintenance in lands elsewhere, on such grievous pain as would be ordained by the lord king with the advice of the lords of the realm.

19 The courts of king's bench (for criminal cases) and common pleas (civil cases).

20 Knights who had a company of followers serving under their banner; senior knights.

21 Young knights serving under the banner of other knights; junior knights.

14. Agreement with the duke of Brittany to lease the castle of Brest, 1 December 1377

The strategic importance of Brest cannot be overstated, for it (along with Cherbourg, acquired from the king of Navarre) guarded the sea route to Bordeaux. Duke John's dire political straits – he was in exile in England – forced him to enter into this agreement; he received Castle Rising (Norfolk) in return. Despite challenges, Brest remained in English hands until 1397, when, following the long truce with France, it was returned to the duke of Brittany.

Recueil des Actes de Jean IV, duc de Bretagne, vol. I, ed. Michael Jones (Paris, 1980), no. 262.

These articles grant to Richard II possession of the castle of Brest and all that depend on it, including the *brefs de Bretagne*,[22] the fish drying sheds and all other profits, and the right to guard it at his own expense for the duration of the wars, and in the event of a treaty or a long truce, to return it to the duke, to his wife or to his heirs, to whom he has made a solemn promise, strengthened by the letters of John of Gaunt and others. If the duke dies without heirs, the king can retain the castle. The king, in return, must assign to the duke a castle in England with lands producing revenue of 700 marks p.a. while Brest remains with the king. The king will also assign to the duke £1,000 which will be remitted to his wife or to his receiver as soon as the king enters into possession of Brest, where the king will guard the right of free access. The duke can also retrieve his jewels and other goods from the castle. Indentures will be drawn up for the food and artillery to be delivered to the castle for the king's men, which will be surrendered when the king leaves Brest. The king will use the *brefs* and other privileges (*noblesces*) of the duke at Brest in his name. The duke will have letters from the king to the royal officers at Bordeaux so that he will be permitted to benefit from the *brefs* there. If the castle is lost or sold before the king gives it back, he must do his best to retake it for the duke. On retaking possession of Brest, the duke must release the castle in England and the 700 marks. The terms of the alliance of 1372 should be confirmed by Richard II.[23] The duke ought to have the right of return of writs[24] and of other franchises in the county of Richmond, for life.

22 *Brefs* were safe-conducts for ships sailing round the coast of Brittany, and a valuable source of revenue for the dukes; see Jones (1970): 5.

23 The alliance of November 1372 was confirmed in April 1378.

24 A right, granted by the crown, to execute royal writs on the grantee's own land, bypassing the sheriff; Clanchy (1967): 59–82; Jones (1970): 127–98.

1378

15. War in France

No other chronicle gives such full and wide-ranging accounts of the continuing conflicts which beset England in this period.

Anon. Chron., 119–26.

It was decided by the Common Council of England that Sir John Neville, lord of Raby, should become Seneschal of Gascony following the capture of Sir Thomas Felton, and should go to Bordeaux with 500 men-at-arms and as many archers; but he was delayed for a long time by lack of ships until 1 September, to his very great disadvantage and loss. During that time, about the feast of the Nativity of St John the Baptist *[24 June]*, the citizens and good people of Bordeaux, because they had had neither aid nor succour from the seneschal, secretly took counsel how they could harass their enemies of France and Gascony, and were advised to make a sortie from the town by night with their forces. After a night was chosen, they carefully and suitably arrayed themselves for war in their best manner and made their way to a most noble and strong town which was hostile to them, which they took by force, and many prisoners and a great quantity of wine and other goods. Next day they took two or three castles and they ransomed all the country round which was hostile to them, and took all the wine which they could find and carried it to Bordeaux, and then filled six large ships with the wine to send it to England. While these ships were sailing they encountered on the high seas the duke of Lancaster with other lords searching the sea for enemies, about the feast of St Lawrence *[10 August]*. The duke took two of the ships full of wine to supply himself and the other lords more suitably than they previously were. Of the other four ships, one was sent to London, another to Bristol, the third to Southampton and the fourth to Hull, in which there were 180 casks.

On Thursday after the exaltation of Holy Cross *[16 September]*, Lord Neville made his way to Normandy; on 1 September he left Plymouth and put to sea and on the vigil of the Nativity of Our Lady *[7 September]* he came to Bordeaux at the hour of Vespers.[25] At this time there was killed a great enemy of England called Owain with the Red Hand, who was a Welshman.[26] He challenged the inheritance of the crown of England

25 There appears to be some confusion about dates here.

26 Owain ap Thomas ap Rhodri (Owain Lawgoch) was grandson of the brother of

and was the principal warrior after the marshal of France at the siege of the castle of Mortain; the marshal and Sir Owain had besieged that castle before Lord Neville's arrival, for a whole year, with 500 lances drawn from thieving and uncouth peasants. When Lord Neville heard about their siege, within fourteen days of coming to Bordeaux he made his way by sea, with his retinue and men of the Bordeaux area with him, that is to say the Captal de Buch[27] and three other lords, towards that castle. At his coming the marshal of France fled, and the rest of his host fled to an abbey which was very well fortified, like a castle. Now Lord Nevill and his men burned four enemy towers. He then rallied his men and mounted an assault both intense and prolonged upon that abbey and finally captured it, to his great honour and the encouragement of his men. At this assault he created three knights Sir William de Hilton, Sir Hugh Heroun and Sir William Thirkeld, and by the relief of Mortain castle by Lord Neville, the very noble knight of Soudyk[28] and the captain of that castle were delivered from their enemies. While returning towards Bordeaux, Lord Neville conquered in the following five days the castle of Lambert, which was most injurious to all the people of the surrounding area. Three other castles were liberated by him on that journey.

16. War at sea: ducal incompetence contrasted with mercantile efficiency

This criticism of Gaunt was toned down in later re-writing after Henry IV's accession. Gaunt received funds for an expedition to Spain to pursue his claim to the Castilian throne.

Chronicon Angliae, 1328–1388, ed. Edward M. Thompson (RS, 64, 1874), 195–6, 199–200.

Llywelyn ap Gruffudd and so represented the line of the princes of Gwynedd. A distinguished soldier who had fought in France, Spain and Switzerland, he was greatly respected in France. In May 1372, Owain declared his intention to recover Wales from English rule, and his threat was formidable; he secured a large loan from Charles V and his invasion fleet set sail to Guernsey, which he captured and where he was wounded in the hand, so acquiring his nickname. In 1377 rumours of another planned invasion backed by Castile prompted the English to send a spy who assassinated Owain at Mortagne-sur-Gironde, on the French Atlantic coast, Davies (1987): 438; *The Times*, 18 Aug. 2003.

27 Buch (Gironde) was a strategically important town on the Atlantic seaboard, southwest of Bordeaux. The archaic hereditary military title of Captal was held by the Grailly family from the late thirteenth century. In 1378 the holder was Archambaud de Grailly.

28 Another military office.

Although the duke had drawn wages-money on the feast of the Purification *[2 February]* for keeping the sea and kingdom, so that he and his
men could be ready to go to sea by 1 March, he postponed his embarka-
tion until after the feast of St John the Baptist *[24 June]*. So those who
were going to go with him, having spent their wages, were assembled
not at sea but in their own land. From dire necessity they turned their
hands to plunder, and, apart from burning towns and killing people, they
did almost as much damage as the French would if they had been there.
In consequence there arose universal grumbling among the people, not
only from those who were harassed by the plundering, but those who
were compelled to steal .... Then also the worst curses and the foulest
invective grew against him, for this reason especially that, ignoring
both the shocked opinions of men and the fear of God, he deserted
the military responsibility which he had assumed, and was seen riding
about the countryside with a depraved bit of skirt (*cum nefanda pellice*),
namely a certain Katherine, surnamed Swynford, and publicly, with his
own hand, holding her bridle, not only in his wife's presence, but also
in full view of his compatriots, throughout the leading towns of the
realm ....

[The defeat of Gaunt's fleet by the Spanish and a sea-borne attack on Scarborough by Scottish raiders provoked the following response.]

John Philpot, a citizen of London,[29] a man outstanding in both thought
and deed, saw the failure of the duke of Lancaster and other lords who
should have defended the realm, and he was distressed by the oppressions of the inhabitants. So, with his own money, he recruited 1,000
armed men to seize ... the ships and goods which the pirates had
stolen, and to protect the realm of England from such raids. This was
done so that the Almighty, who always listens to pious prayers, should
confer great success upon him and his men, and so that, in a short time,
his hired men should capture *[the leader of the Scottish marauders]* by
judgment of war, with everything which he had violently taken away
at Scarborough ... and fifteen other Spanish ships, laden with much
treasure, which were helping him at that time.

29 Mayor of London in 1378–9; a member of the Grocers' Company, he later married
Nicholas Brembre's widow.

17. The violation of the Westminster sanctuary: the case of Hawley and Shakell

The origins of this affair dated from the battle of Nájera, 1367, when the Black Prince, fighting on behalf of Pedro king of Castile, won a victory over Pedro's bastard half-brother Henry of Trastamara. In this conflict two English squires, Robert Hawley and Richard Chamberlain, captured the count of Denia, a kinsman of the king of Aragon, though Chamberlain soon ceded his rights in the prisoner to John Shakell. Since both captors were members of his retinue, the Black Prince had a strong financial stake in the count's ransom,[30] and it was he who fixed the ransom in consultation with the prisoner. The amount was huge: 150,000 gold doubles, or more than three times the prince's annual revenue from the Duchy of Cornwall.

Despite elaborate guarantees, including the count's son being held hostage for his father, the ransom payment soon fell into arrears. The prince, who seems originally to have claimed the whole amount, ceded two-thirds of his claim to Edward III. Meanwhile, Hawley and Shakell continued to press for a share in the spoils, and the prince eventually gave them the one-third share which was his due as their commander. The value of the ransom was continually decreasing as the money was not forthcoming, and in 1374 Edward III decided to sell half of his two-thirds stake to Hawley and Shakell. Originally this share had been worth 50,000 doubles, but was now valued at 33,333 doubles. The following year the king decided to cut his losses and sold his remaining one-third share to the two squires for around 6,900 doubles. Hawley and Shakell were now faced with the twin tasks of recovering the ransom and of paying for the hostage's keep.

By 1377 the crown seems to have regretted disposing of its stake in the count's ransom, for the count had died, and been succeeded by his son who, along with the money he owed, was a potential diplomatic tool. The crown brought a ransom case against Hawley and Shakell in the court of the Marshal (a court of chivalry), claiming a part share. The pair were ordered to produce their hostage, and when they refused they were seized and put in the Tower of London.

Such is the background to the violation of the sanctuary of Westminster Abbey, on 11 August,[31] which provided all the elements a story-teller could desire: good guys; bad guys; a sinister 'Mr. Big' in the background (John of Gaunt, by implication); violence and drama; and a mystery – 'Where is the count of Denia?' – which was solved at the last moment.

(a) The incident according to Walsingham

Walsingham's is not the only chronicle to describe the episode, but it provoked him to produce a brilliant set-piece account of the affair. His mistakes were

30 Hay (1954): 91–109.
31 The feast of St Taurinus, Flete, ed. Armitage Robinson (1909): 137.

surely not deliberate, for this matter was remarkably complex. In 1378 the case of the count of Denia's ransom was by no means over; indeed much more of the saga lay in the future.[32]

SAC I.238–42, 310–12.

Once upon a time there were two squires whose like for valour could scarcely be surpassed either in England or in France. The name of one was Robert Hawley[33] and of the other John Shakell. Ten years before, during that war which the most illustrious Prince Edward[34] had fought against the Spaniards, in which he defeated Henry the Bastard *[Trastá-mara]* and restored to his kingdom Peter his brother *[Pedro the Cruel]*, who had been unjustly dethroned, these men had captured the count of Denia, a man of noble birth, who was declared to be their captive by the judgment of the prince and of John Chandos, the master of these gentlemen. They obtained charters to this effect, attested by the seals of the prince and of that same John, lest afterwards any claim should impede them and prevent them from taking the ransom of so great a personage. This count of Denia, therefore, gave them his son as a hostage, and by their leave he returned to his own country.

But when he returned to Spain he ignored the faith shown by those who had captured him; his son, it was said, remained a hostage, abandoned in England. After the two Edwards, namely the king the father, and the son the prince, had paid their debt to nature, the new king's counsellors arrogantly sought this man for the king's benefit. It seemed to some people that this was done to please the duke of Lancaster who had a right in the Spanish kingdom, so that, with the count in his possession, he could more easily gain possession of that kingdom. But others maintained that it was done on account of Lady Matilda, the king's *[half]* sister, widow of Sir Peter Courtenay, so that, if she were married to him and she was influential with him, peace and concord would grow between the kingdoms through such a marriage. But by no means could the king or the duke manage to prise the prisoner from their power because they had hidden him and had removed him from their presence; whereupon they were captured and thrust into the Tower of London. Escaping from this custody, they sought refuge in the court

32 Workman (1926): I.314–16; Perroy (1951): 573–80; Rogers (1962): 74–108; (1963): 53–78. It was still reverberating in the 1470s, *Cal. … Papal Letters* XIII, pt 1, 241–2.

33 Hawley served the Black Prince in 1365, 1369 and 1374, receiving letters of protection to serve with him in Spain.

34 Richard's father, the Black Prince; Russell (1955): chap. IV.

at Westminster.[35] The duke took this badly, and so did their enemies
the councillors, who disregarded all advice and even scorned equally
the privileges granted by holy kings, the papal confirmations and the
terrible threats against contravening sentences [of excommunication],
and even the fear of God and reverence for Holy Mother Church. They
decided to snatch the fugitives from sanctuary and take them back to
the Tower and keep them there more securely; or, it was thought, to
injure them so severely that they would be driven to death.

So there were sent to Westminster fifty armed men from among the
courtiers in order to commit this attack on men, God and the Church;
but secretly, however, for fear of the Londoners, lest there be an uproar
among the people.[36] They entered into the sanctuary of St Peter,
and by moving swiftly they surrounded the first man, namely, John
Shakell, removed him from ecclesiastical liberty, and led him back to
the Tower. But the same day, when they had come back for the second
man, Robert Hawley, he was present during solemn Mass for the [feast
of] St Lawrence [10 August]. They accosted him to satisfy the king in
this business in which he had offended his majesty; because he was the
king's liege man he had dared to scorn not so much the commands as
the entreaties of the king. But while Hawley strove to accuse, not the
king, but his advisers, of injustice, greed and false counsel, they seized
him in order to drag him violently out of the church. A short sword
was drawn, and soon the unarmed man was compelled to flee all these
armed men. In an effort to save himself he twice ran round the monks'
choir in flight, but finally he was surrounded on all sides in that by very
place by the armed men.

What more need I say? On all sides he was surrounded by men with
unsheathed daggers, making a horrible din, to make him surrender.
They threw into confusion both that most holy convent of monks, and
the priest standing at the sacred altar after the reading of the words of
the Holy Gospel. Their anger blazed up even more, so greatly did they
hold in contempt not only the house of God but even the servants of
Christ who now, as we said, were standing in the Lord's choir. Turning
those vessels of iniquity to their service, they fixed the point of their
swords to each monk's breast, forbidding them under pain of gruesome

35 *SAC* says *in curia ad Westmonasterium* though it is evident that they were actually
within Westminster abbey.

36 The words *ne forte tumultus fieret in plebe illa* echo Matthew 26:5: *ne forte tumultus fieret
in populo*. When the chief priests and elders were plotting Jesus' death they were
anxious not to do this during a festival time, for fear of provoking a riot.

death to give assistance to him whom they were seeking to kill. These men stood round Robert Hawley and while he sought the peace of the church, and while he asked the cause of so much wickedness, and as, finally, with hands crossed, he commended himself in these words to God and the Church, saying, 'I return myself to God, avenger of such injuries, and to the liberty of Holy Mother Church', one of them in the middle of these words, struck his head with a sword, while he was in the choir, standing before the altar, and cruelly brained him. Another of them at the same moment stabbed him with a sharp point from behind. A certain member of the convent of that church, who had endeavoured to prevent the perpetration of so great a crime, by exhortation and warning, lest that venerable temple, miraculously dedicated to the Prince of the Apostles [St Peter] and hitherto unpolluted, should be defiled, soon perished in that same spot by having a spear thrust through his side. He was crowned as a martyr, we believe. But those ministers of Satan, already overhasty, were not content with such cursed deeds; they seized the lifeless corpse of Robert Hawley by the heels, they dragged it horribly through the most sacred place of the choir, and through the church, polluting everything with his blood and brains. Finally, they rushed headlong and threw it out of doors, just like demented Bacchantes who neither fear God nor reverence men.

(b) The political consequences
Anon. Chron., 122–4.

The archbishop of Canterbury, the bishop of London and the abbot and convent solemnly excommunicated all those evildoers who had done such wrong to Holy Church ... by which the church was polluted; neither Mass nor Matins was chanted in that abbey until the feast of Christmas when they had a papal grace because that church was dedicated and sanctified to the apostle St Peter, as is found in the chronicles.

For this reason there was much dispute and discord between the king and the abbot, because the king and his council proposed to revoke the whole royal franchise of Westminster and remove all the abbey's temporalities, from their liberty, for contempt, because they had refused to hand over those squires to the king. The king's council accused the abbey of having received the prisoner who was the cause of this dispute, contrary to the king's will so that he could receive the ransom from him, to the benefit of the realm, and this sanctuary gave absolutely no right to receive those accused of debt or treason. The abbot demanded time for consultation, and the king's council fixed a date for a hearing at the next meeting of parliament, at Gloucester. The abbot came to this parliament and went before the commons when they were deliberating in the monks' chapter house. He showed them how his church was dedicated to St Peter the Apostle and could not be reconciled[37] by any bishop, but only by the holy father the pope or his representative; he explained to them how the abbey was despoiled of these squires, and he showed them its charters of privilege, begging them, for charity, for remedy by their good counsel, so that redress and amendment could be made to Holy Church for the evil which had occurred, and restitution of the squire who had been dragged out of the church and imprisoned in the Tower of London. Because he had laid these matters before the commons, the king and his council were very angry and indignant at the abbot and convent. At the same time there was a distinguished clerk of Oxford, called Master John Wycliffe, who had often preached in Oxford and argued that the king could seize the property of possessioners[38] to assist in his war, and that no church had such a franchise that it could harbour a man for debt. So the king ordered Master John to come to parliament, and when he arrived, on the appointed day, he entered the chapter house among the commons, accompanied by a doctor of laws, at the instigation of Sir Simon Burley, the king's tutor, and Sir Thomas Percy. Master John began to explain to the commons that the king and his council could safely and in [good] conscience drag the squires out of Holy Church for debt or treason, and that God himself could not make dispensation for debt. There followed much disputation by clerical subtlety and declarations on the same matter by these two, because there was no clerk of eminence on that occasion to answer them, because this was arranged at short notice. Those clerks were condemned by the commons and bystanders for their actions in destroying the liberty of Holy Church. The king and council were greatly strengthened by their arguments, and the abbot and convent much discomfited by the folly of these same clerks.

(c) How the matter ended

SAC I.310–12.

By the intervention of certain weighty persons, who piously and justly grieved a great deal for the injury once imposed on certain persons

---

37 A church polluted by the shedding of blood could not be used again until it had been re-consecrated by a bishop.

38 Churchmen receiving profits of endowments of real property.

in the church of Westminster, viz Robert Hawley and John Shakell, peace and freedom were restored to John Shakell. We have described earlier how he was extracted from that church, dragged to the Tower of London, and there imprisoned. An agreement was reached between the lord king and him, at the request of venerable men,[39] by which John Shakell made over to the lord king his captive, the son of the count of Denia, who now, by the recent death of his father, had become count of Denia by inheritance; for no one yet knew of what character he would be, nor where he had been living all this time. Furthermore, it was agreed that the lord king should give the said John, for possession of this captive, lands to the value of 100 marks a year, and 500 marks in cash; and that the lord king would, from his own resources, found a perpetual chantry of five priests for the souls of those whom his ministers had killed in that church. When these conditions had been agreed, the captive would be returned to the king, and John Shakell restored to freedom. When ordered to produce his captive, to the amazement of everyone, he brought forward his servant, who had stood by him and served him as a valet in all his adversity, both before the persecution which landed him in prison, and outside prison; and he had stuck to him so faithfully that he could not be recognised; he ministered to him so faithfully that he could easily have been taken for a hired retainer.

18. A monk's-eye view of the Gloucester parliament

It was almost certainly the court's unpopularity which prompted the holding of the next parliament at Gloucester, a remarkable move because no parliament had been held outside Westminster since 1338. One of the unusual features of Richard II's reign was the number of parliaments held outside London, and the king's ambivalent attitude to his capital was perhaps formed during his minority. In 1378 the Council probably feared popular anger at the recent outrage in Westminster Abbey,[40] but holding parliament in a provincial town was very inconvenient for members, and for this meeting we have an insider's viewpoint of the unwilling hosts.

Historia et Cartularium Monasterii S. Petri Gloucestriae, ed. W. H. Hart, I (RS, 1863), 52–4.

39 The phrase *viris venerabilibus* probably means senior ecclesiastics.
40 Saul (1997): 37–8.

In 1378, during the first year of the abbot [John Boyfeld],[41] a parliament
began at Gloucester on 22 October which lasted until 16 November.
King Richard stayed alternately in Gloucester abbey and in Tewkes-
bury, as he pleased. When he was at Gloucester both he and his whole
household lodged in the abbey, which, what with them and the parliament, was everywhere so full up that the convent for some days ate in
the dormitory. But afterwards it was judged to be more convenient to
eat in the schoolhouse, on both meat and on fish days, for the duration
of parliament, for reasons of absolute necessity; and on those days their
food was prepared in the orchard. So the laws of arms were discussed
in the refectory, while the guest hall was assigned to the commons of
parliament. Furthermore, in the guest chamber, a room which was traditionally called 'the king's room', on account of its beauty, confidential
discussion were held among the magnates, while the commons' discus-
sions took place in the chapter house. ....Truly, all the accessible areas
in the monastery were so crowded by those coming to parliament that
they appeared to observers places of commerce rather than of religion.
Indeed the very grass of the cloister was so flattened by the strenuous
exertions of the wrestlers and ball-players that no trace of greenness
could be found there. On the third day before the end of the parliament, which was a Sunday [14 November], they held a royal banquet,
as custom required; it was held in the refectory. For the occasion the
lord abbot sang High Mass in the choir. The king was no less keen and
enthusiastic about this, and, dressed in suitably regal style, he heard
the Mass devoutly, and he very humbly paid a most worthy donation of
royal magnificence; and, prompted by the duke [of Lancaster], the abbot
blessed him. At this Mass there were present two archbishops, twelve
bishops, the duke of Lancaster with his two brothers, namely the earls
of Cambridge and Hereford,[42] and other earls, barons, knights and an
almost countless number of the common people of differing rank, sex
and age. At last, after Mass was honourably celebrated, the king, closely
surrounded by these magnates, set off with the crowd to the place of
the banquet. On the fourth working day after, namely the morrow of
St Edmund the Archbishop [17 November], everything concerning the
government of the realm was successfully and without disagreement
(somewhat miraculously as was then believed, by divine dispensation)

41 Elected 1377; died 1380.
42 Thomas of Woodstock (earl of Buckingham, 1377) received the third penny of
   Herefordshire from 1380 to 1384, though he was never styled earl of Hereford, HBC:
   465.

happily arranged, and all went to their homes rejoicing. ... No tax was imposed on the common people – happy to relate – nor were ecclesiastical men oppressed by any payments of tenths; but only the merchants, by common consent, supplied a money aid for the king's war, on behalf of the whole kingdom, because they were rich.

19. Decisions of the Gloucester parliament

This parliament took two important policy decisions.

(a) New military strategy.

The renewed military activity which followed the expiry of the Anglo-French truce in June 1377 forced the English, whose military position had been in decline since 1369, to formulate a new strategy, which was outlined in this parliament. The 'barbican' policy meant keeping strong garrisons in a number of places, especially on the French coast (Calais and Cherbourg being notable examples); these would not only defend England and her overseas interests but could also become launch-pads for any later attacks on French territory.

RP III.34, 36; *PROME* 1378, sections 15, 25.

[*On Friday 22 October, Sir Richard Scrope, Steward of the King's Household, introducing the need for a tax grant, said:*] 'It is very obvious to everyone that our lord king, his realm of England and his other lands, territories and lordships, are threatened on all sides by our enemies who are increasing daily, both in Scotland and elsewhere ... and that we have, very recently, opened many beautiful and noble entry-points and ports to harass our enemies, which have not long been in English hands, namely Cherbourg and Brest; not to mention Calais, Bordeaux and Bayonne, which require no small sum to protect, and thus a large sum must be devoted to safeguarding the same. So our lord king spends annually at Calais and its surrounding borders, more than £24,000 and at Brest a full 12,000 marks,[43] and at Cherbourg it is now necessary to spend large sums; also at Bordeaux and Bayonne, for their safety; and in our king's lands and lordships in Guyenne and elsewhere overseas; and also in Ireland ...'

[*In answer to commons' criticisms that £46,000 had been spent on guarding places overseas which were not their financial responsibility, it was said on the king's behalf that:*] Gascony and the other strongholds which our

43 £8,000.

lord king had overseas are and should be like barbicans to the realm of England, and if the barbicans are well guarded and the sea secured, the realm will be safe enough; but otherwise we shall never have security or peace from our enemies, because they will then wage fierce war on us at our very doorsteps, which God forbid; and also in those barbicans our lord king has such good ports and entry-points through which to harass his adversaries when he pleases, and can do so.

(b) Recognition of Urban VI as the legitimate pope

The decision to give English loyalty to the Roman pope, Urban VI, after the election of a rival, Clement VII (the Avignon pope) on 20 September 1378, formed English foreign policy for the rest of the reign. Indeed, the way the secular powers of Europe lined up behind the rival pontiffs dominated international relations until the schism was ended in 1417. With France and her allies giving allegiance to the Avignon papacy, and England being among those who decided to remain with the Roman pope, a new element entered the series of conflicts centred on the Anglo-French war. A common petition, now damaged (RP III.48; PROME 38,78) formed the basis of this important statute.
SR II.11.

Because our lord king has heard, both by letters patent newly arrived, of certain cardinals in rebellion against our Holy Father Urban now pope, and also by common report, that division and discord have arisen between our said Holy Father and those cardinals, who strive with all their might to depose our said Holy Father from the position of pope and to incite and stir up, by their untrue allegations, the kings, princes and the Christian people against him, to the great peril of their souls, and as an evil example; our lord king has caused those same letters to be shown to the prelates, lords and other great men of his realm present at parliament; and having seen and heard these letters, and after much deliberation on this matter, it was pronounced and published by those prelates, for the great and notable reasons shown there in full parliament, both by the matter found in those same letters and elsewhere, that the said Urban was duly elected as pope, and that so he is and ought to be the true pope, and ought to be accepted and obeyed as true pope and head of Holy Church. And all the prelates, lords and commons in this parliament are in agreement to do this. And, further, it is agreed that all the benefices and other possessions which those same rebellious cardinals, and all their other collaborators, supporters, adherents or any another enemies of our lord king and his realm have within the king's power, shall be seized into the hands of our lord king. And that answer should be made to our lord the king for the fruits and profits of those same benefices and possessions, as long as they shall remain in his hands for the above reason. Also it is decided that if any subject of the king, or person within his power, should purchase a provision,[44] benefice or any other grace from any other person in the name of any pope except our Holy Father Urban, or be obedient to any other pope, he shall be put outside our lord's protection, and his goods and chattels seized as forfeit.

20. Bad feeling between Thomas of Woodstock and Nicholas Brembre, former mayor of London

The Gloucester parliament was also the occasion when the king's youngest uncle, Thomas, entered politics, as a complainant with a grudge against Nicholas Brembre, a prominent court supporter in London and formerly mayor.

Riley, *Memorials of London*, 424, 427–8, from London Letter-Book H, adapted.

(a) John Maynard, wax chandler, and other evildoers in his gang recently committed in London an offence against that honourable lord, [*Thomas of Woodstock*] the earl of Buckingham and his servants. For this offence Nicholas Brembre, then mayor of London, was impeached and censured by that lord and by other members of the king's council at the parliament held at Gloucester, and he paid a large sum of money to that lord. All the community of London had for the same reason often been forced to pay damages for the misdeeds of those particular criminals; but those damages should rightly rather fall upon those who were guilty of the offences, than upon others. So it was unanimously ordered, by assent of John Philpot the mayor, the aldermen and a Common Council held at the Guildhall on the Saturday following the feast of saints Simon and Jude [*28 October 1378*], that John Maynard and all others of his gang, should, as soon as they were found within the city, be arrested and detained until they and their sureties made sufficient compensation, both to Nicholas and the whole community, for all the payments, wrongs, losses and damages suffered by any of them for the above reason.

(b) On 25 November [*1378*] John Philpot the mayor and all the aldermen and community, the aldermen and commoners of the Common Council of London, and others of the more reputable citizens of that city, were

44 The appointment to a benefice, when made by the pope.

specially summoned and assembled together in the upper chamber of the
Guildhall by John Hadleye and his colleagues, namely Geoffrey Newton,
John Northampton and William Vanner, citizens of London elected on
its behalf to the parliament at Gloucester. It was reported by William
Walworth, who was also there, and by the four elected members, that
when Nicholas Brembre, mayor of London, had come to Gloucester
at the king's command, he was questioned there and arraigned in full
parliament by Thomas of Woodstock, earl of Buckingham, because in
the same year on Cornhill in London, the men of that neighbourhood
assaulted the earl's servants, beat, wounded and pursued them as they
fled to his town house, where they broke and smashed down its doors
with axes and other weapons. The earl was inside, lying in bed, and was
greatly alarmed by this affray, which caused him grievous damage, and
was a pernicious example to the whole realm. All this, alleged the earl,
had happened through the inexcusable slothfulness of the said Nicholas,
and he requested that redress should be made to him for the same.

Whereupon Nicholas, wonderfully well as it appeared to all his friends,
rebutted and cleared himself of all the acts of injury so imputed to him;
so well that on the same day he returned to his lodging with honour,
as being an innocent man and entirely exonerated. The earl, however,
and his brothers and some other lords who were his friends, seeing
that they could not gain their ends by those means, most grievously
threatened both Nicholas and the whole city of London, so much so
that all the citizens who were present dreaded that some new statute
would be made there, or perhaps [an old statute] confirmed anew
through which London and many of its officers might incur no small
damage, and also the liberties of the city be infringed, and in great
measure perhaps annulled, unless the earl could be appeased in some
other way. So it was agreed through mediators, that, in order to avoid
something worse which otherwise might very probably befall them,
Nicholas Brembre should give the earl 100 marks, on the understanding that he should no longer have any right of action against
Nicholas on those grounds, but would show himself a kind lord
towards him for the future.

These transactions were related in the presence of the mayor and
Common Council, and every one of them gave Nicholas hearty thanks,
for they knew for certain that it was not for his own faults, but to
preserve the liberties of the city and for the extreme love which he
bore it, that he had undergone such labours and expenses. Therefore,
the mayor, aldermen, and all the rest of the commoners, unanimously

and faithfully granted and promised that the city should indemnify Nicholas for the 100 marks, and also for all other expenses incurred by him because of that business. And, that this might be remembered, orders were given to the Common clerk that it should be entered in the record. This was also unanimously agreed and affirmed, at another meeting of the Common Council on the 15 January following *[1379]*.

21. An insult to the king, and its aftermath

Richard is often thought to have been unduly sensitive to personal criticism or slights to his position, but this episode shows that such attitudes characterised those governing during his minority.

Eulogium, 348–9.

A knight of the king's household came from Woodstock to Oxford, and at night some students came and stood outside his lodging, chanting rhythmically in English some insulting words against the king's honour, and they shot arrows at his window. When he got up in the morning the knight complained to the king. Immediately the chancellor and the vice-chancellor *[of the university]* were summoned to London and brought before the chancellor of the realm[45] and the king's Council. When the chancellor of the university was asked why he had not punished those who insulted the king he replied: because he feared disorder.

The chancellor of the realm: 'You provide the evidence that Oxford cannot be governed by the clergy. We cannot have the king insulted like this at Oxford or anywhere else, and if you at Oxford are unable to correct and punish those who insult the king – because of unrest, as the chancellor says – it follows that Oxford cannot be governed by clerics, and the king should withdraw its privileges. You ought to defend the university's privileges as much as you can, both because of your office and because of your oath, yet you speak against these privileges. We dismiss you from your office'.

The chancellor of the university answered: 'I receive my office from the pope and from the king; what I have from the king, the king can take away, but not that which I have from the pope'. The chancellor of England retorted: 'And we have deprived you on the king's behalf, disqualifying you from this office; now see if you can get any joy from

45 Probably Richard Scrope, lord Scrope of Bolton, who became chancellor on 29 Oct. 1378.

the pope's part. The king can remove from Oxford both the university and you'.

The vice-chancellor, a monk, was sentenced to imprisonment because, at the pope's command, he had, as we said earlier, imprisoned John Wycliffe who afterwards was freed at the request of his friends. The deposed chancellor, disguising his dismissal, resigned freely in convocation so that he could say that he was not coerced.

22. An unfavourable view of Alexander Neville, archbishop of York

Before Alexander Neville became a courtier in 1385, he had already made many enemies, including St Albans Abbey and its chronicler.

Thomas Walsingham, *Gesta Abbatum Monasterii Sancti Albani*, ed. H. T. Riley (RS, 1869), III.278–9.

The archbishop of York, called Alexander Neville, was a man as useless to the realm as to the church, grasping towards his own men, but lavish among strangers. When he had consumed the ample resources of his see, he schemed to seize his subjects' money so that he would not lack resources for his dissolute ways. So he pretended to have held a synod at which a large subsidy had been granted to him by his subjects, not by the grace of love, but by the goad of fear. And because the abbot of St Albans held the church of Appleton[46] in his diocese, and had not been present at that synod – because the archbishop had not cited nor summoned him – the archbishop adjudged him contumacious[47] and fined him a large sum of money. Not content with this, the archbishop ordered and caused to be sequestrated a certain sum of money, owed by the abbot and convent for that alleged subsidy granted to the archbishop by the York clergy, at the synod to which neither the abbot nor the convent were summoned, and he harassed them to extort it. And he heaped one wrong upon another: because the abbot and convent had, for the monastery's good, sold the fruits, rents and profits, for one year, of that parish church belonging to the monastery, which had been previously set apart, he ordered and caused those fruits to be sequestrated and he held on to them.

46 Appleton le Moor in north Yorkshire, *VCH Hertfordshire* IV.389.
47 Disobedient to a summons of legal force.

Abbot Thomas [de la Mare], bloody but unbowed by these events, sought remedy by bringing a case of appeal in the Roman curia, and so vigorously and so vehemently did he prosecute this matter that he took vengeance on the archbishop at the start of the case. For he caused him to be cited to the curia by legal process, and when he did not appear, he was judged contumacious. If anyone wants to read the proceedings of this case he should look in the register of that abbot, and in the year 1379 there is the case in full. This is my final assertion: that the abbot, by his courage and constancy obtained the best result in this business, and provided peace for his church, so that never again did that archbishop try to molest the abbey.

1379

This year and the next were dominated by the government's need to raise money in the light of continuing and unsuccessful warfare. Indeed, the years 1371–81 have a unity created by the experiments in taxation that is arguably stronger than the division resulting from the change of king.[48] Starting with the parish tax of 1371, through the first poll tax of 1377 (voted in Edward III's last parliament), this decade of fiscal novelty continued with the graduated poll tax of 1379 – a remarkably subtle and sophisticated measure but one which failed to raise sufficient revenue. These experiments took place against a background of discontent; criticism of perceived financial ineptitude was a feature of parliament in this decade.

23. Continuing warfare on land and sea according to the *Anonimalle Chronicle*

The chronicler begins his account of the year with the parliament of 24 April to 27 May granting the graduated poll tax, and he lists its rates. See Dobson (1983): 107–11. The descriptions of fighting remind us of the reason for the government's constant need for money.

Anon. Chron., 129–32.

In 1379 Sir John Harleston, captain of Cherbourg in Normandy, and the soldiers stationed in the garrison of that town suffered a great food shortage. So the men of the garrison begged the captain to make a raid into the countryside, so that they could seize animals and food, and damage their French enemies. Finally he graciously agreed. On 4 July, which was a Monday, all the men of the garrison gathered and mounted

48 Jurkowski, Smith and Crook (1998): 54–62.

on horseback in the morning and they raided across the countryside
for at least fourteen English leagues;[49] they numbered a good 400
men-at-arms and archers, and they ravaged the whole country round,
took about 1,000 beasts and returned to their town of Cherbourg. On
returning, two hours after nones that same captain, Sir John Harleston,
looked towards a small hill rising up a league from them and there
he saw about forty enemy lances mustering on that hill to spy on
them. Sir John told his companions it was clear that there were many
of the enemy in sight, and it seemed likely that there would be an
encounter with them that very day. Afterwards the enemy assembled
to the number of 600 men-at-arms well arrayed, and 500 bowmen, not
counting foot-soldiers, who took up a good position in order to alarm
Sir John and his men. At this Sir John, seeing their array, comforted his
companions, telling them that he would not leave the field until he had
fought, if that was the enemy's wish, and urging the men to confess to
each other and be clean and pure and of good heart. Then he arrayed
his men wisely, dividing them into two companies of troops with 40
lancers in each part, and the same in the first battle line and vanguard,
ordering them to help him when needed. Shortly afterwards the two
hosts engaged and struck each other hard. Sir John was knocked to the
ground, but was quickly picked up and helped by his men. They were in
fierce conflict and endured a long time, fighting with axes and lances,
swords and daggers. Finally they broke through the enemy lines, vigorously prevailed over them and discomfited them, by divine grace, and
killed a great number of them. There died at that place 100 knights
and squires of high estate; they took many good prisoners that day and
brought them to Cherbourg along with the looted animals they seized
earlier, thanking the Almighty for such a good victory.

A month later, the earl of Salisbury, then captain of Calais, and Sir
Brian Stapleton the deputy captain, heard that the captain of Beaulieu
in Guînes had gone to his Maker (this Beaulieu was a very strong and
beautiful abbey,[50] and for a long time was held by force of arms against
the king of England and the good duke Henry of Lancaster[51] and many
other lords) and that the soldiers of that captain of Beaulieu had left
the abbey for lack of food and payment. So the captain and his men of
the Calais garrison made their way to the abbey to see if they could

---

49 A league's distance is uncertain, but was perhaps about 3 miles, though Knighton
   [98c] makes it 4½ miles and Froissart [121a] uses 'English leagues' of about 4 miles.
50 Beaulieu in Guînes was an abbey of Augustinian canons.
51 Henry of Grosmont, father of Gaunt's first duchess, who died in 1362.

capture it. They came close to the abbey and saw a good thirty armed men on the walls to defend it against enemies. At this the English, by common consent, returned without striking a blow or making an assault, and they ordered certain armed men privately to be concealed to spy if anyone came to help them, by night; those men saw clearly that the defenders had no help and that no one came to them, except only one woman who was their servant. They caught her and questioned her harshly on various matters, and the conditions of those inside. She told them that there were only thirty defenders inside the abbey and that the other soldiers had gone home, and that they could not hold the abbey for much longer without more help, if they were strongly attacked. So the spies informed the earl-captain of Calais what the woman had told them. He therefore assembled his men and hastily came to that abbey, where they made a vigorous assault and soon captured it, and they took all the prisoners and some of the monks with them to Calais. They put the abbey to fire and flame and they razed the walls, so it remained in ruins for a long time afterwards.

It was decided in parliament that Sir John Arundel, son of the earl of Arundel, and Sir Thomas Banaster and Sir John Trumpington,[52] knights of the duke of Lancaster, and many other knights and commons with them, ought to go to Brittany to aid and succour the duke of Brittany against his Breton enemies; and about the feast of St Nicholas they were arrayed, and began their journey to the sea. During their journey through the country side they robbed the poor people of their goods and chattels, causing them great damage, and they took women and girls against their will and raped and villainously defiled them, contrary to the law of God and Holy Church. For this they were excommunicated and were greatly cursed in all the county round; wherefore great vengeance came upon them shortly after. On the feast of St Nicholas [6 Dec.] they came to the coast and embarked and took many girls with them, in great elation of spirit, to their own discomfiture. And when they were sailing on the high seas there arose a tempest so horrible and hideous that it was phenomenal; it lasted nine days, and they were driven from land to land. During that time seventeen ships, laden with men-at-arms and archers, were lost altogether; and finally Sir John Arundel who was their captain and leader, and his companions who had been driven by the tempest to the coast of Ireland, ordered the

52 Walker (1990): 32n., 152, 153, 263 (Banaster); 26 (the Trumpington family), and 35n., 99, 110, 281 (Sir Roger Trumpington, who is probably the individual mentioned here).

master mariner to make a landing. But the sailors advised them to put themselves on the high sea and they could be saved there, otherwise they would perish. They did not agree to this, but made the mariner steer the ship towards the land where they expected to be saved; but to no purpose, because God did not wish to forgive them their wickedness, and as was said by the men, the devil was seen in that same ship pulling a monstrous face to make the ship founder. At that time Sir John, Sir Thomas and Sir John wished they had made land, but they could not, nor did they have the grace to be saved but were drawn out of the ship which was sunk to the bottom, and many good men with them. So the day was lost, and the duke of Brittany was without hope of aid or succour.

24. Grant of an allowance to Thomas of Woodstock

Much of Thomas of Woodstock's political career can be explained by this grant; it was both fragile ('during pleasure') and exceptionally miserly, for the alien priories had been milked by the exchequer for years and their farms formed a very uncertain income,[53] which would disappear if peace was made with France. So this uncle of the king was a victim of the government's weak financial position, and had a vested interest in continuing warfare.

CPR 1377–81, 372.

5 July 1379. Grant, during pleasure, with the assent of the Council, to the king's uncle, Thomas of Woodstock, earl of Buckingham, that he may receive the £1,000 a year granted to him at the exchequer on 17 July 1 Richard II [1377] for the maintenance of his rank as an earl, from the following farms of alien priories, in the king's hands on account of the war with France, viz from the priory of Ware [*Herts.*] £206 13s 4d, from that of West Mersea [*Essex*] £60, from that of Takeley [*Essex*] £133 6s 8d, from that of Stoke by Clare [*Suffolk*] £60, from those of Panfield and Wells [*Essex*] £40, from the farm of the possessions of the abbess of Caen £266 13s 4d., from those of the abbot of Fécamp £200, and from the priory of Swavesey [*Cambs.*] £33 6s 8d.

---

53 McHardy (1989): 277–95, esp. 284–6.

1380

25. The year 1380 according to the *Anonimalle Chronicle*

This short account of the year's second parliament conceals the agonising which went on at that meeting [29], but this chronicle's emphasis on foreign warfare explains much of the domestic tension evident whenever parliament met.

Anon. Chron., 132–3.

King Richard held a parliament at Northampton, which began after the feast of All Saints *[1 November]*. In that parliament there was granted to the king a subsidy for which every archbishop, bishop, abbot, prior, canon of a cathedral church or college, archdeacon, dean, rector and vicar had to pay half a mark *[6s. 8d.]* and each monk, canon or chaplain 3s. 4d., and each clerk 12d., and each lay man and woman between sixteen and seventy years old 12d., and this was to be paid in the following year at the feasts of Easter *[15 April 1381]* and St Peter in Chains *[1 August 1381]*.

Thomas of Woodstock, earl of Buckingham, Lord Latimer, Sirs Thomas Percy, *[Hugh]* Calveley, *[John]* Harleston, *[Robert]* Knolles and many others went to Brittany to the great disadvantage of the commons, because the duke of Brittany did not want to help them with gold or silver, nor by advice, nor with soldiers, but he became French and did homage to the king of France for certain lands which he held of him. When they returned to England Lord Latimer took very ill and died before Pentecost *[13 May]*, and was buried with great honour in Guisborough Priory, in Cleveland. May God of his great grace have pity and mercy on his soul.[54]

By assent of the English king and all the lords, the duke of Lancaster made his way towards Scotland after the feast of Pentecost to discuss a peace between the two kingdoms of England and Scotland; by agreement of the ambassadors the parties concluded a profitable truce for two years so that the peoples could come and go and trade, without disturbance or molestation; and those who were trespassers through larceny or through any felony, from whichever side they came, should be delivered, the Scots to the English and the English to the Scots, until redress was made to the parties to whom the trespass was done, whether

---

54 Not everyone thought so well of Latimer; see Holmes (1975): 101–7, 109–11, 126–33, and McHardy (1989): 277–95. See also **8, 11**.

by ransom or by punishment. But the Scots for their part behaved badly because great redress was made to the Scots and none to the English.

26. The parliament of 16 January–3 March 1380

Even so early in the reign dissatisfaction and calls for reform are evident. *SAC I.342–4.*

On the Octave of Epiphany *[13 January]* a parliament was held at London which went on continuously until 1 March *[correctly, 3 March]*. During this meeting the community of the realm asked that there should be appointed as guardian one of the barons who knew how to make diplomatic answers to foreigners, who should be of mature character, strong in deeds, reasonable and discreet. So by common consent Thomas Beauchamp, earl of Warwick, was selected to live close to the king, who would take from the royal treasury a fitting sum each year for his trouble. For there had been deputed to this business, in the previous year, certain bishops, earls, barons, with judges and many others who were to help his council, and to be useful. They all, in the course of the year, drained off a great sum of money from the king's funds, and showed no or few results, so now, as we said, the community requested that, after the rest had been removed, there should be one man who would fulfil all the roles which previously they had performed. Also in this parliament Sir Richard Scrope relinquished office as chancellor, and the archbishop of Canterbury, Master Simon Sudbury, contrary to the rank of his dignity, as many pointed out, succeeded to that office like a knight.[55] But whether he sought this, or undertook it willingly, God knows.

27. The commons' petition for reform, spring 1380

In that year's first parliament the chancellor explained the serious financial situation, which had resulted in a much smaller expedition being sent to Brittany than had been planned. John de Gildesborough, the speaker, replied on the commons' behalf.
RP III.73; *PROME* 1380 (1), sections 12–14.

55 Chancellors were usually bishops, so this is a curious comment. Walsingham may be expressing disapproval of an archbishop of Canterbury who had not made a career in crown service becoming involved in government.

He said that it seemed to the commons that if their liege lord were well and reasonably governed in respect of his expenses, both inside the realm and out, he would now have no need of their aid by burdening his commons because they were too poor .... He asked that the prelates and other lords of the continual council, who had laboured long on this matter, should be completely discharged, to their great ease, and to save the crown their expenses; and that no such councillors should be retained any longer about the king, considering that he was now of such good discretion and such fine stature, and having regard for his age, which was now almost the same as the age of his noble grandfather, whom God save, who at the start of his reign had no other councillors, except only the usual five principal officers of the realm. He asked also that in that parliament there should be elected and chosen the five principal officers from the most sufficient and capable men in the realm, and who could best fulfil their offices, that is: the chancellor, treasurer, keeper of the privy seal, the chief chamberlain and the steward of the king's household. And the commons wished to be told the names of those chosen during this present parliament, to their very great comfort and for the aid and profit of the king's business, and notified to the same commons; nor should they be removed before the next parliament, save by reason of death, disease or other such necessary cause.

He also asked that in order to remedy the defects of government, if any there were, a sufficient general commission be made, as could be best devised, to certain prelates, lords and others of the most sufficient, loyal and wise men of the kingdom of England, to make diligent survey and to examine in all the courts and places of the king, both in his household and elsewhere, the estate of the household and all the expenses and receipts of each minister in any office of the realm, and of the other lordships and lands overseas, both at home and overseas, from the king's coronation until then, so that if any fault were found by this examination, in any manner, through negligence of the officers or in any other manner, those same commissioners should inform the lord king what to amend and correct, so that he be honourably governed within his realm, as he ought to be, and from his own resources support the expenses of defending the realm and of all other costs.

Afterwards our lord king, on the advice of the lords of parliament, readily granted that such a commission be made ... and that the said commission, made by their advice to the best of their ability, should be rehearsed in full parliament, and assented thereto; also it was agreed that those commissioners would afterwards have new articles for that commission, newly adjusted and with greater power, which was to be amended from time to time as could best be devised; saving always the estate and regality of the lord king in all matters.

28. Edward III's trustees petition for their rights

Although this scandal was not mentioned by the chroniclers, it was a symptom of the new regime's greed, corruption, contempt for property rights and disregard for Edward III's wishes. In autumn 1376, as Edward's health sharply worsened, he made his will and established a trust [4] intending to benefit the Dominican priory of King's Langley, St Stephen's College, Westminster, and, especially, St Mary Graces, a Cistercian abbey beside the Tower of London.

To safeguard his scheme to increase St Mary's landed endowment, Edward selected an impressive group of ten trustees headed by Gaunt and the archbishop of Canterbury. To no avail: scarcely was the king in his grave when the provisions of his will were set aside and the properties involved were seized by greedy courtiers. Especially attractive to them were the extensive lands, mainly in Kent, which had once been held by Juliana Leybourne, countess of Huntingdon: the Leybourne inheritance. In 1378 the trustees petitioned parliament for the return of their properties and, despite an attempt to browbeat the judges, they won their case. The judgment, however, was ineffective. They again petitioned parliament in 1379, but this too resulted in little improvement.

The two following petitions were presented to parliament in 1380: the first almost certainly to the January parliament, the second either then or to the November parliament. Neither has an endorsement saying what action resulted from these petitions; and, despite agreements between crown and trustees made in 1380–82, some courtiers, especially Burley, were able to gain possession of this property from 1383 onwards.

TNA SC 8/100/4995 and 4989; printed, C. J. Given-Wilson, 'Richard II and his grandfather's will', *EHR* 93 (1978), 336–7.

(a) To our lord king and the lords in this present parliament: John, king of Castile and Leon, duke of Lancaster, Simon, archbishop of Canterbury, John, bishop of Lincoln, Henry, bishop of Worcester [*for the five lay trustees see* 4a] show that since our lord the King Edward, whom God save, grandfather of our present lord king, gave and granted to them and to Roger Beauchamp, now deceased, all the castles, manors, lands and tenements with fees, advowsons of churches, regalities, franchises, reversions, parks, woods, warrens, chases, fisheries, rents, services and with all the other appurtenances which the said grandfather had purchased, to have and to hold to them and their heirs in fee simple, unconditionally, as is more fully contained in the charters of the said

grandfather made to them under his great seal; and on this the grandfather had caused to be delivered full seisin of those castles, manors,
lands and tenements, without mention of any condition on the said gift,
either on the gift or on the livery of the said charters or on the livery
of the said seisin; and at the suit of those feoffees to the parliament
held at Gloucester on the quindene of Michaelmas in the second year
of the present king *[13 October 1378]* it was expressly declared that if
that gift was simple, without any discussion before the gift or on the
gift or on the livery of any charge in doing what the feoffees ought to
do, that by no entreaty made to them after they first came into possession of the king's charters, which are the record of that preceding gift
which was simple,[56] could that gift be made conditional. For that reason
it was agreed in the last parliament held at Westminster *[April–May
1379]* that writs, of such kinds and so many as should be necessary,
should be sent to the treasurer and barons of the exchequer, to the
sheriffs and to other ministers of the present king, to cease completely
and to remove the king's hand from occupying these castles, manors,
lands and tenements without any ... interfering with them. This agreement is ineffective and still nothing is done to disturb any of the king's
officers. May it please you, wise persons, to order that agreement to be
entered on the record of this present parliament, and also to put that
same assent into due execution; that also full payment should be made
to those feoffees[57] for all the rents and profits whatsoever of the said
castles, manors, lands and tenements with their appurtenances received
by the officers and ministers of the present king in any way since the
death of that said grandfather, as reason and good faith demand.

(b) To our lord king and the lords in this present parliament: John,
king of Castile *[and the other trustees, as above]* show that as the lord
king *[Edward III]* gave and granted to them, and to Roger Beauchamp,
now deceased, and to their heirs in fee simple, unconditionally, all the
castles, manors, lands and tenements which that grandfather had by
purchase, together with all the livestock, goods and chattels of the
same castles, manors, lands and tenements present or in any manner
whatsoever to be found, as is plainly contained in the charter *[Edward
III]* made under his great seal on 5 October in the fiftieth year ·of his
reign *[1376]*; and on this the said livestock, goods and chattels which
are in the castles, manors, lands and tenements aforesaid, are, by the

56 Fee simple: an estate in land held absolutely and descending to heirs without direction or entail.

57 They would now be described as trustees.

ministers of the present king, without the assent of the said feoffees, to whom those same goods rightfully belong, being taken and carried away. That it may please your wise discretions to order and command in this present parliament that the said livestock, goods and chattels should be restored to those said feoffees completely and without delay.

29. Parliament at Northampton grants a new poll tax, winter 1380

When parliament met at Northampton from 5 November until 6 December it was asked to make a grant of £160,000. The commons replied that this was outrageous and passed to the lords the responsibility for devising a scheme to raise this sum.

RP III.89–90; *PROME* 1380 (2), section 13.

When the prelates and lords had pondered and discussed this matter at length they caused the commons to appear before them again, and gave them their advice on how it seemed that they should now proceed. First, their advice was that they should grant a certain sum of groats from each person, male and female, within the realm, the strong to aid the weak; or, if this did not please them, then their advice was to have, for a time, a certain imposition throughout the realm, and to take [*a levy*] on the pound from all types of merchandise bought and sold in the kingdom, each time that they were sold by the hands of the vendors. And thirdly their advice was to raise a sum by tenths and fifteenths. But because the tenths and fifteenths were very grievous in many ways to the poor commons, and the other impositions were as yet untried, so that no one could know what sum it would raise, and that it would be a long time before any notable sum would be raised, it seemed to the lords that if they wished to grant four or five goats from each person, this would provide a good and notable sum by which the king could be considerably assisted; and each person of the realm could well afford this, because the strong would be compelled to help the weak. And so it seemed to the lords that this kind of levy of groats would be the best and most easy, it was said.

1381

30. Early 1381 according to the *Vita Ricardi Secundi*

This year began with the same lack of military success as in previous years. Edmund of Langley's Portuguese expedition ended ignominiously: he was unable to control his troops (whose destructive behaviour is still remembered in eastern Portugal) and the Portuguese made terms with the Castilians behind his back.[58] The author of this popular chronicle, who covered the years 1377–90, was normally heavily reliant on Walsingham, but his account of 1381 is an exception.

VR, 61.

This year that old hypocrite the heretic John Wycliffe resurrected the damnable opinions of Berenger[59] about the sacrament of the altar, and led many astray. About the beginning of March a certain cardinal came to England ... along with the duke of Teschen and many others sent by the king of Bohemia,[60] who called himself the emperor, to contract a marriage between his sister and the king of England. Here, under the pretext of power which he said he derived from the lord pope, he collected a great deal of money. He accomplished wonderful things in this land, and departed very well rewarded.

At about the end of May, Lord Edmund of Langley, earl of Cambridge, Lord Beauchamp, brother of the earl of Warwick, and Sir Matthew Gournay mounted an expedition to Portugal to assist the king of that land, who was frequently harassed and attacked by the Spaniards, so that, with the help of that king, Langley should conquer the kingdom of Spain in the name of his brother the duke of Lancaster, who had obtained the elder sister in marriage.[61] But our men, who with God's help had arrived there safely, afterwards accomplished nothing that they had come for, except that the son of the earl of Cambridge married the daughter and heiress of the king of Portugal.[62]

---

58 Lopes (1989): 63–151.

59 Berengar of Tours (c.1010–88) held controversial views on the eucharist; Macy (1984): esp. 35–53.

60 Wenzel (Wenceslas), king of Bohemia (r. 1378–1400), was son of the emperor Charles IV, but never became emperor himself.

61 A reference to Gaunt's marriage to Constance of Castile; Langley married her younger sister Isabel.

62 The marriage between the two children was annulled by the pope in 1382.

31. Attacks on northern England

*SAC I.*370–72.

This summer the Scots, mourning the captured ship of which we spoke,[63] planned to inflict revenge on the Northumbrians, and plotted tit for tat. So they entered our borders with a great multitude of madmen. They attacked the peoples of Westmorland and Cumberland, destroying and killing; and, advancing further, they drove away animals of various kinds from Inglewood Forest[64] into Scotland, numbering, it is said, 40,000, everywhere raging, everywhere killing and consigning to the flames everything they could. Not content with this, they made a night raid, furtively and suddenly attacking the town of Penrith where a fair was being celebrated by a large crowd of people. Some were killed there, and some captured, and all the rest were driven away. The Scots carried away the assembled riches.

The Peasants' Revolt, 1381

This uniquely dramatic event generated a large and diverse range of documents. Dobson (1970, 1983) provides a rich collection in translation; the entries here are chosen mainly to supplement what is already available.[65] The rising was an event that no chronicler could ignore, and it features in the works of Henry Knighton and the Monk of Westminster, and in the *Eulogium.* Its fame spread to the continent, and Froissart, always keen to make a drama out of a crisis, included a celebrated account in his chronicle. All these, with notes and commentary, are found in Dobson's collection. Three sources deserve further notice here.

The fullest account of the events in London (13–15 June) was written by an eyewitness, probably a clerk in crown service, and included in the *Anonimalle Chronicle.* Although composed mainly at St Mary's Abbey, York, this chronicle incorporates vivid and detailed eyewitness accounts of both the 'good' parliament and the Peasants' Revolt, written by someone closely linked to the royal administration. These passages may come from a lost chronicle by William Packington, a clerk who served successively Prince Edward, Princess Joan and Richard II, until his death in 1390.[66] Another important narrative was given by Thomas Walsingham, an eyewitness to events at St Albans. A third major source consists of the diverse accounts which can be grouped under

---

63 The ship captured by the men of Newcastle and Hull.

64 Inglewood Forest stretched from Carlisle to Penrith in Cumberland.

65 The exceptions are contained in **34**.

66 Galbraith in Du Boulay and Barron (1971): 46–57, esp. 48–51.

the heading of 'judicial records': indictments, accusations, inquisitions, deposi-
tions, petitions and pardons. These come from the records of courts both
national (parliament and king's bench) and local, for example, of sheriffs and
of town administrations, also the proceedings of *ad hoc* commissions. These
are especially valuable for their information about events outside London and
the extreme south-east of England. A notable example is the great struggle
between the town and abbey of Bury St Edmunds, but such records also tell us
of risings and disorder in places as far from the epicentre of unrest as Cheshire,
Bridgwater in Somerset, York, Beverley and Scarborough.

The rebels' words, demands and opinions are well represented in the sources.
Whether it was the moving speech which William Grindcobbe, leader of
the St Albans rebels, made before his execution,[67] or the sermon and written
'manifesto' of the itinerant firebrand cleric John Ball or the letters of other
rebel leaders,[68] the shocked observers recorded, apparently faithfully, what the
insurgents said as well as what they did. Ironically, the chroniclers publicised
the case for the rebels of 1381 in far greater detail than they did for the king and
his friends in the parliamentary crisis of 1388. There was, however, one subject
on which they were perhaps mistaken: they blamed Wycliffite preaching for the
revolt. Whether they were right to do so is unclear; the evidence for this cause
and effect is inconclusive.[69] However, the fact that they equated religious devia-
tion with social sedition was important and remained so long afterwards.[70]

The Revolt's greatest effects must surely have been psychological, and cannot
be measured, but some political results left observable marks. The main one
is negative: the reluctance of parliament to vote generous taxes in the years
after 1381. No further taxes were collected until 1383, and several times in the
following years (1383, 1384, 1386, 1388) parliament granted a half fifteenth
and tenth, the most miserly grants since 1319.[71] England thus lost the chance to
land a decisive blow on France, where affairs were not only in turmoil but also
mirrored remarkably the English situation: Charles V died in 1380, leaving an
heir Charles VI (1380–1422) eleven years old, and power was wielded by three
royal uncles; experiments in taxation from 1380 provoked a series of revolts
from the Midi to Paris during the next two years [40]. England's inability to
take advantage of French weakness in the early 1380s was caused by parliament's anxiety about social disorder after the Peasants' Revolt, and fear lest the
state's financial exactions provoke more protests.

67 *SAC* I.534; Dobson (1983), 277.

68 *SAC* I.546–8; *KC*, 222–4.

69 See **32–3**, *SAC* I.544, *KC*, 210.

70 Aston (1994): 3–47.

71 Jurkowski, Smith and Crook (1998): 34, 62–6.

32. A brief account from a northern chronicle

The Kirkstall Short Chronicle account may have been based upon other sources circulating at the time when these events were recent, and it is interesting to compare its detail with those accounts written closer to the areas where these events took place. It provides a vivid summary of the rising and some perceived causes.

Kirkstall Abbey Chronicles, ed. J. Taylor (Thoresby Society, 42, 1952), 110–11.

In ... 1381 ... there arose civil disorder among the peasants and other workers in the mechanical arts. They rose together in the greatest number in Kent, Essex, Sussex, Suffolk, Norfolk and Cambridgeshire, and generally throughout all England in the major cities and towns the community of the servile rose against the lords of England and royal officials, and especially against the lord duke of Lancaster and against all justices of the realm and lawyers. They endeavoured to subvert all the laws of the land so that, among other things, all the serfs throughout the province of England would be manumitted and made free, and many other things too. King Richard, impelled by fear of them, promised to confirm everything by his great charter. So, to accomplish their aims, the men congregated in arms, and were like madmen in the greatest wickedness, huge numbers of them, whose captains were Thomas [*sic*] Tyler, Jack Straw and John Ball, a priest of the lollard sect. With staves and cudgels, with swords and rusty arrows, and with other rustic implements unsuited to warfare, they all plundered the land everywhere and beheaded many of the more valuable members of the nation, and stuck their heads on spikes, distressingly, for example, the heads of Sir John Cavendish, chief justice of the king's bench, and of the venerable prior of the noble abbey of Bury [*St Edmunds*], whose severed heads were horribly fixed to a stake in the town of Bury. Finally, on the vigil of Corpus Christi [*12 June*] this wild madness of those traitors advanced so that they entered the city of London, and captured the Tower of London and the city without resistance. They contemptibly dragged from the Tower the archbishop of Canterbury, Simon Sudbury, chancellor of the realm, Sir Robert Hales, a worthy knight and master of the hospital of St John Clerkenwell and treasurer of the realm, and Brother William Appleton OFM,[72] the king's doctor, and beheaded them on some open ground near the Tower. Indeed, the archbishop's head with his cap fixed to his head with a nail, they suspended over London Bridge. They broke all London's prisons and

72 Order of Friars Minor, i.e. a Franciscan.

set the prisoners free, and they found some foreigners and immediately beheaded them. Then they went to the duke of Lancaster's manor outside the city walls, called the Savoy, and razed it to the ground. They threw into the Thames a great treasure in money, jewels, silver coin, bed-hangings and precious tapestries, with arms and instruments of war, in contempt of the lord duke of Lancaster. No one dared to salvage or carry away anything of any value, but all was consumed by fire or deep water.

They came to the hospital of St John Clerkenwell, and after attacking the Hospitallers with invective and threats they burned their very beautiful buildings. Even more remarkable, all the military skill in England was so greatly turned to foolishness that no knight or squire dared to acknowledge membership of the duke of Lancaster's retinue or publicly to wear his badge. Indeed, when the duke heard of their evil excesses he became very afraid and went to Scotland. But blessed be God who hands over the wicked, three days later, in the Londoners' fields, in King Richard's presence, their captain was wounded by the city's mayor John [correctly William] Walworth, because he did not make reverence to the lord king, either by gesture or by word, and was arrested and at once beheaded. His head was raised high on a stake. Because of this the mayor was invested by the king with the order of knighthood, as he deserved. The rest were dispersed, an almost countless number who fled in all directions like wandering sheep. Many of them were captured and beheaded and their heads publicly hung up (*suspensa*) in many parts of England.

33. The *Vita*'s account

This detailed and apparently independent account has not been translated before.

VR, 61–6, 68–9.

The king of England received from his subjects, both clergy and people, a heavy tax, because of which there was raised up in England the upheaval of a great commotion .... Some of the king's ministers wished to please him but to displease the Lord and, driven by greed, they suggested to the royal court that this tax was not being faithfully levied by its collectors for the king's use. So they offered to pay a certain sum – because they wanted to collect more than had already been paid to the king from that tax – if the king would grant them his power for that purpose. And so, after some of them had accepted commissions with royal power, they sat in various places in Kent and Essex, and treated the people inhumanely in order to raise this money, and inflicted upon them many injuries and wrongs. When the people saw this, some of them entered into a secret plan, and when they had gathered strength, they resisted the king's oppressors, and rose up against them, killing some, wounding others. The rest fled in fear.

Because they had done this they were afraid that their force would be met with force and that they would suffer serious injury, so they raised a detestable rebellion, for they incited all the commons, both country-dwellers and others, of Kent and Essex, to rise against the king and lords. They gathered an almost numberless crowd and appointed the wickedest criminals, and those accused of every crime, to be their leaders and spokesmen or captains, giving them the names Jack Shep, John Wraw, Thomas Myllar, Wat Tyler, Hobbe Carter and Jack Straw. So they rushed about in many places, some armed, others unarmed, carrying different kinds of weapons, with fearsome banners and pennons, marching about and looting, burning many manors and sumptuous houses, and razing them down to the very foundations, especially those which they knew belonged to lawyers or the king's ministers, or retainers of the duke of Lancaster. All these were especially loathsome to them, and all these, if they could find them, they wanted to kill and to wipe their memory off the earth.

The advancing rabble of almost 100,000 rustics came, about the feast of Holy Trinity [9 June], to a place outside London commonly called 'Blackheath'. They kept with them for a time some vagrants whom they compelled to swear fealty to them, and others to support them. While they lingered there they sent to the king, who, for fear of them, had fled to the keep in the Tower of London with his household, to come to Blackheath to talk with them. For they thought that if the king came to them, they could take him with them through the whole realm, and by his authority could carry out what they had proposed: namely that all of noble blood of either sex be destroyed and killed, and finally the king himself; and so they would be able to do as they liked with the kingdom. But as soon as they had summoned him, the king collected his chancellor, Simon Sudbury, archbishop of Canterbury, and his treasurer, Robert Hales, prior of the Hospital, a most valiant knight, with others of his household, and sailed across the Thames to meet them.

When they saw him approaching, a great crowd of them rushed towards the Thames. Then the archbishop of Canterbury and the king's treasurer advised him to return to the Tower, saying that it was not certain what the mad people would do to him, if he came within their grasp. So, acting on their advice, he turned round and went back to the Tower. When they saw the king going back they raised their voices crying, 'Treason! Treason', and came as fast as possible into London.[73]

They entered its gate on 12 June, the vigil of Corpus Christi, because the commons of the city held the gate open for them. They filled the whole city; running about everywhere they caused much destruction and killed many, especially Flemings, and plundered them. Next day, the feast of Corpus Christi, they hurried to the duke of Lancaster's mansion called the 'Savoy' and burnt that most beautiful of buildings and razed it to the ground, leaving not one stone upon another. But while it was being destroyed, finding goods and an almost infinite variety of objects, such as cloth, precious stones, gold, silver, both in money and in vessels, arms and other things, which they could secretly carry, they seized and carried these away with them, burning some and reducing others to fine dust. Meanwhile the duke, with certain lords, was negotiating a peace treaty between us and the Scots in the Scottish borders. The rebels would gladly have killed him if they had found him there, because he was then most hateful to them.

When they had damaged it beyond repair, the mad rabble speedily made for Clerkenwell priory where they demolished and destroyed the great part of the church and several houses, and did much other damage, and they poured away all the wine they found there after they had drunk what they wanted. Likewise they destroyed a very beautiful manor of the prior outside London which he had newly built for his recreation.[74] Coming also to the Temple and to other halls where there was a school for those learned in the law of the land, they broke open their coffers, seizing their statutes and books, and many muniments deposited there. Some they tore, others they burned; and taking many goods with them they went away. Meanwhile the lord king was with his household inside the Tower of London, but the very numerous knights and squires, who had such a great reputation for bravery, dared neither to take up arms nor to attempt anything against the unarmed commons, to defend the king and kingdom by any struggle whatsoever ....

73 Both Blackheath and the Tower were outside the city boundary.
74 Highbury, Middlesex.

Next day, Friday, most of these servile people eagerly withdrew to that place outside London called 'The Mile End'. They sent people who complained and spoke to the king, ordering him without delay to come to them unarmed, because unless he quickly complied, they would immediately destroy the Tower, nor would he escape alive. When this message was given, the king, because he then did not dare to resist their commands, rode in great trepidation towards them, along with a few unarmed men. And so, once the gates of the Tower were opened, a great crowd of them entered and searched diligently for the chancellor and treasurer, and others of the king's ministers whom they hated, shouting, 'Where are the traitors?' Finally they found and beheaded the chancellor and treasurer, and butchered a good fifteen more, but many others, whom they had wished to kill, miraculously escaped their clutches. Taking up the archbishop's head, and taking down the head of John Munsterworth – of whom there was mention earlier,[75] which for a long time was stuck on London bridge – they mockingly fixed it in the same place, and fixed his cap on the archbishop's head with nails.

Meanwhile, when the king had come to Mile End, as he had been ordered, he appeared like a lamb among wolves; he even greatly feared for his life, and addressed those surrounding him in an ingratiating manner. Regarding him with a grim expression, the mad rabble unanimously and very insistently demanded, through their spokesmen, that many things be set down in writing to the very great prejudice of the crown and realm of England, and of the prelates, nobles and magnates, and to the disinheritance and injury of the holy English Church, and tending to the manifest disadvantage of the state; these to be confirmed by the king's letters patent. They insisted that he would not depart from them until he had confirmed what they demanded.

First, they asked that it should be confirmed that he should cause everyone, throughout the whole realm of England, to be free and quit of all bondage and the yoke of servitude, so that not a single villein should remain. Then they asked him to pardon all his subjects and lieges for all the insurrections raised by them in riding against the king, going through various places in the kingdom, and all the various treasons, felonies, transgressions and extortions committed by them, or by any one of them on these occasions; and that he should then grant his firm peace to them and to each one of them, henceforward. Also, that the same lieges and subjects should in future be free to buy and sell in all

75 Munsterworth is not referred to in the surviving text. He has not been indentified. See *VR*: 38–9.

cities, boroughs, market towns and other places within the realm of England; and that not a single acre of land, which was held in bondage or servitude, should be had for more than 4d; and if this should be contrary to the previous law, it should not afterwards be increased. They wanted these, and many other things prejudicial to the king, to be granted in full. They said also that before this time he was badly led and governed, and that in future he ought to be governed and led by them. The king, seeing that he could not escape by any other way, gave assent to their petitions, and caused letters patent to be made on these subjects, attested by his seal. And so, when permission had been sought from them, he departed.

On the fourth day, namely, Saturday *[15 June]* the king went after lunch to Westminster to visit the holy king Edward *[the Confessor]* and to see if they had committed any evil there, and, returning through the suburbs in Smithfield, he found the whole place full of this rabble. At once one of their leaders, Wat Tyler, with his head covered and with a grim expression, approached the king, asking him with threatening words to order that the letters which he had granted them should be improved and corrected. None of the king's attendants dared to seize him for his insolence to the king, but finally William Walworth, who was mayor of London that year, inspired by God's grace, rebuked him for speaking so disrespectfully to the king; and striking him with his sword he gravely wounded him, and immediately one of those standing near quickly cut off his head. Then the people at once began to shout, 'Where is our leader?' The king, as God willed, rode his horse in amongst them, answered by shouting, 'I am your leader. Follow me'.

The whole crowd, as one man, followed him out of London and into the open country; then members of the king's household leapt in amongst them, beat them and with their horses knocked them to the ground. The wretched people ran through the fields and hid themselves, nor did any of them afterwards dare to raise their heads. So, with God's help, this scandalous tumult was calmed down. The king immediately knighted the same William Walworth, and three or four others of the more powerful burgesses of London, with a sword, and he appointed Sir Robert Knolles as captain of the city. These men made enquiries, and caused to be beheaded any of the ringleaders of that wretched rabble they could find, and those who had incited them to insurrection. William Walworth also caused the head of the archbishop, which had been raised over London Bridge as a spectacle, to be taken down and guarded with reverence; and he had the head of Wat Tyler stuck up in its place.

While these things were going on, the commons of Suffolk, Norfolk, Huntingdonshire and many other neighbouring areas were making similar uprisings. Rushing about in various places they demolished and destroyed many manors and buildings, killed many people and committed many other wrongs. And among other deeds, they cruelly murdered John Cavendish, one of the king's judges, while he was in the abbey of Bury St Edmunds, also the prior and a chaplain of the abbey. *[Then comes a passage identical to Walsingham.]*

Meanwhile, the letters of manumission, which the king had reluctantly granted them, were publicised in many parts of England. Because of them the villeins were unwilling that year to render to their lords either other obligations or the accustomed dues for the lands which they held of them, or to work in any way, nor would they be persuaded by wages, all insisting that they had been made free; but in many places they rebelled against their lords and resisted them. So the lords remained in fear of them for some time.

Afterwards the king ordered the lords and magnates of the realm to hurry to him at London to consider how so great a popular uprising could be quelled, contained and pacified. It was decided that certain lords, with an armed force, should go into Kent and other places where these insurrections had taken place, to calm down and pacify the people who had risen in this way, so that they would in no way harm those who wished to remain at peace; and they would chastise and vanquish completely with the edge of the sword those who resisted them. The king, with great courage, went to Essex in person, and pacified those parts. But a great mass of people were killed meanwhile before they could be pacified. For by the estimate both of the lords who were putting down these disturbances and of those evildoers earlier, some 7,000 men or more were killed in various places.

Also during this storm a certain chaplain, John Ball by name, one of John Wycliffe's disciples it was said, was captured at Coventry. By his preaching in many places he had persuaded and incited the people to these rebellions, telling them that by these means they could gain salvation for their souls. It was said that, if they had had their wicked way, they would have promoted him to the archbishopric of Canterbury. This chaplain was led before the king, who was then at St Albans, and there was drawn and quartered; he did not wish to seek any privilege[76] from the king but completely despised him. Another chaplain also of

76 Benefit of clergy.

that same sect was captured in Suffolk and there suffered a similar judgment. But afterwards those commons were somehow or other pacified, and the king gave them his peace, which they were anxious to . retain, and he ordered letters to be written which he had despatched to every county, there to be publicly read out; their entire contents, which he had earlier granted at the most insistent demand of the insurgents, he revoked, quashed and completely annulled.

34. Some episodes as reported by the *Anonimalle Chronicle*

These extracts have been selected for their significance to politics later in the reign.

Anon. Chron., 136–7, 143–4, 149–50.

(a) Simon Burley's harsh behaviour.

This story cannot be literally true because Burley was abroad at the time of the revolt, negotiating the king's marriage; he left England for Bohemia on 15 May 1381 and returned in January 1382.[77] It illustrates his bad reputation in Kent, and the harsh actions of (probably) his subordinates.

On Monday after the feast of Pentecost [*3 June*], a knight of the king's household called Sir Simon Burley came, along with two of the king's sergeants-at-arms, to Gravesend where he accused a certain man of being his villein. The good folk of the town came to him to make a reasonable agreement, from reverence for the king, but Sir Simon would not take less than £300 in silver, to that man's great damage. Those good people begged him to exercise moderation, but they were unable to mitigate [*his demand*] nor achieve their purpose for a lesser sum, even though they told Sir Simon that the man was a Christian of good character and so should not be irretrievably ruined. This made Sir Simon very cross and angry, and he greatly despised these good people, and from sheer arrogance he ordered the sergeants to seize the man and take him to Rochester castle for safe keeping. Great evil and mischief later resulted from this. After he went, the commons began to revolt, welcoming to their number the men from other towns of Kent .... At the same time the men of Kent came to Maidstone and beheaded one of the better men of the town, and razed to the ground various houses and tenements of those who were unwilling to join their rebellion, as was done in Essex. On the Friday after [*7 June*], they came to Rochester

77 Tout (1928): III.367–8.

and there encountered a great number of the commons of Essex and, on account of that man of Gravesend, they besieged Rochester castle in order to liberate their friend whom Sir Simon had earlier imprisoned. They vigorously assaulted the castle which the constable stoutly defended for half a day, but finally, from fear of such a mad mob from both Essex and Kent, he surrendered the castle to them. The commons entered and took their companion and all the other prisoners out of the prison. The men of Gravesend departed very joyfully with their companion, and did nothing more, but the others from Maidstone made their way, with others of the commons, through the neighbouring country.

(b) The fearful king tries to placate the rebels.

Richard's decisive action at Smithfield on 15 June is probably the best-known incident in the revolt. Yet other descriptions show him as entirely fearful, cowering in the Tower or seeking the protection of Edward the Confessor at Westminster, though fear and courage are not incompatible. The episode cannot fail to have burned itself on his memory. The insults to Richard's mother, Princess Joan, should also not be forgotten.[78] Richard could pacify and disperse the rebels in London only by offering them the charters of manumission, and pardons for their actions, that they demanded, but these concessions were reversed in the next parliament [45]. Richard may have learnt a lesson in deceitfulness from this ploy, which was to be a feature of his reign to the very end.[79]

On Thursday, the Feast of Corpus Christi [13 June] the king was in the Tower, pensive and sad. He went up into a little turret facing [the hospital of] St Katherine from where he could see a great number of the commons, and he had it proclaimed that they should all go home peacefully, and that he would pardon every kind of trespass.[80] They all cried with one voice that they would not go until they got the traitors in the Tower, and had charters of freedom from all kinds of servitude, and other matters. The king gladly granted these and had a clerk write a bill in their presence, as follows: 'Richard king of England and France warmly thanks his good commons because of their great desire to see and to support their king, and he pardons them all manner of trespass and offence and felony committed until now; he wills and commands that henceforth each one should hasten to his own home; he wills

78 Dobson (1983): 172, 181; Ormrod (2000); 277–92.

79 *CR*: 64–7, 72, 145–6.

80 This was not a generous concession, for trespass covered lesser crimes. Capital crimes (felonies) were what many of the rebels had committed.

and commands that they should set down each of their grievances in writing, and send them to him, and he will enact, on the advice of his loyal lords and of his good council, such a remedy as will bring profit both to himself and to those of his kingdom'. He sealed this with his own signet seal in their presence, and then sent that bill with two of his knights to those who were near St Katherine's and had it read to them. The one who read the bill was placed on an old chair among them, so that everyone could hear. All this time the king was in the Tower in great agitation. When the commons heard the bill they said that it was nothing but a sham and a mockery, so they returned to London and had it cried through the city that all men of law and all who worked in the chancery and exchequer, and everyone who knew how to write a writ or letter should be beheaded wherever they could be found. At the same time they burnt various places in the city. The king himself went up into a high attic of the Tower to see the fire, and when he came down he ordered the lords to give him their advice. But they did not know what to advise, and they were so terrified that it was a marvel.

(c) The knighting of four Londoners.

The energy and courage of the mayor of London stands in strong contrast to the ineffectual behaviour of the nobles and fighting men of the king's household. This extract records Richard's impulsive act of gratitude.

The king ordered the mayor, William Walworth by name, to put a helmet on his head because of what was going to take place. The mayor asked the reason for this, and the king said that he was very grateful to him and therefore ought to advance him to the order of knighthood. The mayor replied that he was not worthy, nor did he have the means to advance to such a rank because he was nothing but a merchant and wished only to live by trade. But in the end the king made him put on the helmet, and took a sword in both hands and gave him a strong [blow] on the shoulder with right good will. The same day he created three other knights from among the citizens of London for that same reason and in the same place. These were their names: John Philpot, Nicholas Brembre and [Robert Launde].[81] The king gave Sir William Walworth £100 of land, and £40 of land to each of the others, for themselves and their heirs.

81 Blank in ms; the missing name is supplied from Calendar of London Letter-Book H, 166. Philpot and Brembre had already been mayors of London; Launde was an alderman.

35. Anti-foreign feeling in London

Flemings living in Southwark and Cheap were targeted simply for being
foreigners; folk memory, preserved in this account written c. 1435, tells us how
they were identified. For consistency this extract has been translated, but the
original English is not hard to understand.

Chronicles of London, ed. Charles Lethbridge Kingsford (Oxford, 1905), 15–16.

On the 11 day of June after Trinity Sunday there occurred the rising of
the commons of England against the lords; at which time they beheaded
the archbishop of Canterbury on Tower Hill, and Sir Robert Hales,
prior of St John's *[Clerkenwell]*. Many Flemings also lost their heads
at that time because they could not say 'Bread and Cheese,' but only
'*Case* and *Brode*'.[82] Jurors[83] too were destroyed, wherever they could be
found. But finally William Walworth, at that time mayor of London,
slew the chief of the rebels in the king's presence; he was called Jack
Straw. Therefore Walworth and several aldermen were made knights
that same day by King Richard.

36. The murder of Archbishop Sudbury, Friday 14 June 1381

This denunciation, which would have circulated throughout the province
of Canterbury, was immensely influential, and its echoes can be detected in
several chronicle accounts. The Kentish jurors offered corroboration for the
allegation that Sudbury was killed by his tenants, the evidence from Kinghamford Hundred being especially convincing. See Du Boulay (1966): 44, 391.

The Church in London, 1375–92, ed. A. K. McHardy (London Record Society,
13, 1977), 91–2.

Mandate of William *[Courtenay]*, bishop of London, to William *[of
Wykeham]*, bishop of Winchester, to publish in all the churches of his
diocese the sentence of excommunication, dated 1 September 1391,
pronounced by John *[Fynch]*, prior of Christ Church, Canterbury, against
those who killed Simon *[Sudbury]*, late archbishop of Canterbury: sons
of damnation who violently entered the palace and other manors of the
archbishop against his wish and the wishes of his staff, drank his wine
and seized his goods; they broke into his prison at Maidstone, seized

---

82 'Cheese and bread'. The inspiration for this way of identifying foreigners may have
   been biblical, cf. Judges 12: 5–6.
83 On jurors, who were then witnesses rather than deciders, see Walker (1980): 686–8,
   s.v. 'jury'.

the prisoners and compelled them to depart; they broke into his chase known as The Broyle[84] in Chichester diocese and the adjacent parks; they hunted, killed and took away the game there; not content with this, they entered the Tower of London, beat and wounded the archbishop and finally took him outside the Tower where they decapitated him, and carried his head, to which his episcopal hat [mitre] was affixed by a nail in the brain, through the city shouting, 'Here is the predator's head'; then they placed it on London bridge. For all this, these persons have manifestly incurred the sentence of greater excommunication.

London, 16 September 1381.

37. The rebels in Kent, according to William Thorne

William Thorne was a monk of the Benedictine abbey of St Augustine, Canterbury, whose chronicle is essentially a domestic history, but who on occasion gives an interesting local view of wider events.

William Thorne, *Chronica de rebus gestis abbatum S. Augustini Cantuariae*, ed. Roger Twysden (Historiae Anglicanae Scriptores Decem, London, 1652), cols. 2156–7.

A turbulent crowd of wicked men of Essex rose in rebellion; they were joined, from all parts of the kingdom, by a huge crowd of scoundrels, to the number of 60,000, whose leaders were Jack Straw, J[ohn] Bank, John Hales, Thomas Mellere and other criminals worse than these. They overran every district, oppressing the innocent and either killing or ill-treating the king's judges, the nobles of the realm and decent men. They broke into prisons, liberated criminals, burned houses, razed buildings; nobility served them willingly and respectable people furthered their designs. Then, after massacres at Canterbury and the neighbouring villages and towns of this county, which they so damnably perpetrated at the instigation of the devil, they gathered all together at Blackheath and sent for the lord king to go there to talk with them, to approve them and their worthless doings. He approached by water, and when from a distance he saw that violent and disorderly company, he was afraid that, if he approached them, he might imperil his royal majesty. Acting upon wise advice, he retreated and went to his Tower of London. So the people turned in a rage and hurriedly journeyed to London on the festival of Corpus Christi, where all that day and

---

84 Broyle Park, Sussex, falls in the two parishes of Ringmer and Framfield, east of the river Ouse, in the Rape of Pevensey. It now covers about 2,000 acres.

the following night the restless and impetuous mob was perpetually intent on destroying beautiful buildings and shedding human blood. At daybreak on 15 June they entered the Tower of London and dragged out the archbishop of Canterbury along with the Master of St John's hospital, then holding the offices of chancellor and treasurer of the realm. On the same day they beheaded them on Tower Hill, and had the archbishop's head, placed on a pole, fixed over London Bridge. And note that, while this false and pernicious confederacy was at Canterbury and in the neighbouring parts, the prudent abbot [of St Augustine's] acted with such wisdom that he kept the goods of his monastery undamaged, and preserved his friends and neighbours from bodily harm, and their property safe from destruction. But when these wicked deeds had been committed, the earls, barons and nobles of the realm took up arms again, and when they had a sufficient force of warriors, seized the multitude [of rebels], along with their leaders and paid them back as their crimes deserved. By this action against the pernicious people the lords calmed the troubled land. Afterwards the monks [of Christ Church cathedral priory] took away the body of their leader, and gave him a fitting burial in his own church.[85] He was succeeded by Master William Courtenay, who was promoted from the see of London.

38. The rebels in Kent, according to some juries' presentments

These presentments enable us to get a detailed view of the rebels' actions as recorded by their neighbours. Although there was clearly some theft and some demanding of money with menaces, a striking theme to emerge is the importance attached to the destruction of documents, whether about the recent tax, the general administration of justice or landlords' rights. The rebels also attacked prisons and freed inmates. At least two men were identified as having been involved in Sudbury's murder. The jurors' ability to identify by name so many culprits reminds us that this was a land of small villages, in which everyone knew everyone else's business.

'The Great Rebellion in Kent of 1381 illustrated from the public records', ed. and trans. W. E. Flaherty (*Archaeologia Cantiana* III, 1860), 71–3, 77, 81–2, 87–8, 92–3, 94, adapted; place-names modernised.

THANET. William Tolone, John Jory, Stephen Samuel, William atte Stone the younger and John Michelat ... raised a cry on the feast of Corpus Christi [13 June] at St Lawrence in Thanet, that every liege man of our lord king should go to the house of William Medmenham,

---

85 Sudbury church in Suffolk contains what is said to be the archbishop's head.

to demolish his house, level it to the ground, fling out the books and rolls found there and burn them; and, if William could be found, they should kill him ....

RINGSLOW [HUNDRED]. The jurors ... say on oath that William the Chaplain officiating in the church of St John in the Isle of Thanet, and Stephen Samuel, on Thursday the feast of Corpus Christi [13 June], rose and proclaimed, against the king's peace, that all ought to unite and go to the house of William Medmenham, under penalty of death and the forfeiture of their goods and chattels, to pull down William Medmenham's house. Whereupon, William and Stephen entered the house of William Medmenham, together with others who were driven by them to this, and burned the books and muniments of William Medmenham at Manston, to the damage of that William of twenty shillings.

CHATHAM AND GILLINGHAM HUNDRED. Memorandum that Thomas Berghestede and Robert Prat of Gillingham, on Sunday the feast of Holy Trinity [9 June], went to the messuage of Thomas Bedemanton in Gillingham and broke open his chambers, entered the house, and took and feloniously carried away the charters, writings and divers muniments found there, and the remainder of Thomas's goods and chattels found there, to the value of 100 shillings.

CALEHILL HUNDRED. The jurors say on oath that John Warener and other unknown malefactors rose on Tuesday, the feast of St Barnabas the Apostle [11 June], feloniously broke into Maidstone gaol and carried off the prisoners that were inside, against their will and against the king's peace.

WYE HUNDRED. The jurors to inquire concerning the malefactors who rose against the king and his people ... [between 9 June and 1 July] say that Bertram de Wilmynton esquire, Roger Baker, John Bergheman, John Chelvertone, Robert Foxtegh, Thomas Bulloc and Robert Cademan, of their own will, on Wednesday following the feast of St Barnabas [12 June 1381], made insurrection, came to Wye and feloniously broke into the house of John Laycestre, plundered it and burnt his muniments to the damage of ten marks ... Also that John Gerkyn, on Thursday the feast of Corpus Christi, rose and made proclamation that all of the hundred should assemble and prepare themselves with divers arms, etc., whereby a multitude of the people assembled and did no harm by that proclamation. But they say that that proclamation was made by order of Bertram de Wylminton. Also that John Henwode, Thomas Steyhame, constable of the hundred of Longbridge, John

Juyke, Thomas Heldeman, John Smyth, piper, Stephen Repton, Stephen
Poynont, unjustly and against the king's peace, made insurrection and
came to the muniment-room of John Colbrand, with other malefactors,
on Tuesday the feast of St Barnabas and feloniously broke into the
muniment-room, plundered it and burnt his books and muniments at
Wye, and assaulted and beat Joan his wife so that her life was despaired
of, to the damage of 100 shillings.

LONGBRIDGE HUNDRED. The jurors say that John de Hendwode,
William Prowde, Thomas Bodesden, John Heldeman, John Sp...
carpenter, Stephen de Repton, John May and Richard Elys made insurrection on the feast of St Barnabas and feloniously broke into the house
of John Colbrond at Wilmington in Boughton Aluph parish in Wye
hundred, and feloniously entered John Colbrond's chamber, and took
and destroyed the roll of green wax[86] of the lord king. Also that William
Prowde, Thomas Bodesdenn, Stephen de Repton, John Henwode,
Alexander Bakere, William Fax, Gregory Egethorn, Thomas Adam,
Adam Rolf of Mersham ... on the same day and year, feloniously entered
the manor of John Brode of Mersham, and feloniously destroyed the
escheat roll of our lord king, and of the receipt of the subsidy of three
groats [12d.] granted to the king, when that said John was escheator.[87]

KINGHAMFORD [HUNDRED]. The jurors say that Richard de
Denne raised insurrection with others unknown, and made proclamation from vill to vill from Monday next after the feast of Holy [Trinity]
... and continued till Friday next after the feast of Corpus Christi on
which day Simon, archbishop of Canterbury, was feloniously killed
at London; and they say that the foresaid Richard was there present,
aiding and abetting in the death of the said Simon.

BOUGHTON [HUNDRED]. The jurors say that Roger Baldewyn of
Boughton under Blean raised insurrection with other malefactors on
Wednesday after the feast of Holy Trinity [12 June], and aided and
abetted when Simon, archbishop of Canterbury, was feloniously killed
and was present then.

---

86 The roll listed fines imposed by the central courts and sums due to the chancery and
    exchequer. Such a roll was sent to the sheriff of each county; it was his duty to collect
    this money. Exchequer writs were sealed with green wax.

87 Escheators were local officials, answerable to the exchequer, whose duty it was to
    collect revenue which came to the crown by virtue of its feudal position, for example,
    from wardships, from lands which had reverted to the crown for lack of heirs or from
    bishops' estates while a see was vacant. The subsidy was the poll tax granted in 1380;
    cf. **29**.

DOWNHAMFORD HUNDRED. *[The twelve jurors]* say that John Halis of Malling, Walter Teghelere of Essex, William Hauker and John Abel, on Monday next after the feast of Holy Trinity, made insurrection against the king and his people and came to Canterbury, and assaulted William Septvantz, sheriff of Kent, and made the sheriff take an oath to them and compelled him under fear of death to deliver up the books, viz the rolls of the pleas of the county and of the crown of the lord king, and whatever king's writs were in the sheriff's custody, and they burnt fifty rolls and the writs on the same day at Canterbury, in contempt of the lord king and to the prejudice of his crown. They feloniously and traitorously broke into the king's castle at Canterbury, and forced John Burgh, an approver,[88] Richard Derby, clerk, a convict, Agnes Jekyn and Joan Hampcok, prisoners fettered and manacled in that castle, to leave, in contempt of the king and to the prejudice of his crown.

PETHAM HUNDRED. The jurors say that Henry Aleyn junior and John Colyn burnt the custumal of Petham,[89] of the lord archbishop of Canterbury, on Sunday next after the feast of St Barnabas.

39. The sacking of the Savoy Palace, Thursday 13 June 1381

During the revolt John of Gaunt's London residence, the palace of the Savoy, was sacked so completely that it was never rebuilt. Afterwards Gaunt brought a case against the destroyers of this property in the court of common pleas, during the Trinity law term, 1383. Although the case was dropped, the record is interesting since it details precisely the persons thought by Gaunt's administration to have been responsible for the destruction. The list of names is printed as it stands.

Similar lists of rebels in Yorkshire towns can be found at TNA SC 8/225/11233 and 11239 (Beverley) and SC 8/139/6949 (Scarborough).

TNA, Plea Roll, CP 40/490, m. 268–268d.

MIDDLESEX. John, king of Castile and Leon, duke of Lancaster, through his attorney Hugh Wombwell appeared on the fourth day against Robert Dyngele, Geoffrey Waryn, Henry Fifian, Henry atte Plotte, Jordan de Bladyngton, Ralph Erlych, Thomas Flemyng, John Poynt, Peter Cook, Ralph Wardale, John Bourne, Simon Corner,

---

88 An approver was an informer; the term was especially applied to accused persons who escaped punishment by informing against their accomplices.

89 A custumal was the written collection of the customs of the manor. For archiepiscopal lands in Petham, see Du Boulay (1966), 17, 96–7.

William atter Kebbel, Robert atte Wode de Depeford, John Lelfred de
Leuesham, Richard Podde, Willing Waryng, Stephen Pruet, William
Kirkeby, John Catel, Richard Catel, John Aleyn the Abbotesquyer of
Lesenes, Thomas Chaundeler de Derteford, Henry Whitewell Trave-
lyngeman, William Bakere de Westram, John Lesle hotiler, John
Taverner de Cantuar, Richard Barbour de Eltham, Adam Thressher de
Elsham, William Lokeman, William Walssh, William Jop' de Wolewych,
William atte Beche de Grenewych, John Gy de Burstede mason,
Laurence Rokesacre de Burstede mason and Richard Rokesacre his son
and Robert Rokesacre brother of the same Richard Rokesacre, William
Cantelowe de Maideston coupere, Thomas Gamen de Geversham
hosiere, Richard Barbour de Maidston, Alan Dyere, Richard Coventre
draper, William Skynnere de Maidston, William Fullere de Maideston,
William Webulton de Maidstone diere, Geoffrey Dru de Maidston
skynnere, John Roghilde, John Bertelmowe, John Thomasyn chaundeler, Giles Westwode webbe, Henry Dyne taillour, Richard Kyng
fullere, Simon Kyng mason, Silvester Smyth Michereno Ferrour [sic],
Walter Gregge glovere, John Hamme tannere, John Frakeman mercer,
junior, John Frakeman mercer senior, Roger Huchon, John Skynnere
the Westhalf the Water, Gilbert Strok mason, John Kympton Skynner,
Thomas Alderman tannere, John Bourne mason, Guy Yonge mason,
Simon Postlyng, Thomas Badere skynner, John Roke mason, William
atte Rugge mason, John Taillour de la Mullelane, John Propynchaunt
taverner senior, John Propynchaunt taverner junior, John Rasshford
glover, John Dene de Maidstone, John Morys de Maidstone, John
Thomas de Maidstone, John Bofeld junior, John Bofeld senior, John
Torner, Thomas Barry de Bokeland, Stephen Phelippot, Simon Cartere,
Roger Heldere, Richard Broun de Grenebrugge taillour, Richard Morys
cordewaner, Geoffrey Coventre draper, John Veek shipman, John Pyk
shipman, Henry Skynner de Mellelane, Stephen Webbe, Gilbertiser-
vant Stork, John Clerk bocher, William Bocher de Maidston, John
Fisshere, Chalmiwebbe Saferner [sic] tanner, Henry Smyth diere,
Robert Gilcote fuller, Thomas Glovere de Shopperowe, Richard Spot
bocher, Walter Bocher cordewaner, William Coryour de Podynglane,
Stephen Kitte bakere, William Gretyng mason, John Crouland fisshere,
John Shether de Shopperowe senior, Mathew Clerk de Maidston, Walter
Pikeman fullere, Thomas Coupere servant of the same Walter Pikeman,
Nicholas Frogge cook, Thomas Wyke de Estlane chaundeler, John
Dyne de Estlane, William Shoppere de Maidston, John Hosier de
Maidston, John Perys webbe de Estlane, John Bakere de Estlane
cordwaner, William Howe de Estlane fullere, John Gravesend de

Estlane, John Froggepole de Estlane brewere, Thomas Wyghtgrom, John Trot glovere, William Wolmonger, Robert Kyng de Estlane bakere, John Wilkyn de Wyke bakere, Thomas Reve, Simon atte Mulle shipman, John Mabbe shipman, Stephen de Lake masoun, Richard atte Mulle masoun, Henry Polyene mason, William Lyndraper de Towefeld, John Prynce de Towefeld, William Towefeld carpenter, Thomas Aylyf carpenter, Peter Mulleward carpenter, Thomas Sheypey de Brodgare, Thomas Gryngent de Brodgar iuxta Newenton, Thomas Germayn, Abel Kyere, Robert Bakere de Derteford, Robert Webbe de Eltham, Robert Osteler de Derteford, Sampsone le Feriere, John Baron de Cretford, John Robbel de Cretford, Robert Cook de Feversham, Robert Cave de Derteford, Robert Swynyngton osteler, Maurice Pardoner de Dertford, William Draper de Derteford, William Bole, John Sharp tanner, John Estlond de Heston in Kant', William White, Thomas Champe de Derteford, John Neylot de Newenton smyth, John Redyng de Newenton osteler, John Taillour de Newenton senior, John Taillour de Newenton junior, Robert Elys de Alford, John Getour, Robert Getour, Thomas Baylly of Byxle, Walter Molkere de Byxle, William Osemere de Byxle, William Broun de Byxle, John Spynan de Wellynges, Thomas Seman de Wycham, John Smyth de Eltham, William Pruet de Modyngham, William Rose de Carleton, Gilbert Berkyng, Peter Stuard de Leuesham, William Hakeneyman de Depeford, John Stonham de Grenewych, John atte Nasshe de Grenewych, John Pye of Grenewych, Joyn Boyn de Grenewych, Thomas Clerk de Greneych, Thomas Swon de Combe, William Doo, Richard Depeden de Plumstede, William le Bocher de Rouchestre, William Haiward de Tottyng taillour, William Litilwil de Rouchestre, Richard Ferthyng in the Doune, William Forthe de Westram, John Reynald de Okholte, John Lonestede, Richard Tuppenden, John Tuppenden, Henry Hammyng de Feversham, Robert Cook de Feversham, Thomas Beauwe de Maideston, John Bailly de Techam, Richard Boucher de Rouchestre, Hugh Stacy de Strode, Nicholas Josep', Richard Wardal de Wycham, John Raude de Eltham, John Holeherst de Eltham junior, Thomas Hasteneleys de Derteford, William Forster de Eltham draper, Severus rector of Cherleton church, Richard Pode de Eltham, William Pode de Eltham, Thomas Auncel de Grenewych, John Mareschall' de Combe, William Richard de Cherlton junior, Walter Kebbel, John Rose de Cherleton tyler, Thomas atte Halle de Creye Beate Marie, John Wytteneye de Depford, Walter Baret de Altham, Simon Cornere de [m.268d] Combe, Robert Rolfe de Depford, Robert Bakere de Depford, Robert atte Millene de Depford, Robert Kakere de Cobeham, William Plomer de Grenewych, John Canon de

Kant, William del Chaumbre, John Kent cordewainer, Thomas Torke-
shoe sadeler, Thomas Spicer atte Rammeshede, Thomas Wyg atte
Bolehed, John Bor milleward, John Auncel cordwaner, Richard Baillif
dwelling Lestnwes atte Flourdelys, John Sherman de Suthwek, John
Abbot cordwaner, Robert Fernyngham taillour, John Mokkyngg de
Suthwerk, Richard Webbe de Suthwerk, John Chaundeler iuxta la
Pilery in Suthwerk, Robert Barbour atte Faukon, John Doresaunt atte
Flourdelys, Robert Kyngeston brokour, Ralph Bassyng travelyngmann,
Ralph Stallard de Lichefeld, Ralph atte Welle, Roger Gaillard de
Holbourn, Simon Smyth de Holburne, Thomas Bedeford charioter,
William Cook de London webbe, John Hundrede soutere, Robert
Andrew de Suthwerk pynner, John Fawe de London brewer, John
Westbury, John Frome, Thomas Shorteman, John Kent cordewaner,
John Alured mulward, Walter Veseook, John Sandale, William
Lyndewod, Peter le Barbour, John Brikkele senior, John Brikkele junior,
Robert Bakere savoye, Roger Beldyng savoie, John Doddele, John
Crabbe, Geoffrey Makea de savoye, John Balle de Lestnwes, Stephen
Mergate, William le Ber boteman, John Michel boteman, John Sampson
bocher, John Priour de Stretham, William Tyler de Stretham, William
Cartere de Stretham, William atte More de Stretham, Robert Devenyssh
de Stretham, William Tubbyng de Stretham, Richard Tubbyng de
Stretham, John Pikestoun de Totyng, Robert Abbot de Totyng taillour,
John Polthorn de Totyng, John Milet de Micham, William Priour de
Micham, John Monnyng de Micham, Nicholas Davy, William Heward
de Merton, William le Haiward de Stretham, John le Smyth de Wande-
lesworth, John Bassyngham de Wandelesworth, Richard Savage servant
of John, John Bassyngham, Thomas Knotte, Roger Albyn de Wandeles-
worth, John Vailaunt de Wandelesworth, Ralph atte Crofte de Lambyth,
Richard atte Crofte de Lambythe, Richard atte Dene de Camerwelle,
Richard Ode de Camerwelle, John Kantebrigge smyth, John Markere de
Pekham, Richard Daiser webbe, John Chamberlayn de Suthwerk,
Richard Gildon de Esshere, Richard Crikkelade de Shire, Alan Tyler de
Southwerk, John Abbot de Southwerk, Walter Walpol de Newenton,
Richard Deynell de Southwerk cordwainer, John Auncel de Suthwerk
cordewaner, John Jernmuth de Suthwerk cordewaner, Baldwin fitz
Geoffrey le Wolpakker de London, William le Smyth of the parish of St
George in Suthwerk, James le Skynner de Suthwerk and Robert Savage
on a plea that by force and arms they broke the close of the said king [of
Castile] in the parish of St Mary le Strand outside the bar of the New
Temple, London, and they took and carried away his goods and chattels
to the value of ten thousand pounds (£10,000) and his charters, writings

and other muniments existing in his houses there and they burnt the said houses and his goods and chattels found there to the value of ten thousand pounds and committed other enormities etc., to the grave damage etc. and against the peace etc. And they did not appear. And the sheriff was ordered to attach them etc. And the sheriff signified that they had nothing etc. And the sheriff was ordered to seize them if etc.

[The sheriff was given dates on which to produce the defendants in court: 25 June 1383, then 3 November 1383. On neither day did they appear, and the case was dropped.]

40. A French eyewitness of the Revolt in London

Michael Pintoin, a monk of St Denys, near Paris, was the author of the chronicle from which this account is taken, and records these events under the year 1382. His account reminds us that England was not alone in experiencing rebellions at this time.

Chronique du Religieux de Saint-Denys, ed. M. L. Bellaguet, 1842, repr. with new introduction by Bernard Guenée (Paris, 1994), I.132–4.

This bold spirit of revolt took hold not only of the people of Rouen but of almost all the people of France. They were aroused to no small fury, especially, as common report had it, by the news and letters of the Flemings who were also suffering from a similar outbreak of rebellion; and also by the example of the English who at that time were rebelling against the king and nobles of the kingdom, whom they put to flight. They came armed into his palace and in the king's presence they violently dragged out five famous knights along with his chancellor the archbishop of Canterbury, and ordered them to be beheaded in public view as disturbers of the common peace. I was then in that kingdom to defend the interests of our church, and when I dared to voice my indignation on learning that, on the same day, the sacred head of the prelate had been kicked around by the mob at every crossroads of the town, one of those assisting said to me, 'You should know that worse things will shortly happen in the kingdom of France'. I replied only, 'God forbid that the ancient faith of France should be perverted into such a show'.

41. The Revolt at Dunstable, according to the Dunstable Annals

Although events at Dunstable were not as celebrated or violent as those at St Albans or Bury St Edmunds, this account reminds us that other religious houses were also on bad terms with their neighbours.

Annales Monastici vol. III, Annales Prioratus de Dunstaplia, Annales Monasterii de Bermundeseia, ed. H. R. Luard (RS, 1866), 415–19.

Memorandum that in 1381, about the feast of St Barnabas the Apostle *[11 June]*, the commons *(communitas)* of Kent and Essex rose in rebellion against King Richard II, on account of an excessive tax imposed on the whole of England, and they impeded ships laden with food and merchandise from reaching London, with the intention that the citizens of London should unite with their confederacy. Afterwards they besieged London, and finally the commons of London gave in to them; and so within three days they threatened the king, who had taken refuge in the Tower of London, that they would overrun the Tower unless he permitted to be handed over to their pleasure the archbishop of Canterbury, Simon Sudbury then chancellor of England, Lord Robert Hales then prior of Clerkenwell, and some others, whom they accused of treason. The apprehensive king, fearing for the life of Simon and Robert, at first refused to agree to their demand. When the commons heard this, they were roused by a spirit of fury; they rushed as soon as they could to the archbishop's manor of Lambeth, and carried away all the goods they found there. Then they hurried to the residence of John of Gaunt, duke of Lancaster, who was then in the north of the country, namely the Savoy, and in similar fashion they completely destroyed it; afterwards they burned, and razed to the foundations, the hospital of Clerkenwell, London, and the manor of Highbury which belonged to that hospital.

Finally the king, with a heavy heart, and brooding on the evil in his kingdom – and because he did not believe that this mob really wished to kill the archbishop and Lord Robert – placed them outside the Tower, with their consent and assent. But the mob, inflamed with a spirit of fury, soon beheaded them without respect or delay. This horrendous wickedness was done on Friday 14 June, on the morrow of the feast of Corpus Christi.

Other horrors followed these: the commons of the lands of St Albans with the commons of Barnet, on learning that the commons of Kent, Essex and London had risen against the king and by force and fear of them compelled him to give in to their demands, rose up in a similar way against the abbot of St Albans. And when the people had assembled and raised aloft their standard, first they broke into the abbot's prison and beheaded a certain man they found there; then they came to the abbot and forcibly exacted a charter of liberties from him. Finally, compelled by dread of death, the abbot sent them that charter just as they had so ruthlessly exacted. The commons of Berkhampstead and Hemel Hempstead did the same at Ashridge. These deeds were done on Saturday 15 June.

But this sort and magnitude of malice was not confined to those places; the devil spread the poison of his malice as far as us, for some merchants of Dunstable were in the market at St Albans on that Saturday, and they saw these dreadful things being done. That very same Saturday they entered into a plan and, as I truly say, a conspiracy, and a little before vespers they broke in upon us. The first executor of this malice, Thomas Hobbes, the depraved mayor of Dunstable, deceitfully greeted the lord prior, that is, Thomas Marchal, on behalf of the lord king, with whom he had never spoken. At this greeting, so mendaciously made, the lord prior put down his hood, bowed his head, and to the lord king, as is fitting, showed reverence. And when the lord prior asked what was the king's will, Thomas Hobbes answered with a grim and menacing expression, 'The lord king', he said, 'wills and commands you that you should make a charter of liberties for his burgesses of Dunstable, as they had in the time of King Henry I'. The prior, briefly considering their stubbornness and falseness and the malice of the time, refused at first to agree to their demand.

But later, thinking over what had been done at London, and what had happened to the abbot of St Albans, namely the many dangers and destructions of those who spoke out against the commons, he yielded for the time being to the flowing fury of the commons, and permitted to be made, as the burgesses demanded, a charter sealed with our common seal. During that time of fury and insanity, there were concealed among us, for our protection, Sir William Croyser knight, and William Bateman, who advised us that, for the moment, we should contradict the mob's wishes in nothing. The prior agreed to their advice, and considering the evil of the time, he permitted a charter to be made for them, as we said. And note that in that charter, which they so forcibly exacted from us, it was contained that they ought to do fealty to the lord prior. But by God's grace, as was written elsewhere, their pride speedily abated, and that charter, so quickly and without deliberation extorted from us, written in so solemn a style, and sealed with much wax, did not last for long. Contained among the articles of this charter was that butchers and fishermen of the neighbouring towns should not sell meat and fish within the borough of Dunstable. And when the burgesses were asked by the prior whether this article pleased them, the response from many was that it did not; so division arose between them so that each one wished to rush headlong at the other. At last, when the factions were pacified, the charter with the other articles in it was sealed, as I said.

For, shortly after, when the king had assembled the nobles of the realm, he caused those insurgents against him and the magnates to be killed, some by hanging and drawing, others by beheading, as was fittingly done to those guilty of the crime of treason. When at last he came to the town of St Albans the king caused to be punished the principal authors of this wickedness, according to the law. Among them John Ball, a priest, was drawn, hanged and quartered because by preaching in the north parts at the time of this uprising, as was said, he incited the people to rebellion. The lord prior [of Dunstable], when he had lit on the opportune moment to revoke the charter so extorted, first spoke sooth-ingly to the townsmen, so that they would bring back that charter; then, despite their opposition, he went quickly to the town of St Albans, and caused the indicted burgesses to come there, and he had that extorted charter cancelled and annulled. He lavished great expenses there, and incurred many perils for the liberation of his people, namely the burgesses of Dunstable.

42. Manumission and pardon for the men of Somerset

This document presents several puzzles. Found among the Westminster Abbey muniments, it purports to be a draft of a royal grant, but should probably be seen as a 'wish list' or 'insurance policy'. It tells us much about the fears and aspirations current that summer.

Barbara Harvey, 'Draft letters patent of manumission and pardon for the men of Somerset in 1381', *EHR* 80 (1965), 91.

Richard, by God's grace king of England and France and lord of Ireland, to all his bailiffs and faithful subjects to whom these present letters shall come, greeting. Know that we, of our especial grace, have manumitted each and every one of our liegemen and subjects the commons and others of the county of Somerset, and we have divested those and every one of them from every bondage, and we make them quit by these presents; and also we have pardoned those same lieges and our subjects all the felonies, treasons, transgressions and extortions done or perpetrated by them or by any of them whatsoever, and also outlawry or outlawries if this or these will be published against them, or any one of them, for these reasons; and we have granted our firm peace to them and to each one of them henceforward. In testimony of which we have caused to be made these our letters patent. Myself as witness at Westminster, 2 July, the fifth year of our reign [1381].

43. Gaunt's quarrel with the earl of Northumberland

Fortunately for him, Gaunt was negotiating with the Scots on the border at this time. He still feared for his safety, though, and the refusal of the earl of Northumberland to offer him shelter provoked a rift between them. Gaunt's duchess and his mistress also felt threatened. It is tempting to think that Gaunt's experiences in 1381 influenced his subsequent decision to concentrate on his Spanish ambitions.

Anon. Chron., 152–3.

In the same year, when the duke of Lancaster had made the truce ... between the kingdoms of England and Scotland, he was returning towards England both glad and happy. But his joy was turned to sorrow and distress because it was announced to him by messengers that the king was his enemy and that all the commons of the south had risen against him, with the king and the lords, in order to destroy him, and that he should never again either enter or live in England, because he was a traitor and schemed by plotting the death of the king from day to day, and he was no use to the king or kingdom. At that time he was invited by the earl of Northumberland to rest and eat with him at Alnwick, but the earl, hearing of the king's will, as he supposed, but without having received any message on this matter, sent Sir John Hothum knight and Thomas Motherby esquire to the duke asking him not to come at all, nor to take it badly, because he did not dare to receive him or entertain him for fear of his liege lord. Because of this the duke was very angry with the earl, and a great quarrel arose between them because of this accusation, as you shall hear later. He was very suspicious of the king and his council, and in consequence retreated towards Scotland where he was most courteously received by the lords of the land. They treated him with great kindness, and sent him large presents of corn, wine and beasts; and further, several lords came to him begging him to be of good cheer and to remain with them and they would seek for him lands and tenements and possessions in great plenty. At this he thanked them warmly with all his heart for their good wishes, and from day to day he assumed that he enjoyed the king's favour because he had suffered no forfeiture, nor did the king act unnaturally towards him.

At the same time some of his men abandoned him through fear of losing their lives through their liege lord, and as each took their leave, which he readily gave them, he thanked them warmly for their good service, begging them not to take it amiss that he could not at this time reward them according to their length of service, as he wished and as they deserved. But the lord of Marmion and Sir Walter Urswyk[90] and others to the number of [blank in ms.] remained with him to take good or bad, whatever would come. At the departure of his men he addressed them piteously and with humble demeanour, and he thanked them for their good service, making daily protestation with a solemn oath that he had never been a traitor nor thought evil towards his liege lord, nor to the realm of England either by plotting or planning; but he supposed that God wished to punish him for his misdeeds and his wicked life because he had lived for a long time, and especially in the sin of lechery, which he had indulged in especially with Lady Katherine Swynford, a witch and enchantress, and several others close to his wife, contrary to God's will and the law of Holy Church. At that time the duchess his wife, a lady of great beauty and virtuous life, while staying with her entourage in Pontefract castle, heard of this matter and of the discomfiture of her lord, and her friends told her that she was in great danger. So she hurriedly left Pontefract in fear, and moved, fleeing to Knaresborough with a few of her people, because some of them left her and completely abandoned her, to the duchess's distress. Lady Katherine Swynford, his mistress, went into hiding where nobody knew where to find her for a long time. And when the duchess came to Knaresborough castle, she was honourably received by a yeoman, the keeper of the castle, Richard Brennand[91] by name, who greatly comforted her until better news could reach her.

90 Sir John Marmion of West Tanfield, Yorks., had been on the Nájera campaign, was constable of Knaresborough from 1377 and was one of Gaunt's most favoured retainers 1372–87. His family had served the Lacy earls of Lincoln and Leicester. Its male line died out in 1311; the earls (later dukes) of Lancaster acquired the lands through marriage to the Lacy heiress. Sir Walter Urswick of Catterick, one of several of his family to serve the house of Lancaster, was retained by Gaunt 1361–94. Walker (1990): 25–6, 32n, 47–8, 58, 88, 91, 274, 287; 31n, 78, 91, 283.

91 *Ibid.*, 89, 236, 287.

44. A favourable view of John of Gaunt

In contrast to some chroniclers, Knighton consistently spoke well of the duke. Gaunt was the lord of Leicester, whose castle was an important administrative centre of his lands, and thus a powerful presence in the town (though not the abbey's patron). Knighton's word for Gaunt here is pius ('godly' or 'holy', but also 'dutiful, conscientious, honest'), here translated as 'excellent'.

KC, 238–40.

In case anyone should fall to wondering why I have constantly called the duke 'excellent', let the diligent reader pay attention and the hearer who is the friend of truth understand that this excellent duke was so grounded in the strength of virtue that, in all his tribulations, and in every tight corner and all the injuries maliciously heaped upon him, he never sought revenge, nor did he order punishment by his men. But he endured patiently, and forgave the wrongs of those who asked his forgiveness.

45. Events during the winter of 1381–82

The deaths of the earls of Suffolk (without a male heir) and March (whose son was a minor), had political consequences. The new queen's arrival provoked no comment from this chronicler.

VR, 70–1.

At the beginning of November the king began to hold a parliament at London. This parliament was almost entirely[92] occupied with making peace and concord between the duke of Lancaster and the earl of Northumberland, that is, Lord Percy. For, while Lancaster was conducting negotiations with the Scots, at the time of that evil insurrection, serious discord arose between them. This could scarcely, and only with the greatest difficulty, be calmed down and ended by the king and all the lords of the land during that whole time, so that few, if any, other matters were concluded. So the parliament was continued until the feast of St Hilary [*13 January 1382*].

In this parliament there was some discussion about the manumission of villeins. For their hope rested upon this: that because at another time the unwilling king had granted this during their insurrection, it

---

92 For measures taken in this parliament as a result of the revolt, see Dobson (1998), 239–42, 325–33.

would now be confirmed by this parliament. But this was reversed, first by the king and afterwards by all the lords. Also in that parliament William Ufford, earl of Suffolk, overtaken by sudden unexpected death, died in Westminster Hall. About the feast of St Thomas the Apostle [2 December] the sister of the emperor of Germany or king of Bohemia, called Anne Wenceslas, the future queen of England, arrived at Dover with a large retinue.

The Lord Edmund, earl of March, after making a vigorous campaign in Ireland in which he had by force of arms nobly subjected almost the whole county of Ulster which had rebelled against him, caught a chill when riding across a large river. He died on 27 December, the feast of St John the Evangelist, in Ireland where he ordered his body to be buried in a certain cathedral church until the time when his flesh should be consumed. And when the flesh was reduced to dust his bones were to be brought back to England and buried in Wigmore Abbey along with his ancestors .... In that year Pope Urban [VI] translated Master William Courtenay from the see of London to Canterbury, and confirmed the election of John Fordham as bishop of Durham, and he gave the see of London to Master Robert Braybrooke.

II: THE STRUGGLE FOR POWER, 1382–87

Because Richard never had an official minority – since no regent was appointed – we cannot tell when the unofficial one came to an end. After 1381 though, he gradually began to assert his independence and to make policy for himself. In the five years 1382 to 1387, Richard's political qualities began to emerge, as did the character of his court, and a group of his leading political advisers took shape. By the middle of the decade, disappointment and disenchantment with the young king became increasingly obvious in the chroniclers' observations.

1382

46. The year 1382, according to the *Eulogium*

In 1382 Richard married Anne of Bohemia, daughter of the Holy Roman Emperor Charles IV (1316–78). The intention behind this alliance was probably to attach her half-brother Wenzel, king of Bohemia, more firmly to the Roman papacy, but in the event Wenzel ('The Drunkard') proved diplomatically negligible. Though the marriage was initially unpopular and ultimately childless, the personal union seems to have been happy. Anne's greatest importance lay perhaps in the cultural links she created, however inadvertently, between England and Bohemia. Her family was cosmopolitan and cultured; her father founded Prague University and was a notable patron of the arts. The Wilton Diptych is probably one indirect result of Anglo-Bohemian cultural links; another is that John Wycliffe's ideas were exported to Bohemia, where they caused considerable interest, and a number of Wycliffite writings have survived only in manuscripts in Bohemian libraries.[1]

In this year events in the Low Countries, where there was civil war between Bruges and England's long-standing ally Ghent,[2] began to impinge on English consciousness. The October parliament discussed a possible indirect attack on France through Flanders, and granted a tax, but on exceptionally stringent conditions.[3]

Eulogium, 355–6.

---

1 Gordon, Monnas and Elam (1997): chaps. XV, XVII; Hudson (1988); Leff in Kenny (1986).

2 Nicholas (1992): 227–31; de Vries (2004): 155–65.

3 Jurkowski, Smith and Crook (1998): 62.

This year the king married Anne, sister of the emperor, that is, the king of Bohemia, without the consent of the realm, and after 22,000 marks was paid for her. Forgotten was the daughter of the count of Flanders; if he had married her he could afterwards have held Flanders in his own right …. In this year dissension arose in Flanders because the cities or good towns of Flanders obtained the removal of the privileges of the Gantois; these rebels sought the aid of the English. In the same year a parliament was held at London in which peace was made with the insurgents, and a tenth conceded by the clergy and a fifteenth by the laity.

47. The king's marriage

(a) The negotiations

The great European chronicler of the period was Jean Froissart.[4] Born in Valenciennes, Froissart served successively the count of Hainault, Queen Philippa (1361-9), Wenceslas, duke of Luxembourg and Brabant, and the count of Blois.

Froissart, *Chronicles* I.593.

Sir Simon Burley, a sage and valiant knight who had been the king's tutor and much beloved by the prince his father, was nominated to go to Germany to treat of this marriage, being a wise and able negotiator …. He set out from England magnificently equipped, and arrived at Calais; from thence he went to Gravelines and continued his journey to Brussels, where he met the duke Wenceslaus of Brabant [and others]. The duke and duchess of Brabant, from the love they bore the king of England, received his knight most courteously. They were much rejoiced on hearing the cause of his journey into Germany, and said it would be a good match between the king of England and their niece. They gave Sir Simon Burley, on his departure, special letters to the emperor, to assure him that they greatly approved of this marriage.

(b) Walsingham's opinion

Anne of Bohemia reached London on 18 January, was married on the 20th and crowned on the 22nd.

SAC I.572, 576.

[*During the meeting of parliament*] … news came of the arrival at Calais

4 See M. C. E. Jones in *ODNB*.

of the new queen, namely the sister of the king of Bohemia, Wenceslas, son of the former king of Bohemia and emperor, who expected to be crowned emperor and described himself as emperor literally everywhere. So when the king had chosen her she was bought for a great price and with tremendous effort, although a great sum of gold had been offered to him for the daughter of the lord Bernabo [*Visconti*], duke of Milan. When ... news of the future queen's arrival was heard, parliament was dissolved, to reconvene after the royal wedding and Christmas. Meanwhile each and every one strove with all his strength to honour these great nuptials with gifts and favour over and above what allegiance demanded. A delegation was sent to meet this magnificent maiden and conduct her with all worldly glory to the port of Dover; she was accompanied by many nobles, both of her own country and of this land. ...

After the feast of Epiphany, all the nobility of the realm gathered at London to be present at the king's wedding and to exercise office according to ancient custom. The imperial girl was anointed queen at Westminster; and she was crowned in royal wedlock by the lord archbishop of Canterbury with glory and honour. Tournaments were also held for some days in order to enhance such celebrations, and in them the English publicly demonstrated their virtue and the queen's compatriots their prowess. In these events, though not without injury on both sides, honour was gained and military matters glorified.

(c) An eyewitness description of Anne

The monastic author would have had several occasions to observe the new queen.

WC, 24.

It seemed to seekers after truth that she was not so much given as bought, for the king of England had expended no small sum of money for such a tiny portion of meat (*pro tantilla carnis porcione*).

48. Appointment of a new chancellor

In July 1382 the very experienced Richard Scrope (treasurer 1371–5, chancellor October 1378–January 1380 and again from December 1381) was dismissed as chancellor. Scrope, a member of a baronial Yorkshire family, was unusual, though not unique, in being a lay chancellor. Walsingham viewed his dismissal as a sinister new development, and blamed the king. However,

Scrope's successor, Robert Braybrooke, bishop of London, was a kinsman of Princess Joan, so perhaps we should detect her hand in this business.

SAC I.620–2.

Sir Richard Scrope, knight ... elected chancellor of the realm by the community of the kingdom and by the assent of the lords, was at this time ejected from the office of chancellor which he had exercised laudably and prudently. The cause of his dismissal was his steadfast resistance to the will of the king who wanted to be rid of him so that he could promote outsiders. For after the demise of Edmund Mortimer, earl of March, and of other lords who had recently succumbed to death, some ambitious men, both knights and esquires and also courtiers of lower rank, came to the king and demanded of him that certain lands and lordships of the deceased should be granted to them for that time in which, by the custom of the kingdom, the king should hold them in his hands. The king, being a mere child, granted their requests without delay, and, sending the courtiers to the chancellor, he ordered that charters, sealed with the great seal, be given to them in accordance with their wish.

But the chancellor, who earnestly desired the profit of the realm and also the king's advantage, flatly denied their requests, arguing that the king, heavily burdened as he was by many debts, needed to keep such windfalls for himself so that, through them, he could in part discharge his debts to the creditors; and alleging that they, who knew with what debts the king was burdened, were not the king's faithful men while they considered rather their greed than royal advantage, by demanding such benefits, and preferring private profit before public necessity. For that reason they should stop these demands and be content with the king's previous grants, which were enough for them; they should clearly understand that he himself would make or seal for them no confirming charters of these gifts of the king, who did not yet exceed the years of childhood, in case by chance in the future he should receive ill will from him. So those who had come as petitioners seeking such grants were sent away empty-handed by the chancellor. They informed the king that the chancellor had an obstinate attitude, and that he wanted to do nothing at the king's command but rather to scorn the royal mandate; and that the king ought quickly to discipline with due severity such outrageous disobedience, or else in the near future the royal honour would be scorned among his subjects, and his rule would not be respected.

The king, who reasoned like a child,[5] paid more heed to the false schemes of those tale-bearers than to the loyalty of his faithful chancellor. In a spirit of fury he sent someone to ask for the seal from him and to bring it back. And when the king had sent again and again by increasingly solemn messengers that he should return the seal to him, the chancellor finally gave this reply: 'I am prepared', he said, 'to consign this seal, not to you, but to him who handed that charge to me; nor shall any intermediary carry it between me and him, but I shall restore it into his hands, who with his own, and not through others' hands, committed it to me'. So he came to the king and handed back the seal, and promised that he would be faithful to the king in future, as before; but he refused to hold office under him again. After receiving the seal, the king for many days did whatever he liked[6] until finally Master Robert Braybrooke, bishop of London, took up the office of chancellor.

When not only the magnates of the realm but also the community heard that the king had – contrary to the custom of the kingdom – summarily dismissed the chancellor whom the whole nobility, along with all the elected representatives, had chosen, they were very angry. But no one dared to say anything about the matter openly, on account of the malice of the king's advisers and because of the youthful foolishness of the king himself. And so the interests of the king and kingdom were set aside by an act of the unwise king and by the malice of those around him.

49. The rise of Robert de Vere, earl of Oxford

Richard was beginning to form strong friendships, of which this would eventually become the most important.

Froissart, *Chronicles* II. 70.

The earl of Cambridge, on his arrival in England, represented to his brother the duke of Lancaster how the king of Portugal had acted, and the state of that country. The duke became very thoughtful, for he saw that the conquest of Castile was very distant and doubtful; besides, his nephew, King Richard, had in his council those who were unfriendly to him, more especially the earl of Oxford, who had the sole management of the king. This lord did everything in his power to make a breach between the king and his uncles. He said to him, 'Sir, if you wish to

5 Latin: *sapiebat ut parvulus*, a reference to I Corinthians 13:11, *sapiabam ut parvulus*.

6 Scrope resigned on 11 July, but his successor was not appointed until 20 September.

support your two uncles, my lords of Lancaster and Cambridge, in their
war with Spain, it will cost you the whole revenue of England, and they
will not at last gain anything. It will be more prudent to keep at home
men and money, than that they should be scattered abroad without any
profit to yourself; you had better guard and defend your own inheritance, which is invaded on all sides from France and Scotland, than
employ your men elsewhere'. The young king was well inclined to
follow this advice of the earl, for he loved him with his whole heart,
they having been brought up together.

50. The bishop of Lincoln seeks support for the bishop of Norwich's expedition

The papal schism had added a new dimension to international affairs, since
France's allies who adhered to the Avignon papacy were considered schismatics.
Any attack on them could thus be considered a crusade, and this was a useful
argument given that a direct attack on France itself was financially impossible.
The only question was, against which schismatic régime would the crusading
army be sent? Naturally, Castile was Gaunt's choice, but Flanders, whose count
was a French vassal and supported the Avignon papacy, was strategically much
more significant for England. It was also the largest customer for English
wool. Flanders was the choice of the commons and of Henry Despenser, the
bishop of Norwich, who already had papal backing for the scheme; the lords
supported Gaunt. No decision was taken in 1382, but the church began to
organise support for a crusade, and the date of this letter shows that Bishop
Despenser began to organise his expedition before the scheme was even
discussed in parliament.

Lincolnshire Archives Office, Register 12 (John Buckingham, Memoranda), f.
253v.

John *[Buckingham]*, bishop of Lincoln, to the archdeacon of Lincoln[7]
or his official, and all abbots, priors, rectors, vicars and chaplains of
parochial chapels, greeting, grace and blessing: our lord Urban, pope
by divine providence, has commissioned Henry, bishop of Norwich,
to proceed against Robert, once cardinal of the Basilica of the Twelve
Apostles, commonly called 'of Geneva', and his favourers and adherents,
and has published a bull and letters giving privileges, indulgences and
full remission of sins to those who contribute, for the defence of the
Roman church and the subjection of those schismatics. We order you to

---

7 A letter to the archdeacon of Lincoln or his deputy was the pattern which was copied
  into the bishop's register. Similar letters were sent to the other archdeacons in the
  diocese.

allow his representatives and special messengers, whose names appear more fully in their letters, to enter the archdeaconries of Lincoln and Stow to publicise and announce to Christ's faithful people everything contained in those apostolic letters, and especially the remissions and privileges, and to receive and collect legacies left in wills and last testaments for the work of the crusade, and alms and subsidies freely given for the health of souls. We order you jointly and severally, by virtue of the obedience which you owe to the apostolic see, and entreat you in the bowels of Christ to allow those proctors or their deputies to approach and explain and expound this matter to the clergy and people, according to the form of the apostolic letters, so that the sign of Christ's cross may be raised up and the cause of God and Holy Mother Church may be advanced, and their imbecile enemies may be overcome, and that these proctors may successfully exhort those who are not able to take part in the journeys in person to contribute of their goods according to their resources. Buckden [*Hunts.*], 15 December 1382.

1383

The question – by way of Flanders, or Spain? – was again debated in the April parliament, and after a brisk discussion it was decided to launch a crusade against Flanders, led by the bishop of Norwich.[8] The 'Norwich crusade', by reason of its legal status and some unusual funding, can claim to be the oddest campaign of the Hundred Years' War. It is also exceptionally well-documented, providing insights into public opinion at several levels. The enthusiastic response to the appeal for support shows us a genuine expression of popular feeling. Indulgences, which have been reviled since the sixteenth-century Reformation, were still popular in the late fourteenth century and proved effective in raising money to support the bishop's army.

51. The year 1383, according to the *Eulogium*

The bishop of Norwich was Henry Despenser, a grandson of Edward II's hated favourite Hugh Despenser the Younger. In some ways Despenser was a model bishop: highly educated, with close ties to the papal court, resident and active in his diocese. On the other hand, he had a fondness for fighting which was both unseemly and uncanonical: as a young man living at the curia, Despenser had undertaken military activity on behalf of Pope Urban V in 1369; in 1381 he was the only repressor of the Peasants' Revolt to hang insurgents without trial;[9] and in 1399 he alone showed any willingness to oppose Bolingbroke's invasion

---

8 Wilks, ed. Hudson (2000): 253–72.

9 *KC*: 224–7, 226 n.3.

with force.[10] In 1383 he eagerly embraced the chance to lead a crusading army to Flanders.

Eulogium, 356-7.

In 1383 the bishop of Norwich, dissolute rather with military light-mindedness than weighty with pontifical maturity, procured from the pope the authority to preach the Cross of Christ and to make war on the antipope and his supporters. The pope granted him that power and indulgence which were granted to all those going to the Holy Land who had taken the Cross and who wished to go with him or who gave him any of their goods. He also gave him the power to take with him, as soldiers, any religious, at the summons of their superiors.[11]

This year the lords in parliament proposed to send an army to France; the bishop exhibited the papal bull and sought permission to execute it; the king did not wish to bestir himself; the commons wanted the bishop to set out. The bishop maintained that a holy war against France was a necessity; the lords put it to him that he should go under the banner of another lord whom the king would send, but the bishop said that the banner of the church would be in command. The lords replied that it was not legal for a bishop to fight. He answered that in the cause of the Lord and of the pope he certainly could; also he and his agents had preached, and they had both promised indulgence to the living and stood over the graves of the dead and absolved them, praying to the Archangel Michael to lead their souls into heaven, and in this way they collected a great sum of money. The men identified themselves with the sign of the Cross, and they arrogantly rearranged everything as if they were in a religious house, and they withdrew from Divine worship into certain places of silence under the pretext, as they said, of fighting the antipope, but in fact to fight against chastity. The bishop, therefore, crossed over with the assembled money and the subsidy he had accepted from the king, along with the armed priests and false religious; and coming into Flanders he killed certain weavers of Dunkirk who crossed his path and called this 'The conquest of West Flanders'. Then he wrote to the king of France calling him a schismatic and the illegal occupier of the French kingdom, and ordered him to desert the schismatic pope. He besieged the town of Ypres, but the townsmen defended themselves

---

10 *CR*: 118, 120, 127.

11 For details of the relevant bulls see *WC*.30 n.1, and 164.n.1.They empowered Despenser only to preach a crusade; it was Lancaster's crusade against Castile which had military authorisation. 'Religious' means members of the religious orders: monks, canons (regular) and friars.

vigorously and killed many [*of his troops*]; and God struck them in the posterior and they died of a bloody flux.[12]

After a short time the king of France arrived with a large army, and those priests and apostates who had come to plunder ran to the sea. The bishop and the knights shut themselves in the towns and, after the duke John of Brittany interceded on their behalf, and by the indulgence of the king of France, they returned with difficulty, flowing with blood and infecting their native land. Blessed be God who confounds the arrogant. The king ordered the bishop to say a psalter for those whom he had killed, and he deprived him of his temporalities until he had paid back the grant which he had received from him.

52. The parliament of 23 February–10 March 1383

The appointment of Michael de la Pole as chancellor was significant; his predecessor, Braybrooke, may have been Princess Joan's choice, but Pole, a former servant of the Black Prince, was certainly Richard's appointment.

WC, 34–6.

In this parliament the bishop of Norwich put forward his plan to take the cross against Robert [*of Geneva*] the antipope, offering that he himself would pay the annual wages of those setting out on that expedition; because, when the papal bulls of indulgence had reached him, he at once despatched certain collectors and penitentiaries through many parts of England, both to absolve the people from the crimes they confessed, and collect the money raised through the hope of obtaining indulgence. As a result, a vast sum of money was raised for him by these agents. But for a long time the lords' envy impeded him …. They said that the king of England's right in France could easily be destroyed if the bishop, under crusading colours, were to subjugate France through warfare, especially since it would seem that he had won her rather for the church's cause than for the king's. Prompted by unfair feeling, many of the lords used these and other arguments to delay his departure. Consequently the commons of the realm, who saw that the lords' laziness had been harmful to the kingdom on many previous expeditions, took the bishop's side. Especially vociferous were two knightly sons of the earl of Devon, namely Philip and Peter de Courtenay. For

12 This was certainly dysentery, and almost certainly shigella dysentery, brought on by drinking unclean water, a scourge of army camps in previous centuries and of refugee camps in our own day.

this reason the duke of Lancaster was moved to anger and spoke certain words which, spread about by rumour, moved the commons to anger. When the duke heard this he rode off with a small escort and fled to other places. And so the business of parliament remained somewhat undecided. Afterwards Sir Michael de la Pole was made chancellor of England following the removal of the bishop of London.[13]

53. The two crusades of 1383, according to Walsingham

Walsingham's account of the impact of these two schemes – the Norwich crusade and John of Gaunt's crusade against the Castilians[14] – upon the religious life shows how individuals took advantage of the combatants' need for men and money to further their own ends. Part of the history of the rule of Thomas de la Mare, abbot of St Albans 1349–96, this account comes in the course of a description of the problem of religious apostates: runaways from the religious life.[15]

Gesta Abbatum Monasterii Sancti Albani, ed. H. T. Riley (RS, 1867), II.416–17.

When these crusaders had left for Flanders with Henry Despenser, bishop of Norwich, many who found the peace of the cloister displeasing sought, either through him or someone else, licence from the abbot, which he was not able to refuse, to turn to military matters and the clash of arms. I will not keep silent about their names: from the monastery *[St Albans]* there set out John de Bokedene, from the cell of Tynemouth *[Northumberland]* John Westwick, from the cell of Wymondham *[Norfolk]* William York, from *[the cell of]* Binham *[Norfolk]* Roger Beuver and John Belle, and from the priory of Hatfield *[Herts.]* the prior of the place himself William Eversdon, who died in Flanders, and William Schepeye. All of these, on account of the summer's heat and through drinking fetid water, contracted various illnesses and infirmities so that they could never afterwards enjoy their former state of health. For all of them, except the prior of Hatfield, it was said, came back, and they all experienced the unexpected forgiveness of the abbot.

13 Robert Braybrooke left office on 10 March; his successor was appointed on 13 March.

14 In March and April 1383, Gaunt's projected expedition to Castile was recognised by Urban VI as a crusade; Gaunt was made 'captain and standard-bearer', his troops were granted plenary pardon of their sins, and he was accorded the privileges and indulgences which Innocent III had granted to those crusading to the Holy Land, *Calendar of Papal Registers: Papal Letters IV (1362–1404)*, 264–5.

15 Logan (1996): esp. chap. 2.

At the time of this abbot, when the schism in the church had already been going on for a long time, and as the fortunes of the antipope rose because of the backing of the French king, the true pope, Urban, who was almost destitute of resources, explored many avenues by which he could obtain money, so that he could at least sustain his life. Observing this, many, both those of the secular habit and those professed in a rule, because they were keen to escape from under the yoke of obedience to a superior, sent money to Rome where they knew that everything was corrupt, and asked to be designated papal chaplains so that by this agreement they would be absolved from obedience to prelates.

Certain men also were promoted to that rank, wonderfully, or rather, miserably, by one Brother Walter Disse, of the Carmelite order, Doctor of Theology,[16] confessor of the duke of Lancaster, to whom he *[the pope]* had granted power to collect money to promote the duke of Lancaster's crusade against the schismatic Spaniards, and among other privileges, the power to create fifty honorary chaplains of the Supreme Pontiff, under a *[papal]* bull of grace, or rather, dishonour.

54. The people contribute generously to the costs of the Norwich crusade

On 5 April 1383, Archbishop Courtenay ordered special prayers and masses to be said on Thursdays and Saturdays throughout the southern province, with explanations of the reason for these efforts.[17] The bishop of Lincoln obeyed on 14 May, ordering explanations to be made in English (which would make them distinct from the Latin of the liturgy); forty days' indulgence would be earned by all those who participated.[18] These instructions of Courtenay and his episcopal colleagues followed a well-established procedure for rousing support for both patriotic and ecclesiastical efforts.[19] In this extract we can see the results of this series of commands; Leicester lay within the diocese of Lincoln. It is possible that Knighton, a canon of Leicester Abbey, was aggrieved that parliament had preferred this crusade over Gaunt's projected Castilian crusade.

KC, 324.

16 For Disse's high-profile international career, see Emden (1963): 188.

17 The bishop of London, who distributed letters from the archbishop to the whole southern province, forwarded the command on 14 April.

18 Lincolnshire Archives Office, Register 12 (Buckingham, Memoranda), ff. 253v, 259v–260.

19 McHardy (2001b): 171–89 and references.

Henry Despenser, bishop of Norwich, took the cross against the adherents of Pope Clement [VII]; for France, Scotland, Flanders and many
other nations favoured and adhered to that antipope. This bishop had
collected a huge and incredible sum of money: gold and silver, also
jewels, necklaces, rings, dishes, cups, spoons and other ornaments,
especially from ladies and other women; for it is said that a single
lady contributed £100, and some gave more, others less. Many gave
more than they could afford, it is believed, so that they could gain the
resulting benefits of absolution both for themselves and their loved
ones. And so the secret treasure of the realm, which was in the hands
of women, was exposed. The men behaved in just the same way as the
women, both rich and poor, according to the value of their goods, and
beyond, so that both their deceased friends and they themselves should
be absolved; for they would not be absolved unless they contributed
according to their ability and resources. Many recruited and equipped
men-at-arms with their own money, and many provided archers at their
own expense, and many went in person and at their own cost. For that
bishop had amazing indulgences, with absolution from pain and guilt
for that crusade, granted to him by Pope Urban VI, by whose authority
he absolved both the dead and the living, if their contribution was sufficient, through himself and his agents. For it was said that some of those
agents asserted that, at their command, angels would descend from
heaven and snatch the souls languishing in purgatory away from their
tortures, and instantly conduct them to the heavens.

55. The start of the Norwich campaign, according to a letter

Parts of this letter, shown here in italics, were incorporated into the *Westminster Chronicle* (44–6), so the letter was probably addressed to the abbot of
Westminster. The writer was certainly an eyewitness with close Westminster
connections. The chronicle's editors suggested that it was Despenser himself, a
frequent visitor to the house whose abbot (1362–86) was his kinsman Nicholas
Litlington. This would explain why Westminster, alone of the monastic chroniclers, looked kindly on the enterprise, blaming greedy captains for its failure.

W. A. Pantin, 'A medieval treatise on letter-writing from Rylands MS 394',
Bulletin of the John Rylands Library 13 (1929), 359–60.

Reverend Father and Lord: Because very often, and especially in this
present undertaking, reckless chattering of careless people obscures
the truth with gossip and spurious rumours, we therefore propose,
Reverend Father, to declare by these present letters to your reverend

lordship, how, in what way, and how much the Most High has lately deigned to work for the consolation of his people in F *[landers]* and its adjacent lands. And because the Lord will praise his people in what is written below, you, Reverend Father and others who are filled with the same fervour and purpose towards our goal, may be overcome by a spirit of happiness, and render thanks to the Almighty. On the eve of Holy Trinity *[16 May]*, taking advantage of times and hours favourable for our departure, along with certain of our captains and other mercenaries in S*[andwich]* harbour, we left port with our fleet. Carried by favourable winds we ploughed through the waves, where after a short delay we entered the port of Calais by skilful rowing; on the feast of Holy Trinity *we entered that town with our captains and others, where we waited during Monday and the Tuesday until noon in order to rest.* On that day we rode with our army to the town of G*[ravelines]*, pitched our tents beside the walls of the town, *drew up our battle-lines* and at once sent our messengers and their heralds to the captain and burgesses of the town to ask them whether they wished to hand over that town of G*[ravelines]* to the illustrious king of England and France and to us, in return for preserving their lives, limbs, goods and chattels peacefully and without any molestation; otherwise they and their goods would be destroyed or led away as booty. But those proud and puffed-up people made the spirited reply that they did not want to hand over their town by any agreement, and they totally despised our force and army. When we had received this response to us and our advice, we rested there the whole night, and in the morning we very carefully prepared ladders and other equipment for an assault. On that day, namely Wednesday, about the hour of tierce, the men of the town of B*[ourbourg]*, after weighing up carefully whether the hand of vengeance would be violently extended both towards us and our men and also towards them, and saying that they wished to be subject to the legality and rule of our lord king and ourselves, returned that town of B*[ourbourg]* into our hands, and after we had received their fealty, and the captured castle of that town returned by negotiation through Sir W,[20] and when that same Sir William had been appointed captain of the castle by us.[21] About the fourth hour after none of that day we arrayed ourselves for the assault, and our knights, squires and others fought vigorously for about four hours. Finally, by the clemency of divine favour, our force prevailed

20 Perhaps Sir William Faringdon.

21 The text appears corrupt at this point. It seems that the castle or citadel surrendered, but not the town itself.

with little death or injury, and at dusk we entered the town by ladders and other machines, and slaughtered many of the enemy, and the stroke of sword devoured them all except those whose female sex and tender age it spared from the slash of the blade. We remained in that town for Thursday, Friday and Saturday and a little of Sunday to rest ourselves and our army. A little after the hour of none on that day we drew up our battle line towards the town of D*[unkirk]*, and at dusk some of our men entered the town, and we camped beside the citadel of M.,[22] and in mid-morning we entered the town in full armour, and there we refreshed ourselves and our men with food which was in abundant supply. When we had stripped off our armour and were resting at noon, suddenly about the third hour after none on the Monday *there came numerous men of Flanders and France, drawn up in the finest battle array, with pennons and lances crowded everywhere, scarcely a mile from the town, their numbers extending to 28,000 at least, as we were more fully informed by some of those whom we captured. The loud call of the horns and trumpets was sounded in our army and with noise and clamour we ran to arms; we left the town in companies and eagerly went to fight. Where the battle-lines clashed there was a shattering of lances, helmets were smashed, buckles burst, the whole battlefield resounded with the screams of the slaughtered and armed riders pursued the fleeing enemy. The dead numbered at least 10,000, scattered over the whole countryside in ditches, cornfields and on the open ground. Afterwards, when everyone had assembled at our standard, we humbly knelt and sang a Te Deum to God, giving hearty thanks for the victory granted us by Heaven. At the end of the hymn there occurred a miracle,*[23] which the bearer of this letter can describe to you, also giving authority to that and the other things which he will relate to you orally, Father, on our behalf.

56. The Norwich crusade, according to Froissart

The expedition started well but ended in failure; the bishop's army disintegrated and Despenser slunk home in disgrace. The fullest account is by Froissart who, without openly criticising him, described Despenser's belligerence, quick temper and refusal to negotiate. Froissart's hero was Sir Hugh Calveley, one of the bishop's lieutenants, whose wise advice Despenser consistently ignored. Calveley was a veteran of England's war glory-days under Edward III, from 1346 to 1369, fighting in both France and Spain.[24] In 1383 the English

22 The text is unclear here.

23 A thunderstorm broke out over the fleeing enemy, while the sky remained clear over the English army, *WC*, 40.

24 See K. Fowler, 'Calveley, Sir Hugh' in *ODNB*.

were permitted to retreat in good order, resulting in accusations of treachery on their return. De Vries (2004): 155–65 explains the course of the campaign.

Froissart, *Chronicles*, I.758–9, 761–3, 765–6; II.1–2, 10–11, slightly adapted.

The Bishop of Norwich, young and eager, and wishing to bear arms (having never done so except in Lombardy with his brother),[25] finding himself at Calais and at the head of so fine a body of men-at-arms, said to his companions, 'For what purpose, my good sirs, are we waiting here so long? Sir William Beauchamp[26] will never arrive, and the king and his uncles have totally forgotten us. Let us perform some deeds of arms, since we have been ordered so to do, and loyally employ the money of the church, since we are living upon it, and make conquests over our enemies.' 'Well spoken', replied those who heard him. 'Give notice to our men that in three days we shall make an expedition, and let us determine to what part we shall march. We cannot leave the gates of Calais without entering enemy country, for France surrounds us on all sides. ... On which account', continued the bishop of Norwich, 'if I may be believed, the first expedition we undertake should be to Flanders'. ... This was adopted by all in the council.

Sir Hugh Calveley was not present at this council, having gone to see a cousin ... *[and when asked for his advice, answered]*: 'Sir, you know on what terms we have left England: our expedition has nothing to do with what concerns the wars of kings, but is solely directed against the Clementists. We are the soldiers of Pope Urban *[VI]*, who has given us absolution from all faults if we destroy the Clementists. If we march into Flanders, notwithstanding that country now belongs to the king of France and duke of Burgundy, we shall break our contract, for I understand that the count of Flanders and all the Flemings are as good Urbanists as ourselves; besides, we have not a sufficient army to enter Flanders for they are prepared and accustomed to war, having nothing else to do .... They are a numerous people and it will be difficult to march through so strong a country. ... I therefore advise, since you are resolved on an expedition, that we march towards Aire or Montreuil; none will venture, as yet, to oppose us ....'

25 Before his promotion as bishop of Norwich in 1369, Despenser spent a number of years at the curia and, with his elder brother Edward, took part in a campaign against Milan on behalf of Urban V (pope from 1362).

26 The earl of Warwick's younger brother and a former associate of the Black Prince, Beauchamp was appointed captain of Calais early in 1383. He was to be the lay commander of this campaign, and Despenser had been ordered to await his arrival.

Scarcely had Sir Hugh done speaking when the bishop, in a rage, hot and impetuous as he was, replied, 'Yes, yes, Sir Hugh. You have learnt so long to fight in France that you know not how to fight elsewhere. Now, can we make an excursion anywhere more advantageous to ourselves than towards the sea, by Bourbourg, Dunkirk, Nieuport, and on to the dependencies of Cassel, Bergues, Ypres and Poperingue? In the country I have named, according to the information I have received from the citizens of Ghent who are with us, they have never been harassed by the war; so we will go there to refresh ourselves and wait for the arrival of Sir William Beauchamp, if he intends coming ....'

When morning came, the trumpet sounded, and all marched off, taking the road towards Gravelines. They were, according to a muster made, 3,000 strong. They continued their march until they came to the port of Gravelines. ... The town could not hold out for long, for it was only enclosed by palisades, and the inhabitants were seamen. If there had been any gentlemen in the town it would have held out longer than it did. The country had no notice of this war, nor had they any suspicion that the English would attack them. The English therefore took the town of Gravelines by storm. *[Negotiations with envoys of the count of Flanders proved abortive. Then news that 12,000 Flemings were camped outside Dunkirk sent the English hurrying there.]*

The archers were ordered to advance on the Flemings ... and shortly the battle began briskly, for, to tell the truth, the Flemings defended themselves very well, but the archers wounded or beat down many when the men-at-arms broke through them, and with their pointed spears killed multitudes at the first charge. In short, the English won the day, and the Flemings were defeated. *[After this victory the English marched down the coast taking, as they went, the towns of Bourbourg and St Venant, and Dixmude castle. Their successes continued.]* When they had so laid the whole country under their subjection that none came to oppose them, and when they were masters of the coast from Gravelines to Sluys, having taken Dunkirk, Nieuport, Furnes and Blanquenbergue, they advanced to lay siege to Ypres. There the bishop and Sir Hugh Calveley and the English halted, and sent messengers to Ghent. When ... the captains in Ghent heard that the English demanded their assistance, and were besieging Ypres, they were much pleased, and prepared themselves to march there as quickly as possible. They set out from Ghent on Saturday morning *[12 July]*, to the number of nearly 20,000, with a very considerable train of carts, and in good array. They marched by Courtrai, and came to Ypres. The English rejoiced at their coming.

... The siege of Ypres continued with great activity on the part of the English and Flemings, who made many assaults which greatly frightened those in the town.

The king of France, who greatly desired to raise the siege and fight with the English, hastened his preparation, set out from Compiegne and marched to Arras. The constable of France with many barons, who formed the vanguard of the army, had already arrived and were quartered in Artois. The duke of Brittany came with 2,000 lances, as he was anxious to assist his cousin the count of Flanders on this occasion. Indeed he was greatly obliged to do so for he had found him, earlier, eager to befriend him in his distress. ... News was brought to the bishop of Norwich, Sir Hugh Calveley and the English besieging Ypres, that the king of France was hastening by forced marches, with an army of over 20,000 men-at-arms, knights and squires, and 60,000 others .... They also learnt that the duke of Brittany was with the king of France and coming against them, which greatly astonished them. They called a council on this information, to consider what line of conduct to pursue. Having weighed every circumstance, and not finding themselves in sufficient strength to wait for the whole force of their king, they judged it to be more prudent for ... the men of Ghent to return to their town, and the English to retreat towards Bergues and Bourbourg, which they were to garrison.... This resolution was adopted and they broke camp.

[When the French arrived, Calveley abandoned Bergues without a fight and made for Calais. The French sacked Bergues and attacked Bourbourg.] The English ... were in a most perilous situation, being surrounded on all sides, without means of escaping by flight .... The duke of Brittany, who was on the opposite side of the town to the *[French]* king, entered into negotiations with the English, aware of the peril they were in. He advised them to surrender the town, on their lives and fortunes being spared. This they were very willing to do, and they entreated the duke, through love of God, and in honour of his gentility, to undertake the business.

The duke sent information of what he had done to the king. ... The king of France and his uncles replied that, in God's name, they would willingly agree to a treaty, if the duke of Brittany and the constable of France would undertake it. In this manner Sunday passed. ... On the Monday this negotiation was carried on in the king's tent, and in his presence. ... The duke of Brittany was very active in this business, and it was settled that the English should leave Bourbourg and Gravelines, and carry away with them as much of their wealth as they could .... The whole of Tuesday they employed in shoeing their horses, and in packing up all their wealth, of which they had much, and in making preparations for their departure. On the Wednesday morning they loaded their baggage-horses and began their march, passing through the army with passports from the king. The Bretons were much exasperated when they saw them so loaded …. Thus the English marched to Gravelines, where they halted. On the Thursday morning, when they left it, they set fire to the place, burned it to the ground, and arrived in Calais with all their pillage. They stopped there to refresh themselves and to wait for a favourable wind to return to England.

57. An impostor punished for circulating false reports about the crusade

Popular enthusiasm for this campaign waned quickly.

Translated, from City of London Letter-Book H, by Riley, *Memorials of London*, 479, adapted.

Hugh de la Pole of Wales was brought before John Northampton, mayor, and the aldermen on 24 July 1383 and examined before them on the charge that, the previous day he came into the street of St Lawrence in the Old Jewry in London, begging for alms, and alleging that he, together with fifteen of his comrades, had come from Flanders, from the town of Ypres, which the bishop of Norwich had taken by assault, and was inside with his men; that the French and other enemies who had held it had withdrawn to a castle within the town and held this; that within the town the bishop and his men had three barrels full of gold; and that in the assault those fifteen comrades of his were so badly wounded and bruised that not one of them could now help himself. He also said that dissension had arisen between the bishop and the other English knights who were with him. And, that the people might more readily believe his words, he showed them his hand, anointed with oil and wrapped in cloth, to appear as though it were wounded, when really it was not hurt, as was plainly shown before the mayor and aldermen. So by falsely and maliciously lying, and making himself out to be poor and feeble, he deceived the whole people, to the manifest scandal of the city of London.

58. Indenture between the duke of Brittany and the English for evacuating Bourbourg, 14 September 1383

The duke of Brittany, England's on–off ally, acted as intermediary in securing the safe passage home of the bishop's defeated forces.

Recueil des Actes de Jean IV, Duc de Bretagne, vol. II, ed. M. Jones (Paris, 1983), no. 462.

It has been discussed and agreed between my lord duke of Brittany on one side, and Sirs Thomas Trivet, William Elmham, William Farringdon and John Cornwall on the other what follows, namely that these knights and others of their company, having and holding the town and fortress of Bourbourg, will return and deliver it to the lord king [*of France*] by order of the said lord duke, and that they, and all those within, will evacuate and abandon it by noon on Thursday, and all the country of Flanders. Further, they will assist and advise, with all their power, that those who are now at Gravelines[27] will also leave that town and district, and if they refuse, will not aid, advise or comfort them in any way, except if the king of England, the duke of Lancaster or any of that king's lieutenants should issue any explicit new order, by which they would no longer be prevented from helping them. ... And if anyone of the town of Bourbourg and of the land of Flanders wishes to remain in the town, they may do so and they and all their goods shall be secure, provided they come and remain at the pleasure of the lord king, and that they shall be and remain in the obedience of my lord of Flanders. By this means the said knights and all those of the town of Bourbourg are to go with all their goods, horses, armour and other property whatsoever, securely and safely, to any place they please, and on this there shall be made good letters guaranteeing this, and during this time there will be good truces and cessation of hostilities on one side and the other, and this will be announced by proclamation, and these things and each of them are to be kept and accomplished in good faith, without fraud or evil intent as both sides have sworn and promised. Monday after the Nativity of Our Lady [*14 September*] 1383.

27 Which capitulated shortly after.

59. The parliament of 26 October–26 November 1383: the impeachment of Bishop Despenser

In the next parliament Despenser was impeached, essentially on four counts of breach of contract. In his vigorous defence the bishop argued that he had been sent to help Ghent, and it was the Ghentois who forced him to divert from his original plans; this may well have been true.[28]

RP III.153–4; *PROME* 1383 (2), sections 18–19.

Henry, bishop of Norwich, was impeached in this parliament on many counts, but especially on four charges, put to him by the chancellor in full parliament in the king and duke of Lancaster's presence. The chancellor said, 'My lord bishop, I am commanded on the king's behalf to address you as follows: although an indenture and covenants were made between the king and yourself, by which you were obliged and undertook to serve our lord king in his French wars with 2,500 men-at-arms and as many archers, well armed, equipped and mounted, from which you would provide a suitable muster at Calais, for an entire year, yet you have not actually served the king for a year, or even a half. You returned and disbanded your host, before the year was up, contrary for the terms of that indenture. The result is great discredit, loss and damage to our king and his whole realm, and for this you are greatly at fault. Also, as for the number of men for which you contracted by indenture, and for making the muster at Calais, you have failed both on both counts, and here too you are much to blame. Also, although in the last parliament it was agreed that my lord of Spain[29] or another of the king's uncles would lead the French expedition, for the honour of the realm, you persuaded the king to grant the command to yourself by the lavish promises you made, and especially because you promised first the commons in that parliament, and then the king himself, that if the king granted you command of that expedition, you would have in your force the number specified above, together with the best captains of England – after the royal princes. The king then asked you particularly to notify him of the names of the captains and commanders which you would have in your company, if the command were granted to you. You answered that for certain reasons you would not reveal their names until you were certain that the command was actually yours. But you made many promises and assurances that if the king put you in command of the expedition you would be accompanied by the best

28 De Vries (2004): 155–65.
29 Gaunt, in his role as king of Castile.

and most worthy captains of the kingdom, after the royal princes, as has been said. In consequence, and because of the other promises you made, which you have since utterly broken as you know, our lord king was greatly deceived, and so the command was granted to you, and you received it on the terms you asked for, and the king's uncles were completely excluded by those deceptions, to the great injury and harm of the king and his kingdom. Also, regarding the grant and levy made to you for that expedition, the king proposed in parliament, for the good governance and security of your army, to appoint a suitable lay peer of the realm as his lieutenant, who would obey you, during this expedition, in whatever concerned the crusade, and you would obey him in matters concerning the lieutenancy. This proposal of the king's did not please you, and in fact you refused it; and what is worse, by those lavish promises of yours the king was greatly deceived, and because he was distracted during that parliament by your other business, you gained both that expedition and its sole command. And it is common knowledge everywhere that it was for the lack of a lieutenant and good captains that the great injuries and terrible disasters suffered by that army, the king and his kingdom, were all your fault. Therefore you are again grievously at fault; to those matters alleged against you by the king, you may now answer as you see fit.'

To these the bishop replied that although by right, with his liege lord's permission, he should have counsel, through whom he should answer the charges ... nevertheless ... he himself, who knew more about the matter than anyone else, would, with his liege lord's permission, answer the charges, humbly requesting his liege lord to give him an audience and a hearing. To the first allegation that he had not served the king for the promised term, nor even half of it, which by the contracts drawn up, he said that he had been bound and charged by his liege lord, first and foremost, to rescue the town of Ghent with his men. And because of that command, as soon as he had arrived overseas he set off with his men towards the town of Ghent; and on the way, as it pleased God, he came upon his enemies at both Gravelines and Dunkirk, and elsewhere. And eventually, when the people of Ghent had met him and they had talked together and discussed the best course of action both for themselves and to accomplish the aims of the expedition, the men of Ghent finally decided that the town of Ypres should be besieged; they assured him that Ypres had insufficient stocks of either men or food to withstand the combined power of Ghent and England. They also said that if the town of Ypres, where the most important Flemings were, were to be won, the rest would be won. So, with the encouragement and support of the men of Ghent, and with the assent of all the English captains on the expedition, the siege was begun there. During it many of his men fell victim to serious illnesses, many were wounded and killed, and many wicked people, disobeying and rebelling against the bishop, returned to England with their booty.

60. Some other episodes in that parliament

Despenser's impeachment was the major event of this session, but other important matters surfaced too.

WC, 50–4.

During parliament there were brought before the king and the lords those knights who, earlier in Flanders, accepted money to hand back to the enemy towns won for the king of England. On this matter they were asked why they had acted thus, or by what authority, and without the knowledge or permission of the king or his lieutenant there, they presumed to embark on that action, and because they gave no acceptable reply to the accusations they were sentenced to imprisonment in the Tower of London. Thomas Trivet indeed put himself in the king's mercy and was glad when his bonds were released. But the others, through the mediation of friends, and after making a fine to the king (because money dissolves everything these days), were reconciled and restored to their former liberty.

About the end of the parliament the chancellor of England *[Michael de la Pole]* addressed the bishop of Norwich in the presence of the king and the magnates of the realm like this: 'Lord Bishop, you have your sword carried before you everywhere, as though you were a temporal lord. Put down your sword because it offends the king, and other temporal lords are making a serious complaint about it; and in future behave yourself as a bishop should. Besides, Lord Bishop, at the commons' request and as you yourself wanted, the king appointed you commander of his wars for one year to make vigorous warfare against these foes, wherever you should come upon them, and you accepted from the king a great sum of money for that purpose; and lastly, you promised to do these things right away. But now, after almost half a year has elapsed, you have left your promise incompletely fulfilled, you have taken the treasure of the kingdom but without *[making]* an expedition, and you have reduced the state of the war almost to nothing'.

The bishop was quite amazed by this, and did not offer an excuse to the onslaught, but was like a man completely fenced in by his enemies, not able to escape without penalty; and immediately there was removed from him everything which he could possibly lose, namely his temporalities, which were immediately seized into the king's hand. But the king consoled the bishop and encouraged him to have no fear, insisting that he himself was favourable enough to him, whatever judgment had been made then. These things were done, it is said, on the last Friday of the parliament [20 November].

Also in this parliament there arose a great dissension between the king and the lay lords; for it seemed to them that the king was following bad advice and on this account would not admit good governance into his circle, so they tried to assume the whole burden of governing upon themselves. For they alleged that his predecessors, the most noble kings of former times, used to rule with the advice of the lords, and while their governance was accepted the kingdom of England basked in wonderful prosperity. But the king thought differently. He declared himself unwilling to be ruled or led by their advice alone, but that it pleased him to be modestly and reasonably advised by his council, that is, by chosen and experienced men of the realm.

1384

This year witnessed renewed unrest in London, and the first attempts by Richard's government to end the French war.

61. John of Northampton and unrest in London

The 1381 revolt left an aftermath of unrest in London which continued throughout the reign,[30] causing England's rulers to fear that London politics would again disrupt national government [63–6, 93, 134]. Class antagonisms, inter-guild rivalries and friction between individuals all contributed to a tense and unstable situation. Most serious was the rivalry between those guilds (labelled 'the victuallers' by their enemies)[31] led by Sir Nicholas Brembre, who enjoyed royal support, and the (mainly) non-food guilds like drapers and mercers. The latter included John (Comberton) of Northampton, a draper who was sometimes backed by Gaunt. After several years in which the 'victuallers' held power, Northampton was elected mayor in 1381 and 1382, but he was succeeded in 1383 by Brembre. In 1384 Northampton tried to regain power by

30 Bird (1949).
31 Nightingale (1995): 230.

force, but failed, and was tried for treason [**63–6**].

WC, 62–4.

On 7 February, while the earl of Nottingham was having dinner with
John Northampton, he asked him whether, after dinner, he would go
with his friends to *[the house of]* the Carmelite friars.[32] Nottingham
was showing him honour because the day of his brother's anniversary
was very imminent; he had recently been buried there.[33] Northampton
accepted, and arrived with about 400 men drawn from various gilds,
while the mayor of London had with him no more than forty companions. On the return journey, the mayor challenged Northampton, asking
him why he was defended by such a big crowd on that occasion. He
explained that not everyone who was there with him had been invited;
indeed they had flocked around him freely and without his prior knowledge. But others said angrily that the reason why he gathered so many
and such sorts of people around him was to incite riot and rebellion in
the population. The result was that unrest arose because of seditious
people, and despite the size of his escort Northampton would have been
killed had not the mayor promptly arrested him. Afterwards a report
of this was made to the king, namely that Northampton was trying to
destabilise the city of London – the king's chamber – and unless he
were removed from the city for a while, it was feared that he would be
the cause of the city's destruction. As a result of this allegation the king
ordered Northampton to be sent to Corfe castle *[Dorset]*, to be held in
custody there until such time as he could purge himself of the charges
alleged against him.

62. The Salisbury parliament, 29 April–27 May

(a) Discussion of peace proposals

When peace proposals (which have not survived) were put to parliament,
its members declined to give their advice. Proceedings, in the great hall of
the bishop's palace, were opened by the chancellor, Michael de la Pole, who
expounded the reasons for calling parliament.

RP III.166, 170; *PROME* 1384 (1) sections 3–4, 16.

32 The Carmelites (White Friars) had a large site near the city's western boundary,
south of Fleet Street, and west of the Fleet River, between the bishop of Salisbury's
inn and the Temple.
33 Mowbray's elder brother John, created earl of Nottingham at Richard's coronation,
died on 10 February 1383.

'About the truce which has been in force for a long time and continues between our lord king and his adversary of France: the negotiators of this treaty on both sides have now agreed a form of a final peace to be concluded between the kingdoms, on the advice of the kings and their councils, on both sides, of which certain articles are made, ready to show you in a convenient time and place. Because our lord king wishes to demonstrate his benevolence and perfect love, and considering the grievous burdens which you have long borne in connection with this war, our lord king does not wish to conclude this business finally without your assent and knowledge, as far as possible.[34] ... The king asks and charges you most earnestly, that – after you have viewed and heard these articles and the terms of this treaty – you would give him your advice about what seems to you would be the best thing to do, for his honour and the profit of himself and his kingdom.

Again, if peace were achieved, which God grant, it is still true that it could not be completed and ratified without the presence of those two kings, and there was no doubt that his adversary would appear with much magnificent clothing, and it would be a great disgrace to him and all his realm if our king were not equally honourably apparelled and equipped. For this, and also because both on the Scottish border and the marches of Calais, Cherbourg and Brest, and for the safety of his faithful subjects of Guyenne and Ireland, our lord king has spent much money, and still ought to continue spending, and nothing now remains of his revenues ....' [The chancellor asked for a tax grant.]

Concerning the command to the commons in this parliament about the peace which, God willing, would be made between our lord king and his adversary of France, on which certain articles have been newly drawn up and settled during the peace negotiations which have taken place in the march of Calais between the ambassadors of both sides: when they were brought to the commons for their better information about this treaty, and of its result, these same commons replied to our lord king in parliament as follows.

In commenting on the outrageous perils which they clearly perceived on every side, they neither could nor dared in any way to advise their liege lord expressly either on the one [course] or the other, inasmuch as that peace, if it please God to grant it so as to be honourable and profitable to the king and his realm, would be the noblest and most

34 The English delegation was led by Gaunt, and a truce was concluded on 26 Jan. 1384 to last for ten months while negotiations for a final peace were proceeding.

gracious help and comfort in the world imaginable. And it seemed that the lord king should and could do in this matter whatever seemed to his noble lordship best to do, because this business concerned his own inheritance, which by right royal lineage had descended to his noble person, and pertained neither to the realm nor crown of England. And they humbly begged their liege lord that for God's sake he would act, with his Council's advice, as seemed to him best to do in this matter, to the honour and profit of himself, and the aid and comfort of his realm. And as for the perils and unbearable mischiefs which might arise, which God forbid, the poor commons should be discharged from giving any other advice than this on the matter at present.

[The peace terms proved unacceptable and envoys were instructed to renew negotiations.]

(b) The affair of the Carmelite friar, according to the *Vita*

This curious affair was also reported by Walsingham, SAC I.724–6, and at greater length and in more grisly detail by WC, 68–80. The torturing to death of the friar prevented any resolution of this inquiry. The episode demonstrates the fevered atmosphere at court and the presence of some aggressive young hot-heads in the king's entourage, who were probably behind the plot.

VR, 81–2.

At the time of this parliament a certain friar, John Latimer, of the Carmelite order, a bachelor in theology, came to the king, approaching him in secret and alleging as true that the duke of Lancaster and others, citizens of London, and of various other towns throughout England, were together plotting his death. He wanted to repeat and to prove this in the duke's presence. So when the duke had been called before the king, the king openly put to him all that the friar had told him, while the friar stood behind a curtain listening to everything. But after the duke had utterly denied what the king had told him, he humbly offered to suffer everything which should rightly be inflicted on such men as had plotted those wicked things against his liege lord, if they could be proved to be true. Suddenly the friar openly joined them, and with a bold expression openly affirmed that everything he had told the king about the duke was true, and that he would prove everything he had said, as he ought, adding the allegation that Lord Zouche of Harringworth was the head and co-conspirator in all this. Then the king ordered the friar to be detained in custody until Lord Zouche had been brought, sending people to bring him back without any chance of flight. Lord Zouche, although ill, was brought, and, coming before the friar, he publicly affirmed and swore that he had never previously known or helped in this matter, of which the friar had accused him. Then the friar, seeing there was no help to be had there, alleged that there was a certain powerful squire of Oxfordshire who was the head and accomplice of these matters. This man was sought and when brought, excused himself with a similar oath about these matters. Then the friar, realising that his plan had failed, pretended to be mad, and was held and hung by his arms, and lead of great weight was fixed to his genitals, and similarly to both his feet, and a great fire was lit under the soles of his feet, and so for a long time he was cruelly tortured, but he never offered to retract his story, and finally he was drawn and beheaded. It was said that the king did not know about the torments which he suffered.

(c) The earl of Arundel's attack on Richard's government

Most notably, this parliament saw the extraordinary attack on Richard by the earl of Arundel, the start of a feud which ended only with the earl's execution in September 1397. Richard's response was dramatic: a terrific loss of temper which reduced the company to shocked silence. This was the first of several occasions when Richard showed himself unable to respond to criticism in a measured manner.

WC, 66–8.

On 29 April the king of England held a parliament at Salisbury which lasted until 27 May, in which some extraordinary things happened at the beginning. First, both the churchmen and the temporal lords quarrelled so amazingly among themselves that they almost frustrated the whole purpose of the parliament; but the duke of Lancaster arrived[35] and with a long speech laced with threats he pacified them. Second, about the earl of Arundel's words: for in full parliament, in everyone's hearing and in the king's presence he spoke these words, or at least some like them:

'My lords, you know that every kingdom which lacks prudent government is in danger of destruction, something which is now obvious because, as you know, this land has for a long time been weakened through bad government and now has almost wasted away. And unless it is quickly helped by practical remedies and is quickly lifted from the dark abyss into which it has fallen there is a real fear that it will shortly be in serious trouble and suffer huge losses and collapse completely, and will afterwards – which God forbid – be beyond help'.

35 After 9 May.

At these words the king turned white with rage and was completely engulfed by fury, and glaring at the earl he said: 'If you are blaming me and saying it is my fault that the kingdom is badly governed you are lying in your teeth. Go to hell!' A complete hush followed this outburst, for no one present dared to speak. Then the duke of Lancaster broke the silence and with soothing speech he wisely interpreted the earl's words in such a way that the king's fury was soothed.

(d) A dispute about badges

The commons' complaint about the badges worn by members of aristocratic retinues recurred in 1388 and 1397 [**122b, 169a**].

WC, 80–2.

Those elected by the community to come to parliament for the common good of the realm complained bitterly about powerful men, dominant in their localities, namely those provided with badges ornamented in various ways (*ornamentis diversis*) by lords of the kingdom and, protected by their favour and much emboldened by this advantage, unjustly oppressed and harassed the poor and needy in their neighbourhood and strove to nullify the laws passed and publicised for the common good of the kingdom, and trusting in their cleverness and their lords' friendship, did not permit them to be rightly observed; so the commons thought it right and proper that such men should in future be constrained by a general statute so that their fraud and cunning should no longer gain strength, to the detriment of the realm. The duke of Lancaster responded to this, saying that this complaint was in very imprecise terms; he asserted also that this and other matters ought to be put forward with complete details, because each lord was well qualified and able to correct and punish his followers for such transgressions …. But when those elected by the community of the realm heard this – that there would be no remedy given to this complaint – they fell silent.

63. The appeal of Thomas Usk

When Northampton was tried for treason in August his secretary, Thomas Usk, defected to his opponents and brought this appeal (accusation) against Northampton and his associates. The document, which is much damaged, was written by Usk 'in his own hand'. These sections have been chosen to show the level of unrest in the city of London.

A Book of London English, 1384–1425, ed. R. W. Chambers and M. Daunt (Oxford, 1931), 24–5, 27–9.

The whole intention of these people was to have the town under their control and to rule it by their advice, and to have held down, or else driven out of town, all those who were powerful enough to oppose them; and the rest, the less powerful, to have kept in subjection for ever. And of this I appeal John Northampton, John More, Richard Norbury and William Essex.

Because the older officers of the town had no love for that mayor's [*Northampton's*] opinions, all the senior officers were to have been removed by process of time and replaced by those who would have supported and approved of his opinions; for they said that those people who held opinions contrary to his were enemies of all good opinion. And there was constant incitement of the poor, to make them more fervent and rebellious against the great men of the town and the officers too; and it was alleged to the people that the great men wanted the poor to be oppressed and lowly; for which words, and their maintenance, dissension has arisen between the worthy persons and the humble people of the town; and of this I appeal [*the above*].

Often, before Sir Nicholas Brembre was elected mayor, the mayor John Northampton, John More and Richard Norbury sent William Essex and me, Thomas Usk, to Goldsmiths' Hall to speak with men of the Common Council about choosing the [*new*] mayor.... And there, among those assembled at Goldsmiths' Hall, it was decided that certain persons of various crafts, who were enrolled amongst the Common Council, should on election day be called in to the Common Council to help get John Northampton elected, and the lesser people were drawn in to be of the same party, with the intention that their support should be fully given to John Northampton; and if, in future, another mayor were to be chosen, who would act against Northampton, he might have them ready to maintain him against all that they would say against him. And, had he been mayor, I am certain that he would have maintained all his enactments, or else have set the whole town in an uproar.

The night before mayoral election day, John More warned all his sergeants and men to be armed at the Guildhall next day, for he declared that he and his supporters would guard the doors that day, intending that no one should come in save only those who would choose John Northampton as mayor. And hereof I appeal John More.

On the day that Nicholas Brembre was chosen mayor, soon after the meal, John Northampton came to John More's house, and there [*too*] came Richard Norbury and William Essex, and there it was agreed that the mayor, John Northampton, should order the people who were then in the Common Council of crafts, and the wardens of the crafts, to go to Goldsmiths' Hall the following day; there the mayor should speak with them, to consider and arrange how the election of Sir Nicholas Brembre might be obstructed. And had it not been for fear of our lord king, I am certain that every man would have been at each other's throat. Then he sent Richard Norbury, Robert Rysby and me, Thomas Usk, to the Neyte,[36] to the duke of Lancaster, to inform him thus: 'Sir, today when we should have proceeded to the election of the mayor in God's peace and the king's, there came in a horrible crowd of rowdies, no one knew who they were, and there, without any proper procedure, but by force, they chose Sir Nicholas Brembre as mayor, contrary to our form of election previously used. We therefore ask you if we might have the king's writ to proceed to a new election'. And the duke said: 'No, indeed, you shall have no writ; take counsel among yourselves'. And of this I appeal John Northampton, John More, Richard Norbury and William Essex.

At Goldsmiths' Hall, when all the people were assembled, the mayor, John Northampton, described as maliciously as he could the election of the previous day, and truly he said: 'Sirs, so are you likely to be overrun; and that', said he, 'I will not tolerate. Let us all rather be dead at once than suffer such villainy'. The commons were roused at these words and said that they would certainly proceed to another election, and not suffer this wrong to be done. ...[37] Then the mayor, John Northampton, ordered everyone to go home and come quickly again into Cheap with all their crafts; and I believe there were about thirty crafts planning to have assembled in Cheap to proceed to a new election. Certainly, if the aldermen had not come to mediate, and compelled John Northampton to order the people to go home, they would have proceeded to a new election, and in that fury would have killed anyone who obstructed it, if they could. And hereof I appeal John Northampton.

36 A royal manor house in Middlesex, about a mile from Westminster, Brown, Colvin and Taylor (1963): I.508.
37 The text is corrupt here.

64. Northampton's trial following Usk's appeal, 18–20 August at Reading

WC, 92.

John Northampton constantly denied the accusations thrown at him, calling Usk, in the king's presence, a false rascal worthy of death; and to rebut the falsehood imputed to him he offered to defend himself in a duel with his own hand; but in this Northampton overstepped the mark, because he did not save the king's reverence, as is fitting in such circumstances. Nevertheless the king, of his special grace, granted him a refund (*refundi*) of 100 marks annually from his rents; but he was not suitably grateful to the king for this, as he should have been. So, seeing him rather obstinate, the king said, 'Let us make an end of this controversy and proceed to judgment according to the findings and proofs'. At this, John Northampton said to him, 'I hope, my lord king, that you do not intend to proceed to judgment in the absence of the duke of Lancaster your uncle, nor to hold a tribunal in this case'.

When he heard this, the king was completely suffused with anger, saying that he was sufficiently competent to judge Northampton, and the duke of Lancaster too. 'Understand this', said the king, 'that I will be your judge despite his absence'. Immediately he ordered Northampton to be drawn and hanged and all his goods confiscated too. … And so because of these three *faux pas* and his disorderly conduct John Northampton would have ended his life in a shameful death had not the queen by chance been present, and, prostrate before the king, she humbly begged for his life. At this intervention the king granted his life but ordered him to be committed to perpetual imprisonment.

65. The further trial and sentencing of John of Northampton

CPR 1381–5, 470, adapted.

6 October. Grant to the mayor, sheriffs, aldermen and community of London that it shall not prejudice them, diminish their liberties or serve as a precedent, that the following proceedings have recently been taken by the king and his authority. By the king's writ the city's coroners, mayor, aldermen and forty of the more substantial and capable citizens were required to appear in person before the king on a given day at Sheen manor, where they were ordered to enquire and

report on the riots and disturbances which had arisen and continued
in the city. Following their report, they were commanded to appear
before the king and his council at Reading, where, when they appeared,
John Northampton, draper, then citizen of London, being charged with
rebellion ... was arraigned, and on the citizens' report and his record,
and on the accusation of Thomas Usk, scrivener, citizen of London,
he was convicted and judicially deprived by the king of the freedom of
the city, and sentenced to perpetual imprisonment. Later, on the same
accusation brought by that same Thomas [Usk], Richard Norbury and
John More, mercers, then citizens of London, were brought before the
king and his council at Westminster, and after the accusation was read
in the king's presence, and indictments declared by William Cheyne,
the recorder, they pleaded guilty, and were remitted for safe custody
to the city. Subsequently Simon Wynchecombe, one of the sheriffs,
was commanded to deliver them to the king's serjeant-at-arms, Robert
Bekerton, to be brought to Windsor Castle, from where they and John
Northampton were afterwards by the king's writ committed to the
Tower to be tried for treason; and on being arraigned on that charge
before John de Montacute, steward of the household, and the other
justices assigned to deliver the prisoners there, they pleaded guilty and
were sentenced to be hanged.

66. Disorder and royal pressure in the London mayoral election

This shows Richard intervening directly in London politics by sending
emissaries to ensure that the 'right' man, Brembre, was elected.

Calendar of Select Pleas and Memoranda of the City of London, A.D. 1381–1412, ed.
A. H. Thomas (Cambridge, 1932), 62–3.

Although on the eve of the Translation of St Edward the King [13
October 1384] proclamation was made throughout the liberty of the
city of·London – both on behalf of the king by virtue of his writ, and
on behalf of the mayor and aldermen – that no one of any rank or
status should go armed or wearing breastplate or padded jacket, or
should lead an armed force against the king's peace, nor that any one
should go to the election of the mayor and sheriffs, except the mayor,
aldermen, sheriffs and good men of the wards who were summoned
there, under penalty of imprisonment and forfeiture of all his goods,
and under penalty of losing the freedom of the city...; and although

the mayor, aldermen, sheriffs and good men of the wards, on being summoned, were present on that feast in the Guildhall for the election of the mayor, and there were present Lord Neville, Lord FitzWalter and Thomas Moreux, knights, who had been sent by order of the king and his council, there came also certain persons of the middle sort belonging to various guilds. These men, forgetting themselves and having no respect for, or fear of, the proclamation, and because they were banded together in a great congregation and assembled in Guildhall, made a great clamour and outcry to the great alarm of the mayor, aldermen and commonalty, and contrary to the proclamation. When these offences had been committed against the king, mayor, aldermen and sheriffs, various good men of several guilds made inquiries about these evildoers, and afterwards brought the names of certain men of their guilds whom they suspected. Other guilty persons were arrested, and yet others surrendered themselves, of whom some were mainprised,[38] and others delivered under bail, as follows: *[19 Oct. 1384]* the good men of the armourers' guild were brought before Sir Nicholas Brembre the mayor, and the aldermen and sheriffs. *[The names of six suspected armourers then follow. They were bailed and bound over.]*

1385

This was the year when Richard openly began to direct policy for himself, in both military and patronage matters. In spring, parliament made a grant of taxation, conditional on the king going to war in person. He fulfilled that condition, though not in the way members had expected: he led an army to Scotland. Why Richard chose Scotland, rather than continental Europe, for his military experience, is open to conjecture,[39] but his grandfather had begun his military career fighting the Scots, and the threat of an Anglo-Scottish invasion was real, for Jean de Vienne, a distinguished French warrior, had arrived in Scotland with a small army in 1384. Fighting a Franco-Scottish force was therefore a way of confronting two foes at once **[69c]** and protecting his realm; it also offered Richard, who had never previously been north of Nottingham, the chance to see the northern part of his kingdom. This costly campaign was not successful enough, however, to silence parliamentary criticism or calls for reform.

38 A form of surety, similar to bail.
39 McHardy (2000): 230.

67. Winter 1384–5: a plot against Gaunt, and Richard's quarrel with the archbishop of Canterbury

Hostility to Gaunt on the part of some courtiers, and Richard's inability to cope calmly with criticism, were again evident during the following winter.
VR, 85–6.

The king decided after Christmas to hold a council at Waltham,[40] to which the lords were summoned. The duke of Lancaster, as the king's principal councillor, was among those invited, but before he hurried to that meeting he was told in secret that he had better beware, if he attended, because some of the king's intimates were plotting to kill him suddenly. On hearing this the duke invented a reason for not going, and sent to the king begging to be excused on this occasion; but the king ordered him, on his allegiance, to attend without fail. So the duke then took counsel about how he could honour his allegiance yet not lose his life. Someone advised him that to save his life and to preserve himself from danger of death he should hasten to the council with a strong force. So, acting on this advice, he went there with a protective retinue, telling the king not to wonder that he came like this because he feared that his death was being plotted. The king protested on oath that he had known nothing of these plots. Henceforward the duke put little faith in that quarter.

In the following Lent, William Courtenay, archbishop of Canterbury, prompted and even egged on by certain lords, it is said, upbraided the lord king about his arrogance and the continuing bad governance of himself and his kingdom; insisting that, unless he allowed himself to be advised otherwise, this bad regime would lead shortly to the undoing of himself and the kingdom. The king was greatly angered by this rebuke, and had not Thomas of Woodstock his uncle intervened, he would have struck the archbishop; he shouted many foul words at him and took the greatest offence against him. So the archbishop left him and took himself to distant parts. Afterwards, neither in the convocation of the clergy at London nor in the council of the lords and prelates at Reading gathered to grant the king a subsidy, did he appear.

40 Probably a mistake for Windsor, where Richard stayed from 28 Dec. 1384 until 3 Feb. 1385.

68. The laws of war: a selection

The higher nobility showed rare unanimity as they approached the border, as shown in the twenty-six rules drawn up early in the campaign, which became politically important in 1388.

The Black Book of the Admiralty, ed. Travers Twiss (RS, 55, 1871), I.453–8.

These are the statutes, ordinances and customs to be observed in the army, ordained and made on the good advice and deliberation of our most excellent sovereign lord King Richard, and John, duke of Lancaster, Steward of England, Thomas, earl of Essex and Buckingham, Constable of England, and Thomas Mowbray, earl of Nottingham, Marshal of England, and of the other lords, earls, barons, bannerets and wise knights whom they had summoned, at Durham 17 July, 9 Richard II *[1385]*.

[i] First, that all manner of men, of whatever nation, estate or condition they are, should be obedient to our lord the king, and to his Constable and Marshal on pain of all that they could forfeit in person or property.

[ii] No one should be so bold as to touch the king's person, nor the conveyance in which he is, on pain of being drawn and hanged, and having his head cut off.

[iii] No one should be so bold as to rob or pillage a church, nor destroy a religious man of Holy Church, nor anchoress, nor any woman, nor take prisoners, if they do not carry arms, nor to force any woman, on pain of hanging.

…

[vii] No one should be so bold as to rob or steal from another whether food, supplies, fodder or anything else, on pain of having his head cut off, nor also any food, nor other goods, merchandise or anything whatsoever which arrive to supply the army, on the same pain; and he who can inform the Constable and Marshal of such robbers or pillagers shall have 20 nobles[41] for his trouble.

[viii] In no dispute about arms,[42] captives, lodgings, nor about any other matter whatsoever should anyone cause a riot, brawl or quarrel within the army, nor should anyone make a faction or assembly of men, or others, whether as leaders or followers, on pain of losing their horses and armour, and their person to be detained at the king's pleasure; and if

41 A noble was a coin worth 6s. 8d., i.e., one-third of a pound (£).
42 This probably referred to heraldic devices.

he is a groom or page, he shall lose his left ear. But if he has a grievance, he shall present his complaint to the Constable and Marshal, and right will be done to him.

...

[x] No one shall be so bold as to cry havoc[43] on pain of having his head cut off, and that he or those who start this cry should also have their heads cut off and his body afterwards be hanged by the arms.

...

[xvii] No one shall be so bold as to raise the banner or pennon of St George, or any other, to attract men away from the army to go anywhere else whatsoever, on those pains that, if the captains do this, they are to be drawn and hanged, and those who follow them to have their heads cut off and all their goods and inheritance forfeit to the king.

69. Accounts of the Scottish campaign

The expedition, though destructive, was inconclusive: Richard reached Edinburgh, quarrelled with Gaunt and marched south again; but the Scots and French were also on bad terms and failed to present a united front to the invaders. Northern reaction to the campaign was sympathetic.

(a) According to a northern chronicler
Kirkstall Abbey Chronicles, ed. J. Taylor (Thoresby Society, 42, 1952), 109.

In 1385 Sir Jean de Vienne, a virtuous but proud French knight, assembled a great French fleet, with the assent and blessing of the French king, and sailed to Scotland, vowing by God and his order of knighthood never to return until by armed force – after the Scots had joined him – he had ridden with a great army the length of England, even to Dover, and they would burn and devastate the Anglo-Scottish borders. King Richard confronted him with a glorious army of Englishmen, eagerly hoping to fight the French and Scots to the death. But the Scots and French, having observed the very strongly-organised battle-lines of the English, took flight like madmen, and found refuge across the Scottish sea [*Firth of Forth*], and were afterwards scarcely seen by the

---

43The earliest precisely dated use of this term, the signal for an army to seize spoil and to pillage, giving no quarter. Only the king could give the order, e.g. 'Caesar's spirit ... shall ... with a monarch's voice cry Havoc and let slip the dogs of war', Shakespeare, *Julius Caesar*, III.i.273 (1601).

English. Sir Jean de Vienne returned with the French to France by sea, his plan frustrated and his vow unfulfilled. King Richard, however, advanced energetically into Scotland with his army, burning towns and woods as far as the Firth of Forth. He destroyed Melrose Abbey by fire because of the plotters concealed there, and even the Scottish royal town called Edinburgh. But after this, King Richard, on hearing rumours of his mother's death, clothed himself in black and returned to England with all his army. The lady Joan, mother of King Richard II, died on St Agnes' day [8 August] in that year. Her body was buried among the Friars Minor of Stamford [Lincs.],[44] in a sumptuous chapel newly built next to the brothers' choir.

(b) According to the *Vita*

It was near York that Richard's half-brother John Holand fatally stabbed Ralph Stafford, heir to an earldom, and a close companion of the king. This left the field clear for Robert de Vere as the king's best friend. This account of the Scottish campaign is much more lukewarm.

VR, 88–90.

At this time the Scots, those haters of peace and concord, sent to the king of France, with whom they were always in an evil alliance against us, asking for his help against the king of England. They promised to do more for him than was in their power to achieve, even alleging that if he would grant them a little help they could easily, with his assistance, destroy both the king of England and his land. So the French king despatched to Scotland 1,500 lances, with all logistical support, appointing over them Sir Jean de Vienne, a most energetic man, so that the French and Scots together would total, it was said, about 10,000 warriors. They encamped near the English borders, poised to ride swiftly over the lands of the king of England. And while they were engaged on this, the king of France, unless prevented, planned to invade the southern parts of the kingdom of England, and so between them they hoped to inflict many evils upon us.

When he heard this, the king of England, about the beginning of July of that year, travelled at speed with his men towards the north. In and near York he waited until his whole army had joined him. From every part of the kingdom, of every kind of fighting men, no small multitude flocked to him, and when the whole army had assembled, he moved

44 No trace remains of the Franciscan church there. She was buried beside her first husband, Sir Thomas Holand.

camp towards Scotland. At his entry into Scotland, the king had with him – according to the common estimate of worthy men – more than 100,000 troops, for it was said that no other king of England was ever seen with so great a multitude. As soon he had entered Scotland the king caused his standard to be displayed, and straight away, it is said, he knighted 300 men with a sword. But the French and Scots, immediately they heard that the king of England had come with so great a horde, ran away from their place of encampment and scattered into many companies, it is not known where. Some of them hid in woods and marshes, following alongside our army, and when some of our men rashly left the army to seek food or for other reasons, they broke out from their hideouts, capturing some, killing others. The rest of the population, except a few women and children, fled to the mountains and beyond the Scottish sea, in the face of our king and his army. While our king and his army were proceeding towards the Firth of Forth, they razed to the ground and burnt to ashes their woods and houses, whatever there was, reducing corn and hay almost to nothing; and they burnt and destroyed the best town which they had this side of the firth, called Edinburgh, with a good abbey[45] next to it. Similarly they devastated and consigned to the devouring fire another noble abbey of the Cistercian order, called Melrose, in the middle of the march towards Edinburgh. The king was advised by some – who got little thanks for their counsel – to cross over the firth in order to defeat his enemies decisively. But the king, who lacked sufficient food for himself and his men, spurned this advice and returned with his army towards England through other regions of Scotland, inflicting similar damage upon them. And, God be praised, he returned with his army intact, so that he did not lose any strength, into England, to those places where he usually lived, about the feast of the Nativity of the Blessed Virgin Mary [8 September].

On this expedition against the Scots the lord Ralph Stafford, son and heir of the earl of Stafford, was killed in a quarrel by Lord John Holand, the king's half-brother through his mother. When he heard of this deed the king was violently and extremely angry and deprived that Lord John of all the lands, rents, offices and dignities which he held …. Besides this, it was said that the king sent letters to his mother that she should neither receive nor comfort his brother John. This caused the king's lady mother such grief, it was said, that within three or four days of receiving it, about the beginning of August, she departed this life, and was buried at Stamford.

45 Holyrood Abbey.

(c) A Scottish view

Walter Bower, an Augustinian abbot, was born in 1385 and wrote his chronicle in the early 1440s, but he used a lost contemporary source for this part of his story. Bower wrote for a Scottish audience – his manuscript ends 'Christ, he's no Scot who doesn't like this book' (*Non Scotus est Christe cui liber non placet iste*) – but his accounts of Anglo-Scottish affairs are remarkably sober.

Walter Bower, *Scotichronicon*, vol. 7, ed. A. B. Scott and D. E. R. Watt (Aberdeen, 1996), 402–8.

In 1385 the French king was amazingly jubilant at the success the Scots were having against the English, and to support and reinforce them he sent his most energetic and experienced knight Sir Jean de Vienne ... admiral of France *[then follow details of his army]*. This admiral lived and worked continuously, with his men, in the company of Earl Douglas; several times they led their armies into England. By the Frenchmen's skill and cunning they captured three fortresses in the English march, namely Wark, Ford and Cornhill,[46] and by main force razed them to the ground. Then the admiral with his Frenchmen joined with Archibald Douglas, lord of Galloway, warden of the West March, and together they invaded England with a large force, and wherever they went they devastated and laid waste without any English resistance. ... For three months the French served with distinction in the war campaigns alongside the princes and magnates of Scotland, but when their purses were empty, about the feast of All Saints, they took ship for France. A little earlier in that year, about the feast of St Lawrence *[10 August]*, Richard II, king of England, greatly saddened that the Scots and French were so dreadfully despoiling his land – assaulting his castles and razing them to the ground – gathered a large army and invaded Scotland. He was then 19 years old. Advancing with an arrogant multitude, he destroyed everything around, sparing nothing. He burned with voracious flames the temples of God and the sanctuaries of the religious, namely Dryburgh, Melrose and Newbattle abbeys, and the noble royal town of Edinburgh with the church of St Giles. Once he had carried out this great destruction in Lothian he returned home unharmed. ... King Richard would also have burned the honourable monastery of Holyrood had he not been dissuaded by his paternal uncle the duke of Lancaster, who had earlier been forced to take refuge there while escaping the peasants' fury.

46 Wark and Cornhill are both on the River Tweed (the present-day border). Ford, 5 miles south, is on the Till.

70. Aristocratic promotions

There are different accounts of the promotions Richard made on reaching Scotland. See also **74**.

(a) According to Knighton

KC, 336–8.

On entering Scotland the king created two of his uncles dukes: the elder, Lord Edmund of Langley, earl of Cambridge, he made duke of York; his younger brother, Lord Thomas of Woodstock, earl of Buckingham, he made duke of Gloucester, and he royally endowed them with lands, rents and other gifts.[47] Also, he made the earl of Oxford marquess of Dublin, and Sir Simon Burley earl of Huntingdon.[48] Sir Michael de la Pole he made earl of Suffolk, and he lavishly enriched all of them with gifts. He also created a great multitude of knights. He ratified these deeds in the parliament following.

(b) According to *Westminster*

WC, 126.

The king entered Scotland on 6 August with a large army and with banner unfurled, and he created knights, earls and dukes: he promoted the earl of Cambridge to be duke of Canterbury and the earl of Buckingham to be duke of Aumâle,[49] and promoted Sir Michael de la Pole earl of Suffolk, and Lord Neville earl of Cumberland.[50]

71. The battle of Aljubarotta, 14 August 1385

In one of medieval Europe's decisive battles, King João I secured Portugal's independence by a crushing victory over Castile, with repercussions throughout Europe, especially England. The site of the conflict, 160 km north of Lisbon, is now called Batalha.

WC, 132.

47 Knighton was mistaken in this.

48 Burley had already received the lands that traditionally went with this title, but his promotion to the title never took effect.

49 Probably the Monk confused Canterbury with *Cantabrigia*, Latin for 'Cambridge'. Thomas of Woodstock was summoned to the next parliament as duke of Aumâle. For further links between him and that title, see Mott (1974): 117.

50 Ralph Neville was not promoted until Sept. 1397, when he became earl of Westmorland.

At this time there came definite news of a certain battle fought in
Portugal between the kings of Spain and Portugal. By divine grace,
victory went to the king of Portugal, who had in his army some English
warriors and archers – about 700. There fell in this battle almost all the
flower of the nobility of Spain *[names of the leading casualties are given]*.
The battle was fought on the vigil of the Assumption of the Virgin *[14
August]*. In this battle more than 7,500 Spaniards were killed. Thus
the king of Portugal recovered by this battle what had been forcibly
removed from him by the king of Spain.

72. Richard is urged to go to Ireland, autumn 1385

Richard's expedition to Ireland lay nine years in the future, but this plea for
his intervention indicates that his decision to go there was a response to the
serious situation in the lordship.

Contemporary official records distinguished between the Anglo-Irish, under
such descriptions as: the English race, English born in Ireland, faithful lieges,
faithful English, degenerate English, English rebels or English traitors; and
the Gaelic Irish, variously described as: Irish enemies, men of the Irish nation
of Ireland, savage Irish, pure Irish, Irish malefactors, fierce Irish or wild Irish.

*Statutes and Ordinances and Acts of the Parliament of Ireland, King John to Henry
V*, ed. Henry F. Berry (Dublin, 1907), 484–7.

From the prelates, lords and commons, assembled at the councils held
at Dublin and Kilkenny[51] this present year: it is shown to them by the
king's lieutenant and council the mischiefs and very great perils which
the land of Ireland, the lordship of the king and his poor lieges suffer in
these parts, and how and in what manner they could help themselves in
time to come, either by themselves, if they should possess the power, or
in any other manner; so those prelates, lords and commons answered
that they – considering the great power of the Irish enemies and English
rebels, both by their own strength and by enemies of Scotland, Spain
and elsewhere allied to them, and also the weakness and poverty of the
English lieges – are not able in any way to help themselves without the
effectual help and recovery of their liege lord the king; that at this next
season, as is likely, there will be made a conquest of the greater part
of the land of Ireland. Therefore, at those councils, the prelates, lords
and commons, with great deliberation viewed and considered the above
matter, and – the conquest appearing so imminent upon the land – they

51 In October and July 1385, respectively.

cannot nor know how to find or think of a remedy except the coming
of the lord king in person. They demanded of the said lieutenant and
council that they should choose certain messengers to show their liege
lord the mischiefs abovesaid and to sue for remedy of them. Whereupon, at the said councils, the prelates etc. were commanded by the
lieutenant to choose suitable messengers to send to the king to inform
him of those mischiefs and perils, and to pray his high majesty very
humbly, on their behalf, to prepare to survey and visit his said lordship
in person, for the rescue and salvation of the same, and to resist its
imminent conquest, and for the safety of his poor lieges in these parts.
The prelates etc. on this command, elected the reverend fathers in
God the archbishop of Dublin and the bishop of Ossory to convey this
message, these messengers being charged to make urgent and painful
representation to our lord king, that it please him to visit his said people
to their perpetual succour. And if our lord king will not consent to that
– which God forbid – then they should urge to come into the land of
Ireland the greatest and most trustworthy lord of England, because it
seems to them that the land cannot otherwise *[survive]* the mischiefs
that it has suffered this present year.

73. A libel against Alexander Neville, archbishop of York

Richard's route to Scotland took him via Bishopthorpe (near York), which had
until then been the main residence of Alexander Neville, the archbishop; but he
joined the military expedition and thenceforth was seen as a courtier,[52] becoming
more widely known from that autumn onwards. This bill, supposedly fixed
to the door of St Paul's cathedral, claims to represent the oppressed subjects
of his Yorkshire archdiocese, but is of uncertain linguistic origin. A sophisticated document, its author had received rhetorical training, as evidenced by
the device called amplification: the series of sequences of three words to make
each point. The reference to Scotland shows that this was composed after the
summer of 1385, and it should probably be dated to autumn 1385.

Printed from TNA C 49/9/22 by William Illingworth, 'Copy of a libel against
archbishop Neville, temp. Richard II', *Archaeologia* 16 (1812), 82–3.

You commons of England, why do you blame the king and his council
for the mishaps and unrest and troubles of this realm of England? It is
not the king's fault, for there is no land in this world which has a more
rightful, more worthy or a more nobly-born king than you have in King
Richard: the worthiest prince's son that ever was seen, for there was

---

52 R. B. Dobson, 'Neville, Alexander' in *ODNB*, and references to his earlier papers.

never a king more willing to do right and create peace in the realm than he is. And this was seen in Scotland.

But there is another king in your land, that is, Black Alexander, bishop of Yorkshire; he destroys the land of the north, and because of his vengeance all the land shall be destroyed, for God knows and the lords know well, and the commons know well, that there has never been such a tyrant in Holy Church nor among the commons of this country; for he oppresses more the country and he imposes more extortion and destruction and oppressions on the country than the king and all the lords of England. And this you know well, but the king does not hear a word about it, and if he knew, he would be as badly pleased with it as the lowest in this land, and no man would be worse pleased than he, for truly he [Neville] destroys the country more falsely and extortionately than the king, even if he taxed the kingdom three times a year. If any man dies in his jurisdiction he will take a thousand pounds or a hundred pounds or else half his goods for proving his testament;[53] if there were a rich priest or parson or vicar in his territory, even if he were as good a man as [St] Thomas of Canterbury, he would be summoned to appear, and would be suspended or deprived or condemned [to pay] the value of his benefice, or a great sum in gold, and other extortions without number. God and you and the world know well, that even though he be a prelate of Holy Church, he is a plunderer, a thief, a traitor both to God and to his king; he behaves to his king as if he were a saint, but all the world knows it well, the fairer he speaks the falser he is. But if any man should say this, it would have to be a southerner, indeed it must, King Richard's man, and not a northerner, King Alexander's retainer; for they dare not say that if King Alexander were well examined on his extortion and his maintenance and his tyranny about that which he has taken falsely against the king's laws, he should forfeit for ever to the king £60,000. Alas that a tyrant of Holy Church should ruin all the land, and the king knows not of it, nor no man dares tell it to him.

Let these be my witnesses.

Black Alexander
King in York   } commons beware![54]

---

53 Complaints about the cost of proving wills were made against several other bishops, Aston (1967): 93–4.

54 These last two words were on a label, attached to the document, but now lost.

74. The parliament of 20 October–6 December confirms earlier promotions

This important meeting is poorly documented.[55] It received little attention from the chronicles, while the parliament roll mainly describes the confirmation of aristocratic promotions made during the summer campaign. commons' anger at financial mismanagement and concern at Richard's unwise patronage, evident in other sources, formed the basis of attempts at reform and restraint. When the promised reforms were not implemented the commons' heightened anger was vented in the parliament of 1386, for yet again the king and his advisers had shown they could not be trusted.

(a) Michael de la Pole as earl of Suffolk

Walsingham's comment is pure snobbery towards the promotion of a man whose family had risen through 'trade'; the chancellor's father was William de la Pole, wool merchant and financier of Hull, but Michael's career was made in (largely military) service to the Black Prince and his widow.

SAC I.782.

Sir Michael de la Pole, who was chancellor of the realm, was made earl of Suffolk, and given 1,000 marks a year from the king's money-bag; a man more fitted for mercantile than military matters, who had grown old in peace with money-changers, not in war with soldiers.

(b) Robert de Vere as marquess of Dublin

The earl of Oxford's elevation to this unheard-of rank took place some days after the others, suggesting that the king had to struggle to get it accepted.

(i) The reason for his elevation

RP III.209; *PROME* 1385, section 17.

The king, considering the nobility of his birth, the absolute integrity and outstanding wisdom of his dearest kinsman Robert de Vere earl of Oxford, and desiring that the excellence of his name should be the consequence of the earl's magnificent deeds ... will confer on the said Robert the name of Marquess of Dublin ...

(ii) One practical consequence

WC, 144.

On 1 December the king conferred the lordship of Ireland, to be held of himself, upon the earl of Oxford, who immediately did the king homage for that, and ordered that he should be called Marquess of Dublin. A

55 Palmer (1969): 96–101; Palmer (1971b): 477–90.

marquess is greater than an earl but less than a duke, so the king made him sit in parliament above the earls.

75. Financial reform

(a) A request for reform

RP III.213; *PROME* 1385, section 32.

That the estate of the king's household should be reviewed once a year, or oftener if necessary, by the chancellor, treasurer and the keeper (*clerc*) of the privy seal, and amended as needful at their wise discretion. Likewise, that the statutes made in times past about that household should be strictly observed and respected in every particular, and duly executed according to the intention of the same.

(b) Proposals for financial reform

'The document which follows is clearly that most rare type of survival, an original parliamentary bill'.[56] This detailed programme of fiscal administration was designed to quash Richard's tendency to grant favours or positions to his friends and other petitioners, regardless of the financial consequences to himself or the recipients' suitability. Failure to implement this scheme caused the anger evident in parliament in 1386.

British Library, Harley roll K.28, printed J. J. N. Palmer, 'The impeachment of Michael de la Pole in 1386', *BIHR* 42 (1969), 100–1.

To the parliament held at Westminster the 9th year of the reign of King Richard II *[1385]*.

[1.] If it please our lord king, the revenues brought by his ministers accountable yearly at the exchequer by right of his crown could be improved by a great amount if it please him to be advised about his gifts from these in future because they belong to his crown, and were so burdened by his forefathers and himself before this time, as can be seen.

[2.] No sheriffs, escheators or other officials accountable for these revenues should be appointed by entreaty or particular request, but solely from good and loyal men on the advice of the king's great council and his principal officers, and according to the intention of the statute.

---

56 Palmer (1969): 99, no. 2.

[3.] The profits of the hanaper[57] can be improved if it please the king to take advice about the gifts or assignments from them, and about the pardons for fees and fines.

[4.] The profits of wardships and marriages would be increased if it pleased him to be well advised by his councillors and officers of their value, without them being granted without notice.

[5.] The profits of his great and petty customs[58] would be greatly increased if it pleased him that customs collectors and other associated officials should be chosen from good and loyal men, on the advice of his council and officers, and not from an entreaty or particular request, and removable if unsatisfactory; and that they should occupy their post [in person] without deputies or attorneys.

[6.] The king's expenses within his realm could be lessened, if he wished, in his household and great Wardrobe and in the sums which various officials take yearly beyond their accustomed fees.

[7.] It is noted that our lord king will have from time to time some escheats to give to those who please him, in [which] case he should be advised about such gifts before confirming them, to safeguard his honour, and specially considering the noble and honourable gifts which he and his noble forefathers have previously given.

[8.] The profits of alien priories could be increased if it please the king to remove the granting of them from those who want them for private profit, and allowed them to be farmed by his councillors and their officers.

[9.] The subsidy on wool and woolfells granted to him could be greatly increased if the king were pleased to permit the customs-officers, controllers and weighers[59] to be chosen from good and loyal men, on the advice of his councillors and their officers, and not by individual petitions or requests, and were removable if unsatisfactory, and they should exercise their office in their own person.

[10.] The annual costs of guarding towns and castles on the various borders and the king's other lordships, and the ordinance for guarding

---

57 The Chancery department into which the fees were paid for the sealing and enrolment of documents.

58 Great, or ancient, customs: the duties on wool, leather and woolfells (un-tanned hides with the wool still on them); petty customs: the duties on cloth and general merchandise.

59 Customs collectors were commissioned in pairs; controllers kept an independent record to ensure collectors' honesty.

the sea, could be greatly lessened if it pleased him to be advised what to do by his councillors and their officers as to good, honourable and suitable captains and men, and not by individuals' desires nor anyone's entreaties.

[Dorse:] The names of the lords who were chosen by the king to survey his estate and enquire into revenues, to reduce costs, as the commons called for: the bishops of Winchester, Exeter, Durham; the earls of Salisbury, Stafford, Northumberland; Lord Cobham; Sirs Richard le Scrope[60] and John Devereux, who made this bill and showed it to the king, and then by his order to the lords and to the commons.

76. The lords' recommendations

This further attempt to improve the conduct of government probably dates from the same parliament of 20 October to 6 December 1385. Although undated, Palmer (1971b): 480–1, plausibly suggests that this was drawn up in early November 1385.

Proceedings and Ordinances of the Privy Council, ed. N. H. Nicolas (Record Commission, 1827–34), I.84–6.

The lords' advice about the good government of the king and kingdom.

First, that it please the king to trust his councillors in those matters which concern the government of the laws and of his kingdom, and to permit them to do and duly to govern what concerns them, as seems best for his honour and the profit of the realm; and not in any way to command his council, either by messenger or by letter, to the contrary.

[2.] If anyone wishes to influence or incite the king to meddle in person with anything which touches the law or a litigant, that it please him to entrust and send all such instigators, with their information and suggestions, to his council, and not to give credence or attention to such proposers, but to allow his council to do what is lawful and for his honour and position.

[3.] If any suppliant wishes to give or promise him anything to have favour, aid or maintain any cause or quarrel against a group, or in prejudice of an opponent, that our lord king be pleased not to receive or accept such gifts or promises from him, nor from another, but utterly to refuse them, so that he is always the most impartial and the most inclined to dispense full and equal justice.

60 The former chancellor; see **48**.

[4.] That it please the king to give suitable times and audience to his council, from time to time, when it desires to talk with him about the good execution and discussion of the business concerning the state of himself and his kingdom, because by doing this he will know and better understand administrative matters, to his honour and advantage, and business will be better and more quickly despatched, to the great honour and profit of himself and all his realm.

[5.] That it please the king that those who occupy the offices of chamberlain, steward of the household and keeper of his privy seal should be sufficient and suitable persons, and that they should liase between himself and his council, and that no other intermediaries should be used for important matters, saving always the right which the earl of Oxford claims in respect of that office of chamberlain.[61]

[6.] That it please the king not to grant any office of justice, sheriff, escheator, steward of land or of lordship, receiver, customs collector, controller or searcher, nor any farms, to any person without receiving first the advice of his council and of his principal officers.

[7.] That it please the king that his position regarding the revenues and the charges on his exchequer should be reviewed and examined by certain lords, with the intention of making good arrangements about how, and by what means, his position can be upheld, and his people paid for the provisions which will be taken for his household, as the statute intends.[62]

[8.] That it please the king that the state of his household be reviewed, and if any insufficient or unprofitable persons are found there, that they should be removed and sent away, and if the council advises that more competent persons are needed, there should be employed those who would be honourable and profitable to him, and who would have the strength and ability to serve him effectively when he needs them.

[9.] That it please the king to refrain from giving or granting lands, rents, farms, wardships, marriages, escheats, annuities, or other profits or revenues from these which he has at present, or others when they escheat from any person, so that they are safeguarded and reserved for his own use, to pay his expenses and discharge his debts. And if any

---

61 Robert de Vere held the office of great chamberlain by hereditary right.

62 This clause was about purveyance: the right of the sovereign to compel the sale to himself (at reduced rates) of food, transport and labour to supply his household as it moved around the country. It was a source of grievance from the twelfth to the seventeenth centuries.

such income be granted, then it should be done by the open advice and assent of his council and with accurate information of its true value.

[10.] That it please the king to be advised not lightly to grant charters of pardon for manslaughter, murder, rape of women, robberies and other felonies, without reliable information and the testimony of competent persons.

[11.] That it please the king to be also warned against granting charters of exemption; because otherwise he will scarcely find any suitable men to hold inquests, or to be sheriff or other officer.

[12.] That it please the king to attract to himself good and honourable men of standing, and to associate with them, and avoid the company of others; because in so doing he will have, in future, great goodness and honour, and so attract to himself the hearts and love of his people. In doing the contrary, he will have the contrary in future, to the great peril of himself and his realm, which God forbid.

[13.] That everyone who is around our lord king should now cease, and refrain entirely in future, from committing any maintenance whatso-ever, or from undertaking and promoting any other quarrel of any kind which concerns a litigant, with our lord king, and taking any bribe or intervening with our lord king in such a case, either secretly or openly, on pain of being shamed and considered disloyal, and of being expelled from the king's household for ever.

77. The king of Armenia attempts mediation between England and France

The year ended with the discernible start of Richard's policy of friendliness to the French, and the visit of Charles VI's emissary, the king of Armenia. After his kingdom was invaded by the Turks, Leo V (1373–93) was a refugee whose aim in attempting to make peace between France and England was to organise a crusade to recover Armenia. King Leo was said to have 'little skill in Latin or fluency in French', which might seem to disqualify him as a diplomat, but was also 'a prince of great vivacity and clear vision',[63] so probably Richard found his personality engaging. Walsingham's bitter comment on Richard's generosity towards this fellow-monarch is corroborated elsewhere;[64] it was noted even in France.

SAC I.784.

63 *Chronique ... de Saint-Denys* (1994 repr.): 1.420.
64 Compare *WC*, 155–61. The Monk called him *valde astutus:* very cunning.

The king spent Christmas with Queen Anne at Eltham, where there came to him the king of Armenia on the pretext of newly making a peace between the kings of England and France, but he alone saw the profits of his arrival. For beside numberless gifts which he took from the king and nobles of the kingdom, the king conceded and granted him a charter for £1,000 for life, payable annually. He had indeed, as he said, been made a refugee from his kingdom by the Turks, and for that reason he wheedled many gifts from Christian kings, to such an extent that he was more fortunate as a fugitive in foreign lands than as ruler of his realm with his own people.

1386

The twelve months from November 1386 to November 1387 saw the turning point of the reign. In this period three decisive events took place: first, the business of government was put into the hands of a commission for twelve months; second, Richard and his friends retaliated by posing ten questions to the judges about the legality of proceedings in the previous parliament; third, Richard's leading critics reacted by formally accusing the king's five leading supporters of treason.

78. The year 1386 according to the *Eulogium*

This was a momentous year with enduring consequences for the whole political community.

Gaunt decided to make good his claim to the Castilian throne by force and embarked with his army, having made an alliance with João, king of Portugal (r. 1385–1433). This illegitimate son of King Pedro (r. 1357–67) succeeded his legitimate half-brother Fernando (r. 1367–83), but faced both internal and Castilian challenges. He was desperate for allies, hence his overtures to England. For England, the support of the Portuguese navy was worth having, and Portugal provided good harbours at which Gaunt could disembark, and a base from which to attack Castile.

Eulogium, 358–60.

The duke of Lancaster, who had earlier married the daughter of Pedro, king of Spain, and also collected a large sum of money by papal indulgence, took ship with the youth of the kingdom for Spain, planning to rule there in right of his wife. The king of Spain, however, declared that he did not want a war but that he alone would fight for himself; he collected all the provisions – except the fruits actually growing on the vines and trees – inside castles and walled villages. The king of France, on account of his alliance with the king of Spain, gathered a large fleet in the port of Sluys, and made himself a red ship as a symbol of the spilling of blood, and lay there for a long time waiting for a favourable wind, he said, to sail over to England. Nothing was organised against him except that the lords lingered around London, and the shrine of St Thomas of Canterbury was handed to Simon Burley, constable of Dover, for safe keeping in Dover castle, and everyone was ordered to evacuate the Isle of Thanet, taking their possessions, leaving it empty; but the monks of Canterbury and the islanders refused to do this. Then wise men sensibly discussed effective resistance to the French king. In the duke of Lancaster's absence the king followed the advice of the earl of Oxford, a young man whom he ordered to be called duke of Ireland, of Michael de la Pole the chancellor, of Simon [Burley] and of other flatterers. However, when the king of France could not get a favourable wind and his horses died at sea, he turned back. So the kingdom of England was protected by God, and not by man.

That same year, as was said earlier, John of Gaunt, duke of Lancaster, set out for Spain with a great company of young soldiers to vindicate his right to the kingdom of Spain, due to him by right of his wife, taking with him his wife the duchess and his three daughters. After a very small delay,[65] and following negotiations between the pretended king of Spain and the duke, an agreement was made that the king[66] should marry the duke's elder daughter, who would be the heir to the kingdom of Spain, in return for an immediate payment to the duke of a large sum of gold and silver; and afterwards in each succeeding year of the duke's life the king should pay, or have paid, to the duke £10,000, which would be transported (by land or sea) to Bayonne at the Spanish king's expense ... and given to the duke and his agents. At the same time the duke married another of his daughters[67] to the king of Portugal.

At Michaelmas 1386 a parliament was held in London where, on the king's behalf, the reason for calling parliament was explained, namely, that measures should be organised against the French king and [other] external enemies. The duke of Gloucester and the earls of Arundel and Warwick, and their supporters, answered that something should

---

65 This suggests that the writer was referring to the negotiations which led to the Treaty of Trancoso in early June 1387.

66 The king's elder son, Enrique, married Catherine, the elder of Gaunt's daughters by Constance of Castile.

67 Philippa, daughter of his first wife, Blanche of Lancaster.

first be done about the internal enemies, namely Michael de la Pole the
chancellor, and many others. The king, on Michael's advice, dissolved
parliament and ordered everyone to disperse. Those who were gathered
there said that they wanted to discuss the safety of the realm, because
it was in danger. The king did not want to come to parliament. They
even sent for that statute by which the middle Edward [Edward II] was
judged,[68] and under pain of that statute they compelled the king to
attend. And when they had accused Michael of many crimes – especially
that he had had a collection made for [the hospital of] St Anthony of
Vienne which was forbidden in the kingdom, a collection he had appro-
priated to his own use;[69] also that he had sealed blank charters (cartas
albas); and he had organised nothing against the king of France; and
that he had used the office of chancellor to the detriment of the kingdom
– they dismissed him from the office of chancellor and from the rank of
earl, and condemned him to perpetual imprisonment in Corfe castle. In
his place they appointed Thomas Arundel, bishop of Ely, as chancellor.
The king, however, sent Michael to Windsor castle.

Then, because in previous parliaments it was said that the crown's
revenues were insufficient for the appropriate honour of the royal
household and that tallages[70] were always levied under this pretext,
they compelled the king to concede to the bishops of Canterbury, York,
Winchester, Ely, to the dukes of York and Gloucester, to the earls of
Arundel and Warwick, to the abbot of Waltham and to John de Cobham
baron, that he would give them a commission before Christmas – unless
parliament intervened – to receive and spend all the crown revenues; to
enter his castles and manors, remove officials and appoint new ones; and
to govern the royal household and the affairs of the kingdom. Parliament also conceded that, if they thought it necessary, they could levy a
tallage. The king had to assent to this commission, and he commanded
Thomas the chancellor to seal the commission, which was done on his
order, under his signet. The earl of Arundel was made keeper of the sea.

68 Although Clementi (1971): 96–115 claimed to have identified this statute, it is not
   clear that it ever existed. The references to 'statutes', both here and in **82**, may have
   been concocted simply to intimidate Richard.
69 St Anthony was an Augustinian hospital dependent on a mother house at Vienne.
   Its purpose was to care for sufferers from St Anthony's Fire (ergotism), a condition caused by eating diseased rye. This 'alien priory' was supported by the sale
   of pardons and was granted to de la Pole in 1382 for 20 marks p.a., though it was
   probably worth over 400 marks yearly; Maxfield (1997): 225–47, esp. 229–31.
70 An arbitrary, essentially obsolete tax that Anglo-Norman kings as feudal superiors
   levied on towns and their demesnes.

After parliament was dissolved the king, by a proclamation in London, ordered that Michael de la Pole be called earl of Suffolk, and he restored him to liberty.

79. The Anglo-Portuguese alliance: the Treaty of Windsor, 12 April 1386

The treaty which created England's oldest alliance resulted from the grudging and reluctant partnership between King João and Gaunt, and went unnoticed by English chroniclers.[71] The text begins with a high-flown preamble dwelling upon the principles of good government, with the expectation that there would soon be peace after all nations were united in obedience to Rome.

Foedera, Conventiones, Litterae, ed. Thomas Rymer, 3rd edn (The Hague, 1745), III, iii.200–1.

[1.] First it is decided and finally agreed that, for the public good and the peace of the kings and subjects of both kingdoms, let there be inviolable and perpetual leagues, friendships, confederations and firm unions, real and perpetual, between them and their heirs and successors, and for their kingdoms, lands, dominions and countries, and their subjects, vassals, lieges and allies whatsoever; so that each of them shall be bound to bring succour to the other and prompt help against all men who in any way strive to violate the peace of the other or to undermine its stability, excepting only our lord Urban, the supreme pontiff and his successors canonically elected, the lords Wenzel, by God's grace king of the Romans and of Bohemia, and John, by the same grace king of Castile and Leon, duke of Lancaster, uncle of the aforesaid most illustrious lord the king of England.

[2.] It is decided and unanimously agreed that each and every vassal or subject of the kingdoms, lands and dominions aforesaid – whether prelates, dukes, earls, barons, knights, clerics, esquires, merchants or others, of whatever eminence, status or condition they be – shall be able safely and securely to enter the kingdom, lands and dominions of the other, and to converse and trade with its subjects and to remain there, and then to return to their own firesides (*lares*), or wherever it pleases them to turn aside, as freely and peacefully as in their own country. And that those of one country should be as amicably received and honestly dealt with in every place in the kingdoms, lands and dominions of the

71 But see Lopes (1989): 189.

other … as men of those parts, of equal status and condition, should or are accustomed to be treated, paying to the king and the other lords of those said lands the customs and dues which in those places are accustomed to be paid, and observing the laws and statutes of the realms and territories aforesaid, wherever … they enter or where it happens that they remain.

[3.] It is mutually agreed that in no way are those kings permitted, nor any of the subjects of their lands and dominions, of whatever status, rank or condition, in any way to give or lend counsel, help or favour to any land, lordship or nation which is hostile or rebellious to either party; nor in any way to hire or grant to the enemies of this nation galleys or any other ships, which could be used to the detriment of the other

…

[9.] It is decreed that all the heirs and successors of the said kings, in all times to come, shall within a year of their coronation, be bound … solemnly and publicly to renew, ratify and confirm these present alliances, and to confirm them by public testimony ….

80. The invasion scare of 1386

That summer, England's nightmare of a French invasion nearly came true. The threat caused disquiet in government and panic in Kent.

(a) According to Walsingham

This is preceded by report of a rumour that the French intended to besiege Calais.

SAC I.792.

When the Londoners at this time discovered that the king of France had gathered a fleet, obtained an army, and was determined to invade England, they grew very fearful, and like frightened rabbits and anxious mice they sought secluded spots and searched carefully for hiding places, and, as though the city would soon be captured … they rushed, like drunkards, to the walls, pulled down, demolished and destroyed the adjacent houses, and in great terror did everything they were accustomed to do in times of dire necessity. Not a single Frenchman set foot on ship, no enemy set sail, but the Londoners, as though all the land around had been vanquished and conquered, were as fearful and agitated as though they could see the enemy before their gates.

(b) Mayor Nicholas Brembre puts London in readiness for an invasion

In contrast to 1381, when London was overrun by rebels from adjacent counties, Brembre was determined that London should be well prepared, both militarily and with sufficient supplies at fair prices.

Calendar of Letter-Books of the City of London: Letter-Book H, ed. Reginald R. Sharpe (London, 1907), 285–6, 288–9, adapted.

4 September: Order to the aldermen to see that the men of their respective wards are arrayed according to their status; that all weights and measures are of the proper standard; and that all foodstuffs conform to the ordinances made about them.

5 September: Proclamation that all those Londoners who have left the city are to return there within twelve days from the next feast of the Nativity of the Blessed Virgin Mary *[19 September]* in view of an expected attack by the enemy, and forbidding those remaining in the city to leave it without permission.

13 September: Order to the aldermen to summon the householders of their respective wards and command them to lay in a stock of provisions for three months. They are also to make a return by Sunday next of the names of the inhabitants of their ward who are absent; and they are to prepare a pennon for their men *[when]* suitably arrayed, as ordered earlier.

[Undated]: Proclamation regulating the sale of hay, oats, ale, poultry, and forbidding armourers, bowyers, fletchers and horse-dealers to sell arms, bows and arrows, and horses at an inflated price owed to the present expedition.

A quarter of coal is to be sold for no more than 9d., on paid of forfeiture.

(c) Simon Burley's activities in Kent

In contrast to Walsingham's detached view, Thorne, a monk of St Augustine's Canterbury, wrote from a very parochial perspective, seeing Burley as a threat to the local community and ecclesiastical rights. This story continues in **113 (b)**.

William Thorne, *Chronica*, cols. 2181–2.

The French people and their king collected a fleet of ships at Sluys, intending – on account of the discord which had arisen in the realm because of a certain very powerful man called Simon Burley, who was both the king's chamberlain and constable of Dover castle and warden of the Cinque Ports and the county *[of Kent]* – to invade this land with their fleet, to lay it waste, and both to wipe out all its people and to destroy its language. So this Simon, ruler of the realm, being a false favourer of the French king, compelled our king to journey to the west regions to fight the Scots,[72] so granting the enemy king free entry to these parts and allowing him to do what he liked here. But the good Lord, through the merits of those saints who defend Kentishmen, considered our king's innocence and the traitor's plans, and by a persistent contrary wind, He prevented the [French] royal fleet from leaving port. Meanwhile, many thousands of the enemy died of hunger. Simon, the crafty turncoat, pretended both to dread their power and that he wanted to make everything safe, but he was motivated by greed, and he craved not relics but riches, not heavenly treasure but the measureless gold of the martyr.[73] He even attempted to despoil St Thomas of his precious tunic, by what ways and means he could, on various occasions, and to carry it away with our other jewels to his treasury at Dover; he alleged that all these things would be safer there than in an unwalled city. But the saints were against him, the monks both prayed and strenuously resisted, and so by God's will he was frustrated in his plan and withdrew empty-handed.

Meanwhile Simon, depressed by the adverse wind, summoned eighteen ships from the aforesaid fleet, which circled our country to strike great terror there. For, circling round the island [of Thanet], they first laid waste, then destroyed with fire, the town of Stoner, which the abbot would have saved if he had had free passage from Northbourne through Sandwich. The abbot, foiled by them in this way, wished with God's help to keep safe his own and his tenants' goods, so at night, by a roundabout route through Fordwich and Sturry, he succeeded with great effort in reaching the island. When they heard he was coming the enemy left the island untouched. Simon, however, unresting and always plotting evil, devised a new trick by which those galleys might more easily attack the islanders and ordered letters patent to be issued, in the following form:

'Richard, by God's grace king of England and France, and lord of Ireland, to his beloved and faithful Simon Burley, constable of his castle of Dover and warden of the Cinque Ports, or his lieutenant: greeting. Know that we have learnt for certain that our enemies of France, Spain, Flanders and Brittany, and others allied to them, have joined together

72 Richard spent July 1386 in Wiltshire, Somerset and Gloucestershire, Saul: 471. Thorne seems to have confused this journey with the previous year's campaign.

73 Burley was thought to be eyeing the magnificent shrine to St Thomas Becket and its riches, later looted by Henry VIII.

and united as our foes, and are endeavouring and planning how they can
lay waste the coasts of our realm of England, and for various reasons
are gathering their forces together to destroy those coasts and our
faithful people, and to invade, capture and occupy our defences and the
fortresses on those coasts in a short time unless you offer effective resistance to their plan. Wishing – with the help of God's grace – to resist
such malice of our enemies, and for the safety and protection of our
realm and faithful people to set guards and organise them all around,
we order you to have proclamation made within the town of Sandwich
and its suburb, that each and every person living within that town and
suburb, and all others holding lands, tenements or possessions there,
under pain of imprisonment and forfeiture of all the other things which
can be forfeit to us, should remain within that town with their families
and servants, to save and defend it and the adjacent area, as stoutly as
they can, or find persons sufficiently armed and arrayed according to
the extent of their lands and tenements and their means, to remain
there continuously for the safety and protection of the town. And all
those whom, after that proclamation, you shall find to be uncooperative
or rebellious in this matter are to be arrested, seized and kept in our
prisons, there to remain, and all their goods, lands and tenements are
to be seized into our hands and kept in safe and secure custody until
ordered otherwise by us and our council, etc. In witness whereof, etc.
in the ninth year of our reign.'[74]

He also ordered and, on the king's behalf, told the abbot to withdraw
with all his force from that same island [Thanet] because the land would
be soon be lost, since he was unable to withstand the enemies' imminent
attack; but the abbot was to leave the island with his whole force, with
all speed, and help him guard the town of Sandwich. All this was done
so that the island, after being duly captured by the French, should be
handed over by royal authority to Simon, and this church be deprived
of it forever. But the heroic abbot was neither deflected by fear of the
foe nor seduced by the traitor's blandishments, but undismayed, he
remained with his men to protect his and his tenants' property, preferring to die among them rather than see evil come upon his people.
The French, however, weakened during this time by hunger and other
miseries, abandoned their ships and returned to their homes.

74 This letter cannot be identified with any one entry in either the Close or Patent Rolls,
    but a flurry of similar mandates to defend the Kentish coast was issued in late April
    and early May 1386.

(d) Froissart on the French plan and its results in England

Froissart gives most detail about the invasion plans, though his description of the size of the fleet massed at Sluys should be treated with caution. Despite the extensive preparations, contrary winds and the approach of winter forced the French to abandon their plans.

Froissart, *Chronicles*, II.74–5, 197, 203, 237.

The king of France, his uncles and council, had been well informed about the duke of Lancaster's intended expedition before he had sailed from England ... that it was meant against Castile. This was the reason the duke of Burgundy had so easily concluded a peace with the Flemings, so that the king of Castile might have assistance; for the king of France was bound to help him, as he had always supported France when called upon, with men and ships. Add to this the great desire the young king of France had always shown to invade England with a powerful army and navy. In this he was joined by all the chivalry of the realm.

By St John's day *[24 June]*, all the great vessels in Holland, Zeeland, Middleburgh and Dordrecht ... and other places near the sea, were sought for, to carry this army from Sluys .... Never, since God created the world, were there seen such numbers of large ships as filled the harbours of Sluys and Blanckenburgh: for, when they were counted, in the month of September that year, there were 1,287 ships. These masts, on coming from the sea, appeared like a thick forest. ... The conversations which were overheard between the French showed that they considered that England would be ruined and destroyed beyond repair, the men put to death, and the women and children carried in slavery to France ....

Sir Simon Burley was governor of Dover castle, and, from his situation, received frequent intelligence from France by the fishermen of the town, who told him what they heard from the French fishermen ... for, even though there were wars between France and England, they were never interrupted in their pursuits, nor attacked each other, but, on the contrary, gave mutual assistance, and bought or sold, according as either had more fish than they needed. ... Sir Simon learnt from the fishermen that the king of France was absolutely determined on the invasion; that he intended to land one division at or near Dover, and another at Sandwich, and that his forces were immense. He, as well as the rest of England, believed all this was true; and one day he set out for Canterbury to visit the abbey,[75] which is very large and handsome.

75 Christ Church (Benedictine) whose church was, and is, Canterbury cathedral.

The abbot inquired, 'What news?', and Sir Simon told him all he knew, adding that the shrine of St Thomas, so respected and rich, was not safe in Canterbury, for the town was not strong, and if the French came, some of the pillagers, through avarice, would make for Canterbury, which they would plunder, as well as the abbey, and make particular enquiries after the shrine, 'and they will take it away, to your great loss. I would therefore advise that you have it carried to Dover castle where it will be perfectly safe, though all England were lost'. The abbot and all the convent were so much angered at this speech, though well meant, that they replied, 'What, Sir Simon!, would you wish to despoil this church of its jewel? If you are afraid yourself, take courage and shut yourself up in your castle at Dover, for the French will not be bold enough, nor in sufficient force, to venture so far'. This was the only answer he had; but Sir Simon persisted so long in his proposition, that the common people grew discontented.

...

England was, at this period, in greater danger than when the peasants, under Jack Straw, rose in rebellion and marched to London; and I will tell you the cause. The nobles and gentlemen were unanimous, at that time, in their support of the king, but now there were many serious differences between them. The king quarrelled with his uncles of York and Gloucester, and they were equally displeased with him, caused, as it was said, by the intrigues of the duke of Ireland, the king's sole confidant. The common people in many towns and cities had noticed these quarrels, and the wisest dreaded the consequences that might ensue; but the giddy laughed at them, and said that these disputes were caused by the jealousy of the king's uncles, and because the crown was not on their heads. But others said, 'The king is young, and puts his confidence in youngsters: it would be to his advantage if he consulted his uncles more, who desire only the prosperity of the country, than that puppy, the duke of Ireland, who is ignorant of everything, and who never saw a battle'. Thus were the English divided, and great disasters seemed to be at hand, which was perfectly known all over France, and caused them to hasten their preparations for invading the county, and adding to its miseries ....

As soon as the English learnt that the camps near Sluys were broken up, and the invasion abandoned, great murmurings were general throughout England. Those who wished mischief said, 'What has now become of our grand enterprises and our valiant captains? Would that our gallant King Edward, and his son, the prince of Wales, were now alive! We used to invade France and rebuff our enemies so that they were afraid to show themselves or venture to engage us; and, when they did so, they were defeated .... Where now are the knights and princes of England who can do such things?'

81. Plans to proceed against Robert de Vere

This translated fragment of a lost chronicle has de Vere as the original target of criticism. The translation was perhaps made in Charles I's reign to use against George Villiers, duke of Buckingham, whose impeachment was planned during the spring of 1626. This would account for its anachronistic language.

Somers' Tracts, ed. Walter Scott, 2nd edn (London, 1809), I.15–16, adapted.

Many of the more experienced nobility and senior gentry represented to the king that the new glory of Robert de Vere, created marquess of Dublin and duke of Ireland, and his exorbitant views, reflected great indignity upon the reputation of the English and Irish nations, to be so unworthily abused and oppressed by a fellow subject; but King Richard sent them home without thanks, his nature being against any whole-some counsels – though as true as oracles – not failing to acquaint either the chancellor *[de la Pole]* or the duke of Ireland, not only with this advice, but the *[name of the]* adviser, which his grace childishly discovered ... de Vere's ambition was now grown to so high a point that moderate persons, much more the haughty, thought it high time to lance it; the lords and ministers of state had many private meetings about it. Most were of opinion that at the meeting of the parliament he should by both Houses be remonstrated against, as the common grievance of the whole kingdom, and consequently be brought to trial, having matter enough in his crimes to compose a weighty charge; but others more experienced in the ways of those assemblies differed in their opinion, holding it best to begin with the new earl of Suffolk, a man in no danger of being pitied .... Besides they held the chancellor to be steersman in affairs of state, and, removing the rudder, the ship would leave sailing of itself; and, consequently, 'twas resolved to exhibit this charge against him the second day of parliament: *[seven charges follow]*.

82. The 'wonderful' parliament, 1 October–28 November 1386

It is unclear whether it was the invasion scare which precipitated the subsequent attack on the chancellor Michael de la Pole, though evidently some members of the following parliament were in an ugly mood by the time it assembled. The warning to Richard that he should co-operate with the assembly provoked another intemperate outburst.

(a) According to Knighton

Knighton's is easily the most complete chronicle account of this parliament; he alone describes the mission of Gloucester and Thomas Arundel to Richard at Eltham. He also includes the articles of impeachment against de la Pole, a summary of the scope of the commission of reform and a copy of the statute which established it. Richard's elevation of Robert de Vere to the new title 'duke of Ireland' on 13 October 1386 would seem, in the circumstances, to have been the height of tactlessness. But this date was of deep significance to Richard, for it was the feast of the Translation of Edward the Confessor, a saint for whom the king had particular veneration, and so the grant to de Vere was put under the saint's protection.[76]

KC, 352–60.

The king held a parliament at Westminster on Monday the morrow of St Jerome *[1 October]*, which ended on the feast of St Andrew *[30 November]*. The earl of Oxford, who was marquess of Dublin, was created duke of Ireland on the feast of St Edward King and Confessor *[13 October]*. At the time of this parliament the king mostly lingered at Eltham. So the nobles and commons of the realm, by common consent, told the king that he ought to remove the chancellor and treasurer from their positions, because they were unprofitable to the king and realm; and also because they had certain business to transact with Michael de la Pole which they could not conduct as long as he remained in the office of chancellor.

This angered the king: he ordered them to keep quiet about these matters, and to proceed with parliament's business, and to hurry up, saying that he would not remove the lowest kitchen boy from his post to please them. For the chancellor had, in the king's name, asked the commons for four fifteenths, payable in a year, and the same number of tenths from the clergy, saying that the king was so in debt that otherwise he could not be relieved of his debts or other encumbering

76 Mitchell in Gordon, Monnas and Elam (1997): 115–24, 310–15.

burdens, both of war and of his household.[77] But by common consent
the lords and commons responded to the king that they could not, and
absolutely did not wish, to proceed with any parliamentary business, or
to expedite the smallest matter until the king came and showed himself
in his own person to them in parliament. The king replied that they
should send him forty knights of the more experienced and weighty of
the commons, who would convey to him the wishes of all the others.

Then each one became more fearful for his own safety, because a
secret rumour was whispered that their death in an ambush was being
planned. For it was said that it was later revealed to them that, when
they had arrived to talk with the king, an armed gang would rush in and
kill them; or that armed thugs would storm in to those who had been
invited to dinner with the king, and kill them; or they would be killed
suddenly in their London lodgings. But Nicholas Exton, the mayor of
London, refused and would in no way consent to such wickedness, so
that vicious act was publicised and the evil plot consequently exposed.
Adopting a safer plan, they sent to the king at Eltham – with the backing
of all parliament – Lord Thomas of Woodstock, duke of Gloucester, and
Thomas Arundel, bishop of Ely, who greeted him on behalf of the lords
and commons of his parliament, conveying their wishes to him.

[*After an elaborate greeting:*] 'On their behalf we hereby inform you that,
according to an ancient statute we have, and by laudable and approved
custom – which cannot be contested – our king can convene the lords
and magnates of the realm and the commons once a year to his parliament as to the supreme court of the whole kingdom, in which all equity
should blaze out without the slightest hesitation or hindrance, like
the sun rising to noonday, where rich and poor, for the refreshment of
tranquillity and peace, and for the redress of injuries, can always find
refuge … It seems also to them that, because they support the burdens,
they have also the duty to supervise how, and by whom, their goods and
chattels are spent.

'They say also that they have, by an ancient statute, that if the king
of his own volition wantonly absents himself from his parliament –
not because of illness or any other unavoidable reason, but through
his unbridled will – by an absence of forty days, as though not caring
about the harassment of his people and their burdensome expenses,

77 A grant of half a tenth and fifteenth, payable by 2 Feb. 1387, was made 23 Oct. ×
   28 Nov. 1386 and a second half tenth upon conditions, which was not collected,
   Jurkowski, Smith and Crook (1998): 65–6. See also **84**.

each and every one of them, without any need of the king's permission, has the right to go home, and every one of them to return to his own country. By now you have been absent for a longer time than this, and, for reasons unknown, you refuse to attend'.

The king said: 'Now we clearly observe that our people and commons intend to resist and struggle to rise up against us. Against such persecution it seems we could do no better than to seek the advice and help of our kinsman the king of France against the insurgents, and rather submit ourselves to him than to succumb to our subjects'.

To this they answered: 'That would be a mad idea, more likely to come to certain grief. For the king of France is your chief enemy and the chief adversary of your kingdom, and if he should set foot in your kingdom, he would more likely strive to despoil you and occupy your realm, and expel you from the eminence of your royal position, than to extend a helping hand .... Remember too how your grandfather King Edward III, and your father Prince Edward in his name, with sweat and suffering, all his life, by countless labours in all weathers, struggled indefatigably to conquer the kingdom of France, which by hereditary right belonged to them and to you after them in succession.

'Remember also how the lords of the realm, the nobles and innumerable commons both of the kingdom of England as of France, also kings and lords of other realms, and numberless people suffered in that war death and the danger of death, and tirelessly poured out goods and countless chattels and boundless treasure to sustain this war. ...

'But there remains one more part of our message which we must tell you on your people's behalf: they have an ancient statute, and one which was used not long ago – sad to say – that if the king, through any evil counsel or foolish refusal or contempt or by his wanton personal will, or any sort of irregularity, alienates himself from his people, and does not wish to be governed and ruled by the laws of the land and statutes, and by laudable ordinances along with the wise counsel of the lords and nobles of the kingdom, but wantonly to exercise his own individual will, in his mad plans, then it is lawful for them – by common consent and with the agreement of the people of the kingdom – to remove that king from his royal throne, and to substitute upon the throne another close relative of the royal line in his place. ...'

(b) The impeachment of the chancellor, Michael de la Pole, earl of Suffolk.[78]

In Edward III's last years, and earlier in Richard's reign – though there had been calls for financial reform, and prosecutions of corrupt or incompetent individuals – there had been no question of the death penalty, nor of the charge of treason. The prosecution of Michael de la Pole was in this humane tradition; he was accused of financial corruption and abusing his office, but of nothing worse. His punishment (imprisonment) was also measured, and it was made much milder by Richard's early release of him, within a few weeks of his conviction.

RP III.216, 219–20; *PROME* 1386, sections 5–6, 12.

In this parliament all the commons assembled together in agreement came before the king, bishops and lords in the parliament chamber, complaining bitterly about Michael de Pole, earl of Suffolk, former chancellor of England, who was present there, and accused him orally as follows:

[1.] First, that this earl, when he was chancellor and sworn to act for the king's profit, purchased from our lord king lands, tenements and rents of great value, as appears on the record of the rolls of chancery, contrary to his oath, more than he deserved, considering the great necessity of the king and realm. Further, because the earl was chancellor when those purchases were made, those lands and tenements were alienated at a lesser value than they were worth annually, by a great sum, thus defrauding the king.

[2.] Also, although nine lords were assigned in the last parliament to view and examine the state of the king and realm, and advise how it could be improved and put into better governance and disposition, and to make examination and to report on this to the king, both orally and in writing, the former chancellor *[de la Pole]* said in full parliament that this advice and these ordinances ought to be put into full execution; but this was not done, and the fault for this was his because he was the principal officer.

[3.] Whereas money was granted by the commons in the last parliament to be expended in a certain way as demanded by the commons and assented to by the lords, and not otherwise, the money so provided was expended in another manner so that the sea was not guarded in the manner specified; from which several mischiefs have befallen the realm and more seem likely to come, and this was the fault of the former chancellor.

78 See Roskell (1984) for full discussion of the charges.

[4.] Whereas one Tidemann of Limburg,[79] who had obtained for himself and his heirs by gift of the king's grandfather £50 a year from the customs of Kingston on Hull, which Tidemann forfeited to the king, and also the payment of that £50 a year was discontinued for twenty or thirty years, the former chancellor, knowing this, bought for himself and his heirs from Tidemann, that same £50 a year, and arranged for the king to confirm that purchase to him, which the king should have had for his own profit.

[5.] Because the Master of [the hospital of] St Anthony [of Vienne][80] is a schismatic, and therefore the king should have the profits which belong to him within the kingdom of England, the former chancellor, who ought to have advanced and obtained the king's profit, took at farm the king's profit for 20 marks a year and so made 1,000 marks for himself; and at the time when the Master of St Anthony in England should have had possession and livery of that profit, he could not get it until he and two people with him had been compelled, by recognisances of £3,000 made in chancery, to pay this former chancellor [de la Pole] and his son John, £100 annually for their [two] lifetimes.

[6.] In the time of the former chancellor, there were granted and made various charters and patents [of pardon] for murders, treasons, felonies, and erasures of rolls, sale of laws, and especially, after the start of the present parliament, there was made and sealed a charter of certain franchises granted at Dover Castle, to the undermining of the crown and the subversion of all places and courts of the king and of his laws.

[7.] Whereas ordinance was made in the last parliament that 10,000 marks should be borrowed on behalf of the town of Ghent and for that a loss of 3,000 marks [of interest] should be incurred, and this was done, but by the chancellor's fault and negligence the town was lost; nevertheless the 10,000 marks were paid and the 3,000 marks lost, as stated above.[81]

To all these articles the commons demanded judgment of parliament.

---

79 Limburg is in Germany, north-west of Frankfurt. 'The story which lies behind this fourth charge ... is both complicated and obscure', and involved Michael's father William, Hull merchant and crown financier. It is described by Roskell (1984): 158–69.

80 Maxfield (1997): 225–47. For the farming of alien houses, see McHardy (1989): 177–95.

81 There is no evidence that the chancellor alone was responsible for either the financial arrangement or the military defeat.

[De la Pole's replies to each charge individually were all dismissed as insufficient.]

After the earl's response to the commons' accusations, and the replies made to them by the both sides, that earl was, at the commons' request – on account of the gravity of the offences charged against him – arrested on the king's command and committed to the custody of the constable of England, and then released on sureties.

(c) Petition for the appointment of a commission of government

It was after the impeachment of de la Pole that the political temper changed so greatly, and this can be seen by examining the commission of government which this parliament established, a commission which was incorporated into a statute. A notable feature is its date; by ordering the commission's powers to run from the feast of another of Richard's guardian saints, St Edmund, the king's enemies were twisting the knife in the wound.

RP III.221–2; *PROME* 1386, section 20.

The commons most humbly pray, for God's honour, for the maintenance of your crown, and for your own profit and that of all the prelates and lords, and for the relief of the poor commons of your realm, that it may please you to ordain and appoint in this present parliament suitable officials, namely, chancellor, treasurer, keeper of the privy seal, steward of your household and also other lords of your great and continual council; and that they may have power to correct and amend all the defects that so greatly blemish your Crown ...; and that to do this, a sufficient commission shall be given to those lords and officers, to last from the feast of St Edmund king and martyr last [*20 November*] until the same feast one year later; and that there shall be made a statute that no one, of whatever rank, status or nation or condition whatsoever, shall dare, either secretly or openly, to counsel or to do anything to bring about the contrary of what those lords and officers see fit to advise, and that on serious penalty. This you have in part, by your benignity, put into execution; we request that now you bring these [*matters*] to a conclusion, also that your officers and councillors should stay continuously at London during that time to have full information, both from the rolls and records, and from the judges and all other persons of the chancery and exchequer, or any other place of record.

ANSWER: The king assents (*Le roy le voet*),[82] provided that the commission and statute demanded in this petition shall last no longer than one

---

82 *Le roi/la reine le veult* are still the words which give royal assent to legislation.

whole year. As to the steward of his household, he will choose a suitable one on the advice of his council.

83. The commission of government

The commission, mentioned briefly in the *Eulogium* [78], was included in full by Westminster and Knighton;[83] one commissioner, Bishop Wykeham of Winchester, had it copied into his register.[84] It was also the target of sharp, well-informed comment by Thomas Favent, who sympathised with the king's critics. The eleven commissioners, named in strict order of precedence, were chosen from each element of the political community represented in parliament. They were to work with the three officers of state (the chancellor, treasurer and keeper of the privy seal), all newly appointed during that parliament. The terms of the commission repay careful study; only by reading it through can we appreciate how serious the king's position was. The commission's powers were comprehensive, unfettered and overwhelming; they smothered the royal prerogative for twelve months. It was small wonder that the nineteen-year-old Richard was resentful towards it and its instigators. His bitterness at this humiliation, as he saw it, persisted to the end of his reign.[85]

(a) The commission's terms.

The commission was first issued as a letter patent on 19 November and then as this statute on 1 December.

SR II.39–43, adapted.

Know that, for reverence to God, and to nourish peace, unity, quiet and harmony in all parts of the realm of England – which we desire above all – with the assent of the lords and commons assembled in our parliament held at Westminster on 1 October last, we have caused to be made a statute, both for the improvement of its governance and for the common profit of the realm in the following form:

Whereas our sovereign lord king perceives, by the serious complaint of the lords and commons of his realm assembled in the present parliament, that his profits, rents and the revenues of his realm are – by wilful and insufficient counsel and evil governance, both by some of his recent great officers and by various other people around him – so greatly withdrawn, wasted, removed, given away, granted, alienated, destroyed and badly spent, that he is so greatly impoverished and lacks

83 *WC*, 166–76; *KC*, 372–80.
84 Wykeham's Register II.396–400.
85 *CR*: 55–6.

treasure and goods; and the substance of the crown is so much diminished and destroyed that his status, and that of his household, cannot
be honourably maintained as it ought, nor the wars which daily abound
and beset his realm be maintained nor provided for without great and
outrageous oppression and unbearable cost to his people; also that the
good laws, statutes and customs of his realm, which he is bound to
uphold and observe, are not, and have not been, duly held nor executed,
nor full justice and right done to his people, so that many deprivations
and divers great evils and damages have happened, both to the king, to
his people and to all his realm.

Therefore he has – to the honour of God and for the well-being of
himself and his realm, and for the peace and relief of himself and his
people, who have in various ways been greatly burdened before this
time, and willing, by God's grace, to provide a good and due remedy
against such mischiefs, of his free will and at the request of those lords
and commons – ordained, made and assigned as his great officers (that
is, the chancellor, treasurer and keeper of his privy seal) those that he
holds good, sufficient and lawful for the honour and profit of himself
and his realm. Also, by his royal authority, certain knowledge, good
grace and free will, and by the advice and assent of the prelates, lords
and commons in full parliament – to assist the good government of his
realm, and good and due execution of his laws, and to improve the
position of himself and his people in times to come, upon the full trust
which he has in the good counsel, wisdom and discretion of the honourable fathers in God [William Courtenay] archbishop of Canterbury and
[Alexander Neville] archbishop of York, his dear uncles Edmund, duke
of York, and Thomas, duke of Gloucester, the honourable fathers in
God [William of Wykeham], bishop of Winchester, Thomas [Brant-
ingham], bishop of Exeter, and [Nicholas Morice], abbot of Waltham,
and his well-beloved and faithful Richard, earl of Arundel, John, Lord
Cobham, Richard Lescrope and John Devereux, knights – has ordained,
assigned and deputed them by letters patent under his great seal, to be
members of his great and continual council from the eve of [the feast of]
St Edmund the Martyr, for the whole following year after the date of
those letters patent, in order to survey and examine, along with the
great officers (the chancellor, treasurer and keeper of his privy seal) the
position and administration of his household and all his courts of the
realm, and of all his officers and ministers, of whatever rank, degree or
condition, both inside and outside the household, and to enquire and
gather information by every means which seem best to them, about all

the rents, revenues and profits that belong and are due to him, and which ought to belong and be due, both inside and outside the realm, and in any manner, way or condition; and of all manner of gifts, grants, alienations and confirmations made by him of lands, tenements, rents, annuities, profits, revenues, wardships, marriages, escheats, forfeitures, franchises, liberties, vacancies of archbishoprics, bishoprics, abbeys, priories, farms of the alien [*religious*] houses and other possessions of foreigners; and of all other possessions, sums of money, goods and chattels, and all other things, and to what persons, for what causes, how and in what manner; and the names of those people who have wrongly taken these things; and also about all sorts of revenues and profits whatsoever in his realm, namely in the lands, lordships, cities, towns, castles, fortresses and in all his other possessions, both on this side of the sea and beyond, and of the profits and receipts of his money and bullion; and of taking prisoners, towns, and places, ships, carracks,[86] goods and ransoms of war, by land and by sea, and of benefices and other possessions of rebel cardinals[87] and all other foreigners, and also of carrying money out of the realm by papal collectors, proctors of cardinals,[88] Lombards[89] and all other persons, both alien and denizen; and of the revenues and profits from the customs and subsidies on wool, leather and woolfells, petty customs and other subsidies on cloth, wine and all other merchandise; and of tenths, fifteenths and of all other subsidies and taxes granted by the clergy and commons; and also of the receipts, profits and payments of the hanaper of his chancery, and of all his other receipts, from his coronation until now; and of the fees, wages and rewards of officers and ministers, high and low; also of annuities and other rewards, grants and gifts made to any persons by him or his father and grandfather in fee, or for term of life, or in any other manner, and whether resulting satisfaction or payment was made, by whom, how and in what manner, and also how much they have released or given to officers or others in order to receive their payments, and to whom, how and in what manner; and of lands, tenements, rents, revenues and forfeitures, bargained and sold to the prejudice and damage of himself and his crown, by whom, to whom, how and in what manner; and of the sale or negotiation of tallies[90] and letters patent for individual

---

86 Large merchant ships.
87 Those adhering to the Avignon papacy.
88 Roman, that is, those on the same side as England in the schism.
89 A term used to denote all international, or foreign, bankers.
90 Exchequer receipts in the form of notched sticks. They were split down the middle,

profit, both in his grandfather's time and in his own, how and by what persons; also of all his jewels and goods, which were his grandfather's at the time of his death, their price or value, what became of them and where they are now, and how and in what manner; and of all agreements whatever made to his use by any manner of persons, and of all losses and damages which he has suffered and sustained by the same, and by whom, how and in what manner; and of charters of pardon, general and particular; and also the sums and payments, and manner of the expenses, both of his household and for protecting and defending his realms, lands, lordships, towns, castles, fortresses and other places, both here and overseas, made and received by anyone, whether soldiers or others, and by any way, how, and how much they have given to have their payments; and of the concealments of his rights and profits, and by whom, how and in what manner; and of maintainers and instigators of quarrels, preventers of inquests; and about officers and ministers advanced by corruption, and of those who have taken bribes, how and in what manner; and also of all the defaults and offences that are committed both in his household and his other courts, places and locations, and in all other places within his realm of England, by any sort of persons, by which the profits of himself and his crown have been impaired and diminished, or the common law disturbed or delayed, or other damage done to him: giving and committing by his royal authority, and by the above-named advice and assent, to those councillors, and to six of them, and to the great officers, full power and authority, general and particular, to enter his household and all its offices and all his other courts and places as often as they please; and to have brought before them, where and when they please, the rolls, records and other muniments and documents, as seems best to them; and – concerning all the defects, wastes and excesses found in his household, also all the defects and wrongs found in the other courts, places, officers and ministers, and in all the other articles and points named above, each of them, and also all the other defects, wrongs, excesses, falsities, deceits, extortions, oppressions, damages and grievances, committed to the prejudice, damage and distress of himself, his crown and his realm, in general or special, neither specified nor expressed above – to amend, correct, repair, redress, reform and put them in good and proper state and order;

---

and half retained by the exchequer. Great numbers of tallies remained in crown hands until 1835 when, in a bout of 'clearing out' and 'tidying up', they were burnt in the boiler of the houses of parliament. The boiler overheated, the building caught fire and both houses of parliament burned down. Moral: treat medieval evidence of all kinds with proper respect.

and also to hear and receive all kinds of complaints and quarrels of all
his subjects, who wish to sue and complain, both on behalf of our lord
king and for themselves, before those councillors and officers, about all
kinds of duress, oppressions, injuries, wrongs and negligence which
cannot be readily amended or decided by the course of the common law
of the land as hitherto employed, and to give and to make good and due
remedy and recovery, for both the king and his loyal subjects; and fully
to discuss, and finally to decide all of them, and make full execution as
seems best to them, for the honour and profit of the king and his estate,
and the restoration of the rights and profits of his crown, the better
governance of the peace and laws of the land, and the relief of his people;
willing also that, if differences or divergence of opinion arise or occur
between those councillors and officers, the judgement and opinion of
the greater party shall have force and predominate, as is fully contained
in those letters patent.

Therefore the king – because he wishes the correction and redress of
those defects and wrongs to be carried out without delay, for his own
and the realm's profit – has with the assent of the lords and commons of
his realm in this present parliament, ordained and established that every
one of his subjects, of whatever rank or condition, shall be obedient, in
whatever concerns those articles and everything dependent upon them,
to those councillors and officers under the terms stated above; and that
every person who is judged and convicted by them of any faults or
wrongs shall take and receive, without any argument, such correction as
shall be imposed upon him by those councillors and officers; and that no
person, of whatever rank or condition, high or low, shall give the king,
either privately or openly, advice, incitement or exhortation to repeal
their power within that specified time, in any point, or do anything
contrary to this grant or to any of the above articles; and if anyone of
any rank or condition goes against that ordinance and establishment,
or procures or does anything in any way whatsoever to impede those
councillors in the exercise of their powers, or who incites or assists
our sovereign lord king to do or command anything by which those
counsellors and officers are defeated in the execution of their judgments
and awards, and if this is duly proved by good and true witnesses who
are widely considered of unblemished good fame and condition, suitably
examined before the king, and those councillors and officers, acting on
the advice of any of the justices of either bench, or such other persons
discreet and learned in the law as please them he shall have this punishment: on the first conviction he shall forfeit all his goods and chattels to

the king, and also be imprisoned at the king's pleasure; and if any such person is duly attainted in the manner specified above of advice, incitement or encouragement given to the king to act contrary to this grant, even if the king does nothing by such advice, incitement or encouragement, he shall still have such punishment as before; and if it happens, which God forbid, that he so acts that he is attainted another time of any of those faults or wrongs, then the same person so convicted or attainted shall have for the second offence the punishment of life and limb, saving always the pontifical dignity and privilege of Holy Church and clergy, in all such things; and that this statute remain in force and effect during the time of this said commission only.

We therefore command you that you cause this statute openly to be announced and publicised in cities, boroughs, towns, fairs, markets and other notable places within your jurisdiction, within franchises and without, according to the intention and form of the same.

(b) Its appointment, according to Favent

Thomas Favent's 'History of the Wonderful Parliament' (the title was not his, but was attached to the text later) covers the period from the start of this parliament of 1386 until the end of the 'merciless' parliament; it was almost certainly composed in summer of 1388. It is essentially a short chronicle sympathetic to Richard's critics, valuable for its detail as well as for its strong opinions. Though his style was loquacious and convoluted, Favent was well informed, as this account of the commission demonstrates.[91]

Favent, *Wonderful Parliament*, 1–2.

In 1386 … when the king should have first blossomed into manhood, a certain archbishop of York called Alexander Neville, Robert de Vere, duke of Ireland, Michael de la Pole, earl of Suffolk and chancellor of England, Robert Tresilian, the king's chief justice, and Sir Nicholas Brembre, formerly mayor of the city of London, were the king's rulers and closest advisers. They were men of vicious character who deceived the king, having an eye to the business neither of the king nor kingdom, but they grasped to themselves the riches of iniquity by many evil deeds. The impoverished king was put into the shadow of their sin, and so the realm was smitten by the levying of a great plague of tenths and subsidies. Because of this, misfortunes without number afflicted the kingdom. The nobles of the land observed the disasters which had happened and they urged the king to hold a parliament on

---

91 For a complete translation, see Galloway (2002): 202–52; for discussion of the text and author, see Oliver (2003): 167–98 and Oliver (2010); see also Dodd (2011).

the morrow of Michaelmas *[30 September]* in order to direct the realm into the path of peace. In that parliament the same Michael de la Pole, chancellor of England, was dismissed from office because of his usurpations and extortions, and was banished for a year and imprisoned in the gaol of Windsor, and all his immoveable property was confiscated as punishment for his greed. Even so, those measures did not satisfy the other advisers of the king, but in the same parliament, with the common consent of the king, all the lords, judges and commons, a commission was given to the following magnates of the realm: the archbishop of Canterbury, the aforementioned archbishop of York, the bishop of Ely, by then chancellor of England, the bishop of Winchester, the bishop of Hereford, then treasurer of England, the bishop of Exeter, the abbot of Waltham and John Waltham, keeper of the privy seal,[92] the duke of York, the duke of Gloucester, the earl of Arundel, Lord Cobham, Richard Scrope and Sir John Devereux. Those men, by virtue of this ordinance and statute, and being in possession of the full power of the king and parliament in this matter, would correct the foolish grants by calling them in. They solemnly promised, with hand on the gospels, that they would well and faithfully serve to ordain, consult and complete all the business of the king and kingdom in the following judicial year. And if anyone would incite the king to contravene this ordinance, they should suffer the penalty of confiscation for the first offence; but for the second the loss of life and limb. So, when everything had been arranged for the best and parliament had been dissolved, everyone took their way from there and returned to their own business.

84. Canterbury convocation's reluctant tax grant, 3 December

The clergy of Canterbury province proved as unwilling as parliament to make a tax grant. Their reply to the king's request for money, expressed through the bishops, shows vividly the distrust in which he was held.

Lambeth Palace Library, Reg. Courtenay (Canterbury) I, ff. 84v–85.

Reverend fathers and lords: as you know, a subsidy is being sought from your clergy by our lord king for the necessary defence of his realm, as was explained. But, not unreasonably, the clergy are explaining their difficulty in granting an accustomed subsidy, because subsidies granted previously for this purpose have been turned to very different uses, as

92 The appointments of Arundel (chancellor), Gilbert (treasurer) and Waltham (keeper of the privy seal) were all made on 24 Oct. 1386.

experience teaches; and also because subsidies in the times of the king's progenitors, when wars were more oppressive and violent, were of rare occurrence. Now they are almost annual. So much so that through them, other more frequent accustomed burdens, epidemics of men and of animals, and other adverse events, and because of the heavy costs of buying horses and various kinds of arms and of other fortifications against the enemy, repelling incursions and making other weapons for this cause, and the demands of this year especially – the same clergy are reduced to such poverty that very many of them could scarcely support themselves and shoulder other burdens without begging and borrowing. Despite this, however, thinking of your reverend fathers' assertion that great necessity for the defence of the realm is pressing ... and the clergy should contribute of their goods; considering also that our lord king, with the advice of his noble council in the parliament last past, at the urging of the commons of the realm of England, specially deputed by the said lord our king for the better direction of himself and his realm, requested that a sum should be granted to him by way of a subsidy, to be used for the defence of the realm and of the English Church ...; the same clergy conceded, from reverence to our said lord king, in the trust and firm hope that the said lord our king, as by his grace was and is, would in future be a gracious lord and protector to the clergy and to the church, the sum granted to him as a subsidy, a half tenth from those benefices accustomed to pay tenths, payable within the quindene[93] of Easter next *[21 April 1387]*. The same clergy also granted another half tenth from benefices as above, payable to the lord king on the next feast of All Saints *[1 November 1387]*, but on the following conditions: *[1]* that our lord king should protect and preserve the clergy and the English Church in all their liberties, just as his forefathers, the kings of England, preserved them in successive reigns; *[2]* the lords spiritual and temporal, elected, co-opted and deputed to the council of the said lord king and the government of the realm, as was mentioned earlier, shall remain in this office of government, and throughout the time fixed in this matter; *[3]* if the grant of the same last moiety of a tenth, for the defence of the realm and of the English Church, seems to them to be entirely necessary, and that the king and defence of the kingdom cannot be otherwise helped or provided for; *[4]* if this half tenth can be expended, by those elected lords, for the use of this necessary defence. Otherwise the grant of the last half tenth shall be null, and shall be considered as utterly nil, because the said clergy, as indicated, is so

93 Within fifteen days from Easter Day: 7 April 1387.

oppressed that they can by no means support either heavier burdens or any other subsidies. *[5]* Also, if our lord king concludes truces or peace with his adversary of France, before the term of the payment of the last moiety, granted conditionally, as specified, then the whole grant and its collection should cease.

1387

The loss of council records means that we know little about the commission's work. Its political consequences became evident during the summer and autumn.

85. Results of the commission

The commissioners' work was not ineffective,[94] but they were hampered to some extent by the king's refusal to co-operate.

(a) The king's response
WC, 184–6.

After the king had yielded to those bishops and lords all power to rule or govern, correct and punish everywhere inside and outside the kingdom, under the influence of the archbishop of York, the duke of Ireland, Michael de la Pole and others sympathetic to his cause, he became sick at heart and was sorry that he had done this. He alleged that he had been forced into it, and it was not his intention, he said, to delegate all his royal power to others and to keep almost nothing for himself. So he indignantly withdrew from them and went further afield, though during the summer he held councils in various places, namely one at Reading,[95] at which Michael de la Pole sought the reversal of the judgment of perpetual imprisonment to which he had been condemned; but, because the duke of Gloucester and the other lords were absent, his petition had no force. The second council was at Woodstock, and the third at Nottingham. These exhausted the lords more than they benefited them or the kingdom. After this the king traversed the parts of Cheshire and north Wales, and he went to Shrewsbury; and while both going and returning he constantly contracted into his service men of the area he was passing through. Also, he sent a certain serjeant-at-

94 For its administrative achievements, see Ormrod (1996): 303–21.

95 For Richard's itinerary, see Saul (1997): 471.

arms into Essex, Cambridgeshire, Norfolk and Suffolk. By virtue of his commission, he would make the stronger and more powerful men of those counties swear that, forsaking all other lords, they would stand by him *[Richard]* as their true king. They were given badges, namely gold and silver crowns, so that they would come to the lord king prepared and armed, whenever needed. This serjeant was finally caught near Cambridge and put in prison.

(b) The commission at work

Some evidence of the commission's activities can be gleaned from chancery and parliamentary records.

CCR 1385–9, 211, 308, 222, adapted.

(i) To the sheriff of Kent. Order to have proclamations made that all subjects and dwellers in the realm, of whatever rank or condition, who have, since the king's coronation, given or paid anything to his officers, or others, to have or to procure assignments or payments by tallies levied in the receipt of the exchequer, shall hasten to the great council in order to sue and declare in detail how much they paid or gave, to whom and how. It is the king's wish that all those willing, on his behalf or their own, to sue any persons of whatsoever rank or condition who have received any money or other profit for making or procuring such assignments, shall have a third of all that is recovered. By order of the Council.

The same to all sheriffs throughout England; the writ addressed to the sheriffs of London directed proclamation to be made within the city and suburbs; that to the sheriff of Bristol within the town and suburbs. 23 February 1387.

(ii) To the collectors of customs and subsidies in the port of London. Writ of *supersedeas*[96] until further order, for particular reasons concerning the king and council in respect of payments of those customs and subsidies to any persons of whatsoever rank or condition, by virtue of any commandments of the king, or assignments of the treasurer previously addressed to them by tallies or otherwise. By order of the Council.

The same to the collectors of the following ports, Kingston upon Hull, Boston, Great Yarmouth, *[King's]* Lynn, Ipswich.

26 February 1387.

96 An order which countermanded a previous instruction.

As soon as the commission was established, the three religious houses which had been named as the beneficiaries of Edward III's will petitioned once more to have their rights restored. The petition which provoked this summons (TNA SC 8/165/8246) was presented by the dean and canons of St Stephens, who were uniquely placed to act quickly, and makes it clear that the property involved was the Leybourne inheritance. Burley had obtained this through dubious legal methods by December 1385. See **4a–b, 28** for earlier instalments of this story.

(iii) To Simon Burley, the king's under-chamberlain. Strict order, on petition of the dean and canons of the king's free chapel *[St Stephen's]* Westminster, postponing all excuses, to appear in person before the king and council at Westminster within three weeks after Easter *[28 April]*, to show cause why he should not restore the manors, income, lands etc., of which he has deprived the petitioners, with damages and costs. They have shown that the late king acquired in demesne and in reversion various manors, lands and advowsons, and gave them to John, king of Castile and duke of Lancaster, and others, for the purpose that they should use them as they were commanded by that king; that gift was adjudged to be lawful and affirmed in the parliament held at Gloucester ... but contrary to that judgment, Simon has unlawfully evicted them from all the property, to the great cost to the king and his heirs, especially as payment of a great annual sum they received from the exchequer should entirely cease *[to be paid]* once they were peaceably endowed with the properties.[97]

20 March 1387.

86. Arundel's successful naval expedition, March 1387

One result of the commission's existence was a more vigorous prosecution of the war. In spring 1387, the earl of Arundel led a naval expedition which was widely reported in the chronicles; it seems likely that a newsletter (the medieval equivalent of a press release) was circulated giving details of Arundel's triumph, since there are striking similarities in the accounts, but interesting differences too, such as the precise nature of his opponents and the numbers of their ships. Arundel's generosity guaranteed his popularity.

---

97 Cash annuities from the exchequer in (small) compensation for their lost lands were paid to the houses concerned.

(a) According to *Westminster*

The wine fleet which sailed from La Rochelle had previously assembled for the invasion of England. See Palmer (1972): 88–92.

WC, 180–4.

Those newly appointed to the council who had undertaken the whole burden of government endeavoured by their good rule to achieve success and honour on many fronts, to the advantage of the king and kingdom. They commissioned a fleet and appointed Richard, earl of Arundel, as commander ... *[who reached the coast on 12 March and put to sea on 23 March]*. The very next day there came the French and Flemish fleet, laden with wine of La Rochelle, and immediately our men rushed at them with a vicious assault. Battle was joined, a long and hard-fought contest between our men and the enemy, but finally, with God's help, our men were victorious and captured fifty ships, great and small, which the earl sent under safe-conduct to the port of Orwell. During the battle another part of the fleet got away, but the earl pursued it and manfully captured some of those ships, sank six and burned five. He went to Sluys where he anchored his forces in the channel used by cogs,[98] and so arrested all the ships coming to that port while he lay there. In this way he captured three carracks laden with various merchandise, two small Norman barges, a goodly Spanish vessel and some Scottish boats laden with wool. Meanwhile, as the earl was anchored there, some of his men landed and burnt mills and villages, devastated the surrounding countryside and carried off captured booty and took it to their ships. The earl would have accomplished more while he was there but the water of that area was so bitter and unhealthy that they were all worn out by violent coughing and suffered other illnesses, so if he had stayed there any longer he would certainly have in the end lost many of his men. So he weighed anchor and set sail, and on 14 April safely reached the port of Orwell with his men and all their booty. The total of the captured ships was sixty-eight, plus carracks, barges and other little boats. These carried more than 8,000 barrels of wine from La Rochelle, which immediately afterwards was distributed across almost all of England and sold for 4d. a gallon.[99]

98 A type of boat broad in the beam, with a rounded prow and stern.
99 This was about half the usual rate, or even a little less; Thorold Rogers (1866): 550.

(b) According to Knighton

KC, 388–90.

Richard earl of Arundel, the admiral,[100] along with the earl of Devon and the – then young – earl of Nottingham,[101] heard, about the feast of the Annunciation of the Blessed Virgin Mary *[25 March]*, that the fleets of France and Flanders were leaving La Rochelle laden with wine. He went out to meet them with his hastily assembled fleet, and by spirited fighting he put them to flight and captured fifty-six ships carrying wine. After he had sent those ships in custody to England, he himself with his comrades chased the enemy and again fought fiercely with them; and when he had overcome them he captured seventy wine-ships. The total of captured ships was 126. In them it was estimated that there were between twelve and thirteen thousand containers[102] of wine. The Flemish commander was also captured in that conflict, along with many others.

Meanwhile the admiral returned to England in triumph with his comrades to revive themselves and their men, who had suffered heavy casualties. And after a very short time he went back to sea, strengthened by many new men, and directed his battle line of ships towards Brittany, to the town of Brest, which was being besieged by the duke of Brittany for the second time. The duke of Brittany had constructed a wooden fort on the seashore to impede food supplies coming in by sea, and two stone forts on the land side to prevent help coming by that route. So, when the earl of Arundel arrived there, he first captured the fort beside the water, broke it and dismantled it to the foundations, and captured one of the landward forts and razed it to the ground; and with the provisions which were in them he lavishly revictualled the town for the next two years – especially with salt. (The earl of Nottingham was not with him this time.) While returning to England the earl captured many ships. He even reached the port of Sluys in Flanders and there captured some Flemish and Scottish ships which had anchored there. Upon landing he despoiled, devastated and burned the area for ten leagues around.

100 There were normally two admirals, of the north and the west. Arundel was admiral of both parts at this time (about 10 Dec. 1386–18 May 1389). He had previously been admiral of the west, Dec. 1377–Sept. 1378; *HBC*, 139.

101 Arundel's son-in-law.

102 *Vasorum*, literally 'vessels'. Wine was traditionally carried and measured in tuns: barrels containing 252 gallons.

(c) Arundel's success, and domestic reactions

In contrast to popular approval of Arundel's success was the courtiers' sour reaction. Walsingham's comment is celebrated, but not original.

SAC I.810–14.

The captured boats, large and small, numbered 100, and – more important – they were carrying wine; the number of barrels was 19,000 or more. The wine and vessels were speedily despatched to Orwell and other ports of the realm, except those set aside as the king's portion, although citizens of Middleburg had approached the earl and begged him to allow them to buy that wine, and promptly to pay 100 shillings a barrel, because they were our friends and needed the wine. But the admiral answered that it seemed more just that those who had met the cost of his naval expedition, namely the commons of England, should enjoy the wine, than that others should carry it away for profit. 'However,' he said, 'because you are friends and have come a long way, we will give you twenty barrels, so that you are not seen to return completely empty-handed'. Indeed the earl was so generous, giving to several of his allies, that it is believed that he kept not one barrel for himself. So praise of the earl grew in strength among the common people because, setting aside what he could have gained by selling the captured wine to foreigners, he placed public good above private advantage, so that the common people especially realised, as a result, that what they had paid for his expedition was not entirely lost. *[His actions at Brest also won approval.]*

But some of the king's friends hated such honesty: the duke of Ireland, the earl of Suffolk and Simon Burley, along with Richard Sturry. They belittled the earl's deeds to the king, saying that he had accomplished nothing out of the ordinary except that he had attacked merchants whose good will would have been more beneficial to his country than the implacable hatred which he had aroused. And certainly many of these were knights of Venus rather than of Mars, more active in bed than in battle, quicker with the tongue than with the lance, alert for talking, but asleep for doing martial deeds.[103] ... It was at their instigation that

103 This famous criticism of the character of Richard's court draws on a long history of complaint whose origin was probably in the letters of Peter of Blois (c.1135–c.1204). Later generations of preachers and poets made 'Carpet-knights' and 'Liouns in halle, and hares in the feld' a favourite theme, Owst (1966): 331 and nn. Walsingham later criticised Henry IV's knights for being more like Dionysis (drunk) than Mars (warlike), more like Laverna (greedy) than Pallas (wise), *SAC* II.383. He enjoyed showing off his classical knowledge.

the king took so much against those who had fought on this expedition that when the earl of Nottingham came to him – who was the marshal and was always a companion of the king, and a contemporary – hoping to receive warm thanks from the king, the king was unsmiling and completely dismissive.

87. Robert de Vere causes offence by his divorce and remarriage

By divorcing Richard's cousin and marrying one of the queen's Bohemian ladies, de Vere caused a rift in the royal family.

(a) According to Westminster
WC, 188–90.

That fellow Robert de Vere, duke of Ireland, had married the daughter of Ingelram de Coucy[104] and the lady Isabel, daughter of King Edward III. Having taken a great dislike to her, he sent John Ripon, a cleric, to the Roman court to get a divorce. He worked so hard at this that he brought back a sentence of divorce obtained by false witnesses assembled for that purpose. This behaviour greatly displeased the dukes of Lancaster, York and Gloucester, the lady's uncles. After she was finally repudiated, that same Robert de Vere, duke of Ireland, wickedly united in matrimony with a certain Bohemian woman of the queen's chamber called Lancercrona,[105] though the queen always strongly disapproved.

(b) According to Walsingham
SAC, I.822.

At this time Robert de Vere, puffed up by all the honours which the king loaded upon him, promptly repudiated his young and beautiful wife, the daughter of Isabel, daughter of the illustrious King Edward, and married another who had come from Bohemia with Queen Anne. She was said to be a saddler's daughter – certainly not noble – and ugly too. This was a great cause of scandal. Her name was commonly rendered as 'Lancercrona'.

104 A French refugee, created earl of Bedford, May 1366, who renounced his allegiance and title 26 Aug. 1377.

105 A woman of mystery, though possibly a German of noble birth.

88. Peace between Gaunt and the Castilian king: the first Treaty of Trancoso, 12 June 1387

While politics in England were becoming more aggressive, Gaunt was preparing to make peace in Spain, where his campaign against the king of Castile in 1386 had proved inconclusive. Military stalemate and the cost of the war to Castile led to a compromise settlement. On 10 June 1387, Gaunt issued instructions to his ambassadors, and the resulting treaty, concluded at Trancoso, Portugal, is dated two days later, suggesting that negotiations had already been proceeding for some time. A second version was concluded on, or soon after, 29 June; a third version probably dates from July 1387. Although it was not until 1388 that a definitive treaty between Lancaster and the king of Castile was ratified, the main points of their agreement appear in this first accord.

The Treaty of Bayonne (1388) with preliminary Treaties of Trancoso (1387), ed. John Palmer and Brian Powell (Exeter Hispanic Texts, XLVII, 1988), 7–15.

[The agreement begins with an elaborate preamble setting out the names and titles of the protagonists.]

[1.] First: each of the two men aforesaid, both the king of Castile, Leon and Portugal,[106] and the duke of Lancaster, will swear on the Holy Gospels, touching them with their hands, that they will faithfully strive, setting aside all fraud and guile, for the unity of Holy Mother Church,[107] so that there may be one shepherd and one flock,[108] by giving the task to a general council or by other suitable ways through which the church may be restored to unity.

[2.] Each of them will faithfully labour for peace or for a long truce between the king of France and Don Juan, king of Castile, on the one side, and the king of England on the other, proceeding in every way allowed to them which they honourably can.

[3.] Each of them, both the king of Castile, and the duke of Lancaster and Lady Constance his wife, shall swear on the Holy Gospels, touching them with their hands, that they will promote and faithfully work towards – without any fraud and guile – a marriage soon to be contracted in legal form between the prince Don Enrique, the first-born son and heir of the king of Castile, on one side, and the noble Lady Catherine, daughter of the duke of Lancaster and Lady Constance

106 King Juan is described by all three titles every time he is named in the original treaty.

107 To heal the schism.

108 A reference to St John's Gospel, 10:16.

his wife, on the other; and that this marriage shall be solemnised in the sight of the Church within the two months immediately following, reckoned from the time when Lady Catherine is handed over to the custody of the king of Castile.

[4.] The king of Castile shall make a wedding gift to his son Don Henrique and Lady Catherine, to sustain the obligations of this marriage, of the places *[five towns were named]* which shall all be held and governed by the prince or in his name. Moreover, after Lady Catherine is handed over to the king, she shall be maintained in seemly and secure conditions at the king's expense by those deputed by the lord king or by the duke of Lancaster, most of whom the duke himself will choose, until the time when the marriage shall be physically consummated.[109] If by chance it happens, which God forbid, that the prince should die before then, leaving Lady Catherine a widow, she shall hold and govern those said lands and territories under the lordship and sovereignty of the king of Castile, and Lady Catherine shall be maintained by their rents for her whole life. After her death, those lands and territories ... shall freely revert to the king of Castile and his crown. This gift shall be made within the two months from the time when Lady Catherine is handed over into the power of the king of Castile.

[5.] Within those two months, the king will cause Lady Catherine to receive solemn oaths *[acknowledging her status]* of the *Cortes* to be solemnly held, according to custom, so that after the king's death, when the prince is received and recognised as king, Lady Catherine shall be received and recognised as queen[110] equally as the wife of the Prince Enrique then reigning, and for the time of his life and reign.

[6.] The king of Castile, either in person or though his ministers, shall pay the lord duke and his duchess, or to another or others at their command, 600,000 francs of the currency now *[used]* in the kingdom of France, of good gold and true weight, of which 64 *[francs]* shall make a mark of gold, or he shall pay their weight or value in gold, in this manner: 200,000 eight days from the time when Lady Catherine ... has been really and truly handed over to Juan, king of Castile, or to another at his command, in a secure place; also another 200,000 francs thirteen months after the handover of Lady Catherine; also another 200,000

---

109 Catherine was born in 1372 and Enrique in 1378.

110 This became important when Enrique died in 1406, leaving Catherine joint regent for their son Juan II (born 1405); see A. Goodman, 'Katherine [Catalina] of Lancaster' in *ODNB*.

francs one year after the said 13 months. So that the whole payment of those 600,000 francs shall be made within 2 years and 39 days; the time to commence at the moment Lady Catherine is handed over into the keeping of the king of Castile, as stated above.

[7.] The king will pay, or cause to be paid, to the duke of Lancaster and Lady Constance his wife, 40,000 marks annually of currency now [used] in France, of good and legal weight, at the rate of 64 marks to the mark of gold, or shall pay their weight or value in gold, while both, namely the duke of Lancaster and Lady Constance his wife, shall live ....

[Most of the remaining seventeen clauses elaborate on these. An exception is:]

[9.] King Juan of Castle will help the king of France against the king of England by sea with the number of galleys and ships as contained in the treaties and alliances concluded between the kings of Castile and France; but he will not help the king of France against the king of England by sea with more than the number of galleys and ships which are contained in those treaties and alliances.

89. The succession, 1387

This is the only comment on the succession to the throne that was certainly written during the reign. It follows a list of Gaunt's children and their spouses. *WC*, 192–4.

It must also be noticed that the lord Lionel,[111] second son of King Edward III in order of birth, took as his wife the heiress of the county of Ulster and lordship of Clare, and by her had one daughter who was married to the earl of March.[112] She bore the earl two sons; the elder of them[113] married the daughter of the earl of Kent, [half] brother[114] of the present king. To one of these brothers, by hereditary right, the kingdom of the England would descend if – which God forbid – the king were to die without children.

111 Lionel of Antwerp, born 1338, married Elizabeth de Burgh, daughter of the earl of Ulster.

112 Edmund Mortimer, earl of March and (in right of his wife Philippa, daughter of Lionel and Elizabeth) earl of Ulster; died 1381.

113 Roger Mortimer, born 1374, died 20 July 1398. His heir, Edmund, was born in 1391.

114 Thomas Holand, a son of Princess Joan's first marriage, born c. 1350, styled earl of Kent from 5 June 1380; died 1397; see **170**.

90. The councils of Shrewsbury and Nottingham

During the summer the king's clique of advisers, whose names Knighton constantly repeated, egged him on to take revenge on the architects of his humiliation in the previous parliament. The king's critics identified five court-iers whom they especially blamed for the evils of government, so we must try to discover what made each so obnoxious. This exercise is particularly valuable since three of the accused escaped into exile and were never brought to trial. Despised by chroniclers because of his background in 'trade', Michael de la Pole's promotion as earl of Suffolk [70a–b] was perceived as unjustified. His case is the easiest to explain because he had been brought to book once before [82b]. He was back at court, though not in office [78], because the punish-ment after his impeachment had been very lenient. His enemies evidently felt that he had not suffered enough.

Robert de Vere, by contrast, was the ninth earl of Oxford. He could with justice be called the king's favourite and, as has been rightly observed, 'A favourite has no friends!'[115] This is especially true of de Vere, who seems not to have attempted to build up a supporting faction, but to have relied solely upon the king's goodwill; his influence over Richard was notorious, and he was blamed for Richard's bad relations with his uncles [49]. Though of aristocratic lineage, de Vere was insignificant as earls went, and his insulting behaviour to his first wife, who was a member of the royal family [87a–b], and his ridiculous over-promotion [70a, 74b, 80, 82] and influence [78, 81, 92a] combined to make him unpopular, and not only at court [95b].

The Cornishman Sir Robert Tresilian, chief justice of king's bench, was notable for his success as a lawyer, his harshness as a judge[116] and his corruption in manipulating the law for financial gain. Already in 1384–5 he was something of a 'court creep' and retained for life by the king, but it was the belief that he was responsible for the questions to the judges which sealed his fate [90].

The case against Sir Nicholas Brembre, London merchant and former lord mayor, was one which the Appellants found most difficult to make [108], yet more precise charges were laid against him than against his co-accused [107b, nos. 12, 26]. Brembre was a *nouveau riche* whose rise had caused wide resent-ment. A member of the Grocers' Company, he was a court favourite from the start of the reign, because in summer 1377 the incumbent mayor was removed on royal orders and replaced by Brembre, who then held office until October 1378.[117] Friction between him and Thomas of Woodstock dates from this time [20]. Brembre was knighted during the Peasants' Revolt [34c], a promo-tion perhaps engineered by Joan of Kent, and this advancement evidently went to his head and gave him social ambition. The four Londoners knighted in 1381 were given landed property to support their new status, which surely

115 Thomas Gray, 'On a favourite cat, drowned in a tub of gold fishes' (1748).
116 Dobson (1983): 276, 312, 314, 373, 378.
117 October 13 was mayoral election-day, Bird (1949): 143.

rankled with Gloucester. During the stormy 1380s, Brembre was mayor in three successive years (1383–5), and made enemies in the city [**61, 63–6**]. He seems to have become isolated from many of his fellow Londoners and more closely associated with court outlook and culture, and after Radcot Bridge he failed to hold London for the king [**99**]. Dazzled by the court, and perhaps dreaming of a dukedom [**105, 108**], Brembre paid the price for being seen as a royal favourite, despite his active service as mayor and importance in the history of his guild.[118] At the start of the 'merciless' parliament, Brembre was the only accused in custody, having been hustled off to Gloucester's prison (*in carcerem de Gloucestre*),[119] and since he and Gloucester were old adversaries, this probably means that Gloucester had charge of him.

The role of Alexander Neville, archbishop of York, in political life is not entirely clear, but he certainly had a talent for making enemies. Aristocratic, well-educated, young, tenacious and recklessly ambitious, he was a surprise choice as archbishop of York (1373–4), probably owing his promotion to family influence and his own residence at the papal curia. Lacking any experience in either church or crown government, which might have taught him caution or moderation, Neville antagonised his subjects in York diocese and beyond [**22**]. The anonymous warning about him [**73**] was probably posted at the 1385 parliament. Neville had made powerful enemies among men who were not only canons of York and Beverley minsters, but also senior clerks in the royal chancery. His dispute with the canons of Beverley was a cause célèbre in which Richard took Neville's side.[120]

KC, 392–4.

[After 20 August] the king came to Shrewsbury, and on his orders certain judges of the realm gathered there. They were questioned by those seducers of the king, namely Alexander, archbishop of York, Robert de Vere, duke of Ireland, Michael de la Pole, Robert Tresilian and their clique, about whether it was compatible with the law of the land for the king to obstruct and resist the ordinances concerning the king and kingdom enacted in the last parliament by due process and by the commons of the realm, with the king's assent, but, they alleged, under duress. They replied that the king could annul and change such ordinances at will, to improve them, because he was above the law. ... All the judges were then ordered to convene at Nottingham at the king's council which was soon to be held there. Then the king went into the northern areas, and finally returned in August having visited many places.

118 Nightingale (1995) *passim* offers a rehabilitation of Brembre, whose 'intelligence, energy and powers of leadership' were crucial in the founding of the Grocers' Company.

119 Favent, 14.

120 Leach (1896): 1–20.

After this the king returned from the north and came to Nottingham, and at Nottingham he held a council on the morrow of St Bartholomew's Day [*25 August*]. At that meeting were present five evil seducers of the king, viz Alexander, archbishop of York, Robert de Vere, duke of Ireland, Michael de la Pole, earl of Suffolk, Judge Robert Tresilian and Nicholas Brembre. All the judges of the realm were commanded to attend there, but William Skipwith who was prevented by illness was absent. The judges were then ordered to put their seals to the questions written below, so that then those oft-mentioned seducers could seize the chance to kill the duke of Gloucester and all the others who, in the last parliament, were appointed to govern the king and kingdom, and everyone in parliament who agreed with them in that matter. Some of the judges declined to affix their seals, but they were coerced. Judge Robert Bealknapp refused with great vehemence, but the duke of Ireland and the earl of Suffolk compelled him to do it, for they threatened him with death if he would not comply, and it seemed to him that he could not have evaded their clutches.

91. The questions to the judges

Revenge for the proceedings of the 'wonderful' parliament came in the form of ten questions put to the judges about the legality of those proceedings. These turned the king's critics from angry into desperate men.

(a) The Statute of Treason, 1352

The 1352 statute is essential for understanding the significance of the questions which were intended to circumvent it. While Edward III was campaigning abroad, his judges had been defining treason increasingly widely. The statute was intended to check this practice and to offer reassurance to the political community by defining treason precisely; only parliament could add to the list of treasonous behaviour. The statute had indeed been legally amended once before during the reign, when parliament declared it treasonous to restart the 'riots and rumours' which had occurred during the Peasants' Revolt.[121] The 1352 statute was extremely enduring, and was the act under which William Joyce was hanged in 1946.

SR I.319–20.

Whereas there have been various opinions before this time about what cases should be adjudged treason and what not, the king, at the request of the lords and commons, has had the following declaration made:

121 *SR*, II.20.

When a man plots or plans the death of our lord king, or our lady his wife, or their eldest son and heir, or if a man violates the king's wife or the king's eldest unmarried daughter, or the wife of the king's eldest son and heir; or if a man levies war against our lord king in his realm, or adheres to the king's enemies in his realm, giving them aid and comfort in the realm or elsewhere, and be provably attainted of this open deed by men of his rank; and if a man counterfeits the king's Great or Privy Seal, or his money; and if a man brings false money into this realm which counterfeits the money of England ... knowing it to be false, to trade or make payment to deceive our lord king or his people; and if a man slays the chancellor, treasurer or the king's justices of either bench, justices in eyre[122] or of assize,[123] and all other justices assigned to hear and determine, while going about their duties. All these cases described above ought to be adjudged treason; and in such cases the forfeiture of the escheats[124] belongs to the king, both the lands and tenements held of others, as of himself.

[Then follows a section on petty treason: murder of husband by wife, or master by servant.]

And because many other similar cases of treason may happen in time to arise, which man cannot imagine or declare at present, it is agreed that, if any other case, supposed to be treason, which is not identified [here], does come before any justices, the justice shall delay giving any judgment of treason, until the case is brought before the king in his parliament, and it is demonstrated and declared whether it ought to be considered treason, or other felony.

(b) The questions to the judges, Nottingham, August 1387[125]

The object of the questions was to evade the statute by having the king's critics branded as traitors, outside parliament, because summoning a parliament was something the king could not do during the commission's period of power. The judges' answers show how carefully and maliciously they sidestepped the 1352 statute, declaring the critics to be 'like traitors', and deserving of punishment 'as though they were traitors'. Whether or not the judges were correct in law is irrelevant, because their answers constituted a peculiarly nasty piece of casuistry, designed to pave the way for Richard's revenge on his critics.

---

122 The eyre was the most important and wide-ranging commission to itinerant justices.

123 The most usual kind of itinerant justice.

124 All the property and chattels of the convicted person.

125 It was this second occasion when the questions were put, and answered, that became the definitive event.

The questions were posed twice, almost certainly because one judge was not present the first time, since it was important that the opinions should have no procedural weakness.

The questions to the judges were among the most widely copied documents of the century, being found in *SR*, II.102–4, *RP*, III.233, *KC*, 394–8, *WC*, 196–202, *Eulogium*, 361–6, *VR*, 106–9, and, in abbreviated form, in Favent, 7. Latin words in italics show how the judges circumvented the provisions of the 1352 statute.

[1.] They were asked whether that new statute and ordinance and commission made and promulgated in the last parliament held at Westminster were derogatory to the regality and prerogative of the lord king. To which question they replied unanimously that they were derogatory, because they were promulgated contrary to the king's will.

[2.] They were also asked: How should those be punished who procured the aforesaid statute, ordinance and commission? They replied unanimously that they deserved to be punished with capital punishment, that is to say, death, unless the king wished to show them mercy.

[3.] They were asked: How should those be punished who incited the king to consent to the making of this kind of statute, ordinance and commission? They replied unanimously that unless the king showed them mercy, they deserved to be punished with capital punishment.

[4.] They were asked: What punishment do those men deserve who compelled or induced the king to consent to the making of that same statute, ordinance, and commission? They replied unanimously that they deserved to be punished as though they were traitors (*ut proditores*).

[5.] They were asked: How also are they to be punished who have hindered the king from exercising that which belongs to his regality and prerogative? They replied unanimously that they also should be punished as though they were traitors (*ut proditores*).

[6.] They were asked whether, after the business of the realm and the cause of the summons of parliament have been explained and declared in the assembled parliament, and certain articles have been specified by the king, upon which the lords and commons of the realm ought to proceed, but the lords and commons wish to proceed wholly upon other articles and not at all upon the king's articles – even though they have been enjoined by the king to the contrary – whether the king ought in this respect to have the control of parliament, and indeed to control proceedings, so that the king's articles ought to be proceeded with first,

or whether the lords and commons ought first to have a response from the king to their articles before proceeding further?

They replied unanimously that the king should have control of the matter, and thus successively, in respect of all other articles touching parliament until the end of parliament. And if anyone acted contrary to this kind of control by the king he is to be punished as if he were a traitor (*tanquam proditor*).

[7.] They were asked whether or not the king can dissolve parliament when he pleases, and command the lords and commons to depart. They replied unanimously that he can, and if anyone thereafter acts contrary to the king's will, as though he were in parliament, he is to be punished as a traitor (*tanquam proditor*).

[8.] They were asked whether or not the lords and commons can impeach in parliament officers and justices for their offences, without the king's will, inasmuch as the king can – whenever he pleases – remove any of his officers and justices and bring them to justice for their offences and punish them. They replied unanimously that they cannot; and if any one does to the contrary he is to be punished as a traitor (*ut proditor*).

[9.] They were asked: How is he to be punished who proposed in parliament that the statute should be sent for by which King Edward, son of King Edward [*Edward II*] the great-grandfather of the present king, had formerly been adjudged in parliament, by an inspection of which statute, the new statute,[126] ordinance and commission aforesaid was initiated in parliament? They replied unanimously that he who had moved this, as well as he who on pretext of such a motion had carried that statute into parliament, deserve to be punished as traitors and criminals (*ut proditores et criminosi*).[127]

[10.] They were asked whether or not the judgment rendered in the last parliament held at Westminster against the earl of Suffolk was erroneous and revocable. To which question they unanimously replied that if that judgment were now to be rendered, the justices and the serjeant[128] aforesaid would not wish to give it, because it seems to them that it is revocable as being erroneous in every respect.

126 The 1386 commission was established by statute, **83**.

127 Clementi (1971): 96–115, speculated that this was a lost statute of 1307–10; it evidently envisaged plural traitors.

128 John Lockton, identified from the questions recorded in the proceedings of the 'merciless' Parliament. A serjeant-at-law from 1383, he was appointed a judge of king's bench in Oct. 1387, but did not serve long enough to be paid.

In testimony of all of which the judges and the serjeant aforesaid
affixed their seals to their answers in the presence of the following
called as witnesses: Alexander, archbishop of York, Robert *[Wikeford]*,
archbishop of Dublin, John *[Fordham]*, bishop of Durham, Thomas
[Rushock], bishop of Chichester, John *[Swaffham]*, bishop of Bangor,
Robert, duke of Ireland, Michael, earl of Suffolk, John Ripon, clerk and
John Blake, esquire.

92. Rising political tension

We know more about Richard's actions that autumn than those of his critics;
see **93–4**.

(a) According to Walsingham

Alone of the major chroniclers Walsingham did not list the questions to the
judges, though he evidently heard a rumour about them and supplies details
of their aftermath.

SAC I.826–30.

The judges were called to decide whether such indictments would
be legal, and to apply their seals to them. This was done by Robert
Tresilian and John Blake, an apprentice at law whom Robert Tresilian
had brought to the king's court to effect this. With the desired indictments swiftly made against those lords and many others, nobles and
barons, those who had been called to this meeting were sent away.
The king and the duke of Ireland promptly despatched messengers to
muster those capable of supporting them against the lords, if necessary, in the day of battle. ... Meanwhile rumour of this move reached
the lords and filled them with great sorrow; they were alarmed at the
intensity of the king's hatred, since they were unaware of any wrong-
doing.

It was mainly in response to this that Thomas, duke of Gloucester, the
king's uncle, tried to lessen the king's hatred, and to direct his mind
towards peace and concord. In the presence of the bishop of London[129]
and many other nobles of the realm, he swore an oath on holy relics
that he had never plotted any injury to the king, but had intended and
accomplished everything, as far as he could, to contribute to the king's
honour, advantage and pleasure, except that he did not look kindly upon

129 Robert Braybrooke, a kinsman of Richard's mother.

the duke of Ireland, whom the king loved, nor was he ever going to, because this man had dishonoured not so much his own kinswoman as the king; for which he was firmly determined to punish him.

But when the bishop of London retailed these things to the king, as he had been ordered, and was somewhat minded to give some credence to the duke's oath, Michael de la Pole, who feared that an accord between the king and the duke would be to his disadvantage, made a speech against the duke which turned the king's mind against him. At once the bishop said to him, 'You should be quiet, Michael; you ought to keep your mouth shut in future'.

'Why are you saying this?', Michael asked.

'Because you were condemned in the last parliament, and it is only by the king's grace that you are alive'. At this the king became very angry, and ordered the bishop to leave, and to go back to his church. He left immediately and told the duke what he had seen and heard.

This roused rancour and indignation in the duke, and his allies; likewise, in the king and his worthless counsellors, inexorable hatred [grew] daily, because the duke of Ireland, Michael de la Pole, Robert Tresilian, Alexander Neville, archbishop of York, and many others increased, incited and strengthened anger against the duke. Seeing the way that things were going Gloucester secretly called together the earls of Arundel, Warwick and Derby,[130] who would be subjected to similar condemnation if they did not look out for themselves in good time; he unveiled his scheme, stressing the danger which equally threatened them all. At once they gathered their retinues, and determined to confront the king about these matters and the favour which he had shown to those who were not so much his servants as public traitors, and also about the peril to the realm which was imminent unless mature counsel came to its aid.

The king for his part, egged on by the traitors, wondered how to remove those men before they could strengthen themselves with armed force. First he sent the earl of Northumberland with many others to Reigate[131] castle, where the earl of Arundel was living, to arrest him; but observing the earl's angry mood, and his large crowd of attendant militia, Northumberland was afraid to carry out his order, and withdrew with the task undone. Several others were afterwards sent to capture him at night and bring him to the king's presence, or actually

130 Henry Bolingbroke, Gaunt's heir.
131 Surrey; one of the Arundel family castles.

kill him, if they possibly could. But a messenger from the duke of Gloucester arrived before they did, and urged him to ride all night so that by early morning he might reach Haringey wood.[132] By a great effort he traversed the thirty miles with his army and there found the duke of Gloucester and the earl of Warwick gathered with many people.

(b) Reported by the *Eulogium*

Eulogium, 363–6.

The king sent for the duke of Gloucester and the earls of Arundel and Warwick, setting ambushes in their paths to capture them. But, forewarned of these by friends, they gathered with a strong following in the wood of Haringey near London. The king, on the advice of one of the London burgesses, came to Westminster, hoping to attack them with Londoners' help. The archbishop of Canterbury begged the king to admit the lords to his presence without any harm, and to negotiate with them. When he had obtained the king's oath he went and conducted them into the presence of the king who was seated in the Great Hall. Their army was outside.

The king said, 'How dare you rebel and take up arms against the peace of my kingdom?' The duke of Gloucester replied, 'We are not rebels, nor do we arm ourselves against the peace of the kingdom but to protect your life against the enemies of ourselves and of the realm, for which cause any man may bear arms. We ask and insist that you should hold a parliament immediately after the Purification of the Blessed Virgin [2 February], and we place ourselves under the judgment of parliament; and that you should take into custody our enemies, your sycophants and cause them to be present there'.

'You shall have a parliament', said the king, 'but I shall not harm them, and I shall treat you as less than the lowest of your kitchen-boys'.

'You should treat me as no less than a king's son'; and kneeling he said, 'I am a king's son'.

The archbishop of Canterbury begged the king to admit the lords next day, in the same place, and to consent to reform, and this the king granted. But next day he changed his mind and went to the Tower. The next day, however, the lords came with their army into St John's Field and sent for the mayor of London, who conducted them into the Guildhall of the city, and they accepted the city's friendship. But

132 The area is now in part of north London, in the N8 postal district.

the king sent for them to come and talk with him in the Tower. They replied that it was not a safe place, but that they were prepared to talk to him outside the Tower. The king sent for the mayor and ordered him to arm the city.

'My lord, your lieges and faithful men and friends of the kingdom are not here', said the mayor. The king threw him out, and sent the duke of Ireland with his letters patent and his standard to bring the Cheshiremen and other westerners. And the lords, now joined by the earl of Derby, son of the duke of Lancaster, and the earl of Nottingham, the marshal, and their growing army, marched across to intercept the duke who was coming with the king's banner unfurled, near Oxford.

A certain prudent knight left the duke of Ireland's army to see who they were, and on returning said to the duke, 'Here are the constable and the marshal of England and the lord king's best subjects; what is your authority for this commission?'

The duke said to him, 'Don't you want to fight them?'

'By no means', replied the knight.

Then the duke urged his horse across the Thames, along with his confessor, a master in theology of the Franciscan order, and he fled. The Cheshire men, having cut their bowstrings, and with their bows broken, shamefully retreated. They beheaded the chief knight advising the duke of Ireland, took from them the king's banner, rolled it round and folded it up. The duke of Ireland hurried to the Isle of Sheppey and from there fled to Germany. Michael de la Pole likewise escaped. Alexander Neville, archbishop of York, also went overseas. And they never came back. The aforementioned five lords, namely the duke of Gloucester, Richard, earl of Arundel, Thomas,[133] earl of Warwick, Henry Bolingbroke, earl of Derby, and Thomas Mowbray, earl of Nottingham, in destroying those rebels and others who came with them to Radcote Bridge, captured and killed many – almost all of them – except for those who fled.

93. Unrest in London: an illegal fraternity

Nothing illustrates the anxiety of authorities at this time better than the fear of groups of any kind.

Riley, *Memorials of London*, 495–6, adapted (translated from London Letter-Book H).

133 Wrongly called Richard in the text.

On 17 August 1387 John Clerk, Henry Duntone, and John Hychene, arrested on the accusation of the overseers of the cordwainers[134] guild ... appeared before Nicholas Exton, the mayor, and the aldermen in the Guildhall of London. They were charged that, whereas it was enacted and proclaimed in London, on the king's authority, that no one should make congregations, alliances or covens, privately or openly, and especially that those belonging to the trades should not, without the mayor's permission, make alliances, confederacies or conspiracies;[135] yet these three men of the cordwainers' trade, together with other accomplices, on the Feast of the Assumption *[15 August]* last, at the Friars Preachers in the city, brought together a great congregation of men like themselves and there conspired together, to the common detriment, to the prejudice of that trade and in rebellion against those overseers; and there, because Richard Bonet, cordwainer, would not agree with them, they assaulted him, so that he narrowly escaped with his life, to the great disturbance of the king's peace, to the alarm of the neighbours there and against the oath by which they were bound not to make such congregations, unions or sects, to avoid the resulting dangers. When interrogated, the men could not deny the charge. They also confessed that a Friar Preacher, Brother William Barton, had agreed with their companions to petition the Court of Rome to have that fraternity confirmed by the pope; so that, under threat of excommunication, none should dare to interfere with the fraternity's well-being. For doing this he had received money which their companions collected, an action which seriously contributes to weakening the liberties of the city, and the power of its officers. The mayor and aldermen committed the accused to prison until they decided what to do with them.

94. Richard seeks papal excommunication of those challenging his authority, c. August 1388

Urban VI was himself a fugitive at this time. In January 1385 he had discovered a plot to depose him; one of the six cardinals behind the plot was Adam Easton, which made Urban distrust all Englishmen.[136] When the king of Naples, an ally of France, besieged Rome, the pope fled (July 1385); after stays in Genoa and Lucca, he returned to Rome only in September 1388. This letter

134 Shoemakers.

135 The proclamation against congregations, conventicles and assemblies was made in 1383.

136 *SAC* I.741–9; Harvey (1999): 39–40.

was addressed to an unknown official at the papal court; in florid diplomatic language it requests papal support, suggesting that the recipient would know best how to rephrase the king's request to make it acceptable to the pope, and hinting at the rewards to the addressee which would follow.

Edouard Perroy, *The Diplomatic Correspondence of Richard II* (Camden Society third series, vol. XLVIII, 1933), 52.

Dearest friend: since we firmly believe that you are always desirous and keen to hear good tidings about the situation and position of ourselves and of the queen our dearest consort, we want you to know that both we and our said consort are, by divine favour, enjoying the benefits of bodily health, and we eagerly wish to have tidings of your state of health. Therefore, trusting in your affection we beseech that you, through the ripening of your providence ... will place before the holiest father in Christ the lord high priest some of your anxiety, urgently seeking on our behalf apostolic letters through which each and every one who attempts, or who seeks to attempt, anything prejudicial against the right of our crown or regality and our liberty, or who presumes maliciously to defame our person by imputing, either publicly or secretly, anything sinister which could bring scandal upon our name or reputation, should by that fact damnably incur the sentence of major excommunication, so that by dread among the perpetrators of such things others will be deterred. The foregoing might be redacted into better form *[language]*, if it needs to be, by your greater knowledge of such things, and concerning our other business, the promotion of which we committed to your discretion, and also your own state,[137] you should revive our desires as quickly as you can. In return we will return to your belovedness abundant deeds of thanks. May your friendship ever flower in prosperity.

95. The appeals of treason

Richard's critics were forced onto the defensive by the judges' answers; declaring impeachment to be illegal forced them to find another method of bringing royal servants to book. Against a background of rumour and rising tension, Gloucester, Warwick and Arundel demanded a meeting of parliament and accused of treason Richard's five chief advisers; the form of accusation they used was the appeal. They actually made this appeal three times: on 14 November at Waltham Cross before emissaries from the king; on 17 November at Westminster in the king's presence; and again before the king on

137 An oblique reference to the recipient's reward.

27 December in the Tower. The accusers, who became known as the Appellants, did not have the benefit of the judges' expertise, which was at the king's disposal, but they had other lawyers who could advise them, both laymen – they would shortly appoint their own set of judges – and sympathetic learned clerks in the royal chancery.[138]

(a) The first appeal, 14 November 1387

WC, 206–12.

On 28 October the king sent the archbishop of York and Michael de la Pole, earl of Suffolk, to the mayor and citizens of London to ask if there was unity among the citizens of London, and whether or not they were prepared to stand by the king, if necessary. The response to this was that they were united and wished to obey their king in everything, as his majesty demanded and required, and to adhere to him against all others. When they heard this answer, they returned joyfully to the king. The king was exhilarated by this reply, and on 10 November he entered the city of London. The mayor and other citizens all together came respectfully to meet him, dressed in red and white. They rode before him in procession through the middle of the city as far as the Mews of Charing, where the king took off his shoes and he, and the archbishop of York, Robert de Vere, duke of Ireland, and Michael de la Pole, earl of Suffolk, all, like him barefoot, processed to the church of St Peter, Westminster. The abbot and convent of that monastery also came robed in solemn fashion to meet him at the royal gate, and led him over carpets laid from there to the church. Having made his devotions he returned to his palace in the usual fashion.

Next day the king sent for the duke of Gloucester and earl of Arundel to come to him, but they excused themselves, alleging that their mortal enemies were at his side, so that they did not dare to approach him. So, on 12 November, the king had it proclaimed in London that no citizen, on pain of forfeiting all his possessions, was to sell anything to the earl of Arundel, or assist him with any necessities. This order was widely unpopular because he was one of the most valiant nobles in all the land. Also Michael de la Pole, earl of Suffolk, wickedly and constantly advised the king to give priority to having the earl of Warwick killed, because, when the lords were ordered to come to the king, it was through his wicked persuasion that they refused to come, and were now preparing to resist him as though rebels (*tanquam rebelles*) ....

138 See Tout (1928): 432n.1; McHardy (2009): 77.

On the advice of the archbishop of York, Robert de Vere and Michael de la Pole, the king proposed to send his followers against those lords who already, he believed, were rising against him. But they were tipped off about this by their friends and at once flew to arms, that is: the duke of Gloucester in Essex, the earl of Arundel in Sussex, and the earl of Warwick who was then with his retinue in Middlesex; they gathered all together at Hornsey Park,[139] north of London, with all their armed retinues on 13 November. When this was widely known, there flocked to them from every side a huge crowd of gentry. Next day they left that place and retreated to Waltham Cross. The king was amazed at this sudden coalition of strong supporters so, after taking advice, on 14 November he sent to them the archbishop of Canterbury and the duke of York, also the bishops of Winchester and Ely, John Waltham, keeper of the privy seal, Sir John Cobham, a nobleman, and Richard Scrope and John Devereux, wise and shrewd knights, to discuss with those lords why they had risen with such a multitude. The lords' answer was that they saw clearly that the kingdom of England would shortly be destroyed by the traitors always at the king's side, unless a speedy remedy was applied. ... So they unflinchingly appealed of treason, Alexander, archbishop of York, Robert de Vere, duke of Ireland, Michael de la Pole, earl of Suffolk, Robert Tresilian, justice, and Nicholas Brembre, knight of London. They wished to prove against any opponent, sparing no one except the king, that these were the wickedest of traitors.

(b) Both sides seek support

KC, 406–12.

[Richard approached individual nobles.] It is said that Ralph, Lord Basset answered the king, 'My Lord, you know that I am, and always will be, your faithful liege man, and my body and chattels will be yours and lie within your jurisdiction, but if I have to take the field, you know that I would rather support wholeheartedly the party of truth and righteousness, and I do not intend to risk breaking my head for the duke of Ireland'.

It is also reported that the earl of Northumberland said to the king, 'Lord king, these lords in the field always were, and still are, faithful to you, and always intend to be, nor do they plan anything contrary to your status, advantage or honour, but they feel themselves much saddened by the very wicked plots and wrongful violence of some of

139 South of Finchley; now a district in the London borough of Haringey.

your people. And you should know, without any doubt, that your whole kingdom is troubled by them for this reason, and unspeakably shaken, and both greater and lesser, both lords and commons, and will risk themselves, with them, to the brink of death.'

[In response to the royal embargo on food sales to Arundel, he, Gloucester and Warwick addressed this letter, in French, to the Londoners, under the terms of the 1386 commission.]

To the mayor, sheriff, aldermen, citizens and all the good commons of the city of London: greetings. We wish you to know that we have been, are and always will be, obedient and loyal lieges of our most redoubtable lord king, and that you should not marvel at the reason for our assembling in this way. Although it was ordered by our lord king, in his last parliament, that certain lords, chosen there and sworn for God's honour and the good of king and kingdom to have due governance of his council and realm and beyond, for one entire year, this governance was and is greatly impeded (*desturbez*) by Alexander, archbishop of York, Robert Vere, duke of Ireland, Michael de la Pole, earl of Suffolk, Robert Tresilian, false justice, Nicholas Brembre, false knight of London, all false and traitors, each and every one of them traitors to the king and realm, who falsely and traitorously have alienated the king, and by their crafty advice have led the lord king's honourable person into many places far from his council, to the damage of himself and his realm, and have falsely advised him to do many things in contravention of his oath, to the disinheritance and dismemberment of his crown, to the point of losing his overseas inheritance, to the great shame and destruction of the whole realm, and have falsely created divers dissensions between our lord king and the lords of his council so that some of them were in fear and peril of their lives, as we have partly shown to our redoubtable lord king through the very reverend father in God the archbishop of Canterbury, the duke of York, the bishops of Winchester and Ely, and various other great lords of the land; and, God willing, we will also show the whole realm. It is to redress these wrongs and to prevent them in future, and duly punish those traitors as the law permits, that we are assembled.

We require and charge you, by virtue of your allegiance, that you have a proclamation made throughout the city that we intend nothing save the honour, profit and salvation of the king and realm and all his loyal lieges, and that you should aid and comfort us as much as you both should and can, not favouring nor aiding those traitors, or any of them, as you wish to honour God, king and realm, and the salvation of your city. Do not cease from this as you wish to escape the peril which would otherwise befall in the future, and certify us fully of your intention in this matter on Friday [15 November].

(c) Another account of events of November 1387

Favent, *Wonderful Parliament*, 9–10.

Meanwhile, those three lords [*appellant*], namely the duke and two earls, assembled their forces that week (*septimana*), which was 14 November[140] at Waltham Cross in Hertfordshire, and they sent for the other commissioners who were with the king in Westminster palace. There they appealed in writing those five false lords, namely the archbishop of York, the duke of Ireland, the earl of Suffolk, Robert Tresilian and Nicholas Brembre, of the crime of treason, and offered to prosecute the appeal and to prove that this indictment was legal by pledging their goods, and with competent guarantors; and they caused all the other commissioners to be associated as partners in that appeal; then they commanded them to refer these matters to the king. When this deed reached the king's ears he sent to them, asking them to send their plan and desire, and they replied, 'It is in the public interest that certain traitors gathered around you ought to be arraigned and punished, for it is better that certain men should die for the people than that the whole nation should perish'.[141] They also asked that they should come and go in complete safety to confer. Then, when the king knew what they wanted, he replied by ordering them to come to him. When they arrived at Westminster, and the king was in the great hall sitting in state in the midst of his commissioners, those three lords appellant entered the hall with a great crowd of gentlemen, and on bended knee they saluted the king, bowing three times. Again the case was made, in the way and form as was previously done at Waltham Cross, about the crime of treason for which they appealed the said archbishop, duke, earl, Tresilian and Brembre, who at that time were lying low in obscure corners in the palace and in hidey-holes, as Adam and Eve hid from God in the beginning; then they absconded, having no wish to be caught. The king accepted that the appeal should be proved and prosecuted, announcing to them a day in the forenamed future parliament, on the

---

140 A Tuesday. Cf. Galloway, translating *septimana* as 'Sunday', making the date 17 November, but this is unlikely.

141 Alluding to John 11:50: 'better that one man should die for the people, than that the whole nation should be destroyed'.

morrow of the Purification of the Blessed Virgin Mary *[3 Feb. 1388]*. Meanwhile the king took both parties, with their goods and men, into his special protection to ensure that nothing else should cause unrest until the coming parliament. This was publicly and continuously proclaimed throughout England. Consoled by this, they withdrew.

(d) The second appeal, 17 November 1387

WC, 212–14.

Meanwhile, it came to the lords' attention that Sir Thomas Trivet had advised the king to take the field and unfurl his banner against those rebel lords, advice which greatly displeased them. However, at the churchmen's persuasion, on 17 November they came with 300 horsemen to the king, who was seated on the throne in the Great Hall at Westminster. On entering the hall and seeing the king, those three – the duke of Gloucester, the earl of Arundel and the earl of Warwick – instantly prostrated themselves to the ground, and did so three times, before they approached him. Finally, on the king's order, they stood up and told him that he should not be surprised that they had arrived so late, nor that he should marvel at their coming with such a large escort, because – as they had learnt from others – their worst enemies remained constantly at his side, so it was no wonder that they were reluctant to approach him, because above all they were keen to preserve their lives as long as possible, saving always their allegiance. After some exchanges between them and the king, the lords asked the king to hear what Sir Richard Scrope would say on their behalf before a public audience. The king agreed.

Scrope said forcefully that the lords' disaffection had arisen chiefly because of the five persons named above who were always at the king's side, whom the lords had appealed of the treason committed by them against both king and kingdom, and they wanted to stand by that appeal, despite opposition. 'We therefore beg your highness that these persons should be kept in a safe place until the next parliament, and by no favour should they be spared the common law punishment for their misdeeds, if they are found guilty'. The king agreed to their petition and he took the matter into his own hands, and fixed the date of parliament as 3 February.

96. The growing crisis, from London records

(a) Proclamation made in the city by the king's command

This most unusual English entry, in a book[142] whose entries are overwhelmingly in Latin, or occasionally Anglo-Norman, indicates how seriously the authorities were promoting the king's cause at this very tense time.

Riley, *Memorials of London*, 500 (printed from London Letter-Book H).

[*Undated: 28 Nov. × 3 Dec.*] Oure Lord the kyng, that God save and loke,[143] comaundeth to alle his trewe liges in the cite of Londone, and the suburbe, of what condicion that ever thei ben, up[*on*] the peyne of here lives and forfaiture of here godes, that non be so hardy to speke, ne moven, ne publishe, ne prive ne appert, onithyng that might soune in evel or dishoneste of oure lige Lord the Kyng, ne of oure Ladi the Quene, or ony lordes that have bien dwelling withe the Kyng bi for this time, or of hem that dwellen aboute his persone nowe, or shul dwelle, in hindering of here state in any manere: ne that non of his trewe liges melle him of such matirs, but that oure Lord the Kyng, oure sovereyn juge, mowe ordenye thereof that him semeth best.

(b) The king orders investigation of disloyalty in London

Calendar of Letter-Book of the City of London: Letter-Book H, ed. Reginald R. Sharpe (London, 1907), 321, adapted.

To Nicholas Exton, the mayor: order to command the aldermen to take steps to safeguard the City on the king's behalf, and to make a return of the names of all disloyal persons they may find. Windsor Castle, 3 December 1387.

---

142 *City of London Letter-Book*. H. Riley printed this extract from the manuscript, and not from the printed *Calendar*.

143 Guard.

The Radcot Bridge campaign, 1387

The process by which the original three Appellants were joined by Henry Bolingbroke, Gaunt's heir, and Thomas Mowbray, earl of Nottingham, a favoured courtier, is mysterious; the Westminster Chronicle placed the alliance too early, while Knighton gave unlikely prominence to Bolingbroke.[144] It was only in mid-December, with de Vere already on the march from Cheshire, that the Appellant coalition was certainly complete. The five lords and their retinues had the strategic advantage over de Vere and his army, forcing him to approach London and the Thames crossing in the area of their choosing. 'The plan was brilliantly conceived and as brilliantly executed'.[145]

There are several accounts of this crucial but very confusing episode, but considering that there were six forces involved this is hardly surprising. A clerk of the bishop of Worcester knew the route by which de Vere and his army approached the river Thames; Walsingham described a preliminary skirmish at Burford; Westminster also knew of these first encounters; Knighton was ignorant of the earlier skirmishes, but knew about events at Radcot Bridge itself. The classic commentary on this episode is Myers (1927): 20–33; but see also Davies (1971): 547–8.

97. Two views of the crisis from the west midlands

When so much of our knowledge of this crisis comes from sources which are openly partisan, it is interesting to note these two accounts by writers with no obvious political affiliations. Local interest in this episode is explained by geography, for de Vere's route from Cheshire to Oxfordshire would have taken him through this area, and by the fact that the earl of Warwick was a major landowner and ecclesiastical patron here.

(a) By a monastic observer

This cartulary, a collection of charters and other written evidence of the possessions of Stoneleigh Abbey (Warks., Cistercian), also contains a short chronicle of notable events in Richard's reign, followed by a list of kings from William I.

The Stoneleigh Leger Book, ed. R. H. Hilton (Dugdale Society, 24, 1960), 95–6.

In 1387 Robert de Vere, earl of Oxford and duke of Ireland, came with a great army from Cheshire into Oxfordshire, in breach of the king's peace, shortly before Christmas. And Thomas of Woodstock, duke of Gloucester, Henry, earl of Derby, and Richard, earl of Arundel, Thomas, earl of Warwick, and John [*correctly Thomas*], earl of Nottingham,

---

144 *WC*, 208; *KC*, 420.
145 Myers (1927): 25.

marshal of England (John, duke of Lancaster, being then in the kingdom of Spain seeking that kingdom) with their followers intercepted him in the county of Oxford at a bridge called Radcot Bridge near Bampton, where the duke of Ireland abandoned his men and escaped alone through the water, and where Thomas Molyneux[146] was killed, and the rest surrendered to those said lords, and having shamefully despoiled their property and goods in the county of Chester they returned home. Afterwards in parliament held at London that year,[147] after the [feast of the] Purification of the Blessed Mary, which the duke of Ireland and Alexander, archbishop of York, and Michael de la Pole, earl of Suffolk, did not dare to attend, they were convicted of treason because of the treasons they had committed, and their goods were forfeit. They later died overseas.[148] The rest of their confederates, that is, Sir Simon Burley, knight, John Beauchamp of Holt and Robert Tresilian, chief justice of the king's bench, Nicholas Brembre, knight, and divers of their other accomplices, were captured and, for treason, were hung, drawn and beheaded. Also certain of the king's judges, namely Robert Bealknap, Roger Fulthorp, William Burgh and John Holt, along with Thomas [Rushook], bishop of Chichester,[149] who was a member of the order of Friars Preachers, were convicted of treason by the king and peers of the realm and sent into exile in Ireland.

(b) By a clerk of the bishop of Worcester

For four folios of this bishop's register the clerk interspersed copies of royal letters, such as summonses to parliament and mandates to collect taxation, with political comment. His account adds to our knowledge of the strategy of the campaign. Wakefield, bishop of Worcester 1375–95, was a career administrator and Edward III's last treasurer. Did he know what his clerk was entering into this formal record of his episcopate?

Richard G. Davies, 'Some notes from the register of Henry de Wakefield, bishop of Worcester, on the political crisis of 1386–1388', *EHR* 86 (1971), 547–58.

In 1387 and the 11th year of the reign of King Richard II, there arose an open scandal and grumbling about Alexander, archbishop of York,

---

146 A former retainer of Gaunt in Lancs., who went into rebellion against the Lancastrian administration. He then moved to Cheshire and allied himself with de Vere. Walker (1990): 118, 265–9.

147 The calendar year then began on 25 March; by contemporary reckoning, parliament began in February 1387.

148 This dates the account to after 1392, when de Vere and Neville both died; de la Pole died in 1389.

149 Richard's confessor.

Robert, duke of Ireland, and Michael, earl of Suffolk, who continually
stayed in the king's household, about Robert Tresilian, the king's chief
justice, and Nicholas Brembre, knights associated with them, who like
traitors badly ruled the king's person and his regality, and because they
brought the king under their rule and influence and gloried in their
treason, with their propensity for trickery and deceitful disposition they
incited the king to break divers statutes of a certain commission which
were written [in] this book in French, made during the last parliament
by the counsel and assent of themselves, and of all the lords and the
commons of the realm. Furthermore, they took the king to Shrewsbury
and there in a gathering called and assembled by them, they denounced
the lords bringing forward those statutes to be like traitors (*tanquam
traditores*) to king and kingdom to be seized, drawn and hanged because
of those pronouncements, to the subversion and near destruction of
the realm and the English Church, had not the grace of divine favour
intervened to provide a swift remedy in this matter. The result was
that serious discord arose between that most excellent prince our king
of England and that most noble man the lord Thomas of Woodstock,
son of the most excellent prince the lord E[dward] III lately king of
England, duke of Gloucester, uncle of that King Richard, those noble
men Henry, earl of Derby, son of the most noble man the Lord John,
duke of Lancaster, likewise son of the King E[dward], Richard, earl of
Arundel, Thomas, earl of Warwick, and T[homas], earl of Nottingham.
So that most noble man the lord T[homas], duke of Gloucester, and
those said noblemen, directing their attention lest worse should
happen to the kingdom and the English Church out of this treason
and discord, gathered together in force to capture these traitors and
to resist their malice with a great multitude of armed men and other
instruments of war. And on 19 December of that year at Hartlebury,[150]
Thomas Barwelle, then sheriff of Worcester, showed the lord bishop of
Worcester, on behalf of those lords, this letter, explaining the cause of
their gathering, to which they had each applied their great seals, and it
follows in French, word for word in this form. [*A 12–inch gap was left
here for the letter, which was never entered. It may have been the same as, or
very similar to, that recorded by Knighton: see* **95b**.]

Once this gathering of the lords had been announced like this throughout
the kingdom, Robert, duke of Ireland, withdrew from the king's household into the counties of Cheshire and Lancashire and gathered together
armed men to the number of 4,000 to make war on those same lords.

150 Hartlebury, Worcs., was a castle of the bishops of Worcester.

While travelling with this force from Chester towards Windsor to join the king, he came to Chipping Campden on 19 December and spent the night there. Meanwhile, the lord Thomas, duke of Gloucester, and those same nobles, on the next day, Friday *[20 December]*, assembled in the morning near Moreton-in-the-Marsh ready to capture Robert, duke of Ireland. When this intelligence had been relayed to him, he took up a defensive position between Blockley[151] and Bourton-on-the-Hill and warned his followers to prepare more urgently for combat against those lords. But Almighty God the giver of all goodness did not wish him to triumph in his treason and malice; the great majority of those whom he led deserted him and refused to fight. Seeing that everything was against him he fled, and his enemies followed him in flight to Radcote Bridge but he miraculously evaded the pursuers' grasp.

Also, on the following Friday on the Feast of St John the Evangelist, namely 27 December, the lord T*[homas]*, duke of Gloucester, and those nobles, with a multitude of armed men camped in the field commonly called St John's Field near London and in various wards (*custodiis*) energetically prepared for battle in order to discover more clearly who wanted to fight to defend and protect the traitors. This reached the ears of our lord king, who was in the Tower *[of London]*. He sent to them the most noble man, Lord Edmund de Langley, duke of York, the king's uncle, the venerable fathers in Christ the lord bishops William Winchester, Thomas Ely, the chancellor of England, and John Hereford, the treasurer, to negotiate and speak with them. They came to the king in the Tower and they all came, praise the living God. They ordered that a parliament be held for these and other serious and urgent matters concerning the state of the king and kingdom. And on Saturday 28 December the oft-mentioned lords at London seized and arrested the above-named Nicholas Brembre, to answer the charges in this parliament and to bring everything about by legal means (*iuri per omnia pariturum*). The same day Simon Burley, John Beauchamp of Holt, John Salisbury and James Berners, knights of the king's household, were arrested.

---

151 Blockley was site of an episcopal manor, much frequented by the bishop.

98. Four further accounts of the fighting

(a) Walsingham: a preliminary encounter

SAC I.836–42.

With the king's connivance, the duke of Ireland gathered a great rabble in Wales and Cheshire, whose leader was the constable of Chester, Thomas Molyneux, a rich and bold man, whose will was law in that whole region. But such great guile could not be concealed from the lords for long. Being warned about all this – and that the duke of Ireland was hurrying to London with this great mob so that, in conjunction with the Londoners, he would make from those two forces an almost invincible army – they immediately armed their followers …. They set out to intercept the duke of Ireland, but stealthily, and despatched their troops of horsemen to block all the roads by which he hoped to travel. The duke of Ireland was puffed up and conceited as he rode with the army he had assembled, because he believed that no one would dare to obstruct him. Suddenly glancing sideways, he saw the lords' army not far distant, and waiting for him in the middle of a valley.[152] When he saw it his courage failed. *[Walsingham then inserted a speech allegedly made by de Vere in which he proposed to flee, both for his own safety and to spare his men, with whom the lords had no quarrel.]*

Present then was Thomas Molyneux, who prepared himself for battle because not all the lords had arrived at that place, but only one, the son of the duke of Lancaster, Henry, earl of Derby. But when Molyneux had fought for a long time, and was exhausted and despairing, he entered the nearby river. But among many others Sir Thomas Mortimer[153] urged him to climb out, or without doubt he would pierce him with arrows in the river.

'If I climb out', said Thomas, 'will you spare my life?'

'I'm making no promises', said the knight, 'but you must either climb out or else soon be killed'.

To which the reply came, 'If that is so, permit me to climb out so that I can fight with you or one of your men so that I can die like a man'. But as he climbed out the knight grabbed him by the helmet and pulled it off his head, and at once drew his dagger and split his brain.

152 The valley of the river Windrush.

153 An illegitimate son of Roger Mortimer, second earl of March, he was Arundel's steward, Gillespie (1975): 161–73.

Meanwhile the fleeing duke of Ireland reached the river, but found the bridge broken which he wanted to cross, and when he came to another bridge he found archers blocking his crossing. So turning aside, he looked for a ford and drove his horse into the river; and, by becoming a swimmer on horseback, he soon reached the further bank. It was night, so the servants did not follow the fugitive commander, especially as they were in unfamiliar territory, but his horse, along with his helmet, gauntlets and breastplate came into the lords' possession, so it was thought for long afterwards that he had drowned. In addition, the leaders intercepted his wagon and pack-horses in which they found many things, especially the king's letters to him, in which were contained the order to hurry and come to him in London, with a large army, and that the king was prepared, and his heart was set on living and dying with him. Such evidence greatly enhanced the lords' belief in the king's inconstancy and fickleness.

(b) *Westminster:* probably from a follower of Arundel
WC, 218–24.

When the lords heard how the king was intent on threatening them, they proposed to dethrone him, both because he was not observing the agreement promised to them and also because, it seemed, he preferred to be governed by the falsest traitors than by his most faithful friends – the nobility and lords of the realm. The earl of Warwick opposed them and at once recalled them from this opinion. 'God forbid', he said, 'that I should see so glorious a prince, born of such distinguished pedigree and so noble a lineage – to whom I, with other lords of this kingdom, did personal homage and took a sacred oath at his coronation – now being deposed and overthrown. ... You should turn your mind from this plan of yours and strive manfully to resist that perfidious traitor, the duke of Ireland, who is coming from Cheshire with a strong and resolute force through the centre of England and trying to reach the king. ... First let us deny him the means of getting through, by so blocking the roads and bridges everywhere that he does not evade our clutches'.

These words pleased all the lords; they unanimously decided to do this, and to drop any other plans. So the troops of armed men were again reassembled along with those of the earl of Derby and the earl of Nottingham, and shortly after the beginning of December they took horse. Crossing Newmarket Heath, where a certain [*judicial*] session was being held, they seized Sir John Holt, justice, Serjeant Robert

Pynchebek[154] and Richard Skelton, serjeant-at-law. They kept those men with them for some time saying that, in the difficult business just begun, it would be useful to have those skilled men always at hand. Then they went through several other places to Northampton; in some of them they made proclamations that their whole wish was to stand by the king and all the faithful men of the realm, to the death, but to extirpate traitors from the land. ....

Those lords[155] were enthusiastic about their plans, and sent their spies skilfully to find out which route the duke of Ireland proposed to take. When he learnt of this he turned aside from them and went *via* a certain manor of the abbot of Evesham, near Stow *[-on-the-Wold]*. The weather was very overcast and foggy. The lords occupied all the countryside round about, namely Banbury, Brailes,[156] Chipping Norton, *[Chipping]* Camden, Blockley and Bourton 'under Cotswold'.[157] So on 20 December the duke was making his way with his Cheshiremen and Welshmen, numbering 5,000 soldiers, towards Witney, where in an open field the earl of Arundel and his men first encountered him. Seeing them, the duke urged his men to fight, drew them up in battle formation and raised the standards of the king and St George. Realising this, the earl of Arundel and the other lords who were present sent to their opponents saying that they supported the king as his liege men, nor did they at all wish fight them unless they intended to stand by the traitors to the king and kingdom, who had been legally appealed of certain treasons. In response the others said that they had by no means come to fight, 'but they should know that at the king's command and for the protection of the king's person we are riding with the duke of Ireland, but we do not wish in any way to offer support or give encouragement to traitors to the king and realm'. At once they gave the sign of peace by holding up their bows and other weapons. Then the lords ordered them to return home and to proceed no further with the duke if they wished to save their lives. But Sir Thomas Mortimer, despite this truce, rushed at a certain man called Molyneux, chief councillor of the said duke, and instantly killed him. But then the rest of the lords, with their armed

154 Perhaps a mistake for Thomas Pynchbeck, a serjeant-at-law 1383, appointed chief baron of the exchequer 24 April 1388, discharged 12 May 1389, Sainty (1993): 93; Baker (1984): 533. Skelton has not been identified.

155 *Prefati domini*: 'the aforesaid lords', the Monk's habitual description of the Appellants.

156 Lower and Upper Brailes, Warwickshire.

157 Either Bourton-on-the-Hill or Bourton-on-the-Water, both in Gloucestershire.

men, arrived at the spot; they had been further away, but now they arrayed themselves as though for mortal combat. So the duke, who was amazed at this sight, and reckoned that his men would be beaten, took to flight. He came to the bridge called Radcot Bridge, which he found broken; so he rode into the river Thames and swam across it, and disappeared from their sight. Some of his men were drowned in the current; many were trampled down by the duke's pursuers in the marshes beside the river's channel; but the rest abandoned their weapons and horses, and walked sadly home; so all the duke's equipment was brought to the lords. The duke of Ireland, after escaping the lords' clutches, reached the king dressed as a servant and, after some talk together, he hurried to Queenborough[158] castle, where he quickly found a ship and withdrew to foreign parts.

(c) Knighton: the fight at Radcot Bridge

'We can hardly doubt that we have here the account of a Leicester citizen serving with Derby, and eyewitness therefore of what took place at Radcot Bridge.'[159]

KC, 420–4.

Robert de Vere, duke of Ireland, with all his men, in number between four and five thousand warriors, came on the vigil of St Thomas the Apostle [*20 December*] into Oxfordshire, making his way towards Radcot Bridge, which is four leagues [*it is 18 miles*] from Chipping Norton. Had he crossed this bridge he would have been safe from all fear of all his enemies. But his plan was foiled, for the earl of Derby had placed guards at the end of the bridge, men-at-arms and archers who prevented the duke's crossing, and who ripped up the bridge's paving-stones in three places so that only one horse could cross at once; and for even greater security they fortified the bridge in three places with obstructions.

When the duke of Ireland was hurrying like this towards that bridge he espied Henry, earl of Derby, close by with a big crowd of followers. At once he halted and ordered the king's banner, which he had there all ready prepared, to be unfurled and raised aloft on a lance. With a keen countenance and almost joyful spirit he ordered the trumpets to sound and other musical instruments to play loudly, and with a cheerful voice

---

158 The Isle of Sheppey, Kent, whose name was changed to Queenborough in honour of Queen Philippa, in 1366.

159 Myers (1927): 25.

he urged his men to prepare for immediate engagement. Some of them, indeed, wanted to fight, but others declined, saying that they could not because their numbers were small compared with their opponents', nor did they dare to offend in a contest against so many lords and nobles of the whole kingdom, nor did they wish in any way whatsoever to put themselves in so much mortal peril for an unjust cause.

On hearing this, the duke of Ireland, constantly spurring on his horse, rode ahead of them all with hurrying steps, meaning to cross the bridge first, and his men to follow him. But when they reached the paving of the bridge and saw that it was broken and was defended by an armed force, he called, 'We have been tricked'. He wheeled around, jumped off the horse he had been riding, and mounted another courser,[160] hoping to flee from his adversaries along the bank of the river Thames.

And then there suddenly rushed upon him the duke of Gloucester with his exceedingly large troop of men, and the duke of Ireland was caught beside the water of the Thames on one side, and on the other by his enemies everywhere; and the earl of Derby was closing in to capture him. He took a life-or-death gamble: spurring on his horse, he threw away his gauntlets and sword and other equipment which otherwise would have burdened and slowed down his horse, and jumped into the river Thames, and by this marvellous daring he escaped from them. Thomas Moleyns wanted to follow him, [but] was pulled back by Sir Thomas Mortimer, by whom he was killed. ... It was reported that about 800 of the duke's followers were drowned in the marsh, namely men of Cheshire and Lancashire. There was also captured, it was said, one of the duke's horses laden with £4,000 in gold, and this they [the lords] retained for themselves for their followers' expenses. [The commanders took possession of de Vere's baggage train, while their men robbed and pillaged his followers.] So our said lords, sadly frustrated in capturing the duke of Ireland, Robert Vere, returned to Oxford, where they took counsel about what they should do. From there they went to St Albans, and stayed there for Christmas Eve and Day with their men.

(d) The victors' summary of the campaign
This was the 39th and last charge by the Appellants.
WC, 268.

The duke of Ireland, with a great force of men-at-arms and archers from those counties [of Lancashire and Cheshire, and Wales], rode across

160 A swift-running horse.

the realm until they came to a place called Radcot Bridge, which is near Cotswold, and accroaching to himself royal power, he ordered the king's banner to be displayed among his troops, contrary to the dignity of the king and his crown. At this time the duke of Ireland and his force were by God's grace frustrated in their evil plan.

99. Brembre tries to hold London for the king

Favent, *Wonderful Parliament*, 11–12.

When [*news of*] this action reached the ears of the other traitors lying low with the king at Westminster, they fled in great fear with the king – in the silence of night, along the river Thames – into the Tower of London, for greater safety. Nevertheless, Nicholas Brembre, with a fierce and firm demeanour, ordered constant watches to be kept, in the king's name, to exclude those five vigorous appellants from all the gates of the city of London by armed force. But those undaunted appellants hurried briskly with their armies towards London to speak with the king. So when they heard how, on Nicholas Brembre's instruction, the city gates were guarded by continual watches in order to repel them, they wondered whether the city would resist their arrival, and their resolution wavered. So in the field behind Clerkenwell, within the city limits, on 27 December of that year, each of the lords appellant with his army, preceded by a sweet parley of instruments, formally displayed himself in warlike mode; they did not wish through sudden or rash daring to enter the city by a chance error, or to refrain out of paralysing fear, but with a sober mind, so that by wisdom and with careful deliberation they should achieve everything all in good time. So when the mayor and citizens of the city, with welcoming speech and smiling countenance, had helped and comforted them, and pleased them continually, saying that they would be able to use everything at their disposal which was reasonable and fair within that city, the duke of Gloucester said, 'Now I know truly that no one can prevent tale-bearers from telling falsehoods'. Soon by mutual consent, because of the need for greater security, each lord with his army was accommodated separately before the different gates, as night fell.

100. After the battle

After his army's defeat, Richard was totally defenceless, for the Londoners proved disloyal.

SAC I.842–8.

It happened at that time that a certain messenger of the French king, 'Lustratus' by name, was captured. He was carrying letters in which the king of France gave safe-conduct to the king of England, the duke of Ireland and some others, up to a certain number, to go to Boulogne. There the French king and his assembled army would await his arrival, and greet him with great pomp, and would receive from him Calais and all the fortifications which the king of England possessed in those parts. For all these the king of France would pay [*blank in ms.*]. Also, the king of England would perform liege homage to the king of France in respect of Gascony. But the lords kept quiet about this news and hurried towards London where the king was going to celebrate Christmas, not at Westminster, but in the Tower, because he thought this would be a place of safety if the situation became threatening. An army was gathering of about 40,000 doughty warriors who came forward eagerly in the hope of plundering the Londoners. They reached London the day after Christmas and showed themselves in warlike battle array in fields where they could be seen from the Tower.

So ended this year of plenty, fruitfulness and of moderate healthiness. England was turbulent save that the wine captured by the earl of Arundel made glad the heart of many.[161] Spain was happy at the withdrawal of the duke [*of Lancaster*] on selling the kingdom, and at the pitiful ruin of his men.[162] France was gloomy and despondent because not only was wine lost but vessels, along with men. Flanders was melancholy because of the lost wine and goods in common with the French.

The king spent Christmas in the Tower ... and near there the lords gathered along with their men; they were lodging in the suburbs, to avoid the townsmen's tricks. The Londoners were then in great fear, weighing up various dangers, namely the king's wrath if they opened up to the lords, but if they excluded them, the indignation of the unruly mob which had come with them and was ready to break down the walls or gates of the city, if they should be in the least bit provoked. There

---

161 Surely a deliberate echo of 'wine which makes glad the heart of man', Psalm 104:15.
162 A reference to the treaty of Trancoso, **88**.

THE REIGN OF RICHARD II, 1377–97

remained also another grave peril, because unless the city fathers let the lords in, the commons and poor of the city, who favoured sedition rather than peace, would be prepared to admit the lords themselves, along with their followers, and to seize whatever there was of value in the houses of the rich. After deliberation the mayor of London finally went out and promised the lords lodgings within the town and all necessities, in good faith, if they wished to accept them, and he distributed wine and ale, and bread and cheese to everyone in the army. This was afterwards of no small benefit to the town.

The king meanwhile, hearing and understanding all this, pretended both that he made light of the assembled multitude and did not fear the lords, saying to the archbishop of Canterbury and to others who were going back and forth as peacemakers, 'Let them remain here with their rabble until they have consumed all their supplies, and then at last they will go back to their homes empty and destitute, and then I will speak with them, giving individual judgments'.

When they heard this, the lords were very indignant and swore that they would never retreat until they had obtained a face-to-face discussion with him, and they quickly sent word to those guarding the river Thames in case the king slipped out of their clutches and afterwards mocked them. When the king saw that he was surrounded on all sides he began to talk to the messengers and told them to report to the lords that he was willing to negotiate with them. They insisted that he should come the next day to Westminster where they wanted to lay their demands before him. 'I don't want to negotiate with them at Westminster', said the king, 'but here in the Tower'.

The lords sent back the message that this place would be suspect because an ambush could be planned and dangers devised for them there. The king's response was, 'Let them send 200, or as many as they like, of their own men to reconnoitre all round, looking at everything, to see that there is no hidden trickery'. So this was done. Then the duke of Gloucester, with his allies, entered the Tower and, after holding an open, but short, meeting with the king, they went, at the king's request into a room where, in his presence, they related his conspiracy by which they were indicted, and they showed him the letters which he had sent to the duke of Ireland ordering him to assemble an army to destroy them. They also showed him letters from the king of France, which they had intercepted, in which either safe-conduct was granted to the king to go to France, or confirming other matters by which the king's honour would diminish, his power fade and his reputation perish.

When he had seen these, the king did not know what to do, particularly because he knew that he was evidently guilty. Finally, with his permission, they left the confused and tearful king on condition that he came to Westminster next day to hear more, and to discuss the necessary business of his kingdom ....

Next day ... the king returned to Westminster. After a little discussion the lords said that, for his honour and the good of his kingdom, he should remove from his palace and household the traitors, tale-bearers, flatterers, malicious slanderers and useless people, and replace them with others who would be more honourable and faithful companions to him. When the king granted this, though reluctantly, they ordered that there should be excluded from the court Alexander Neville, archbishop of York, John Fordham, bishop of Durham, and Brother Thomas Rushook, the king's confessor of the Order of Preachers, bishop of Chichester; but he, being informed, took flight, and *[the archbishop of]* York went into hiding.

[Walsingham then lists the four lords and five knights expelled from court but ordered to appear before the coming parliament; the three ladies expelled from court; the eight knights and the four king's clerks and a serjeant-at-law who were arrested.]

101. An attempt at mediation

This is the only source to mention this episode.
The Kirkstall Abbey Chronicles, ed. J. Taylor (Thoresby Society, 42, 1952), 114.

The *[Appellants']* armies ... laid siege to the city, sending prudent and discreet lords to the king as mediators who protested that they proposed to do nothing against their lord king, nor against justice or the just laws of the land, but would defend him, them and theirs, and would destroy the destroyers of just laws, and would, as far as they could, maintain justice and the laws of the land. They also demanded that the king should convene his parliament at London at the next Purification of the Blessed Virgin Mary *[2 February]*. Indeed, the venerable earl of Northumberland, Lord Henry Percy, the only earl who was living with the king in the Tower of London, mediated most wisely as a negotiator between the king and those noblemen of the realm, although at his peril, and by God's grace averted a likely civil war – the worst kind – which was then feared to be imminent.

102. An alleged deposition of Richard during the winter of 1387–8

The copy of Ranulph Higden's *Polychronicon* once owned by Whalley Abbey, Lancashire, contains this account of the Appellants' treatment of Richard, inserted into the description of his deposition in 1399. Though the precise date of this episode is unclear, it was evidently after Radcot Bridge and before parliament began. The writer calls Woodstock 'earl of Buckingham', rather than 'duke of Gloucester', which he had become in August 1385, yet mistakenly describes Bolingbroke as 'duke of Hereford', a title granted only in September 1397. This story is corroborated by an article of Gloucester's 'confession' read, after his death, to the parliament of September 1397.[163] There may also be a coded reference to it in *WC*, 234: 'On 1 February near Abingdon, the bed of the river Thames was empty of water for a bowshot's length, and remained so for an hour, conveying a striking portent of events to come'.[164]

M. V. Clarke and V. H. Galbraith, 'The deposition of Richard II', *Bulletin of the John Rylands Library* xiv (1930), 125–81.[165]

Here I have interpolated what was left out of its proper place: When Thomas of Woodstock, earl of Buckingham, the earl of Arundel [and] the earl of Warwick with other magnates had risen in revolt together against certain of the king's councillors, and had beheaded Simon Burley, and had put the duke of Ireland to flight at Radcot Bridge, and had killed Thomas Molyneux and many others there, they came into the king's presence and they deposed him from his royal throne and he remained so deposed (*discoronatus*) for three days. But when they came to discuss the succession, the majority wanted to promote Thomas of Woodstock to be king, but Henry, duke of Hereford, took a contrary position, protesting that he was the son of the elder brother, and claiming that for this reason he ought to be king. The magnates viewed with alarm the discord between these two, and fearing that they would be perceived as traitors, they joined in the deliberations and reinstated (*recoronant*) Richard as king again, [but] removing all his friends and counsellors, from the highest to the lowest, assigning others to him, by whose advice the king would be governed; but how the king revenged himself on these is made clear above.

---

163 *CR*, 81.

164 Abingdon, Oxon., had a large Benedictine abbey.

165 Reprinted in Clarke, *Fourteenth Century Studies* (Oxford, 1937), 53–98.

103. Robert de Vere in exile

The kindness shown to de Vere in exile may in part explain Richard's friendly attitude to the French king.

Chronique du Religieux de Saint-Denys, ed. M. L. Bellaguet (repr. Paris, 1994), I.496–7.

Because his uncles desired the death of some of his friends by any means, King Richard gave careful thought to their safety. Then he sent them to the king of France with royal letters in which he earnestly begged him, by reason of their common kinship, to protect the exiles in peace and plenty. Among the assembled exiles were many distinguished knights, but the duke of Ireland surpassed the others in authority. The French king, on his uncles' advice, received them all honourably; he continually entertained them lavishly and showered them with gifts, demonstrating by both word, expression and a cheerful manner his pleasure at the arrival of them all. Wishing to show, most particularly, the joy which their arrival had given him, he ordered a military tournament to be held in St Katherine's fields. The king of England was glad when he heard this; he praised the French king's graciousness, and despatched high-ranking ambassadors to convey his grateful thanks and to confirm the truce with him up to the month of March.

III: THE RULE AND FALL OF THE APPELLANTS, 1388–89

104. Power passes from the king

These appointments to crucial offices, and the judges' removal, show that effective power had passed to the Appellants before parliament met.

(a) *CPR 1385–9,* 381.

John Devereux, knight, is appointed constable of Dover castle and the Cinque Ports, at a payment of £300 a year, in place of Simon Burley. By command of the king and council. Mandate to Simon to deliver the castle to him. 3 January 1388.

Appointment during pleasure of William Hornby as justice of Chester.[1] By command of the council. 4 January 1388.

(b) *WC,* 306–8.

On 1 February four judges were removed from office – namely Sirs Robert Bealknap, John Holt, William Burgh, Roger Fulthorpe – and were sent to the Tower of London. The same day Sir John Cary, chief baron of the exchequer, was removed and despatched to the Tower for safe custody; and one John Lockton, serjeant-at-law, was also sent to the Tower along with them. On that day new judges were created, namely Walter Clopton,[2] chief justice of the king's bench, and Robert Charlton, chief justice of common pleas.

The 'merciless' parliament, 1388

The well-named 'merciless' parliament, the most dramatic and bloody episode in the reign, presents the historian with peculiar difficulties, for it illustrates vividly the axiom that 'history is written by the winners'. No contemporary account supports the king's position. A short chronicle from conservative Lincolnshire said of the Appellants that 'contrary to the king's will and the

---

1 The previous justice was de Vere; Richard had appointed him in Sept. 1387, Morgan (1987): 187.

2 This west countryman was a serjeant-at-law at the time of this appointment; see A. Tuck, 'Clopton, Walter', *ODNB.*

equity of the law, they inhumanely put to death certain knights and judges',[3] while the Dieulacres Chronicle for 1388, which was written after 1403, is suffused with pro-Ricardian nostalgia.[4]

Among the major chroniclers, Walsingham [105a] is curiously brief. The *Eulogium* [105b] was lukewarm in attitude, while Knighton had an independent view of the proceedings. Already in describing the second appeal, 17 November 1387, he said that the subsequent parliament was 'called merciless (*parliamentum sine misericordia*), no mercy being shown to anyone without the lords' consent'.[5] Most of his description consists of charges against the Appellants, drawn from the parliament rolls, preceded by short notices of foreign affairs, and some account of ecclesiastical controversy, but immediately before the charges against the courtiers is a long petition [115] which appears to date from early summer 1388.

From the Appellant side the material is abundant: Favent's partisan account was written in early summer 1388, shortly after the parliament ended, but the two most substantial accounts are in the parliament roll and the Westminster Chronicle. The parliament roll was composed by clerks of the chancery, a department containing strong factional interests,[6] and naturally clerks allied to the winning side wrote the record of this session; the partisan nature of the 'official' account should always be remembered. More particularly, there is abundant evidence to link the clerk of the parliament, John Scarle, with the Appellant cause.[7] Westminster is easily the most informative chronicle; besides the parliament roll, it contains two accounts, one drawn largely from material supplied by chancery clerks, and another, more personal one, composed by the monastic author himself.[8] Here too we may well detect Scarle's influence, for he had a long association with Westminster Abbey, which paid him an annual retaining fee from 1370. Scarle gave legal advice and produced legal documents for the house, which not only paid him in quarterly instalments, but gave him some lavish meals as well. Inside information is evident in several parts of the chronicle, but above all in the account of this parliament, and it is plausible to identify John Scarle as the source.[9]

The selected material is arranged as follows: first two brief descriptions of the whole meeting, followed by a chronology drawn mainly from the parliament rolls and Westminster, supplemented by passages from other accounts.

---

3 *Chronicle of Louth Park Abbey* (1891): 41, whose description of these proceedings was misdated by the editor.

4 This was printed by Clarke and Galbraith under the title 'The deposition of Richard II', (1930): 167–8.

5 *KC*, 414.

6 Biggs (2000): 57–70; McHardy (2009): 68–93.

7 He was the clerk of parliament 1384–94, McHardy (2009): 68, 77.

8 *WC*, li–lv.

9 McHardy (2009): 90–3.

105. Two short accounts of the parliament

(a) According to Walsingham

SAC I.850–2.

After the feast of the Purification *[2 February]* a parliament began at London, but the king dearly wished to slip away stealthily from this parliamentary session. The nobles gathered with an army sufficient to quell any rebellious protests which might occur. This parliament continued until the feast of Pentecost *[17 May]*, causing much care and dread for many. First, Robert Tresilian was captured, most unfortunately for him because he was quickly dragged to the gallows and hanged. Then the lords decided to proceed against Nicholas Brembre, knight, who suffered the same condemnation, although he had more intercessors. It was alleged that he had planned to abolish the name 'London', and put in its stead a new name, 'Little Troy', and planned to be created and called duke of this city.[10] To put his plan into effect he had tablets or rolls drawn up, in which were noted down several thousand names of citizens whose resistance in this matter was feared. All these would quickly have had their throats cut. But he was hanged before he could carry out his plan.

After this John Salisbury and James Berners, both knights, both young, but both traitors, were by parliament's judgment drawn and hanged. Then James *[correctly John]* Beauchamp of Holt, the king's steward – for many years false and fraudulent, unfaithful both to the lord Edward of Windsor, the king *[Edward III]*, and to his son Lionel, duke of Clarence – was by the judgment of that parliament drawn and hanged. Then John Blake esquire was hanged, who in the council at Nottingham stood out against the lords in that unlucky hour.[11]

Finally Simon Burley was beheaded, although the earl of Derby put every effort into rescuing him. For that reason much dissension arose between him and the duke of Gloucester but, God be praised, it was soon smoothed over. Wherever he paraded, Burley presented himself not as of knightly rank, but as a duke or prince in all his finery. He was keeper of Dover castle, which at the king's command he had agreed to

10 *KC*, 500, makes the same charge, perhaps derived from a newsletter. The story that London was called the second or New Troy came from Geoffrey of Monmouth's twelfth-century *History of the Kings of Britain*. Caroline Barron tells me that interest in the legend of Troy was a court enthusiasm, not shared by even literary Londoners.

11 The serjeant-at-law who drafted the questions to the judges.

sell to the French, and he had been intolerably proud and arrogant, an oppressor of the poor, a hater of the church, a fornicator and adulterer. The judges too were condemned to exile in this parliament: Robert Bealknap, John Holt, Roger Fulthorpe and William Burgh. To each of them was granted a sum of money for life, for daily subsistence.[12] Then an oath was exacted from the king to adhere to the lords' judgment; and the same oath was demanded not only from the king but from all the inhabitants of the kingdom.

(b) According to the *Eulogium*

Eulogium, 366–7

The five lords [*appellant*] held a parliament at Westminster where Robert Tresilian, justice, Nicholas Brembre, knight, citizen of London, and many others were adjudged to death, and because of charges of treachery, they were drawn and hanged. In that same parliament Simon Burley, a valiant knight of the garter, and John Beauchamp, knight, steward of the king's household, James Berners, knight, and others were seized and were beheaded at the Tower of London. Then those five lords stood before the justices and were vindicated in everything imputed to them. ... They caused parliament to appeal certain men of various crimes, such as making truces with the king of France to hand back overseas lands, and for other things of which they were not guilty. They condemned the duke of Ireland, Michael [*de la Pole*], and Alexander, archbishop of York to perpetual exile, and caused John Blake to be drawn and hanged. Furthermore, they consigned the bishop of Chichester, a Friar Preacher,[13] and the other justices, with a serjeant at law [*John Lockton*], to exile in Ireland. This parliament lasted from the feast of Purification [*2 February*] until the feast of St John Baptist [*24 June*],[14] the king arguing with them and saying that the accused had committed no felony and that the appeal was false, but he could not save anyone. They made everyone and the burgesses of the cities swear to observe the statutes of this parliament, and that no one would contravene those statutes nor plead for any revocation. Finally, they made the king swear anew that he would observe the laws of the realm and would

12 Their individual annual allowances were generous: Bealknap and Fulthorpe got £40 each, Holt and Burgh £26 13s 4d., Cary and Lockton £20, *CCR 1385–9*, 515–16.

13 Thomas Rushook (Rushock) O.P., Richard's confessor, was translated to the see of Kilmore, Ireland, in 1389.

14 It actually ended on 4 June.

adhere to the counsels, not of flatterers, but of parliament and the lords; nor would he bear any grudge against them for what they had done. In testimony of which the king caused to be made letters patent of plenary indulgence.[15] However, he always felt these things very deeply, and the lords said among themselves that all three should never gather in his presence at the same time.

The first session of parliament, 3 February–20 March

106. The opening, and protestations of loyalty, 3 February

(a) According to *Westminster*
WC, 234–6.

On 3 February the king held a parliament at Westminster in which T*[homas]*, duke of Gloucester, Henry, earl of Derby, Richard, earl of Arundel, Thomas, earl of Warwick, and Thomas, earl of Nottingham, publicly explained before the whole parliament that they never sought, planned or plotted the king's death, either covertly or openly. They wanted to prove this with their own hands against any contradictor, and to defend themselves against these accusations against any man alive, the king only excepted; and since no one contradicted this, they were considered by everyone to be blameless. So they earnestly sought that Alexander, archbishop of York, Robert de Vere, duke of Ireland, Michael de la Pole, earl of Suffolk, Robert Tresilian, justice, and Nicholas Brembre, knight of London, should be brought before the whole parliament and respond orally to the articles set out in their appeal. But because it was almost Lent the king prorogued the matter until the Thursday after Ash Wednesday *[13 February]*.

(b) According to Favent
Favent, *Wonderful Parliament*, 14–15.

A great parliament began on 2 February,[16] like this: everyone of both estates, lords and distinguished men of the kingdom, assembled in the king's white hall at Westminster. After the king arrived and sat at the tribunal, the five Appellants of most noble reputation, the merits of

15 An ecclesiastical term meaning the removal of all penalities for sin, indicating that the king granted them a general pardon.
16 A slip for 3 February.

whose personal integrity resonated throughout the land … along with a great multitude, identically dressed in gold, and arm-in-arm, entered the hall with a fixed gaze, though as one man they greeted the king on bended knee. There was a huge press of men, the hall was packed to every corner. …When the laity had sat down on the king's left, and the clergy on his right, according to long-established parliamentary custom, the chancellor in full view, and standing with his back to the king, gave a speech setting out the reasons and business of parliament by categories, as is the custom. After this was done, those five lords stood up and gave their opening speech through Robert Plessington,[17] a prudent knight, who said, 'Here is the duke of Gloucester who has come to purge himself of the charge of treason made against him by those fugitives'. The chancellor, in fact, taking the words out of the king's mouth, excused the duke and said, 'My lord duke, you have arisen from so worthy a royal line and we find that you are so closely related to him in the collateral line that no such a plot could be suspected of you'. The duke, supported by his four allies, thanked the king on bended knee. Finally, when silence had been imposed, those same lords put forward in writing their articles of accusation about this treason. So Geoffrey Martin, clerk of the crown, stood up in the middle of parliament and briskly read out those charges for the space of two hours. The hearts of many were smitten by the horrible contents of those accusations, and many had swollen faces and tears running down their cheeks. When the reading of the charges was finally over, they courteously insisted to the king that a just and fitting sentence be imposed on such false treachery, according to what was alleged and proved, so that due execution would be done upon the persons of those runaways; and this the king promised.

107. Proceedings against the five accused

Parliament had immediately to discuss the matter of proper procedure, a problem raised by the use of the appeal (as opposed to impeachment) which the judges' answers had forced on the five lords. Appeals, which were essentially private accusations, were not unusual, and were routinely used in two areas. In common law, criminal case appeals – though less common than indictments (public accusations) – were perfectly normal [**107b, charge 12**] and actually

17 Lancastrian servant in the 1370s; chief baron of the exchequer (Dec. 1380–4 Nov. 1386); Mowbray's chief steward by 1383, A. Goodman, 'Plessington, Sir Robert', *ODNB*.

produced a higher conviction-rate than indictments did.[18] Appeals were also used in the civil law, especially in enforcing the laws of war [68], which covered not only safe-conducts, ransoms and armorial bearings, but treason too.[19] Those cases were heard in the Court of Chivalry, presided over by the Constable of England. In 1388 the Constable was Thomas, duke of Gloucester.

But Gloucester and his allies had made their appeal before any fighting took place. Moreover, a private prosecution for political treason seems very contradictory. Appeals of treason in a non-military context had indeed been made, though back in the previous century.[20] Political, though non-treasonous, appeals had been used recently (1384) in connection with the unrest and power-struggles which shook London at this time [63, 65],[21] and those were heard before the Council. It was the use of parliament in such cases that was novel about this situation, and a number of different, and competing, traditions were involved. The fact that three of the accused were peers was an additional complication.

(a) Legal arguments and protestations, 4 February
RP III.235–7.[22]

On 4 February the justices, serjeants and others learned in the law of the land, and also those learned in civil law, were charged by the lord king to give loyal counsel to the lords of parliament about \due/[23] process in the matter of this appeal. The justices, serjeants and those learned in the law of the land, and also those learned in civil law, deliberated and answered the lords of parliament that they had viewed and carefully heard the matter of this appeal; they said that this appeal could not be made or prosecuted under the procedure required by either one law or the other. In response, the lords of parliament deliberated and took advice, and with the assent of the king and his commons it was decided to declare that, in so high a crime as was alleged in this appeal – which concerned the king's person and the estate of his realm, perpetrated by those who were peers of the realm, with others – the matter could not be \decided/ anywhere except in parliament, nor by any

---

18 Powell in Cockburn and Green (1988): 104–7.

19 Keen (1962): 85–103.

20 Vernon Harcourt (1907): 348–52, 363–9.

21 Strohm (with Prescott) (1992): 145–77.

22 *PROME* is especially difficult to reference for this parliament. The documents are presented in three parts, 1 (Roll), 2 (Appeal of Treason), 3 (Attainders). The sections used here may be found at 1388 (1), Part 3: (Attainders) membrane 14; Part 1 (Roll): section 9.

23 Words within these signs are later additions.

law except the law and procedure of parliament; and it was up to the lords of parliament, by their right and liberty of ancient parliamentary custom, to hear and adjudicate in such cases, with the king's consent. That was how it would be done in this case, by judgment of parliament, because the kingdom of England was not, never had been, nor did the lord king and lords of parliament intend that it ever should be, ruled or governed by civil law; thus their intention is not to rule or govern so great a matter as this appeal is (which will not be tried nor determined anywhere except in parliament, as they said) by the course, process and order used in any court or place within the same realm, because those courts and places are only executors of the ancient laws and customs of the realm and of parliament. The same lords of parliament, with the king's assent, were advised that this appeal should be made and affirmed well and sufficiently duly, and the process of the same well and effectually, according to the laws and course of parliament, and so they should award and adjudge it. ....

By reason of certain matters discussed by this present parliament which obviously concerned felony,[24] the archbishop of Canterbury and the other prelates of his province made a protestation as follows: In the name of God, Amen. Since by right and custom of the English realm, the archbishop of Canterbury ... and his suffragan brothers and fellow-bishops, abbots, priors and all other prelates holding by barony of the king, belong in all the kings' parliaments \as peers/ of the realm, attend parliament in person, there to discuss business and other matters, along with the other peers of the realm, and have the right of being there to consult and discuss, to command, legislate and define, and to do the other things which have to be done during the time of parliament, We, William archbishop of Canterbury ... on behalf of ourselves and our suffragans and all the aforesaid prelates declare, and it is declared by each of them \who/ is now present, whether in person or by a proctor,[25] publicly and expressly, that we intend ... as \peers/ of the realm, to be present in the usual way, to consult, discuss. ... But because in this present parliament some business is to be conducted at which we are not permitted, nor are any of them, according to canon law, to be present in person, we therefore protest on our own behalf ... and each of them here present also protests, that we neither intend nor wish ... to be

24 The clergy were not permitted to be involved in cases in which the penalty was death; these included felonies.

25 The spiritual peers were often represented by deputies; many of the appointments of these survive in TNA series SC 10.

present in any way in this parliament while such matters are or may be dealt with …. Further, we protest … that, because of this absence, we do not intend or wish that the process conducted and to be conducted in this present parliament on those matters aforesaid, in which we neither can nor ought to participate … should in times to come, be in any way attacked, weakened or revoked.

(b) Selected charges against the accused

The 'merciless' parliament was essentially a clearing-out of courtiers and other royal servants who were displeasing to the Appellants and – since the persecution reached to men at a comparatively modest level – their supporters. The prosecutions came in a series of waves: first the infamous five, of whom three, de la Pole, Neville and de Vere, had already fled the country.

Many of the charges against the courtiers were of a general nature: accroaching royal power, manipulating crown patronage, coming between the king and his natural advisers, perverting the course of parliamentary business, plotting the deaths of the Appellants or larger groups. The following are examples of more precise accusations.

WC, 248, 258–9, 262–4; *RP* III.231–5; *PROME* 1388 (1), part 2: (Appeal of Treason): 6c, 4e, 3f, 2g, 1h.

[*12.*] Whereas under the Great Charter and other good laws and customs of the English realm no man should be arrested, imprisoned or put to death without due process of law,[26] Nicholas Brembre etc. by the same accroachment [*of royal power*] by night took certain persons from Newgate gaol, chaplains and others to the number of twenty-two, some indicted, some appealed of felony, some approvers in felony cases, and some arrested and imprisoned there on suspicion of felony, and took them outside London, into Kent, to a place called Foul Oak and there, accroaching royal power to himself … without warrant or [*due*] process had all except one beheaded …

[*25.*] The traitors Alexander etc. … to accomplish their treasons more completely, and also to make the king believe in them and their advice and consider them more loyal to him, and more wise, than any others of his kingdom … made the king call before him in various places in the realm various justices and men of the law, namely [*the seven judges*], John Lokton, serjeant and with them John Blake, referendary[27]…. who

---

26 'No free man shall be arrested or imprisoned or disseised or outlawed or exiled or in any way destroyed, nor will we proceed against him or send against him, except by the lawful judgment of his peers or by the law of the land', *Magna Carta*, clause 39.

27 Someone who gave legal advice in a disputed or difficult case.

were asked by these evildoers and traitors if the ordinance, statute and commission was made in derogation of his regality and prerogative, or not, and other questions to which the justices, serjeant and John Blake replied.

[26.] *[After questioning the judges]* it was then decided among the traitors that some of those lords should be, first, arrested and then by false inquests indicted and attainted of certain treasons falsely devised by them ... and then sent to a dreadful and disgraceful death, and their descendants perpetually disinherited; and that these illegal arrests, indictments and attainders should be made in London and Middlesex and for that reason they appointed a false and evil member of their clique, Thomas Usk, as under-sheriff of Middlesex, who with their assent ... undertook that these false indictments and attainders should be made and carried out. ... And to accomplish that treason completely those traitors caused our lord king to send his letters of credence by one John Ripon, false clerk,[28] directed to the mayor of London, telling him to arrest the duke of Gloucester and other named persons. ... Afterwards Nicholas Brembre and John Blake, by virtue of that letter of credence, took to the mayor a bill which gave information about the false indictment, commanding and ordering the mayor to do all in his power to effect those arrests. ... Also, those same evildoers and traitors ordered a sharp watch to be kept for the coming of the duke of Lancaster who was to be arrested immediately he arrived.

[29.] ... Alexander etc. and their associates by their advice caused the king to send letters of credence to his enemy of France ... requesting and begging the king of France to aid him with all his power and counsel to destroy and put to death those lords and other Englishmen whom the king considered his enemies and traitors ... to the great disturbance and dishonour of the king and kingdom.

[34.] Nicholas Brembre ... Alexander etc. and other traitors ... on their own authority, without warrant of the king or his great council, caused it to be cried and proclaimed everywhere in the city of London that none of the king's subjects should sustain, comfort or aid Richard, earl of Arundel and Surrey, peer of the realm and one of the lords of the king's great council, during the *[term of office]* of that commission, or sell him weapons, food or any other necessities ... and that all those around him should avoid him as a rebel against the king on pain of forfeiture ....

28 For another of his missions, see **87a**.

(c) Judgment on the absentees, 11 February

Favent, *Wonderful Parliament*, 16.

On 11 February ... John Devereux, marshal of the court, the king's representative, gave judgment that the said archbishop, duke, earl and Tresilian should be dragged from the Tower of London to Tyburn through the city, then immediately hanged on the gallows and all their goods confiscated, so that their successors should not enjoy them afterwards.

(d) More judgments, 13 February

In his account of this parliament the Monk refers to the five Appellants as 'the aforesaid lords' (*prefati domini*), here translated 'lords' to distinguish them from lords of parliament in general.

WC, 308.

In full parliament, proclamation was made three times about the treason of those lords appealed by the lords, and, because they did not appear, but had cunningly withdrawn from parliament, parliament proceeded to judge them on 13 February, condemning them as though they were traitors (*tanquam proditores*)[29] to be drawn and hanged, and their goods, moveable and immoveable, confiscated and their heirs disinherited forever; and anyone able to capture them could kill them with impunity. But they judged Alexander Neville to be the most notorious traitor possible; they confiscated his temporalities and all his goods, moveable and immoveable. They were unwilling to pronounce the death sentence on him, for reverence of his position, but left it to the lord pope and other prelates of the church to consider and decide the matter of his deposition. Meanwhile the archbishop remained in hiding because he did not dare to appear in public.

108. Brembre's trial and Tresilian's capture, 17–19 February

Brembre's request for trial by battle reflects the unusual and hybrid nature of the proceedings.

WC, 308–10.

On 17 February, Sir Nicholas Brembre was led before the lords in full parliament and compelled to make a brief answer confirming or denying

29 Surely a reference back to the judges' answers of 1387; see **91b**.

the charges against him. He asked to seek counsel on this, but that was absolutely not allowed. Then he denied that the allegations were true, and he was quite prepared to prove this by fighting a duel against any opponent except the king and other members of the royal family. The answer to this was that battle was not applicable in this case,[30] especially where witnesses had testified that all the charges against him were true – because indeed all the commons kept shouting out that everything was true with which he was charged – and the lords wanted to prove it by their own efforts. But by the end of the day matters had made very little progress.

Next day [18 February] the king was seated in parliament and the five lords who were the principal Appellants stood below him and on the other side [of the hall] – as they always did in all the articles described above whenever, in the presence of the king or his representative, they accused anyone of treason. When those articles against Sir Nicholas Brembre and others had been clearly read out, the king excused Sir Nicholas in many ways, protesting that he had never known him to be a traitor, nor was he culpable of those charges, nor had he himself ever known him to be guilty in such great matters. At this the lords threw down their gauntlets, and a supporting multitude of others did the same, affirming the truth of the accusations against him. At last, to pacify the disputes and discord about this, it was finally agreed that certain lords should decide whether, on the charges laid against him, he was worthy of death, or not. So to examine these charges twelve great lords were chosen, namely the duke of York, the earls of Kent, Salisbury, Northumberland, and other barons to make up that number. After deliberation, and finding no case for his death in these accusations, they returned with this response to the lords, who, for that reason, became angry with them.

But then, unexpectedly, they were notified that Robert Tresilian was in the Westminster sanctuary. At once those lords dropped everything for the time being and quickly went to the sanctuary with a close-packed crowd. The duke of Gloucester took a mace and promptly arrested Robert Tresilian and defended him from those who were fiercely trying to rush at him. Without doubt, serious discord would have arisen at this time among the lords had it not been for this chance happening.

30 See **68**.

109. Accounts of Tresilian's discovery

Despite his proximity, the Westminster chronicler was laconic about this episode, perhaps from disapproval at violation of the Abbey's sanctuary. Years later, John Paule, an odd-job man at the abbey, confessed that it was he who had 'wickedly' betrayed Tresilian's secret hiding place to the lords.[31] More detail is provided in the extracts below. The story became known in Europe, and Froissart (chapter 82) worked it up into a colourful drama.

(a) From Bishop Wakefield's register

Richard G. Davies, 'Some notes from the register of Henry de Wakefield, bishop of Worcester on the political crisis of 1386–8', *EHR* 86 (1971), 558.

On Wednesday the morrow of St Matthew the Apostle *[25 Feb.]*[32] ... at Westminster, in the house of a tenant of the sacristan of Westminster, Robert Tresilian was captured by an ambush, wearing the garb of a hermit, and was led into full parliament to be seen by everyone. The same day he was drawn by horses from the Tower through the middle of London and was hanged at Tyburn.

(b) From exchequer records

TNA E 403/519; printed Margaret Aston, *Thomas Arundel* (Oxford, 1967), 346 n.4.

14 May 1388. To William Forester esquire:[33] in money given to him by gift of the king's own hand as a reward for the labour and diligence exercised by him in finding Robert Tresilian, lately chief justice of King's *[Bench]*, condemned to death for certain causes in the last parliament held at Westminster; by this discovery of William's the said Robert was captured, and was led into that parliament before the king, lords, nobles and commons of the realm. By writ of privy seal among the commands of this term: £10.

(c) Favent's description

Favent, *Wonderful Parliament*, 17.

---

31 Paule, a prolific offender from 1377, was finally executed in May 1392, and while being led to the gallows confessed his betrayal of Tresilian and the luring of others from the sanctuary, *WC* 496–8, and n.3.

32 Every other account places this a week earlier, 19 Feb.

33 Froissart's assertion that Forester was in Gloucester's service seems plausible.

Before they had reached a conclusion in the trial of Nicholas Brembre, the unfortunate Tresilian came before them; he was discovered above the gutter of a house abutting the palace wall at Westminster, looking out at the lords coming and going from parliament while lying hidden among the roof-tiles. So, when some squires had entered the house, and on looking round saw no one, one particular squire, with a stern face approached the head of the household, grabbed him by the hair, drew his dagger and said, 'Show us where Tresilian is or you are a dead man'. The trembling householder said, 'Here he is'. The unfortunate Tresilian was miraculously discovered under a round table which had been covered with a tablecloth to protect him, in disguise. His tunic was of old russet and came down to his mid-calf, like an old man's; his beard was bristly and thick; and he wore red boots with 'soles of Joseph'.[34] He looked more like a pilgrim or beggar than a royal justice. News of this arrest soon reached the lords' ears, and on this pretext the five lords appellant immediately left parliament, giving no reason for their departure and surprising everyone in parliament; many followed them with their minds in a whirl. When they had arrested Tresilian at the palace gate, they led him to parliament and announced with a loud voice, 'We havet hym! We havet hym!' He was asked in parliament how he could excuse himself of this charge of treason and other deeds he had committed, but he remained completely silent, stony-hearted even in this desperate situation, unwilling to confess to anything. Soon, for this reason, parliament was interrupted, and Brembre, who was present, was sent away because of Tresilian. Tresilian was immediately led to the Tower of London so that execution of his sentence could be carried out on him. [*The account describes his wife's distress but Tresilian's refusal to repent.*]

110. The judges' fate

The other judges were also condemned to death, but their sentence was later commuted to banishment to Ireland.

(a) The fullest account of their trial[35]

The Kirkstall Abbey Chronicles, ed. J. Taylor (Thoresby Society, 42, 1952), 115-16.

---

34 Joseph was usually depicted as old and poor.

35 See 'The Kirkstall chronicle, 1355-1400', ed. Clarke and Denholm-Young (1931): 127 and n.

The judges were imprisoned separately in the Tower of London awaiting
trial, and because parliament was prorogued until the octave of Easter
[*5 April*] they were sustained during Lent with bread and a pittance,[36]
and with a modest measure of drink. After Easter they were brought
before the lords of parliament in Westminster Hall, and in the hearing
of all parliament they received their sentences as follows: first, that all
their goods, moveable and immoveable, were forfeit; second, that those
judges and sergeants-at-law, as though they were traitors (*tamquam
proditores*)[37] to the laws of the kingdom of England, should be dragged
from the Tower of London at the tails of horses through the city to the
gallows and there, on account of their sins, should end their lives by
hanging. All the judges immediately blenched, and quaking with fear at
the shameful death they were condemned to, knelt in submission before
the lords of parliament, telling them that by their just judgment they,
the judges, would deservedly suffer this well-deserved death. Then the
archbishop of Canterbury, the Reverend Master[38] William Courtenay,
with the other bishops and great prelates,[39] immediately after the
judges' condemnation, entered the parliament hall[40] lamenting, in a
most humble way, that so many men so learned in the laws of England
should be killed, and begging that, for God's sake, they should be spared
life and limb. This was done, on condition that they all suffered permanent exile in Ireland, within a short designated time. So they were
all banished to Ireland, and some of them died there, but some were
brought back nine years later, by order of King Richard then reigning
as though for the first time.[41]

(b) Knighton's summary

KC, 502.

On the intervention of Anne, queen of England, with the archbishop
of Canterbury and other bishops, the king – with the consent of the
lords against whom they had sinned – pardoned them their lives. But
they were disinherited like the rest, both they and their heirs, and were

36 A pittance was a little treat adding variety to a plain monastic diet. In Lent everyone's diet was more austere than usual.
37 Surely an ironic reference to the language of the judges' answers of 1387.
38 An Oxford graduate; Courtenay was a doctor of civil law, Emden (1957): 502.
39 The parliamentary abbots.
40 The spiritual peers could not take part in a judgment involving the death penalty, and
so had withdrawn earlier.
41 Richard's rule from summer 1397.

outlawed to Ireland, by a published statute, never to return. They were assigned two by two to certain places to live in perpetuity, and were not to cross certain limits and boundaries.

111. Proceedings against other supporters of the king

(a) The trial of Usk and Blake, 3–4 March.[42]

The Appellants then reverted to the well-tried mechanism of impeachment to condemn to death the probable drafter of the questions to the judges (John Blake) and Thomas Usk, who, like Brembre, had been active in London politics and had been recruited as a tool of the courtiers. Both were executed. Richard's confessor, Thomas Rushook, Dominican friar and bishop of Chichester, was also condemned, deprived of his see and translated to an Irish bishopric.

Favent, *Wonderful Parliament*, 19–20.

On 4 March, Thomas Usk and John Blake were led into parliament ... These two, although men of modest rank, had nevertheless both been coerced into the above-mentioned treasons with those grandees. For Usk was a royal sergeant-at-arms, ... and had very recently become [under]sheriff of Middlesex, in order to indict the lords appellant, and he indicted the other commissioners and [their] adherents as traitors by their deeds. Blake was Tresilian's associate; he ran errands for the traitors and, as an adviser, was often consulted about accomplishing the business of the five condemned men. And when, in the trial, no excuse could be made for them, they were given that heavy sentence and, as their masters had earlier made the walk to death, they reaped the reward of fate and were led to the Tower. Soon, separately but within a short time, spattering the surroundings with their flesh, as traitors do, they came to Tyburn and there among the gallows they quickly fell asleep.

(b) The trial and execution of four chamber knights, 12 March–12 May

On 12 March four chamber knights, John Beauchamp of Holt (steward of the king's household, 5 February–31 December 1387), John Salisbury (who had also been involved in negotiating with the French), James Berners[43] and Simon Burley, were impeached. The two months between their accusation and

---

42 They were brought into parliament on 3 March; judgment was given on 4 March.

43 The only one whose portrait is known, though it is not necessarily a likeness. He was lord of the manor of West Horsley, Surrey. His portrait in one of the church windows is reproduced in Alexander and Binski, eds (1987): 537.

execution were not entirely taken up with their trial; a grant of tonnage and poundage was made on 20 March, and parliament was then adjourned until 13 April.

Favent, *Wonderful Parliament*, 20–21.

On Thursday 12 March ... the *[chamber]* ... knights Simon Burley, John Beauchamp, James Berners and John Salisbury were led before parliament. Soon those things which were to be charged were charged and those things to be proved were proved, and they were not able to clear themselves. From that time almost to Ascension *[7 May]*, parliament was troubled solely with that Simon because the undivided trinity of the three lords appellant, namely the duke of Gloucester and the earls of Arundel and Warwick, along with the whole commons of parliament, were firmly insistent on carrying out the just judgment according to the charges and proofs against Simon's person. But the king, the queen, the earls of Derby and Nottingham and the prior of St John *[of Jerusalem]*, his uncle,[44] and many others among the greater part of the lords of parliament worked hard for his life, from the opposing view. So because the commons were tired by the long period of labour and expense in that parliament ... they petitioned the king to dismiss them so that they could freely depart from parliament to their own affairs. ...

But there was uproar among the people, and parliament heard that the common folk in various parts of England, for example in Kent and its surroundings, had risen up from silence, on account of this Simon. At once everyone on Simon's side drew back from, and ceased, their continual protestations. Finally, on the Monday before Ascension, which is 5 May, sentence was pronounced against Simon alone, namely that he should be dragged from the Tower to Tyburn, like his predecessors, and, after hanging, his head should be cut from his body. But because he was a knight of the garter, powerful and humane in bearing, gracious, a kinsman of the king and always found at his court, and *[because of]* the pleading of many lords, the king, of his special grace, in imposing this sentence of execution, mitigated it, so that only beside the land wall on Tower Hill, London, as a penitent was he decapitated and suffered fatal agony.

(c) Selected charges against the knights, 17 March

Sixteen charges were levied against the four chamber knights; their gist was that the accused took unfair advantage of the king's youth and incited bad

44 For Raddington, see Lewis (1937): 662–9.

government through association with the five Appellants. Burley and John Beauchamp were named as 'the principal makers of all the previously mentioned treasons',[45] while Burley alone was named in six of the charges (numbers 4, 5, 6, 7, 11 and 12). Two of the charges against him were factually incorrect: that Burley had reinstated Pole as chancellor in October 1386 so that he could seal a letter patent giving Burley lucrative privileges arising from his constableship of Dover castle – Pole had not been dismissed by that date – and the charge that he let Pole escape before parliament assembled in February 1388; Pole had been at liberty, and at court, during the previous year.[46] Burley was finally convicted and condemned to death for his opposition to the 1386 commission. His execution was a defining moment for the king – just as the questions to the judges had been for his critics. In 1397 when Richard arrested Gloucester, the duke said, 'I hope you will have enough mercy as to spare my life'. The king replied, 'You shall have such mercy as you showed to Simon Burley'.[47] The complete text of the charges exists only in Westminster material, though most are also found in RP.[48]

WC, 272–8.

[6.] After the duke of Gloucester and other lords appellant had reaffirmed their appeals at Westminster, in the king's presence, against those five convicted traitors [17 November 1387], there came to Simon Burley, knight, a prelate of the realm who begged him to advise and entreat the king to command Robert de Vere, duke of Ireland, not to make, nor cause to be made, this great levy of men-at-arms and archers within the realm, which could result in the destruction of king and kingdom. Simon replied in a lofty manner that if he said this again he [Simon] would ensure that he received great suffering and spite at the king's hands which he would find unendurable. Thus was Simon an abettor, maintainer and sustainer of the duke's treacherous plan.

[7.] When Simon was chamberlain to our lord king in his tender years, and was bound to counsel him wisely for the profit of himself and his realm, Simon by his evil schemes advised him to have in his household great numbers of foreigners, Bohemians and others, and to grant them large gifts of revenue and products of the realm by which our lord king is much impoverished and the people utterly oppressed.

[8.] Simon, John Beauchamp, John Salisbury and James [Berners], along with the five convicted traitors, conspired and traitorously plotted

45 Article 2, *WC*, 270.

46 Letters patent 16 Oct. 1386, dismissal of Pole 23 Oct. 1386, *WC*, 272, and 273 nn.3, 4.

47 *CR*, 65.

48 *WC*, 269, n.3.

the death and destruction of those who assented to the making of the commission and statute made in the last parliament.

...

[12.] Simon remained about the king's person during the times of his youth until at a certain time he was banned from the king's presence by the king's good council because of his bad governance of the king's person and for other bad deeds, [but] afterwards he returned to the king's company, without the good council's consent. And it was through Simon's procurement that Robert de Vere, then earl of Oxford, was brought into the king's circle; this earl later committed numerous treasons for which he is attainted. [There then follow accusations about Burley's obtaining the lordship of 'Lyonshall, Wales' (correctly Herefordshire), and securing property worth 500 marks p.a. formerly belonging to Saer de Coucy, father of Robert de Vere's wife, Philippa.]

...

[14.] Whereas in the last parliament certain commissions and a statute were made by assent of the king, the lords spiritual and temporal and by the commons of the realm for the good governance of the king and kingdom ... [the four knights] hindered the execution of that commission because they advised the king to go to distant places, namely Nottingham, Chester and elsewhere, to assemble a great force of men-at-arms and archers to kill and treacherously destroy the lords and others named in that commission, and other knights of the shire, serjeants-at-law and others named in that last parliament ... to the destruction of king and realm and annulment of all the good ordinances made in parliament.

(d) Efforts to save Burley, and the fate of other household knights

It was perhaps surprising that Burley was not a member of the original group of accused, though his prosecution, when it came, was to prove controversial. His unpopularity with some of the Appellants requires explanation. Burley had progressed from service to the Black Prince to become Richard's tutor; his importance to Princess Joan and his standing in the royal household had been dramatically demonstrated at the coronation [10]. 'Pushy' might well have described him in 1377; in 1378 the Gloucester parliament showed his political prominence [15], and his role in negotiations for Richard's marriage cemented his importance [47a]. Soon it was his greed which was noted, for it was he who had benefited most from the disregard of Edward III's will [28]. He had also benefited from casual grants by the crown,[49] while his social ambition was well known [70a, 105a] and his magnificent lifestyle widely observed [113a]. His

49 McHardy (1989): 286.

behaviour (or that of his employees) during the Peasants' Revolt had shown his cruelty [**34a**], and during the 1386 invasion scare he attempted to use the panic to his own benefit [**80b**]. What gave him an institutional basis for the influence he had over the king was the office of sub-chamberlain, which he held from 16 July 1377 until the day of his trial, 12 March 1388.[50] It was through the chamberlain that many petitions were presented to the king – petitions for patronage, generosity and grace.[51] Burley made sure that the prime recipient of royal generosity was himself, which explains his unpopularity not just with Gloucester, but also with the commons. Though Burley's execution caused dissension at Westminster, his fall was welcomed elsewhere, especially in Kent [**113b**].

WC, 330–2.

The king and the other lords were very keen to save Sir Simon Burley's life; they sent the duke of York and Sir John Cobham to the commons to ask that he be allowed to make another full response to all the previous charges. The commons answered that this was now absolutely impossible because his replies had been set down as a permanent written record. John Cobham retorted that he *[Burley]* had been ill then, and so should be treated more mildly and gently. He advanced these and many other arguments on Burley's behalf, but they were not accepted by the commons. ... On 5 May, despite the prayers and arguments of the king, queen and the other magnates, Sir Simon Burley was by process of parliament sentenced to being drawn and hanged and finally decapitated, but because he was a knight of the garter he was excused everything, except only the beheading; and so, with hands tied behind his back, he walked along the king's highway though the middle of the city of London to Tower Hill, where he was beheaded, and he was buried in the new abbey[52] nearby. On 12 May Sirs John Beauchamp, James Berners and John Salisbury received the same sentence. John Beauchamp and James Berners were excused everything except the beheading, because they were very well-born, and because John Beauchamp had a short time previously been steward of the king's household. So these two made the same walk and were beheaded beside the Tower of London. John Beauchamp was buried at Worcester in St Mary's abbey, and James Berners was interred at Westminster in the chapel of St John Baptist. John Salisbury, because he had been appealed of treason committed by him both inside and outside the realm, was drawn from the Tower of

50 Tout, vol. VI (1933): 49.

51 Dodd (2008a): 107, 118–19.

52 St Mary Graces, beside the Tower: the very house which Burley had defrauded. See **4a, 28**.

London through the middle of the city to Tyburn and there hanged. He was buried at Westminster next to James Berners in the same chapel. On the same day the bishop of Chichester was deprived of his temporalities and all his goods, moveable and immovable, by judgment of parliament.

112. Oaths to uphold the proceedings of this session, 20 March

After these executions the appetite for bloodshed was sated, and some men in custody were later quietly released, but so anxious were the Appellants to safeguard both the deeds of this parliament and their own persons that they arranged for oaths to uphold the actions of parliament to be taken both at Westminster, and in each county.

RP III.244; *PROME* 1388 (1), Part 1, section 13.

You will swear that you will keep and cause to be kept the good peace, quiet and tranquillity of the realm; and if anyone wishes to act contrary to this you will resist and obstruct them with all your power. And if any one wishes to do anything against the bodies of the persons of the Five Lords, that is to say Thomas, duke of Gloucester, Harry, earl of Derby, Richard, earl of Arundel and Surrey, Thomas, earl of Warwick, and Thomas, earl marshal, or any one of them, you will stand with the said Five Lords until the complete end of this present parliament, and you will maintain and sustain them with all your power, to live and die with them against all men, no person and nothing excepted, in the manner aforesaid; saving always \your/[53] allegiance towards our lord king, and the prerogative of his crown, and the laws and good customs of the realm.

The second session of parliament, 13 April–4 June

113. Comments on Burley's death

(a) The Kirkstall Chronicle

The Kirkstall Abbey Chronicles, ed. J. Taylor (Thoresby Society, 42, 1952), 116.

No one of his rank could be compared to him in all the fine trappings of his horses, and he excelled the other lords in all worldly pomp. But this knight – despite the humble prayers upon her knees of the lady queen

53 Interlined.

of England for his life – was condemned to death against the king's will, and was beheaded on level ground beside the Tower of London.

(b) A Kentish 'obituary'

This assessment views Burley as a neighbouring landowner to St Augustine's Abbey, Canterbury.

Thorne, *Chronica*, ed. Twysden, col. 2183.

He handed over, indeed sold to the French king, by a deal made between them for an agreed sum of money, all the overseas lands with the town of Calais, and Dover castle with all the villages and castles as far as Rochester Bridge. All these he fraudulently caused to be confirmed in writing by the king and certain others. He verbally threatened the abbot, under pain of death, that he would permanently deprive him and his church of the Isle of Thanet. Also, he harassed the servants on their manors and the tenants at harvest time and at other times, fined them heavily as though they were rebels, and imprisoned them without cause. When he had done these and similar things, and had so gravely offended God and his saints, and had thrown the kingdom and people into confusion, since there was no man who dared to resist his wish to have everything under his thumb, suddenly, it seemed, he was seized by the leading men of the kingdom. He was condemned to death by them ... and was led through the middle of the city of London, as a prisoner, with his hands tied behind his back. As the reward for all his labours, at Tower Hill on 15 May ... this worker of iniquity was killed by being beheaded. Had not God or his servant Augustine shortened his days, our property would have sustained serious losses. But Almighty God destroyed Simon's plan, and justly rewarded him with the pains of death. So blessed be he who so quickly destroyed that wicked man.

114. Popular discontent

Both Palmer (1972): 136–7, and Tuck (1973): 126n.3 noticed this petition, which amplifies the reference to a Kentish rising, **111b**, and deserves more attention. These extracts give a flavour of the document, which only Knighton recorded. Vague, wordy and repetitive, this is a text-book case of 'how not to complain'. With its sinister echoes of the Peasants' Revolt it is scarcely surprising that this was not included in the rolls of parliament, though its complaints were revived at the next parliament, in September 1388.

KC, 442–6.

The humble commons of your realm put forward the matters and the damage resulting ... from the rising and rumour lately happening among the lower classes (*les petitez gentz*). ... First because peace and right justice in your land, which you are bound to maintain, is not administered equally between rich and rich, poor and poor, and especially between rich and poor, as God and right demand; your poor people are harassed by the extortion of your officers in the localities, for example, escheators and others ... and especially by the three or four in each county called 'Second Kings', so that your poor people cannot survive, nor bear the burden of aiding you and your realm as they should do, by which defaults you and your realm are greatly discredited in every land. Further, your great judges of the laws of your land do not always treat all persons equally, according to the laws' demands; so they are inclined to play down an offence on the orders of the privy seal, or great seal, contrary to your good laws, or at the prayers of other lords or members of their retinues ....

Whereas your said poor commons were not accustomed, in the days of your noble ancestors, to bear taxes or tallages or other special impositions except once in every four or five years, every year during the last five years they have been subjected to various tallages, not equitably adjusted according to each person's wealth, but always and continually the greater burden of these taxes is wrongly put upon your poor commons, but never applied to the winning nor reduction of your wars, or in coastal defence of your realm, for which purpose they were granted .... There are many other reasons ... why the said commons should rebel, especially for the long time your lordship and your other lords have tarried in this present parliament, trusting God that a good remedy should be ordered for these faults ....

To remedy these faults ... it seems to your humble commons, that by your leave and command, there is need first to change the governance of yourself and of your land, that you, our liege and natural lord, shall, inside and outside your land in your other lordships, be honoured and feared and perfectly loved by the people for the good and just governance, that is, most honoured lord, in doing right justice to all persons as well to the poor as to the rich equally, according as they deserve, both in your high courts as elsewhere in every land ....

115. Petition for a general pardon

The decision to exempt some individuals from the general pardon was not as serious for these men as we might imagine; none, apparently, were executed, and several prospered exceedingly.[54] This document formed a precedent, however, and was later used to much more brutal effect by the king. When he announced in the parliament of September 1397 that a general pardon would be granted to all the rebels of 1387–8, excepting fifty people, Richard was copying this procedure, except that he refused to divulge the name of the luckless fifty, thereby creating a general climate of fear.[55]

RP III.248; *PROME* 1388 (1): part 1, section 35.

May it please the lord king in this present parliament to consider the great costs which his people of the kingdom of England have suffered and borne during his whole reign; also the great quarrels and troubles between lords and lords, and commons and commons, which occurred and arose during this time; and, to renew the secure peace and unity of all ranks within the kingdom, to grant all his subjects of his realm a general and full pardon for every kind of treason, insurrection, felony, trespass, conspiracy, confederacy, champerty,[56] double-dealing, fraud, deceit, concealment and any other action whatsoever committed until now or arising within the kingdom of England, for which the penalty is loss of life or limb, or forfeiture of lands, tenements, goods, chattels, or imprisonment, or payment of a fine, ransom or other financial penalty; except John Ripon,[57] Henry Bowet,[58] William Monkton,[59] clerks; John Lancaster,[60] Henry Ferrers,[61] knights; Richard Clifford,[62]

---

54 The clerks Metford, Clifford, Lincoln and Slake were bailed on 4 June 1388, *CCR 1385–1389*, 414.

55 *CR*, 55.

56 A kind of maintenance: supporting legal action by another person, on the promise of a share in any resulting profits. It is still illegal.

57 He witnessed the questions to the judges and had represented de Vere at the papal court in his divorce case.

58 A distinguished ecclesiastical lawyer; later bishop of Bath and Wells (1401–7) and archbishop of York (1407–23).

59 Pardoned in 1390.

60 He was alleged to have been involved in a plot, masterminded by Alexander Neville, to lure Gloucester, Arundel and Warwick to France and murder them there.

61 Lord of Groby, where he had entertained Richard before the Nottingham council in 1387. He died on 3 Feb. 1388.

62 A clerk of Richard's chapel; bishop of Worcester 1401–7, bishop of London, 1407–21.

Richard Mitford,[63] John Lincoln of Grimsby,[64] Nicholas Slake,[65] clerks; John Holcote, squire;[66] Nicholas Southwell,[67] James Lustrak,[68] Henry Clerk of Thaxted, Simon Shiryngham; John Fitzmartin,[69] clerk; William Chesterton, rector of Rattlesden [Suffolk],[70] Brother Richard Roughton, Franciscan [friar],[71] and Thomas his brother, and all those who are overseas with the traitors, or decide to go over to them later ... and all those who support the our lord king's enemies of France and Scotland. Provided always that our lord king is answered for money and debts owed to him ... so that no one in the kingdom, high or low, great or small, of whatever rank or status, shall in future be prosecuted, molested, harmed, tried, indicted or accused either by the king or kingdom, either alone or with others, of any of those aforesaid actions, except and provided as above; but that every man of the kingdom of England shall be quit and discharged forever.

116. The king renews his coronation oath at the end of parliament

Just as parliament's actions were secured by oaths, so these rituals of reconciliation were designed to restore the king's authority and soothe his wounded pride.

(a) According to the parliament roll

RP III. 252; PROME 1388 (1): part 1, sections 48-9.

The commons humbly begged the king in full parliament that it would please him of his benign grace, for reverence to God, and to

63 Mitford (Medford), the king's secretary; bishop of Chichester 1389-95, bishop of Salisbury 1395-1407.

64 A long-serving exchequer clerk. In 1388 he was one of the chamberlains of the receipt, recording money paid into the exchequer.

65 Dean of the king's private chapel.

66 His arrest was ordered in July 1387 to secure his appearance before the Council; released from prison 19 May 1389.

67 A personal servant of Alexander Neville.

68 Probably a Gascon; he brought safe-conducts from Charles VI for Richard and de Vere in autumn 1387.

69 FitzMartin alias Taverner was a Lincolnshire man whose faults are unknown.

70 During the course of this parliament he sent the pope a defamatory letter about Thomas Arundel, bishop of Ely.

71 Robert de Vere's confessor.

nourish greater love, peace, tranquillity and concord in times to come throughout the whole realm, to renew the oath which he took at his coronation, and that the prelates should renew their fealty to him, and that the lords temporal should renew their homage, despite having done this previously. ... This prayer our lord king graciously and benignly granted in every particular.

Whereupon, on Wednesday 3 June, which was the 121st day of this parliament, after a Mass of the Holy Spirit[72] chanted in the church of Westminster, and a sermon preached by the archbishop of Canterbury, our lord king, wishing to perform what he had agreed, of his own free will renewed his oath with great solemnity, in the church of Westminster, in the presence of all the prelates, temporal lords and commons there assembled.

(b) According to *Westminster*
WC, 342.

On 3 June at Westminster, after a solemn Mass and sermon, while the chief men of the kingdom and all the other lords stood round a royal throne specially prepared before the high altar, also a book and cross placed on a little altar table, the king renewed his oath which once upon a time he took at his coronation. The lords both spiritual and temporal offered him, with complete subjection and a good grace, what they were accustomed to promise to the king at his coronation. When this was completed, all the bishops gathered under one canopy and pronounced sentence of excommunication on those who afterwards dared to violate this oath, or to incite the king against the lords or to provoke him by their false allegations; and, at the request of the lords and commons, the king ratified inviolate, in perpetuity, everything done in the present parliament. ... And so on 4 June parliament was finished.

72 A votive Mass: a Mass for a special occasion, with particular prayers. It was used especially to invoke good government, justice and renewal.

The Appellants in power

Had the Appellants got what they wanted? The court was purged, and de Vere had no successor as favourite. The judges were punished, serious attempts were made to reverse the direction of recent patronage and there was some redistribution of property.[73] The Appellants recovered their expenses handsomely and Gloucester finally received the grant of landed endowment he had always longed for [119].

117. The earl of Arundel's expedition, 10 June–2 September

Control of the government gave the Appellants direction of foreign policy, but their attempts to inject more aggression into the French war were unsuccessful, for, despite enthusiastic 'spin' by both Walsingham and Westminster,[74] Arundel's expedition that summer was essentially pointless.[75] He campaigned for only ten weeks, yet he insisted on being paid for the four months at sea which he had promised.[76] The Appellants then initiated peace talks with France, for which Richard later took the credit.

SAC I.852–4.

After the feast of Pentecost *[17 May]*, Richard, earl of Arundel, put to sea with a strong force and sailed in all directions looking for the enemy. Finally finding the enemy ships, he fought them and won, and either sank, captured or burnt eighty of them. He landed on the Isle de Batz which he plundered and burnt. He also invaded, captured and plundered *[six more]* islands ... taking a ransom from some, but devastating others with fire. He overcame and put to flight Frenchmen or Bretons who offered resistance, and having completed this task with the utmost success he returned to England.

118. The Treaty of Bayonne, July 1388

The final treaty between Gaunt and the king of Castile was concluded in July 1388,[77] and followed closely the agreements previously made at Trancoso. The thirteen months' delay in implementation was probably caused by King

73 Tuck (1973): 127–9.

74 *WC*, 350–2.

75 Jones (1970): 107–12.

76 Tuck (1969): 233.

77 For the first treaty, see **88**. Gaunt and Constance ratified the final one on 8 July, King Juan and his sons on 17 July.

Juan's inability to gather the required money any sooner.[78] The conclusion of Gaunt's Spanish ambitions freed him to return home, not only to intervene in English politics but to participate in diplomacy, and it opened the way for a potential ending of the Anglo-French war, yet this very important treaty went unnoticed in England. This official chronicle of the dynasty was commissioned from Lopes (died 1459), archivist and confidential secretary to the king of Portugal.

Fernão Lopes, *The English in Portugal, 1367–87*, ed. Derek W. Lomax and R. J. Oakley (Warminster, 1989), 299.

Because all that was necessary had already been worked out in the agreements made in the village of Trancoso, it was not now necessary to have a long delay but only to arrange the treaty in such a way that it would be valid. So, leaving aside many of the treaty's provisions, we shall mention now only … *[The most important addition was:]* 'Prince Fernando, the second son of the king of Castile, shall not marry or take a wife until his brother, the said Prince *[Enrique]*, is fourteen years old' (for he was then nine years old, and that was so that he could validly agree to the wedding and consummate the marriage) 'and that Prince Fernando should swear to do this; and that if, God forbid, the Prince were to die before he reached the age of fourteen, without consummating this marriage, the said Lady Catherine should marry his brother, Prince Fernando'.

119. A grant to Gloucester

Gloucester finally obtained landed endowment appropriate to his rank.

CPR 1385–9, 473.

Grant, at his supplication and with the assent of the Council, to the king's uncle Thomas, duke of Gloucester, of the manors, lands and tenements, fees and advowsons, formerly belonging to Robert de Vere, duke of Ireland, Michael de la Pole, earl of Suffolk, and others, which have become forfeit because of the judgment against them in the last parliament, to the value of £2,000 a year, such value to be agreed between the king and council, and the duke; provided that deduction be made of the yearly value of manors and lands previously granted to him by the king, by letters patent, giving him £1,000 a year when he

---

78 *The Treaty of Bayonne*, xiv. How King Juan raised the money is described by Lopes, 307.

was created earl of Buckingham, and the same sum afterwards when was created duke of Gloucester. 3 July 1388.

120. The Scottish invasions of 1388

The Appellants' image as patriots was seriously damaged by three Scottish invasions that summer. There was a raid on Ulster, and an incursion into the west march, which did the most damage, but it was the third invasion, on the east march, that was best remembered. Its result was sensational: the first Scottish victory over the English in a pitched battle since Bannockburn in 1314. This battle caught, and long fascinated, people's imagination because of being partly fought by moonlight, the long rivalry between the families of the two commanders, the capture of Percy and the death in victory of Douglas. 'I never heard the old song of Percy and Douglas that I found not my heart moved more than with a trumpet', wrote the Elizabethan courtier, Sir Philip Sidney.[79]

> This fray began at Otterburn,
> Between the night and day;
> There the Douglas lost his life,
> And the Percy was led away.[80]

This became the theme of the border ballad versions, 'The Battle of Otterburn' of the early sixteenth century, and the later version, 'Chevy Chase', which Sydney so admired. Walter Bower's account of his countrymen's overall activities in 1388 is balanced, sober and detailed, and he was not ashamed to admit ignorance, for example, of the identity of Douglas's killer.

Bower, *Scotichronicon*, 7.412–18.

In 1388 Robert, earl of Fife, along with Lord Archibald Douglas,[81] father of Sir William, gathered a large army and invaded England. A short time earlier Sir William sailed to Ireland with 500 warriors to fight the English there. He dropped anchor and landed at Carlingford, a very strong walled town, where he made a bold assault on one of the town gates. Those inside negotiated with him fraudulently to save the town and for him to make peace with them; so they promised him a certain sum of money. He, a gracious man, made peace, and was intent on obtaining cattle and necessary food in the neighbouring coastal area for the [return] voyage, so he barely escaped the townsmen's trap; for

79 Philip Sidney, *The Defence of Poetry* (1595).

80 *Border Ballads* (1991): 117. See Reed in Goodman and Tuck, eds (1992): 94–123.

81 Archibald 'the Grim' was an illegitimate cousin of the first Earl Douglas; he became the third earl on the death of his kinsman James at the battle of Otterburn.

they secretly sent a messenger to the neighbouring town of Dundalk asking for help to be sent quickly, and promising that the Scots would be completely wiped out. Because of this 800 armed horsemen came to Carlingford next day, and joined up with many local people. *[Douglas had sent most of his men on a raiding expedition, so was very vulnerable when attacked, but the Ulstermen likewise divided their forces into two.]* To cut a long story short, the result was that victory was granted to the Scots. They captured the town, seized booty and burnt houses, plundered the castle and loaded up fifteen Irish ships, which were anchored in the harbour, with all the goods from the town. Wonderfully enriched by these, they sailed for home with a large fleet. ....

Sir James *[Earl]* Douglas had made a promise, some said, that he would himself join the earl of Fife's army on the west march, but I do not know on whose advice he reneged on this. After collecting his friends and followers he found that he had 7,000 strong warriors whose help he could rely on, and because he was then more optimistic than usual, he thought he could easily overrun the whole north of England. Making an expedition southwards, he led his army, burning and devastating, to Newcastle, where his men made an assault, fought fiercely hand to hand with the townsmen and acquitted themselves in a praiseworthy and spirited manner.

Inside Newcastle all the militia of Northumberland from the city of York *[northwards]* lay in readiness with Sir Henry Percy the younger, son of Henry, earl of Northumberland, commonly called Henry Hotspur, a fierce and battle-hardened knight; they were lying in wait to discover how to gain advantage over the Scots. So when Earl Douglas and his men were returning home, Henry Percy ordered the earl of Fife's army to be reconnoitred, but because it was large he turned to the army of Earl Douglas which was then camped at Otterburn in Redesdale. All unsuspicious of the enemy's malice, Earl Douglas with his two brothers the earls of March and Moray and very many knights and nobles, disarmed. They put on jerkins and full-length robes and on St Oswald's day *[5 August]* thy sat down to dine. When they had taken their places a Scotsman came riding bareback and wildly calling them all to fly to arms because, he said, 'The enemy are bearing down upon you'. At the sound of his voice they all got up from dinner and, flying to the safety of their armour, they were scarcely able to protect themselves with basic armour. So quickly, indeed, did Earl Douglas concentrate on organising his army, that he forgot to fasten his own armour. Because of this he was fatally wounded that night in the face and neck, it is not known by whom; so in the morning, alas, he was discovered dead, leaving no heir of his body. Sir Archibald, lord of Galloway, succeeded to the earldom. ...

So Sir Henry Percy, surrounded by 10,000 armed men, divided his army into two. One part he led himself with his brother Sir Ralph; the other he committed to Sir Matthew Redmayne and Sir Robert Ogle to overturn the pavilions and tents. He himself hurried onto the field. As the noise of the English advance increased, the majority of the Scots ran away, and were vigorously pursued by Redmayne and Ogle. But while Percy observed the fleeing Scots, and was absolutely delighted by seeing their flight, and believed he had won a victory without resistance, Earl Douglas and his men mounted their horses and, concealed among the thorns and thickets, they hurried to the field unseen by the English for some time. Finally, they suddenly erupted beside the English line with twelve banners unfurled and glowing in the sun's reflection just before sunset.

When the conflict had just begun, suddenly a certain very doughty, strong and robust knight, John Swinton, a Scot, jumped out from the battle line, and when each side attacked each other with lances, he withdrew a little from both sides, and vigorously raising his long and dreadful lance, hitting the iron tips of many English lances from the side, he knocked them to the ground with every blow. Because of this the Scots first penetrated the English with their lances, and by brute force compelled them to retreat. So when the fighting had gone on for a while, the English soon turned tail, whereupon the Scots cut down and pursued their enemies and took captives all night. Henry Hotspur, the English commander, was captured along with his brother. Those who neither saved themselves by flight, nor were killed, were overpowered by the Scots; they were led into captivity in Scotland in such large numbers that prisoners outnumbered the captors. On the English side 1,500 were killed, by their own estimate; many also fell on the Scottish side, among them the noble Earl Douglas. ... On the morrow of St Oswald [6 *August*] this news depressed the earl of Fife and his army, especially about the death of Douglas. But the victory granted to the Scots cheered them up and they returned home in triumph.

121. The Battle of Otterburn, 5 August 1388

(a) According to Froissart

The story of Otterburn reverberated round Europe, and Froissart's is easily the longest account of the Anglo-Scottish warfare of 1388. He liked Scotland, which he had visited in 1365, reaching Aberdeen and beyond. Froissart's account of this campaign was the first to be written, and used information from eye-witnesses. A site visit today confirms his description of the marshy terrain, but subsequent changes in land use have destroyed the original vegetation.

Froissart, *Chronicles*, II.366–8, adapted.

The Scots left Newcastle and, taking the road to their own country, they came to the town and castle called Ponteland. ... After they had burnt the town and castle, they marched away to Otterburn, which was eight English leagues from Newcastle *[in fact, about 30 miles]*, and camped there. They made no attack that day but very early next morning their trumpets sounded and they prepared to assault, advancing towards the castle, which was tolerably strong, and situated among marshes. They attacked it so long and so unsuccessfully that they were exhausted, and so sounded a retreat. When they had retired to their quarters, the chiefs held a council about how to act. Most wished to leave next day, without further assault on the castle, to join their countrymen in the neighbourhood of Carlisle. But Earl Douglas overruled this, saying: 'Despite Sir Henry Percy, who the day before yesterday declared he would take from me his pennon that I conquered by fair deeds of arms before the gates of Newcastle, I will not leave here for two or three days; and we will renew our attack on the castle, for we ought to capture it: we shall thus gain double honour, and see if within that time he will come for his pennon: if he does, it shall be well defended'. Everyone agreed to what Earl Douglas had said, both because it was honourable and he was the principal commander. ... They made huts from trees and branches, and strongly fortified themselves. They placed their baggage and servants at the entrance of the marsh on the road to Newcastle, and the cattle they drove into the marsh lands. ...

The English imagined that Earl Douglas's army was only the vanguard of the Scots, and that the main body was behind. For that reason the knights most experienced in fighting and best acquainted with warlike matters strongly opposed Sir Henry Percy's proposal to pursue them. *[Discussion between the Percy brothers, who wished to pursue the Scots, and the other commanders, who advised restraint, was interrupted by the arrival of reconnaissance riders who had followed and observed the Scots.*]

'Sir Henry and Sir Ralph Percy, we come to tell you that we have followed the Scottish army, and observed all the country where they now are. They first halted at Ponteland, and took Sir Raymond de Laval in his castle; then they went to Otterburn, and took up their quarters for the night. We are ignorant of what they did next day, but they seem to have taken measures for a long stay. We know for certain that their army does not consist of more than 3,000 men, including all sorts'. Sir Henry Percy, on hearing this, rejoiced greatly, and cried out, 'To horse! to horse! for by the faith I owe to God, and to my lord and father, I will seek to recover my pennon, and to beat up their quarters tonight'. Those knights and squires in Newcastle who learnt this were willing to join the party, and made themselves ready.

The bishop of Durham was expected daily at that town, for he had heard of the Scots' incursion. ... The bishop had collected a number of men, and was hastening to their assistance, but Sir Henry Percy would not wait; for he was accompanied by 600 spearmen, knights and squires, and upwards of 8,000 infantry, which, he said, would be more than enough to fight the Scots, who had only 300 lances and 2,000 others. When they were all assembled, they left Newcastle after dinner, and took the field in good array, following the road the Scots had taken, making for Otterburn, eight short leagues distant. But they could not advance very fast, in order that their infantry might keep up with them.

As the Scots were dining (some indeed, had gone to sleep, for they had laboured hard during the day at attacking the castle, and intended renewing it in the cool of the morning) the English arrived, and mistook, at their entrance, the huts of the servants for those of their masters. They forced their way into the camp, which was, however, tolerably strong, shouting out, 'Percy! Percy!' In such situations, you may suppose an alarm is soon given, and it was fortunate for the Scots that the English had made their first attack on their servants' quarters, which checked them somewhat. The Scots, who were expecting the English, had prepared accordingly; for while the lords were arming themselves, they ordered a section of their infantry to join their servants and keep up the skirmish .... Meanwhile the night advanced but it was sufficiently light because the moon shone, and it was August, when the weather is temperate and serene.

When the Scots were quite ready and properly arrayed, they left their camp in silence, but did not march to meet the English. They skirted the side of a mountain which was close by; for during the preceding day, they had carefully reconnoitred the country around and said among themselves, 'Should the English come to beat up our quarters, we will do such and such', and so settled their plans beforehand, which was the saving of them, for it is of the greatest advantage to men-at-arms, when they are attacked in the night, to have previously arranged their mode of defence and to have carefully weighed the chance of victory or defeat. The English soon overpowered the servants, but as they advanced into the camp they found forces ready to oppose them and continue the fight. The Scots, meanwhile, marched along the mountainside, and fell on the enemy's flank quite unexpectedly, shouting their cries. This was a great surprise to the English, but they formed themselves in better order and reinforced that part of their army. The cries of Percy and Douglas resounded on each side. The battle now raged; great was the thrusting of lances, and very many of each party were struck down ....

I was made acquainted with all the particulars of this battle by knights and squires who had been actors in it on each side. There were also, with the English, two valiant knights from the county of Foix, whom I had the good fortune to meet at Orthès the year after this battle had been fought ... I met likewise at Avignon a knight and two squires of Scotland, of the party of Earl Douglas. They knew me again, from the recollections I brought to their minds of their own country; for in my youth, I, the author of this history, travelled all through Scotland, and was full fifteen days resident with William, Earl Douglas, father of Earl James, of whom we are now speaking, at his castle of Dalkeith, five miles distant from Edinburgh. ... I had my information, therefore, from both parties, who agreed that it was the hardest and most desperate battle that was ever fought.

(b) According to Knighton

A brief and dispassionate account of the two invasions of England, though inaccurate about the death of Douglas.

KC, 504-6.

The Scots entered England on the west march near Carlisle; they plundered and burned the whole countryside and committed many evil deeds. They captured about 300 men from that district and carried them off, and they captured Sir Peter Tyrioll, sheriff of Carlisle, and other knights of the area, and escaped without coming to any great harm. And on the east march, on 3 August, the Scots entered with the whole might of Scotland .... They devastated the land and burned it, and laid waste many northern areas to an extent unheard of in England for a many a day.

Sir Henry Percy, son and heir of the earl of Northumberland, went to confront them. The Scots called him Henry Hotspur on account of his energy because, when others had fallen asleep, he was accustomed to be on the lookout for his enemies. Henry fought with them at Elsdon,[82] near Newcastle on Tyne, and here with his own hand slew Earl Douglas and mortally wounded the earl of Moray. Henry himself was captured there, with his younger brother and another twenty-one knights, and many other armed men and archers, and were taken into Scotland. But many of the Scots were captured … The battle took place on the Wednesday [5 August] before the feast of St Lawrence, in the evening.

(c) According to Walsingham

Walsingham's description of Otterburn as essentially a contest between the Percy and Douglas families, at whose heart was a duel between the two leaders, began a tradition which continued in the early 16th-century ballads.[83] Douglas's death led Walsingham to present the campaign as an English success.

SAC I.854–6.

The Scots, those strangers to peace, believing that the English could organise nothing against them, put themselves into a state of readiness so that, as soon as the truces had expired, they would be all prepared to invade the north. This they did, and with a large army entered the kingdom before the English could make any dispositions against them. So, meeting no resistance, they advanced, committing slaughter and rapine everywhere, taking many prisoners, and burning the towns which stood in their way – unless their lords redeemed them with money. By the time they reached Newcastle upon Tyne they were very arrogant, and they pitched camp close by. There was then in that town Henry Percy the younger, and Ralph his brother, both of them knights, both anxious for military glory, both haters of the Scots. This was especially true of Henry who, because of his aggressive personality, was greatly feared by the Scots. Henry considered it shameful that the Scots were carousing here with such impunity, and especially because he had been challenged to fight by them. He promised that he would certainly come to engage in close combat with them, within three days,

82 Otterburn lies within Elsdon parish, and those killed in the battle were buried in Elsdon churchyard.

83 *Border Ballads* (1991): 107–17.

although his numbers would be much inferior to their multitude. So he attacked them suddenly, as promised, rushing at them while they were in their tents, and inflicting great carnage on them.

The Scots' commander, William [*sic;* correctly James] Douglas, himself an ambitious young man, seeing the answer to a thousand prayers, namely Henry Percy within his camp, quickly rode against him. Then could be seen a fine sight: two outstanding young men fighting hand to hand and striving for glory, and though neither lacked manly spirit, victory went to Henry, who killed the Scotsman, the leader of the Scots, with his own hands. However, the earl of Dunbar came at him with a great crowd of Scots, captured Henry himself and his brother, and killed many of the English. But the Scots had suffered irreparable damage in the killing of their most powerful men by Henry and the few men who had followed him into this battle.

(d) Richard's reaction to the battle

These incursions were prompted by the turmoil in English politics, and moved the king to anger, though he was persuaded against leading an army of retribution.

WC, 350.

When the king heard this news, his anger flared up and he wanted to punish the Scots. For this reason he convened a council at Northampton on 22 August; he wanted to go to that region and wipe out every Scot. But because winter was already close at hand the councillors considered it would be more advisable to wait for the next year, and in the meantime to organise everything needed for so large and difficult an enterprise well in advance. This advice won unanimous approval as being sensible and good.

122. The Cambridge parliament, 9 September–17 October 1388

The Cambridge parliament in September is often taken to mark the start of the king's rehabilitation. It is unclear why Barnwell Priory, outside the small town of Cambridge, was selected as the venue, because it was uncomfortable and inconvenient. Uniquely among Richard's parliaments no parliament roll has survived, but Westminster has preserved the commons' petition which formed the basis of the legislation it enacted,[84] and describes the king's intervention

84 *WC*, 356–68.

in disagreements between commons and lords, or perhaps lords appellant. The insecurity of government is well illustrated by the inquisition on all gilds ordered that year.[85] The clergy were eternally distrustful of all gatherings of laymen (except in church) and this, added to the experience of the Peasants' Revolt, infected the government also.[86]

(a) Expenses incurred by London's representatives attending this parliament

Riley, *Memorials of London*, 511–12, adapted.

Expenses incurred in attending the parliament at Cambridge by Adam Bamme, Henry Vanner, William Tonge and John Clenhond:

For timber and carpentry, tilers and daubers,[87] in preparing the house for their lodging, both for the chambers and the hall, buttery, kitchen and stables for the horses; and for making stools and benches throughout, and for throwing out the rubbish – this house being quite ruinous; also for payment made to the good man of the house, for that lodging: £6 9s.

For cloth bought for table-cloths, for canvas, tapestries and bed-hangings for the hall, of striped worsted; and for all the other utensils, many in number, that belong to the hall, kitchen, pantry and buttery; excepting only vessels of pewter, which were bought by the Chamberlain of the Guildhall: £6 16s. 8d.

For firewood, charcoal, turf and sedge: £5 13s.

For the hire of horses, and for hay and oats, and for straw for the beds, as well as for litter for the horses; and for horse-shoeing, £12 15s. 7d.

For expenses incurred by the aforesaid Bamme, Vanner, etc. and their servants, in riding on horseback to Cambridge and back; and for carriage of their wine, and all their harness, there and back: £7 16s. 8d.

For two pipes of red wine taken there from London, and for other wine bought at Cambridge: £9 2s.

For clothes for themselves and their servants, dressed in the same way, £22 15s.

Expended at Cambridge, throughout the time of the parliament, on bread, ale, meat, fish, candles, sauces, the laundryman, and in gifts to the minstrels of the king and of other lords, together with various other

---

85 *English Gilds*, ed. Lucy Toulmin Smith (Early English Text Society, original series, 140, 1870).

86 Forrest (2005): 163–4.

87 Those who plastered the wattle frame with a mixture of straw and mud.

outlays made: £23 5s. 9d.

For payments to their officials, such as steward, butler, cook and others; and to scullions helping in the kitchen, and elsewhere: £7 13s. 4d.

Sum total: £112 7s.

(b) A chronicle account of the Cambridge parliament

Westminster gives the fullest account of this and preserves some of the resulting documentation.

WC, 354–6.

On 10 September at Cambridge the king opened parliament. First they decided that all the bishops translated by papal provision should proceed immediately to their sees and take possession in the persons of their vicars-general. Then they consecrated John Waltham, keeper of the king's privy seal, as bishop of Salisbury.[88] They also decided that the wool staple should move from Middleburgh and be established at Calais, as soon as possible. ... Also the commons in this parliament complained bitterly about the lords' badges, 'because those who wear them on account of their lords' power are puffed up with such stubborn pride that they do not hesitate to commit widespread extortion in the surrounding district, with bold rashness; the result is that they damage and distress poor folk in the courts of princes and of others, every-where, and they even rip off and make helpless the middle and other classes without distinction, in every place where justice is dispensed, because they do not permit right to proceed with justice along the route of reason; so they are not afraid to commit these and other acts by the audacity prompted by these badges'. When they heard this the lords (*prefati domini*)[89] wanted to crush this general complaint; they ordered the commons to be specific, and hand over to them those committing such evil deeds, and they would so punish them that others would not dare to behave like that. But this promise displeased the commons, who even wished them to give up badges completely if they really wanted the kingdom to enjoy peace and quiet. At this point the king, who wanted tranquillity in the realm for the sake of peace and to give an example to

---

88 Waltham was consecrated on Sunday 20 Sept. in the conventual church of Barnwell, by William Courtenay, archbishop of Canterbury, in the presence of the king and many lords and magnates; Robert Braybrooke, bishop of London, and William of Wykeham, bishop of Winchester, assisted, *Register of John Waltham*, 1.

89 This text had not mentioned the lords for some time, so probably 'the appellant lords' are meant here. See **107 (d)**.

others, offered to give up his badges. This greatly pleased the commons;
but the lords, after shouting much abuse at the commons, refused to
consent to their enthusiastic demand, and so discord arose between
them. When the king saw the dissension between them on the subject
of the giving up of badges, and, wanting to avoid common discord, he
first calmed them down, and then, so that all cause of dissension should
be removed, he permitted those oft-mentioned lords (*dominis sepedictis*)
to use their badges until the next parliament, as in idiomatic French is
more fully contained here [*Then follows the long and multi-subject common
petition, starting with a complaint against liveries, and then against all guilds
and fraternities.*][90]

90 The complaint against guilds prompted an inquiry whose returns are printed in
    English Guilds, ed. Smith (1870).

IV: FROM APPEASEMENT TO TYRANNY, 1389-97

1389

123. The year 1389 according to Walsingham

On 3 May, Richard staged a bloodless coup, seizing power back into his own hands at a meeting of the council. His actions took the councillors completely by surprise; Richard not only indulged his love of the dramatic gesture, but also prevented the planning of any opposition. Walsingham and Westminster (390–2) reported the occasion almost identically, though the former included an extra theatrical flourish. Richard immediately replaced the chancellor and treasurer, astutely choosing senior bishops who had served his grandfather and were remote from recent factional conflict.

SAC I.862–8.

This year, representatives were sent on the king of England's behalf to seek peace, or at least a truce, from the king of France: Master Walter Skirlaw, bishop of Durham, and John Clanvow and Nicholas Dagworth, knights. They spent a long time at Calais, and now this way, now that, going backwards and forwards across the sea to negotiate acceptable terms and conditions for a truce, only to receive a final response that the French would not consent to a truce unless the Spanish and Scots enjoyed similar peace under the same truce. So for a long time the business of peace was held up, because our envoys insisted that the Scots were liege men of the king of England who had wickedly disturbed their king's peace, and so should be punished as law-breakers, as the king and nobles of the kingdom wanted; nor was it right for the king to concede so much to his subjects – transgressors too – that he should meet with them like this, exacting no vengeance. So a truce was delayed. Meanwhile the Scots, making light of our boastful threats, burst into Northumberland, creating great slaughter among the people, leading away many captives, and carrying back much booty into their own country. At the same time the lord Thomas Mowbray, earl of Nottingham, the Marshal, was sent with an armed force to check the Scots' rebellions; but because of his lack of troops, he did nothing. In fact, he had with him not more than 500 lances against 30,000 of the enemy.

That same year the king, led on by the advice of certain whisperers, assembled the magnates and many weighty men of the realm. He suddenly entered the council chamber where the nobles were awaiting his arrival and, sitting down, he asked them how old he was. The answer was that he had already passed twenty years.

'In that case', he said, 'I am of full age to govern my household and retinue, and even my kingdom. For it seems to me unjust that my own situation should be worse than the situation of the lowest in the land. Truly, every heir in my kingdom who reaches twenty years of age, if his father is dead, is freely permitted to manage his own affairs. So why am I denied what is allowed by right to someone of every lower rank?' When the astonished barons had answered that none of his rights should be denied him, but that he should have the ruling of his kingdom, owed to him by right, he said this: 'Look, you know that for a long time I was ruled by tutors; I was not allowed to do any but the most trivial thing without them. Now in future I will remove them from my council and, like an heir of full age, I will call whom I wish to my council and I will conduct my own business. So first of all I order the chancellor to resign the seal to me.'

When the archbishop of York [Thomas Arundel] had handed back the great seal, the king gathered it into his robe, and suddenly got up and went out; and after a very short time he came back and sat down and handed the seal to the bishop of Winchester, William of Wykham,[1] making him chancellor, unwilling though he was. And he appointed many new officials,[2] dismissing the old ones, using his own will and power entirely. He removed the duke of Gloucester and the earl of Warwick and many other worthy men from the council, and brought in others who pleased him. At the same time the king created five new judges.

Meanwhile certain detractors in the king's circle made him so paranoid that he believed his uncle, the duke of Gloucester, had gathered troops to attack him. But finally the king, after he had sent for the duke and

---

1 Wykeham (c.1324–1404; bishop of Winchester from 1367) had been in crown service since at least 1356, and was chancellor 1367–71. Although sympathetic to the Appellants, he was essentially a discreet and loyal crown servant, and remained chancellor until Sept. 1391. See P. Partner, 'Wykeham, William', in *ODNB*.

2 The new appointments included the treasurer Thomas Brantingham, bishop of Exeter (1370), an exchequer clerk since 1349 and treasurer 1369–71 and 1377–81. The elderly Brantingham found the duties too burdensome and resigned in Aug. 1389. He died in 1394. See R. G. Davies, 'Brantingham, Thomas', in *ODNB*.

discovered that the story was untrue, blushed with embarrassment. There were certain people present who broadcast this lie, whom the duke wished to challenge and whose treachery he wanted to expose publicly, but the king, with protestations of affection, asked him to proceed no further in this matter. The duke agreed to this request ... but, when he had returned home, suspicion grew again on both sides ...

About the feast of the Nativity of St John the Baptist [*24 June*] a three-year truce was concluded between the kingdoms of England and France. John Clanvow, knight, and Richard Ronhale, clerk, received an oath on the French king's behalf, and shortly after – about the feast of St Lawrence [*10 August*] – there came to England the Count of St Pol, who had married the king's [*half*] sister Matilda Courtenay,[3] with other honourable men, to receive the king of England's oath that the truce would be observed faithfully.

124. Announcement of the king's new role, 8 May

We do not know how carefully this coup had been planned by Richard beforehand, nor if he had any co-conspirators,[4] but the king's new status was widely publicised.

CCR 1385–1389, 671.

To all the sheriffs of England: Order to cause proclamation to be made that with the advice, assent and counsel of the prelates, lords etc. the king has taken upon his own person the governance of the realm, purposing to rule with deliberation of the council more prosperously than heretofore, to the greater peace of the people and fuller exhibition of justice, and that all pardons granted in the parliament at Westminster in 11 Richard II [*1388*] shall remain in force, no man being hereafter impeached for any act so pardoned; also that no man, of whatsoever estate or condition, shall under pain of forfeiture make, procure or maintain unlawful assemblies, oppressions or maintenances which may tend to disturbance of the peace, commotion of the people, or to obstruct the common law or the execution thereof, and that if any of the people shall feel aggrieved by such assemblies etc. he shall sue the

---

3 Matilda (or Maud) Holand married first Sir Hugh Courtenay (d. 1374), then Waleran III of Luxembourg, count of St Pol, in 1380. She died in 1392.

4 *Register of John Waltham*, ed. Timmins (1994), ix–x and no. 32, suggests that Waltham, keeper of the privy seal, an Appellant supporter, knew that he was shortly to be removed from his government post.

king and council, and the king shall cause a remedy to be given upon his complaint, and those guilty to be punished. By the king.

125. Action against the king's critics

Sensitivity to criticism was a feature of government throughout the reign; see **21, 135**.

Issues of the Exchequer, ed. Frederick Devon (London, 1837), 239.

14 July 1389. To John Ellingham and Robert Markeley, king's serjeants-at-arms, sent to Worcester with a commission under the great seal to arrest certain persons in the forest of Dean for allegedly blaspheming the king's person, and to cause them to appear before the king's council: £2 13s. 4d.

126. Routine government: minutes of a council meeting

From summer 1389 in periods of political tranquillity, our knowledge of everyday government is much helped by the earliest surviving minutes of council meetings. Considerable documentation shows us the kind of business the council dealt with, who was present and the decisions taken.

Proceedings and Ordinances of the Privy Council of England, ed. N. H. Nicolas (London, 1834), I.6–9.[5]

20 August 1389 in the king's presence at Windsor. Present: the bishops of Winchester (chancellor), St Davids, Durham; the duke of York; the earl of Northumberland; sirs John Devereux, John Clanvow, William Neville, Nicholas Sharnesfield, Lewis Clifford, Richard Sturry, Edward Dallingridge; and the keeper of the privy seal. It was agreed as follows that:

[1.] Letters under the privy seal be sent to the duke of Brittany stating that he *[the king]* had received the duke's letters … that he clearly recognises the goodwill and entire affection which the duke bears towards the king and his realm, and especially how he desires and is always ready to fulfil his part of the treaty between the king and himself concerning the handing over of his castles in Guyenne to the king and the restoration of the earldom of Richmond to the duke, for which the king heartily

---

5 Also printed in Chaplais (1982): II.706–7.

thanks him; indicating that he was always previously well disposed to consent to the treaty, but the business had not yet taken effect according to the wishes of both parties. And indeed the king is still of the same mind as before that it can be fulfilled, saving the honour of himself and the estate of his realm, having consideration that without infringement of the truces concluded between the king and his adversary of France the matter could take no effect during these truces, but that afterwards the king could receive these castles by virtue of that treaty, saving the form of those truces, he would be ready to accomplish the duke's desire in that matter, and to do this the king will find surety on his part, if the said duke will find surety to do the same, on his side, on which the king desires to be notified as quickly as possible.

[2.] Sir John Stanley to have the keeping of the land of Ireland for three years, taking yearly [payment] for himself and his subordinates in the manner more fully specified in the indentures made between the king and himself.

[3.] The bishop of Durham, the earl of Northumberland, the earl of Huntingdon, Sirs William Beauchamp, John Devereux, John Clanvow, Edward Dallingridge, and Master Richard Ronhale, clerk,[6] should be sent to Calais to negotiate peace between England and France.

[4.] The bishop of Durham, Sir William Beauchamp, Sir John Clanvow, Master Richard Ronhale and the treasurer of Calais [Roger Walden] should be sent on an embassy to negotiate a treaty between England and the Flemings if the peace treaty between England and France is not agreed.

[5.] The treasurer of Calais ought clearly to inform the Council of all the sums of money which he has received and the payments made by him, and if it is found that he has made any payment contrary to the authority given to him previously by the Council, that is to say to make payments firstly to the garrison of Calais, that he shall be required to make restitution.

[6.] Sir Richard Sturry should be sent to Calais to enquire into the number of soldiers there and what wages they have received for their services, and to make payment to them, so that they can be removed because of the truces,[7] and if he finds the number of those taking wages there has not been according to the indentures made between

6 For his distinguished diplomatic career, see Emden (1963): 487–8.

7 Namely, that the garrison be reduced or removed to reflect the peaceful situation.

the king and the captain of Calais, the payments should be deducted as appropriate.

7. The treasurer[8] will enquire into payments made by the collectors of customs, and if they are in arrears with their payments they should be arrested as defaulters until they have paid what is owing.

8. The king, with the assent of his Council, has granted Sir John Stanley 100 marks for his fee.

9. Sir Edward Dallingridge shall have a fee of 100 marks to be a life retainer of the king; for this fee he will have Wilmington Priory in wartime,[9] and if the priory be removed because of peace or otherwise, in that case he shall have the 100 marks elsewhere where they can be quickly paid, paying for that farm ten marks above the 100 marks.

10. Sir John Clanvow shall have £100 reward beyond his costs incurred on his embassy to France in connection with the present truces.

127. Truce with France

Shortly after seizing control of government, Richard ratified the truce with France which had been organised by the Appellants. The solemn ceremonies to ratify the truce impressed contemporaries more than its terms. This truce was the first of several.

Chronique du Religieux de Saint-Denys, I.606.

The bishop of Bayeux, councillor of the king and president of the *chambre des comptes*,[10] announced that the king of England had consented to a truce for three years, and that he would soon send one of his principal knights to ratify it. The king received the English ambassador with much honour and courtesy, promising orally to observe the treaty inviolate, and sending him home loaded with gifts, in his usual way. He despatched the count of St Pol to go and receive the same oath from the king of England.

---

8 Thomas Brantingham was replaced by John Gilbert, bishop of St Davids, on 20 Aug. 1389, the day of the meeting.

9 Sussex; a Benedictine priory dependent on Grestain Abbey, Normandy. Dallingridge was granted the profits of this alien priory (in crown custody because of the French war). Successive governments were over-optimistic about the profit in farming such houses: paying the monks an allowance and keeping the income from the landed endowments.

10 The finance department of French royal administration, similar to, but not exactly the same as, England's exchequer.

128. Guarding the northern border

After the coup, Richard turned his attention to Scotland. Mowbray, now back in favour, was appointed warden of the East March and keeper of Berwick, for one year from 1 June 1389.[11]

(a) Mowbray's tactlessness

Bower, *Scotichronicon*, 7.442.

After Sir Henry Hotspur was captured, the English wanted to provide a guardian or warden of their marches. They replaced him in this office with a high-sounding aristocrat, namely 'Earl Marshal', a very suitable person – they thought. Immediately on getting the post he spoke very arrogantly and scornfully to the English borderers, criticising them for allowing the Scots – who were subhuman, he said – to gain a victory over them at Otterburn, since they had been much more numerous than the Scots and also had attacked them unexpectedly. He often added: 'If I could get the supplies for fighting the Scots, even if they were two to one, I would try to attack them'. Hearing this, the new governor of Scotland[12] called these threats to mind and quickly gathered an army ....

(b) Continuing warfare

WC, 394–6.

The previous year's account told how it was decided that certain nobles whose family estates were in the north should defend the region from all attacks – though as it happened this command was ineffective because those northern lords most experienced in war against the Scots lacked sufficient men and money to defend the area, which were refused them. So the earl of Nottingham, Lord Neville, and the other powerful men of the area invaded Scotland with 1,500 men-at-arms on 25 June, but achieved little because they immediately found a large force prepared against them which they did not dare to attack by reason of the great number gathered there. But the Scots, virtually ignoring them, entered England by another road with about 30,000 warriors and devastated the land everywhere as far as Tynemouth. They ordered the prior there to pay them a ransom for his cells and other neighbouring property

11 He was paid £12,000, and was to retain 400 men-at-arms and 800 archers during June and July (the campaigning season), *Calendar of Documents Relating to Scotland*, ed. Bain IV (Edinburgh, 1888), 86, no. 389.

12 Robert, earl of Fife.

or they would consume these by fire and destruction. This they did
everywhere, despite the king having been forewarned of it. The earl
of Northumberland, who foresaw how things were likely to turn out
for those lords, cautiously withdrew and joined the king, and became a
leading member of his council. When he heard of the damage which the
Scots were inflicting on the whole area, the earl of Nottingham, with
his men, hurried to Berwick and remained there. *[Some English raids on
Scotland are described.]* The cause of discord among the northern lords
was this: because all were gentlemen or noblemen, although one was
called an earl, another a baron and others lords, nevertheless in the
taking of money they wanted to be equal. This was denied them, so
they went away to their homes, and therefore the whole area, except
the castles, was left unprotected, giving the Scots absolute freedom to
do as they liked in destroying the countryside.

129. Results of the Scottish invasions

It was not until 1389 that the economic effects of the 1388 invasions became
evident. The most serious damage was in the west, where full recovery had not
taken place even after 1500.[13]

TNA, E 159/166 (Memoranda Roll), *Brevia directa baronibus, rotulus* 17.

For the sheriff of Cumberland. The king to the treasurer and his barons
of the exchequer, greeting. Our dear and faithful Peter Tilliol,[14] our
sheriff of Cumberland, petitioned us that, since he will be completely
unable to levy any profits, farms or rents from very many of our
demesne lands and other lands of serjeanty,[15] assarts and of our petty
farms in that county because these are recently destroyed and wasted
by our enemies of Scotland and by the costs incurred in fortifying our
city of Carlisle against the aggressions of those enemies, we wish him to
be exonerated for his account payable before us, and now due, for these
profits, farms and rents …. We order you that, if by inquisition made
on this matter, or by other legitimate ways, it can be shown to us that
this sheriff cannot have levied nor cannot levy these rents, farms and

13 Cumberland, Westmorland and Northumberland were exempted from taxation in
   1489 and 1514, Jurkowski, Smith and Crook (1998): 122; Schofield (1965): 483–510.
14 Sheriff, 30 Nov. 1387–1 Dec. 1388, Roskell *et al.* (1992): IV.614–15.
15 A form of feudal tenure which obliged the vassal to perform a personal service to the
   monarch, e.g. carrying his lance or banner. The great officers of the king's household
   held their lands in this way.

profits from that county on account of that aforesaid destruction, you should not burden him in any way to answer us in his account for any rents, farms and profits which he cannot collect, but that he should be exonerated and quit, as is just. 5 October 1389.

1390

130. Council instructions to the peace negotiators, 28 April 1390

A three-year truce with France was agreed at Leulinghem in June 1389; it was not allowed to expire but extended by stages to 1396. The absence of warfare allowed serious negotiation towards a permanent peace. Richard's foreign policy presents problems: chroniclers, even Westminster (the best-informed), have comparatively little to say on the subject; a chronology must be assembled from government records. Above all, we can only infer what Richard's policy was, and it may well have changed in the years 1390 to 1396. The sticking point in all negotiations was the status of Aquitaine.[16] Palmer thought that Richard intended to solve the problem by permanently detaching the duchy from the crown and giving it to Gaunt and his descendants. This would have been unacceptable to Gascons, and his theory has been challenged by other scholars; it remains unproven.[17]

These instructions appear to take no cognisance of the fact that Richard had granted the duchy of Guyenne to Gaunt for his lifetime on 2 March 1390, but they show the negotiators wrestling with large questions of sovereignty over wide territories as well as precise instructions about individual castles. These instructions survive in several copies; this one has the autograph signature of John Prophet, clerk to the council, beside every clause.

Pierre Chaplais, *English Medieval Diplomatic Practice*, Part I (London, 1982), I.191–3.

Instructions given to the bishop of Durham, the earl of Northumberland, sirs John Devereux, Edward Dallingridge and Richard Sturry, Masters Raymond Guilliam and Richard Ronhale, the king's envoys and ambassadors sent to Calais to treat with the French ambassadors about peace between our lord king and his adversary of France.

---

16 Aquitaine, Gascony and Guyenne are here treated as interchangeable terms for the area of south-west France whose natural capital was Bordeaux.

17 Phillpotts (1990): 363–86 argued that an independent duchy of Guyenne for Gaunt was Gaunt's policy, not Richard's, and that Gaunt was effectively running a private foreign policy after 1389; when this failed, Richard took charge and negotiated the long truce of 1396. For a thoughtful critique of Palmer's theory see Saul: 212–15.

First, the envoys will demand that the peace made at Calais and solemnly sworn by the two kings and other nobles of each realm should be re-established and observed in all points, and that it should be well and carefully considered on which points or articles the peace was broken, and the party found to be at fault in not keeping the peace and guarding it, according to the purpose and the substance, should be compelled to amend it well and loyally without fraud or evil intention. And if the French do not wish to agree to this, but to enter into a new treaty without having regard to the peace made at Calais, the envoys should enter into a treaty with them in the manner which follows, namely first that the article concerning sovereignty and jurisdiction should be put into the treaty.

[2.] The envoys will urge that the said jurisdiction should be so limited, modified and restrained that the war cannot be revived nor the lands be confiscated by any means in future for this reason, except only for the crime of treason committed against the person of the king of France by the king of England, duke of Guyenne.

[3.] That this crime should be clearly and duly proved by good and just process of law before any pronouncement or declaration or other prejudicial deed is done against the said king and duke.

[4.] If the French do not wish to grant such good, strong and general restrictions to the modification of that jurisdiction, as there should be, the envoys shall strive to discover and extract from the French greater and stronger restrictions and limitations which they can eventually have from them, and report to the lords of the Council.

[5.] The envoys shall demand the whole of Guyenne and of the other lands assigned to the king in the previously mentioned peace; and as for homage and fealty, it pleases the king that such homage should in future be performed by the duke of Guyenne of the day, as was done in olden times, without regard to the liege homage performed by his grandfather king Edward *[III]*, when he was under age and without the consent or advice of his kingdom.

[6.] It is not the king's intention to perform homage in person for the said duchy, or for any other lands which he holds and ought to have overseas, but to hold them freely, absolutely and quit for the term of his life.

[7.] That no demand or challenge nor any service is, or can be, demanded, unless of the persons who hold at the time that said duchy and lands of him. And if the French do not wish to give the whole of Guyenne

and the other lands, the envoys shall report back to the king's Council.

[8.] The king wishes, before the treaty is broken, that after his death his heirs should do homage for the duchy and other services for the lands overseas.

[9.] If it happens that the duchy is in the king's hand or in the hand of any of his sons, the king does not agree that he should come to parliament or Council or in any other manner to a court of France in person, but [only] through his proctor.

[10.] If, while negotiating the peace treaty, the French wish to talk about extending the last truces made at Leulingham, the king will assent as far as the parties can agree.

[11.] It is the king's intention that Calais and other fortresses in the marches of Picardy should remain with him. And if the French do not wish to release Ardres, Oye (*Poyle*), Audruicq (*Oterwyk*)[18] and other fortresses, the envoys must report this.

[12.] If the French want the Scots to be allowed to negotiate, our envoys shall not receive them to discuss anything concerning Scotland.

131. The year 1390 according to the *Vita*

From 1390 this chronicle was continued by a second author, much more independent than the first. He alone described the first distribution of the white hart badge.

VR, 131–2.

On 8 May, there came to London the duke of Guelders,[19] whom the king honoured magnificently and installed as one of the knights of the Garter at Windsor. In July of the same year the king came to Leicester, where, at the duke of Lancaster's prompting, John of Northampton and his allies, who had been recently banished from London, were restored

---

18 Ardres is a town 15 km south of Calais; Oye (or Oye-Plage) and Audruicq (or Ouderwijk) are castles in the Calais Pale, both in the *département* of Pas-de-Calais to the west and south of Gravelines.

19 William of Juliers, duke of Guelders (1379–1402), whose duchy was both large and strategically important, was a staunch ally of England against France. This was the first of three visits which he paid to England (the others were in 1392 and 1396). The ducal household is very well documented, and detailed accounts survive for this visit, showing that Duke William brought 117 members of his court; Nijsten (2004): xviii–xix, 13, 42.

to their former liberties. A king's judicial enquiry called trailbaston[20] sat
this year in the duchy of York. On 10, 11 and 12 October the king held
his great court in the diocese of London, and a tournament at Smithfield. Foreigners flocked to this court from France, Zeeland, Germany
and other lands,[21] bringing with them their best horses and weapons,
and there was distributed for the first time the distinguished device or
badge of the White Hart, with crown and gold chain.

To demonstrate his excellent kingship to these foreigners, the
king observed the feast of St Edward the Confessor *[13 October]* at
Kennington, sitting solemnly in his *[coronation]* regalia, both at Mass
and at table; the queen did likewise. There were present at these solemnities the count of St Pol along with his wife, who was the *[half]* sister
of the king of England, and the count of Ostrevant, who then was made
a knight of the garter. ... At the start of October, Thomas Arundel,
archbishop of York, became chancellor of England and John Waltham,
bishop of Salisbury, treasurer. In the same year the earl of Stafford
married the daughter of the duke of Gloucester, and the noble king's
knights Sir John Clanvow and Sir *[William]* Neville died in the orient.[22]

132. The Smithfield tournament

This was the social highlight of the reign[23] when Richard hosted a glittering
social event which attracted participants from many parts of northern Europe,
though the king himself did not joust, either in 1390 or in any of the other
major or seasonal tournaments.[24] The impetus for this event may have come
from France, where in spring 1390 the French held an international tournament near Calais.[25] Froissart, naturally, provides the most detailed description.

(a) Froissart's account

Froissart, *Chronicles*, II.477–81.

---

20 An inquiry into disorder and perversions of justice.

21 Scots who came included the earl of Moray and the lord of Glen Esk, whose absence
allowed the earl of Buchan ('the Wolf of Badenoch') to rampage in the lands on the
south side of the Moray Firth. The stark ruins of Elgin Cathedral still testify to his
orgy of destruction: Boardman (1997): 175.

22 On their journey and tomb, Düll, Luttrell and Keen (1991): 174–90; on their beliefs,
McFarlane (1972): pt 2, ch. 5.

23 Lindenbaum (1990): 1–20.

24 Saul (1998): 12.

25 *WC*, 432 n.1.

News of the splendid feast and entertainments made for Queen Isabel's public entry into Paris was carried to many countries, and rightly, for they were most honourably conducted. The king of England and his three uncles had received complete accounts about them, for some of his knights had been present, and reported all that had passed with great accuracy. In imitation of this the king of England ordered grand tournaments and feasts to be held in the city of London, where sixty knights would be accompanied by sixty noble ladies, richly ornamented and dressed. The sixty knights were to tilt for two days: on the Sunday after Michaelmas day, and the Monday following [10 and 11 October. Details of the planned jousting follow.]

Heralds were sent to proclaim this feast throughout England, Scotland, Hainault, Germany, Flanders and France. ... Many knights and squires from foreign lands made preparations to attend, some to see the manners of the English, others to take part in the tournaments. When the feast was made known in Hainault, Sir William de Hainault, count d'Ostrevant, who was at that time young and gallant and fond of tilting, made up his mind to be present and to honour and make acquaintance with his cousin King Richard and his uncles, whom he had never seen. He therefore engaged many knights and squires to accompany him. .... The count Waleran de Saint Pol, who had married King Richard's half-sister, assembled a handsome body of knights and squires. ... On Sunday [10 October] ... about three o'clock there paraded out from the Tower of London ... sixty armed war-horses ornamented for the tournament, each ridden by a squire at walking pace; then came sixty high-ranking ladies, mounted on palfreys,[26] most elegantly and richly dressed, each leading by a silver chain a knight armed for tilting; and in this procession they moved through the streets of London, attended by numbers of minstrels and trumpeters, to Smithfield. The queen of England and her ladies and damsels had already arrived and were installed in chambers handsomely decorated. The king was with the queen....

The count de St Pol with his companions now advanced, handsomely armed for the occasion, and the tournament began. Every foreign knight who pleased tilted, or had time for so doing, before the evening set in, for the tilting continued until night forced them to break off. The lords and ladies then retired .... The queen was lodged in the bishop of London's palace near St Paul's church, where the banquet was held.

26 A saddle-horse for ladies.

Towards evening, the count d'Ostrevant arrived,[27] and was kindly received by King Richard and his lords. The prize for the challengers was adjudged to the count de St Pol, as the best knight at this tournament, and that for the defenders[28] to the earl of Huntingdon. The dancing was at the queen's residence, in the presence of the king, his uncles and the barons of England. The ladies and damsels continued their amusements, before and after supper, until it was time to retire, when all went to their lodgings, except such as were attached to the king or queen, who, during the tournament, lived at the palace of the bishop of London.

On Monday afternoon, King Richard entered Smithfield, magnificently accompanied by dukes, lords and knights, for he was chief defender of the lists. The queen took up her position as on the preceding day, with the ladies, in the company of knights and squires fully armed for tilting …. The tournaments now began, and every one tried his hardest to excel: many were unhorsed, and more lost their helmets. The jousting continued with great courage and perseverance until night put an end to it. The company now retired to their lodgings or their homes, and when the hour for supper was near the lords and ladies attended it, which was splendid and well served. The prize for the challengers at the tournament was adjudged – by the ladies, lords and heralds – to the count d'Ostrevant, who far eclipsed all who had tilted that day; that for the defenders was given to a gallant knight of England called Sir Hugh Despenser.

Next day, Tuesday, the tournament was renewed by the squires, who tilted in the presence of the king, queen and all the nobles, until night. … The supper was as magnificent as before, at the palace of the bishop where the king and queen lodged. The dancing lasted until daybreak, when the company broke up. The tournament was continued on the Wednesday by all knights and squires indiscriminately who wished to joust; it lasted until night, and the supper and dances were as the preceding day.

On Thursday, the king entertained at supper all the foreign knights and squires, and the queen their ladies and damsels. The duke of Lancaster gave a grand dinner to them on the Friday. On Saturday, the king and his court left London for Windsor, where the count d'Ostrevant, the

27 He had diverted from his direct route to make a pilgrimage to the shrine of St Thomas Becket at Canterbury.

28 That is, the 'home team'.

count of St Pol and the foreign knights who had been present at the feasts were invited. Everyone accepted the invitation ... and went to Windsor. ... The entertainments were very magnificent in the dinners and suppers King Richard gave, for he thought he could not pay honour enough to his cousin the count d'Ostrevant. He was invited by the king and his uncles to be one of the companions of the order of the blue Garter, as the chapel of St George, the patron, was at Windsor.

(b) *Westminster*'s account

This is the only source which asserts that Richard took part in tournaments.[29] The Monk probably misunderstood the report that one of the king's representatives, either the earl of Huntingdon or Sir Hugh Despenser, had won the prize (as Froissart reported) and believed that the king himself had competed. *WC*, 450.

On 10 October at Smithfield there were solemn joustings, to which earls and gallant knights came to the city of London from many places. There came, among others, the count of St Pol with his wife, who was the king's *[half]* sister, with other warlike Frenchmen; there came also the count called Ostrevantz with others of Germany in noble array, because he brought with him by sea all the equipment for himself and his men. The cause of these tournaments was as follows: when the duke of Guelders had been here in England he greatly wished to see our king in arms, and so at his departure he promised to come back and to be present at these jousts on this day and place, but he was prevented, and not able to accomplish what he wanted. This tournament lasted three days; and on the first day the prize was awarded to the king.

On the feast of the translation of St Edward *[the Confessor; 13 October]* the king was in Westminster Abbey at prime, vespers and compline with all his chaplains; he was also there for matins at midnight with his chaplains; he was at the procession during the day, and at High Mass he sat in the choir, crowned, with his chaplains around him. Soon after the start of High Mass the queen, solemnly crowned, entered the choir and withdrew into the north side. The bishop of London was the celebrant.

29 On tournaments during the reign and the king's attitude to them, Saul (1999): esp. 10–12.

133. The parliament of 12 November–3 December 1390

Despite this extravagant interlude, old problems remained: the income of two
royal uncles, an uncompleted war with France and the unreliability of the duke
of Brittany as an ally.

(a) York and Gloucester petition for the arrears of their allowances

RP III.278; *PROME* 1390 (2), section 12.

At this parliament the duke of York and the duke of Gloucester delivered to the king a petition in the following form: May it please you,
most gracious and redoubtable lord king, to remember how you were
pleased to make your uncles, one the duke of York, the other the duke
of Gloucester, and by the assent of your parliament you promised them
for the maintenance and governance of those honourable estates and
names, to each of them severally and to the heirs male of their bodies,
£1,000 of land and rent per annum, and to take that £1,000 from
your exchequer and from other places designed by you, until you had
assigned to each of them and their said heirs, lands and tenements to
the value of £1,000 a year; the suppliants are now so impeded in this
that they cannot get payment of those said sums, resulting in their
great anxiety about the future, in which they or their heirs may suffer
similar impediment.

Therefore they beg that your highness may be pleased, with the assent
of your parliament, to grant and command that each of your said uncles
should be as legally secure as possible, to have for himself and the heirs
male of his body, by this gift, the £1,000 in land and rent annually,
within the realm of England, to maintain and sustain their honourable
names and estates; and to take those £1,000 p.a. from your exchequer
or elsewhere as they are designated, until each of them should have,
by gift of yourself or your heirs, lands and tenements to the value of
£1,000 annually ….

This petition our lord king granted with the assent of parliament in
all points, and charged his justices to command and see that surety be
made to the suppliants, as requested in this petition, and he granted
also, with parliament's assent, that sufficient new charters be made
for the suppliants and the heirs males of their bodies for the £1,000
granted severally to them … together with letters patent and writs of
execution of the said new charters, in numbers and kinds as are neces-

sary; and that those suppliants should be paid the arrears both of the
£1,000 p.a. and other annuities granted to them by our lord king in
those places assigned to them by *[letters]* patent, notwithstanding any
command made to the contrary.

(b) The duke of Brittany is deprived of his English lands

Duke John IV of Brittany adopted an increasingly independent attitude to
England from 1389. The coolness between him and his former allies explains
this confiscation of his valuable English possessions.

RP III.279; *PROME* 1390 (2), section 14.

It was declared by the king and lords in this parliament that, in the
parliament held at Westminster on the morrow of Martinmas in the
eighth year of the present king's reign *[12 November 1384]*, the earldom
and lordship of Richmond, with all appurtenances, should be judged by
the king and lords to be forfeit to the king, because of the adherence
of John, duke of Brittany, then earl of Richmond, to the adversary of
France, in contravention of the alliances made by that duke, both with
our lord king and with his most noble grandfather, whom God absolve;
for which alliances the duke had that earldom and lordship. That
judgment was not enrolled on the roll of that parliament held in the
8th year *[1384]* for certain reasons well known to the king and lords.

1391

134. Continuing disputes in London

Unrest in London was another of the perennial problems for government. John
of Northampton [61, 63–5] was pardoned on 2 December 1390, but remained
a cause of contention.[30]

Riley, *Memorials of London*, 526–7, adapted (translated from London Letter-
Book H).

Many dissensions, quarrels and false reports have prevailed in the
city of London, both between trades and between persons, because
of various controversies which recently took place between Nicholas
Brembre, knight, and John Northampton, both former mayors of the
city, who were men of great power and wealth, and had many friendships and friends within the same, to the peril of the city and perhaps
of the whole realm, to the displeasure both of God and of every good

30 *CPR* 1388–92, 335.

man. Because of these, unless some remedy is applied, with God's help, the destruction and annihilation of the city may readily ensue, and peril and damage to all the realm – which may God avert. Therefore Adam Bamme, the mayor, and the aldermen of the city, after considering the mischief and great damage that has resulted from this cause, and desiring to maintain the peace of the king and all the realm for the common profit, have ordained and established that no man, great or small, of whatever estate or condition he be, shall speak from henceforth or agitate upon any of the opinions concerning either Nicholas or John, or shall by signs, or in any other manner, show that such person is of the one opinion or the other. But let the folks of the same city be of one accord in good love, without any speaking one to another on the said matter in a reproving or hating manner; on pain – if anyone speaks or acts against any of those matters – of imprisonment in Newgate for a year and a day, without remission, and of being subject to further penalty and ordinance in the Guildhall.

135. A Londoner offends the king

For similar episodes see **21, 125**.

CCR 1389–92, 527, adapted.

Memorandum that on 9 December, 15 Richard II *[1391]*, William Mildenhale of London appeared in chancery where, freely and without compulsion, he acknowledged that he had heard Peter Mildenhale his father, now deceased, say that the king was not able to govern any realm, and wished that he were in his latrine where he might stay for ever without doing any further governing; that he also said that it would be easy, if he wished, to seize the king with twelve men and take him wherever he wanted; and this would be all the easier because the king often rode from his manor of Sheen to London with a small escort, able to put up little resistance; and he spoke many other disrespectful words disparaging the king's person. Because William, contrary to his allegiance, had concealed from the king and council his father's iniquity, unlawful wish and abuse, he was committed to prison. Afterwards he was set free by the king's kindness, because he willingly acknowledged his fault, and because Robert Mildenhale, Robert Barton and Henry Barton of London and John Frank of Somerset had that day given surety for him in chancery under a pledge of £300. William also gave an undertaking under the same pledge that in future he would, as far

as he reasonably could, speak respectfully of the king's person; and, if
he heard unlawful words or abuse of the king spoken by any person of
the realm, he would declare it as speedily as he could, either to the king
himself or to one of this counsel [*sic*] whom he trusted to reveal this
to the king.

136. Trouble in Cheshire

In Cheshire, as in Yorkshire, the rebellions of 1394 [**144**] did not arise out of
the blue.
CPR 1391–6, 77–8, slightly adapted.

Commission to the justice of Chester or his deputy, the chamberlain and
the sheriff of Chester [*and twenty-five others named*] upon information
that, whereas the good men and commonalty of Chester lately granted
3,000 marks to the king, whereof 2,000 marks should have been paid
some time ago for the confirmation of their charter by the king, yet
when the sheriff was busy levying that 2,000 marks by the king's
mandate, divers lieges of the county rose in insurrection and obstructed
him, taking from him the moneys already levied – to enquire and arrest
those persons and commit them to prison until further order, and to
compel restitution of the sums taken from the sheriff; also to proceed
with all haste to levy those 2,000 marks and pay them to the treasurer
and chamberlains of the exchequer at Westminster at the octaves of St
Hilary next [*20 January 1392*], and the remaining 1,000 marks after the
Annunciation [*25 March*]; or failing that, they themselves to be present
in person before the king and council at Westminster at the first date,
bringing with them the letters patent of confirmation to show cause
why they should not be revoked. By the privy seal. 8 December 1391.

137. A diplomatic delegation from Gascony

It is unclear whether Richard envisaged ceding Gascony to the house of
Lancaster in perpetuity, or only for Gaunt's lifetime. This delegation may have
been objecting to long-term peace plans or simply to the person of Gaunt.
VR, 132.

The king spent Christmas at King's Langley and there the Gascons
came to him saying that from ancient time they were accustomed to be
governed by the king of England and to hold of him, or else of his eldest

son, and of no other. They made it clear that they did not wish to have the duke of Lancaster as their lord, but only as the king's lieutenant.

1392

A council at Stamford in April addressed the problems of concluding peace with France; French demands were considered unacceptable and a truce was agreed instead. Westminster's account of Gaunt's report on his diplomatic meetings, and the subsequent discussion, is one of the few places in any chronicle where the issues at stake between the two realms are set out, though efforts were made to keep the nation informed about international affairs. The rest of the year was dominated by an episode entirely of Richard's making. Whether for financial reasons or because of continuing unrest – the 'defects' in the city which Richard detected – the king revoked London's privileges, installed his own nominee to govern the city and demanded a large fine from its inhabitants. He also, at great trouble and expense, moved the law courts to York. The king's displeasure was bought off by money, albeit less than he had originally demanded,[31] and by magnificent ceremonial which was reported in detail.

138. The year 1392 according to the *Vita*

The major domestic upheaval of this year was the quarrel between the king and London; see Barron (1971): 173–201.

VR, 133.

On 7 May, John, duke of Lancaster and Aquitaine, who was honourably supported by the king, was granted Aquitaine. On 25 May a council was held at Stamford at which many things were decided, including an enactment that men of good birth possessing rents to the value of £40 should become knights. At this council a truce was concluded between the kings of England and France to last for some years, and there was much discussion about making a perpetual peace. Also at this council all the courts were transferred from London to York, and royal writs were sent to the mayor and sheriffs and twenty-four aldermen, and twenty-four of the weightier men of the city of London, to be at Nottingham to answer before the king's council to those things of which they were accused. So on 11 July John Hende the mayor of London was deposed and imprisoned in Windsor castle. Likewise the sheriffs were deposed and imprisoned, one in Wallingford castle, the other in Oakham castle.

31 For attempts to raise the money for this, see *The Church in London* (London, Record Society, 1977): xv–xvii.

Meanwhile Edward Dallingridge was appointed warden of the city of London. On 23 November, there died the duchess of York[32] whom the king, on 14 January [1393], caused to be honourably interred at King's Langley.

139. Council meeting at Stamford, 25 April

This gathering was so large that it was almost indistinguishable from a parliament. The visiting duke of Guelders was greatly impressed by the assembly and urged Richard to lead his people against the French, expressing a readiness to join any fighting on the English side.[33] The Monk's account is probably based on an eyewitness report.

WC, 490–2.

At the start of the council the duke of Lancaster ... clearly explained the French demand, saying that they first sought that the English king should completely renounce to them his right and claim which in any way he had or could have had to the French kingdom in perpetuity, and that he should completely remove the fleur-de-lis from his arms. Secondly, they sought that the duchy of Normandy and the county of Artois should be returned to them, in perpetuity, with all their appendages (*appendiciis*). Thirdly, that everything in Aquitaine they had acquired by whatever title, or that had come into their hands in any way whatsoever and was then in their possession, should be possessed by the duke of Berry peacefully and unchallenged, just for his lifetime; but once the duke of Berry was dead, the whole of Aquitaine and Gascony, with all their appurtenances (*pertinenciis*) should revert to the duke of Lancaster and his heirs in perpetuity, provided that the duke and his heirs rendered the customary homage for all Aquitaine to the king of France. These by no means pleased the commons of England because, they said, it would be stupid and very damaging to the king and his crown that, for one person's advantage, he should forever forgo such large and lovely lordships which had been in subjection to the kings of England for so long, with all their hereditary rights. In the arguments about this the king, on the duke of Lancaster's advice and despite the commons, wanted to meet some of the French demands, for

---

32 Isabella of Castile, younger daughter of Pedro the Cruel, was sister of Constance, duchess of Lancaster. She was 37.

33 For the duke's quarrel with the French and their invasion of Guelders, 1388, see *Chronique du Saint-Denys*, 522–54.

the sake of peace, and to refuse others, because he wished to moderate their demands in order that everyone on both sides would be satisfied. He therefore sent envoys to the French about this matter, so that a truce might be concluded during which each side could meantime better deliberate on this. This was done; a truce was concluded between the English and French, from the forthcoming Michaelmas until the same feast the following year [29 Sept. 1392–29 Sept. 1393]. And so, meanwhile, there was respite from the tumults of war.

140. National proclamation about extension of the truce with France

Pierre Chaplais, *English Medieval Diplomatic Practice* (London, 1982), II.654–5.

Be it remembered that the truces and suspensions of war formerly made at Leulinghen between our lord the king of England, for himself, his kingdom, his lands, lordships, subjects and allies on one part, and his adversary of France for himself, his lands, lordships, subjects and allies on the other part, made 8 April 1391, with the assent of the ambassadors of one side and the other, having sufficient power and authority for that, have been extended and prolonged, that is to say, from 16 August next until Michaelmas following [29 September] and from that Michaelmas until a year after, in the form and manner in which the said truces are worded.

The king to the sheriff of Kent, greeting. We send you the form of the prorogation of the truces to be made between us and our adversary of France, in a certain schedule enclosed with these presents, ordering that, immediately you have received this, you have those truces publicly proclaimed in all the ports and places within your jurisdiction where you think best, on our behalf. Do not fail to do this. Westminster 1 May [1392]. By the king and council.

[The same order was sent to the sheriffs of fifteen other counties, and of Bristol and London, to Gaunt as duke of Aquitaine, the constable of Dover castle and warden of the Cinque Ports, and the captains of Brest, Cherbourg and Calais.]

141. The quarrel with London

(a) According to *The Brut*

The Brut was the most popular of all chronicles, judging from the number of surviving manuscripts. This English continuation, written in London, was probably derived from a local chronicle.

The Brut, or the Chronicles of England, ed. F. W. D. Brie, vol. II (Early English Text Society, Original Series 136, 1908), 345–8; modernised.

In the 16th year of King Richard's reign,[34] when John Hende was mayor of London, and John Walworth [*correctly Shadworth*] and Henry Vanner were sheriffs, a baker's man was carrying a basket full of horse-loaves[35] into Fleet Street, towards an inn. Along came a yeoman of the bishop of Salisbury, called Romayne,[36] who took a horse-loaf out of the baker's basket, and the baker asked, 'Why did you do that?' At this, Romayne turned round and broke the baker's head. The neighbours came out and tried to arrest Romayne, but he broke away from them and fled into his master's house. The constables would have had him out, but the bishop's men shut fast the gates, and secured the place so that no one could enter. Many more people gathered, and threatened to pull him out, or else to burn the place down, and everyone in it. Then the mayor and sheriffs and many more people came, and calmed the commons' anger, and made everyone go back home, and keep the peace. Romayne's master, the bishop of Salisbury, John Waltham, who at that time was treasurer of England, went to Thomas Arundel, archbishop of York and also chancellor of England, and complained to him about the people of the city of London. Then the two bishops, out of malice and vengeance, came to the king at Windsor and made a great complaint about the mayor and sheriffs.[37] ... Soon afterwards, the king suddenly sent for the mayor of London and the two sheriffs, who came to him at Windsor castle. The king savagely rebuked them for the offence they

34 In fact this was the 15th year of the reign. Hende, Vanner and Shadworth were elected in 1391, on the customary day, 13 October.

35 A horse-loaf weighed as much as two white loaves and could contain, besides flour, ground peas and beans, *OED*: 401. It was the lowest quality of bread.

36 Possibly a relative of Henry Romayne, a long-serving vicar-choral of Salisbury cathedral, and rector of Alton and of Langton Maltravers; an unsatisfactory incumbent, *Register Waltham*, nos. 111, 668, 783, 974, 1070.

37 The precise date of this episode is unclear, but the consultation between Arundel and Waltham probably took place between mid-January and late April; both were present at a council meeting at Rotherhithe on 4 March, for example; *Register of John Waltham*, 221; Aston (1967): 387–8.

had committed against him and his officers, in his chamber of London. He therefore deposed the mayor and two sheriffs of London. This was done fourteen days before the feast of St John the Baptist *[Tuesday 11 June 1392]*.

The king then summoned a knight called Sir Edward Dallingridge[38] and made him warden and governor of the city and chamber of London, over all his people there, but he kept that office for only four weeks because he was so kind and gentle to the citizens of London. For that reason the king deposed him and made Sir Baldwin Raddington,[39] who was controller of the king's household, the warden and governor of his chamber and of his people there, who chose worthy men of the city to be sheriffs with him, to govern and keep the king's laws in the city. One was called Gilbert Maghfield,[40] the other Thomas Newington. These three good men had the governance of the city until the time to elect the next mayor *[13 October 1392]*; he was William Staundon, and the sheriffs were Gilbert Maghfield and Thomas Newington. Then the mayor, the two sheriffs and all the aldermen, with all the worthy crafts of London, went on foot to the Tower, and there the Constable of the Tower came out and administered their oath *[of office]* to the mayor and sheriffs, such as they should have taken in the exchequer at Westminster in the king's court of the justices and barons of the exchequer. Then they went home again.

Then the king and his council, out of malice and spite to the city of London, removed all his courts from Westminster to the city of York, that is to say, the chancery, the exchequer, the king's bench and also the common pleas, and there they held all their courts of law from midsummer until the following Christmas. The king and his council then saw that it was not so profitable there as it was at London; and he soon moved them back to London, and to Westminster, for his officers' great convenience and to the advantage of the king and all the commons of the realm.

When the people of London saw and knew that these courts had returned, and the king and his people also, the mayor and aldermen and

38 A former adherent and councillor of Arundel who apparently went over to Richard's side in 1389, Dallingridge is today best remembered as the builder of Bodiam castle, Sussex, Goodman (1971): 19, 115–17; Roskell *et al.* (1992), II.738–42.

39 Simon Burley's nephew, Lewis (1937): 662–9, and the husband of Brembre's widow, Idonia.

40 Maghfeld (Mayfield) is unusually well-documented, thanks to the survival of one of his account books. Translated extracts in Rickert (1948): 185–93.

the chief commons gathered a great sum of gold from all the commons of the city, and ordered and made great preparations for his coming to London, in order to have his grace and good lordship, and also to have their liberties and franchises returned to them again, as they previously enjoyed. Then, at the great insistence and entreaty of Queen Anne,[41] and of other lords and ladies, the king granted them his grace. This was done at Sheen in Surrey. Two days later the king came to London, and the mayor, sheriffs, aldermen, with all the worthy citizens following after, rode to meet him in fine style, to the heath on this side of Sheen manor, and submitted themselves humbly and meekly, with all manner of obeisance to him, as they ought to do. Thus they brought the king and queen to London.

When the king came to the gate of London bridge, they presented him with a milk-white steed saddled and bridled, and wearing trappings of white cloth-of-gold and red together, and to the queen they gave a pure white palfrey wearing trappings of the same design of white and red; and the conduits of London ran with white and red wine, for all manner of people to drink. Between St Paul's and the cross in Cheapside a high stage was erected, on which were many angels, [*singing*] various melodies and songs. An angel came down from the high stage, by a device, and set a crown of gold, precious stones and pearls upon the king's head, and another on the queen's. Then the citizens conducted the king and queen to Westminster, to his palace there, and presented him with two silver-gilt basins, full of gold coins, totalling £20,000, begging him, of his mercy, lordship and special grace, that they might have his good love, and their liberties and franchises as they had before, and confirmed by his letters patent. The queen and other worthy lords and ladies fell on their knees and begged the king of his grace to confirm this. The king raised the queen up, and granted all she asked. Then they thanked the king and queen and went home again.

(b) The possible cause
WC, 496.

The reason which goaded the king against the Londoners, according to some people, was as follows. It is a known fact that the king is sometimes short of money; so the king sent to some citizens of London to ask if they would advance him 5,000 marks or pounds, on the security of a

41 Also mentioned by *WC*, 502.

certain jewel of great value .... But the citizens excused themselves, alleging that after losing their liberties they had gained only meagre prosperity, since in the city outsiders were enjoying the same liberty as they, and therefore, since their profits were reduced, they could not stretch to such a large sum. The king was no little amazed at this, and finally consulted a certain Lombard about this matter, who immediately promised to satisfy the king's wishes and next day came to the king with the aforementioned sum. The king asked him how he had managed to get such a big sum so quickly. 'I borrowed it from some London merchants', he said. When he heard this, the king bore a grudge against Londoners, because they would rather lend such a great sum of money to a foreigner than to him.

(c) The law courts moved to York, 30 May

These commands, all made on the authority of the king and council, show what an upheaval the removal was. The process began on 18 May, CPR 1391–6, 65. *CCR 1389–92*, 466–7, slightly adapted.

To the treasurer and barons of the exchequer: order, for urgent causes affecting the king and the estate of the realm to be at York on the morrow of St John Baptist next *[25 June]*, and thenceforward to hold pleas, summonses, accounts and processes, and to do everything belonging to their office; and to the treasurer to send and have there, then, all pleas, records, processes, rolls, writs and memoranda of the exchequer; as ... the king has ordered all such pleas etc. held before them to be heard at York, and has commanded all sheriffs throughout England to return there, before them, on that day all writs returnable at Westminster on the morrow, octaves and quinzaine of Trinity, and all writs returnable at Westminster on later days ... causing proclamation to be made on the king's behalf that all who by writ, roll or otherwise have days[42] at Westminster ... shall keep their day at York on *[25 June]*, and all who have later days shall similarly keep them there; and he commands that all pleas etc. held before them shall have the same force as if held at Westminster, that all who ought to make payments on those days at the receipt of the exchequer shall make them on those days at Nottingham, and all who ought on those days to account at the exchequer should be at York on *[25 June]* to render their accounts. The king has sent similar orders to the sheriffs.

---

42 The day named in the writ of summons on which the person should appear.

To Robert Charlton and the other justices of Common Bench: similar order to be at York on the same day; and order to Robert to have there all the rolls, records, writs and memoranda in his custody. The king has commanded all sheriffs to return there all original and judicial writs returnable at Westminster.

To Thomas Haxey, king's clerk, keeper of the writs of Common Bench: order to be in person at York on *[25 June]* to execute his office in the accustomed form, causing all writs etc. in his custody which concern his office to be brought with him.

To Roger de Saperton, warden of the Fleet prison: similar order to be at York, bringing with him all prisoners in his custody for whatsoever cause, and the cause of their imprisonment, as the king has ordered that all pleas, summonses, accounts and processes pending before the treasurer and the barons of the exchequer, and before the justices of the Common Bench, shall be held there.

(d) Ceremonies marking the reconciliation between Richard and London

This letter survives as a copy in the register of Llanthony Secunda Priory, Gloucester. Its noble recipient and the writer are both unknown, but it claims to be an eyewitness account of the events of Wednesday 21 and Thursday 22 August by someone who rode in the royal procession. It was probably composed soon after the events, and includes as recent news the mental collapse which Charles VI of France suffered on 5 August. Similarity between this account and that given in *WC*, 504–6, suggests that the writer may have bolstered his own memory with information from a newsletter which was also available to the Westminster chronicler. Richard Maidstone, Gaunt's confessor, wrote a poem on this subject.[43]

Helen Suggett, 'A letter describing Richard II's reconciliation with the City of London, 1392', *EHR* 62 (1947), 209–13.

My most honoured lord, may it please you to have the news that the king ordered me to be at Sheen on Monday following the Feast of the Assumption *[Monday 19 August]*. On Sunday *[18 August]*, on arriving in London I was informed of the accord between the king and the city, and at my coming I was a little out of sorts in my head. Because of this I sent to the king to be excused from coming for two or three days, and to learn his will .... He commanded me to be with him on Wednesday *[21 August]* beyond Wandsworth to ride with the Queen through the

---

43 *'Concordia'*, ed. and trans. Rigg and Carlson (2003); extract Rickert (1948): 35–9.

city, and this I did. As soon as the king was a little past Wandsworth, the guardian of the city, with the aldermen, approached the king on foot. The guardian carried in his hand a sword whose pommel[44] was in the air and the point was in his hand, and the keys of the city. When they came before the king the guardian said (he and his companions kneeling): 'My liege lord, these your subjects put themselves into your grace and mercy, their lives and bodies and all their goods, asking for your grace and mercy'. It was answered on the king's behalf that they must come to the palace of Westminster and there they would have their answer. And the king had Percy take the sword and the keys and carry them with him, and then the king rode on. A bowshot's length nearby the king found the city guilds dressed all alike, each one by itself, and they were drawn up on horseback on each side of the road, all staying in their place until the king had passed them ..... When the king had passed them all he turned aside from the road and let all the men of the town pass in front of him and then he himself rode after them in the same company. As he came nearer the town he was met by all the religious, friars, monks, priests, clerks and boys, some singing *Te Deum Laudamus*[45] *[We praise you, O God]*, and others *Summe Trinitati*[46] *[To the highest Trinity]*.

At his entry to the bridge the warden (*gardeyn*) and aldermen presented him with two large coursers, with trappings of cloth of gold, mixed with red and white, a large palfrey for the queen with trappings of the same design. At his coming into Cheap, between the two crosses, there came two angels out of a cloud, one carrying a crown for the king – and the guardian took it and presented it to the king – and the other a crown for the queen. At St Paul's the procession from the church met him, and the king dismounted and went into the church and made an offering. He then rode on, and at Ludgate the guardian and the aldermen presented the king with a beautiful tablet of pure gold for an altar, and the queen with another. And then, around the Savoy, the men of the town were waiting, and they let the king pass. At Westminster the procession met him and he went in there to the palace and clothed himself in a long gown, because he had ridden all day in a short one. Next he went into his chamber and sat on a high seat which was made in front of the great throne, decked with cloth of gold, and the entire room was hung with tapestries, and all the commons stood before him. Then there came the

44 Handle.
45 A very ancient hymn to the Father and Son, in rhythmical prose.
46 A responsory, or liturgical chant.

queen and the archbishop on one side and the bishop of London on the other side; they went on their knees before the king, begging him to take his lieges into his grace and mercy. There was said on the king's behalf, by the steward, that the king was grieved that London, which was almost his household, had been so badly guarded, and some other words which I do not know how to write. But the result was that the king took them into his grace and granted them all their privileges as freely as they had ever had them, except two or three which ought to be shown to, and discussed by, his great Council. Then he ate spices and drank wine, and everyone went away, and the king went to Kennington to dine.

Next day he ate in the town with the guardian and the queen also, and there was presented to the king a large tablet of silver and enamel which was big enough for the reredos[47] of an altar, and to my lady the queen a crystal goblet and a ewer inlaid with gold. After their departure for Westminster certain crafts of the town were arrayed in boats and barges finely decorated, and in them the people of the craft dancing and making loud music, and they went with the king right to Westminster. And as they went along they made the king and queen drink with them. After this the king invited all the guildsmen to come with him to his palace and there he gave everyone something to drink, and then afterwards they departed with very great joy and comfort. And, about several other matters which were ordered in the city, I know not how to assure you that the conduits of the town which were variously decorated, were running with wine and adorned with various painted images and angels making great melody and minstrelsy, and this in many parts of the town, and the streets were adorned with hangings, everywhere of gold and silk. There was offered to him £100,000, which the king pardoned except £10,000 which he took at once, and for the ten years after 2,000 marks a year. Also, Sir, news has come that the king of France has lost his reason ....

---

47 The decoration behind an altar, usually of painted wooden panels, but could be of rich cloth or jewelled metalwork.

1393

142. Selected terms of a draft treaty with France, 16 June

The eighteen articles agreed on this day suggest that England and France were on the verge of signing a final peace treaty by summer 1393. By clause 2, England agreed to renounce sovereignty over Aquitaine, the sticking point in previous negotiations. It is also possible that the English king's nominees (clauses 4 and 5) were understood to refer to Gaunt and his successors, and that it was this projected separation of Aquitaine from the English crown that caused these peace plans to fail.

J. J. N. Palmer, 'Articles for a final peace between England and France, 16 June 1393', *BIHR*, 39 (1966), 182–5.

[1.] These are the articles which have been discussed and negotiated to arrive at a good and final peace between the kings of France and England, their realms, lordships, subjects and allies, by the lord dukes of Berry and Burgundy, having sufficient power for the king of France on one side; and by the lord dukes of Lancaster and Gloucester, having sufficient power for the king of England, on the other.

[2.] First, for the French side the following protestations were made, namely that in everything that will be done in the present treaty it will include the allies of the king of France according to the form of letters of alliance between the king and them .... And that everything that the king of England holds in the kingdom of France, and what he will hold under the treaty of good and final peace, shall be held of the king of France and of his successors by liege homage under his jurisdiction and of his sovereignty.

[3.] The lords of Lancaster and Gloucester made protestation on the king of England's behalf that everything to be concluded in this present treaty should include the allies of the king of England according to the form of the alliances between them. .... The tenure of Calais and its territory shall not be included among the other tenures of lands and places which will be delivered to the party of England; but its tenure shall be decided at a meeting of the two kings.

[4.] It is agreed that the king of France will retain the fealty and liege homage, the jurisdiction and the sovereignty of all that will remain to the king of England or those taking his side, except Calais and its territory, as is said; so that good modifications and ordinances can be advised and ordained on the said jurisdictions and sovereignties before a dispute, war or confiscation might arise plausibly because of them;

and on this should be made good sureties for one side and the other. The king of England, with what he holds in Guyenne or in Gascony, or his nominees, shall have for himself and his heirs in perpetuity the cities, castles, towns, lands and territories which follow: the city and castle of Saintes; the land and country of Saintonge which is beyond the river Charente; the city and castle of Agen; the land and country of the Agenais; the city, castle and county of Perigord; the city and castle of Limoges; the land and country of the Limousin; the city and castle of , Cahors; the land and country of Quercy; the city of Montauban and the lands which are between the rivers Veron and Tarn; the city, castle and county of Tarbes; the land, country and county of Bigorre; the county and country of Gavre; the city and castle of Angoulême; the city and castle of Rodez; the land and country of Rouergue, as Prince Edward held them by virtue of the peace in the year sixty[48] ....

[5.] Because in several articles of this present schedule the party of England has decided that the king of England or his nominee will have the lands which are granted to him by this treaty, and that the king of England or his nominee will perform fealty and homage to the king of France, the party of France has said that if the king of England grants the duchy of Guyenne to the duke of Lancaster to hold for his lifetime, it will be necessary for the king of England himself to do homage to the king of France for the lordship, and the duke of Lancaster perform homage for the usufruct.[49] The party of England has said that there should not be two homages for one thing. *[After consultation with the two monarchs]* ... this is left to be decided by the two kings.

[6.] It is agreed that the king of England should have for himself and his heirs perpetually the castle and town of Calais *[also of Marck, Sangatte, Coulogne, Hames(-Boucres), Wale, Poyle and Guînes]*.

[17.] The islands which are nearest to the places and lands which will stay with France should remain French, except the islands of Guernsey, Jersey, Oléron, and others which ought to stay with the king of England,

[18.] It is agreed that when the articles touching the modifications of the liege homage, jurisdiction and sovereignty, and the other precedents written therein are subsequently agreed and the sureties ordained for one party and the other, and the letters written and sealed as said, the king of England for himself and his heirs and successors will renounce

48 A reference to the Treaty of Brétigny (or Calais), 1360.
49 The right to enjoy the property of another for life, without changing its character or lessening its value.

the title of king of France and all right which he has in the crown and realm of France, and to all that he can demand in other lands which are not ceded to him by this present treaty. And also the king of England will acquit the king of France and his successors and all his subjects for damages which have been done to him, his predecessors and subjects during the wars between them. And there will be advised and ordained good modifications and declarations on the articles touching the said homage, jurisdiction and sovereignty, and good sureties for one party and the other, ceasing entirely all fraud and bad intent in the things above said and every one of them.

Concluded at Leulingham between Boulogne and Calais, 16 June 1393.

143. The condition of Ireland

Well before the expedition of 1394 this evidence shows that Ireland badly needed attention. Most of the surviving 213 petitions to Richard's council in Ireland during the regnal year 1392–3 concern personal or routine matters, but five have been selected from those which illustrate vividly the serious state of the English lordship. All petitions were addressed to the Lord Justice (James Butler, earl of Ormond) and the king's council in Ireland.

A Roll of the Proceedings of the King's Council in Ireland for a portion of the sixteenth year of the Reign of Richard the Second A.D.1392–3, ed. and trans.[50] James Graves (RS, 1877), 6–9, 12–13, 120–2; adapted.

[1.] John Fitz Nicholas Lumbard petitions that during the period when Alexander [Petit *or* de Balscot], bishop of Meath, was justice of Ireland, John was charged and entrusted with the office of Warden of the Peace in county Kilkenny, at which time Macmurgh, O'Nolan, O'Ryan and other Irish enemies[51] there were openly at war, and in discharging that office, during an assault which he made on Macmurgh in the marches there, he was seriously wounded and despaired of his life, in which assault ten of Macmurgh's best men were beheaded; also John often served the king in his wars in both Munster and Leinster, at his own expense, losing some of his kinsmen and horses who were killed in those wars, to John's great injury; in consideration whereof may it please you graciously to order some suitable compensation for him.

[*Answer*]: Let the suppliant, by the king's special grace, have £20 for the reason contained in this petition. Dublin, 1 November 1392.

50 Translated from Anglo-Norman.
51 For a note on racial terms see **72**.

[2.] The commons of the town of Carlow make known that recently
that town, houses and all the corn and other goods were burned, wasted
and destroyed by Macmurgh, O'Carroll and all the other Irish enemies
of the king in the parts of Leinster and Munster, so that they cannot as
yet build in that town nor sustain the people there without aid, succour
and relief from the king, and also that the inhabitants have mostly left
the town for various other places, to the very great injury of the entire
land of Ireland, and the enemies' great comfort; and those who still
remain there are planning to leave: therefore the commons beg you to
… grant them a sufficient allowance to rebuild that town and houses …
considering that this town is the head and mainstay of Leinster; also,
may it please your lordships to order that the gates and barriers of that
town be repaired.

[Answer:] Let the suppliants have £20 by the king's gift, to be paid to
William Burton and Thomas Taillour of Carlow to spend and to divide
fairly amongst those who are willing to repopulate the town there, each
in proportion to his building. … *[Same date]*

[3.] Henry de Wattenhull petitions to be granted the office of attorney
of the lord king before the justices of the Common Bench of Ireland
and in his exchequer there, to hold during good behaviour, receiving
annually the fees, wages and rewards usual to the office; and that Henry
may have power to appoint a deputy, for whom he will be answerable, to
execute this office in his absence, because the roads toward Carlow are
often so dangerous that Henry cannot approach the court on the first
day *[of sitting]* without danger …

[Answer:] Let the suppliant have the office mentioned, taking the usual
fees and wages for it, by royal letters patent under the great seal. *[Same
date]*

[4.] John Desmond petitions that, because the king's cities of Cork
and Limerick and the town of Youghal are situated in the marches,
and the country round them is so destroyed and ruined by the king's
enemies and by the English rebels that the people there cannot support
themselves for lack of food, except with the help of the people of
county Limerick, and the sellers and carriers of victuals, corn and other
merchandise to those parts do not dare, and cannot go, to comfort and
supply those cities and towns without safe-conduct; may it please you to
grant John a patent under the king's seal to convoy these carriers and
sellers in going and returning from these cities and towns, and receive
the customary fees, and to command the king's faithful lieges to obey

John in making that convoy, to aid the king's lieges in these parts.

[*Answer:*] Because it is a known fact that the way between the city of Cork and the county of Limerick is most difficult and perilous, it is granted and agreed by the justice and council of Ireland that the suppliant may have the convoy of the carriers and sellers going and returning between that city and county, during the king's pleasure, receiving reasonable fees and customs from the carriers and sellers for his pains … Kilkenny, 26 January 1393.

[*5.*] Because the people of Castle Dermot have made a bargain with Macmurgh for 84 marks, to the king's profit and to save the town and its inhabitants, a sum which the people assessed among themselves by general consent; and they have granted the prior of the Hospitallers there, and the guardian of the Friars Minor, and various other peaceable people of county Kildare and county Carlow, that they and their goods and chattels may seek help and refuge within the town; may it please you, as a work of charity, to grant a commission to Thomas Brodoke, John Bateman, Esmond Horn, John Chamberlain and John Yonge, to levy that same sum, considering that Macmurgh would not cease his evildoing until Thomas had placed his person in pledge for that money.

[*Answer:*] Let a commission be made to David Wogan, knight, and Thomas Tailour to enquire about the assessing and the matter described in the petition, and report their findings to the chancery; and if they find that this is true, let a commission under the king's great seal in Ireland be made to the persons mentioned, in accordance with this petition. Kilkenny, 27 January 1393.

144. The 'Cheshire rising'

It may have been the prospect of peace – and thus reduced opportunities for military service – that prompted this insurrection, though some causes of discontent were local: long-standing grievances [136] or recent financial demands.[52] Yet the 'Cheshire rising' was not confined to Cheshire, and the episode remains mysterious. It perhaps also indicates popular dismay at the direction foreign policy was taking, animosity to Gaunt's administration and friction among the aristocracy [145b]. It was not mentioned by the Monk of Evesham or by the local chronicler at Whalley in Lancashire, while Walsingham in his revised shorter chronicle referred to it only in passing.[53]

SAC I.944–6.

52 Saul: 258.
53 See Bellamy (1965): 254–74; Walker (1990): 271–3.

That year, while negotiations between the kingdoms still continued overseas, a great rebellion arose in Cheshire against the dukes of Lancaster and Gloucester and the earl of Derby, at the instigation of certain trouble-makers of that district, who told the people there that those lords had, for their private advantage, removed dominion over the kingdom of France and the county of Chester from their liege lord the king of England, and wanted to remove their ancient liberties. They announced these matters not just privately among themselves, but in writings fixed to the doors of parish churches; they also sent them everywhere to the adjacent counties, asking for their help in common collaboration. Their actions soon grew so great that the crowd of armed men and archers, gathered in various places and groups, swelled to more than 20,000 men, it was said ....

But although the king and his council were repeatedly informed about this, they delayed applying a remedy so as not to disrupt the negotiations, nor did they in any way inform his[54] friends about this, so that he first learnt about this through the dukes of Burgundy and Berry, and was promised help and the necessary finance by them, because of their blood ties and their natural goodness. They broke off negotiations, returned home and demonstrated to the king and council their innocence of the allegations against them.

Next, with the king's leave and permission, the duke of Lancaster took himself to Yorkshire, with a commission and royal judges, and with even the chief justice himself, to pacify the land and the rebels. Then he turned towards the counties of Lancashire and Cheshire, with a sufficiently strong armed force, for in Yorkshire a great dispute had arisen between the worthy knight R[obert] Rockeley[55] and a certain aggressive squire called Beckwith, supported by their family clans, in which the knight was killed first, but the squire refused to submit to the rigour of the law. Along with many of his adherents in that faction, he sought to save his life by main force, and after he was indicted he remained an outlaw for a long time, but finally he was killed by the knight's friends. The result was that much unrest arose in that area, so that it seemed to be in a measure divided. Their stubbornness increased the Cheshire men's insolence further; they were united in mutual support.

---

54 Here Walsingham probably has just Gaunt in mind, so goes mostly into the singular in this and the next sentence.

55 A wealthy landowner, steward of Knaresborough, Gaunt's retainer since 1369, Walker (1990): 69n., 79, 119n., 279.

When that land had been pacified to his satisfaction by his usual shrewd-
ness, and he had afterwards obtained both the Lancastrians' support
and their goodwill, he moved against the Cheshire men in order to
return them to their dutiful allegiance, or else to chastise them strongly
with a firm hand. But first he decided to show them his innocence and
so to recall them from their previous disobedience and blood-shedding
to their dutiful subjection. He therefore sent some of his wiser knights
to them and sufficiently satisfied them about the accusations against
him, so that he sent the people home once they were suitably penitent
about their opposition. Not only did he absolve the ringleaders who
had raised this rebellion and who repented of their wrong, but he
graciously restored them to the bosom of their families, contrary to
general expectation and advice; but [persistent] rebels he very wisely
remanded to royal justice. The poor of that area, who were opposed to
peace in the land and who had raised this rebellion, and for that, among
other reasons, had nothing to look forward to, he not only received into
his good books, but also trained them in arms for his own use and sent
them to Gascony and other places under his command, with generous
wages.

1394

145. The earl of Arundel in trouble again

Ten years after his outburst at the Salisbury parliament [62c], Arundel again
showed himself to be abrasive and tactless.

(a) The accusation against him
SAC I.956.

On the octave of Hilary [20 January][56] the leading men of the realm
were called to a meeting of parliament at London, where, after a little
discussion of general matters, inconvenient things were proposed,
namely, subsidies for the king who wanted to cross over to Ireland.
… Nothing else of moment happened at this parliament except the
famous dispute between the duke of Lancaster and the earl of Arundel.
Lancaster accused the earl that, about the feast of the Exaltation of
Holy Cross [14 September 1393], and a little before, he encamped with
a retinue of knights in his castle of Holt, otherwise called Lion's Castle,

56 Parliament met 27 January–6 March, HBC.566, but the grant was made in the
   Canterbury convocation meeting of 14–21 May, CCR 1392–6, 251, HBC.558.

on the Cheshire border, at the time when that area had risen in rebellion against Lancaster. ...The earl explained this vigorously and clearly enough. He also arranged that the king excused him from coming to parliament again, or to the council wherever it was convened, so he went home happy with that freedom. But shortly afterwards the sentence was reversed and he was recalled.

(b) Arundel's complaints about Gaunt

If this criticism was made before a small group, it is surprising that it was recorded in the parliament roll. Richard's measured response, in contrast to his outburst against Arundel's attack ten years before, perhaps suggests that it was given in writing. 'Mautalent' is old French for 'ill will'.

RP III.313–14; *PROME* 1394, section 11.

After parliament had begun, Richard, earl of Arundel, told the king, in the presence of the archbishops of Canterbury and York, the duke of Gloucester, the bishops of Winchester and Salisbury, the earl of Warwick and others, that there were certain matters close to his heart which he could not in conscience conceal, for the honour and profit of the king and realm. He then explained these matters to the king, making his detailed declaration as follows: the earl thought it was contrary to the king's honour that his uncle the duke of Guyenne and Lancaster should be so often and so closely in the king's company; that the king wore his uncle's livery-collar; that members of the king's retinue wore the same livery; the duke of Guyenne used often such harsh and rough words in council and in parliaments that the earl and others often did not dare to speak their minds fully; that granting the duchy of Guyenne to the duke was very detrimental to the king; that the king gave the duke such a large sum of money for his expedition to Spain. He also spoke about the peace treaty.

The king answered the earl about these: (1) it was the king himself who caused this same uncle of his to stay close by his side, as he made his other uncles do, during that uncle's absence; (2) soon after his uncle of Guyenne last returned from Spain to England, the king himself took the collar from his uncle's neck and put it on his own neck, and said that he would wear it as a sign of the great love and unanimity between them, as he had done with his other uncles' liveries; (3) it was by the king's choice and desire that the men of his retinue wore and used the same livery and collar; (4) the king said that the earl and all others should fully speak their mind, no matter what they had heard about this

uncle in council or in parliament; (5) the gift of the duchy of Guyenne
had been made with the assent of all the estates in full parliament; (6)
half the money for the expedition to Spain, namely 20,000 marks, was
given and granted by the assent of all the estates in parliament; the
other half was a loan. Afterwards the duke was in the king's service,
and he rescued the castle of Brest, and thus the king owed him for that
service much more than the 20,000 marks which were loaned. ... (7)
nothing about the peace treaty had been done in any way except as the
duke had been commanded by the king and his council, of which the
earl was one ....

When these articles and answers had been read and explained in the
presence of the king and the lords of parliament, and examined and
considered by them, it was their opinion that these matters were of no
substance or relevance, and that the duke of Guyenne should suffer no
disgrace or disrepute because of these words, nor that they provided any
grounds for impeachment, and that his honour was entirely untainted.
Then the earl was asked, in parliament, if he knew or wanted to say
anything more about the duke of Guyenne and Lancaster. He replied
that he did not. It was therefore decided by the king, with the lords'
advice, that the earl should address these words to the duke: 'Sire, sith
that hit semeth to the kyng and to the other lordes, and eke that yhe
ben so mychel greved and displesid be my words, hit forthynketh me,
and byseche yowe of your gode lordship to remit me your mautalent'.
The earl spoke these words to the duke of Guyenne and Lancaster in
the presence of the king and the lords in parliament.

(c) Pardon of Arundel, 30 April

CPR 1391-6, 406.

Pardon to Richard, earl of Arundel, for all treasons, insurrections with
the commons and others contrary to his allegiance, felonies, harbour-
ings of felons and traitors by himself or by other persons at his instigation, and of all champerties,[57] conspiracies, confederations, embraceries,
maintenances of false quarrels, trespasses, false alliances, falsities,
deceptions, procurements of false indictments, unjust imprisonments
of the king's lieges and subjects, and of all negligence, misprisons,[58]
ignorances and other demands, and of any consequent outlawries.

---

57 Supporting a quarrel in return for a share of the proceeds.
58 Neglect, oversight or undutiful behaviour towards the sovereign.

146. Queen Anne

Queen Anne died on 7 June after a short illness. Her elaborate funeral was marred by Arundel's tactless behaviour which provoked the bereaved king's understandable wrath. Two chroniclers alleged that Richard immediately ordered the manor of Sheen, where the queen had died, to be pulled down, implying that he was so grief-stricken as to be unhinged,[59] but the truth [158] was much less dramatic. Richard's sorrow is understandable, for there is no suggestion that the royal couple were on anything but affectionate terms; Anne was, moreover, the only person of equal status to himself. Partly by policy [68] and his own exalted view of his royal position [161, 171],[60] but partly through family circumstance, Richard was an isolated figure and there is some evidence[61] that, like other royal persons throughout history, he was lonely and lacked confidants of high social standing. Anne's death raised more acutely than ever the problem of the succession, but there is no reliable evidence that this was ever discussed in public [89], nor that Richard designated an heir. Allegations that he named either Bolingbroke or March as his successor probably derive from fifteenth-century Lancastrian or Yorkist propaganda.[62] Richard's grief did not prevent him from quickly starting the search for a new queen, possibly in Germany, and certainly in Spain and France.[63]

(a) Her death
VR, 134.

On 7 June, the feast of Pentecost, Anne, queen of England died at Sheen. Because of this the king, in grief at her death, caused that noble and royal manor to be razed to the ground.[64] Nor, for a whole year afterwards, would he enter any place that he knew she had previously been, except a church. She was buried with the greatest solemnity in the church of Westminster, on the morrow of St Anne's day [27 July], the feast which the queen begged the lord pope to be more solemnly celebrated in the English Church. Although she died childless, this queen was held to be glorious and beneficial to the realm of England, insofar as she could be, so that both nobles and commoners greatly mourned her death. From Bohemia, there came with the queen into England that execrable abuse namely shoe-soles with long points, called in English 'cracows' or

59 Usk: 18.
60 Saul (1995).
61 *CR*: 211; Saul: 335–6 and nn.
62 Stow (2004): 679.
63 Palmer (1971a): 1–17.
64 But see **158**.

'pyks', half a yard long, so that it was necessary to bind them to the shin with silver chains, before one could walk with them. This year, about the feast of St Matthew the Evangelist [21 Sept.], the king journeyed to Ireland to put down their wild rebellion, if he could. He spent the winter there with his army.

(b) Her funeral

SAC I.960–2.

The lady Anne, queen of England, died on 7 June and was buried at Westminster; a woman exceptionally dedicated to God, a lover of almsgiving, friend of the poor and the church, a supporter of true faith and justice, and practitioner of secret penance; yet defamed by the slanders of many. Her funeral rites were notable for their cost, outdoing all others of our time. The king, for some trivial or non-existent fault, was annoyed with the earl of Arundel. He seized an attendant's staff and hit him [Arundel] so violently on the head that he fell to the ground, and his blood flowed copiously over the flagstones; the king would gladly have killed him in the church, had he been allowed. This was done at the start of the funeral office, and he was compelled to postpone the office of the dead while the priests of the church hastened with the rites of reconciliation; it was late at night before the funeral's completion. The cause of the king's anger was that the earl was not present at the procession and bearing of the queen's body from St Paul's church to Westminster, and because, when he had arrived late, he was the first of all to ask the king for permission to leave for certain pressing reasons.

The expedition to Ireland, 1394–95

That autumn Richard made his first expedition to Ireland. Its precise timing was probably influenced by the queen's death, but he had been interested in the lordship since 1385 [72], and de Vere's promotions in 1385 and 1386 [70, 74b] reflected this concern. In July 1389, the indenture to John Stanley as chief governor had stated that he would be freed from office if the king, or a close relative, came to Ireland.[65] That 'close relative' was Gloucester, who in April 1392 was appointed lieutenant in Ireland for five years. Gloucester made extensive preparations for departure, but in July his commission was cancelled for reasons unknown. Richard's attention to Ireland was unusual[66] but not eccentric, for Ireland was already a problem during Edward III's reign. By

---

65 Johnston (1980): 3.

66 The last English king to visit Ireland was John, in 1210.

1393 the situation was desperate [143], and the king feared that the lordship, which was integral to his royal title, was in danger of being lost.

The study of Irish history in this period is bedevilled by the loss of sources. The record store of the Irish Record Office was burned during the civil war in 1922 and its contents destroyed, but there had been serious losses before that, including the Patent and Close Rolls for 1395 onwards, which had disappeared by 1828.[67] English chroniclers were poorly informed about Ireland; Walsingham's is the longest account of the expedition; Knighton included the briefest mention; the *Vita* mentioned it only in passing. Froissart, knowledgeable about Scotland, suspended his critical faculties when writing about Ireland; his account of what happened to an English knight who was taken prisoner there is literally fantastical, and resembles the stories of people who today allege that they have been abducted by aliens.[68] The surviving Irish annals are mostly concerned with very local feuds. Irish historians therefore rely heavily upon the records of the English crown.

Fortunately, two other sources come to our rescue. One consists of letters written by Richard and others on his expedition. Although these survive in what is ostensibly a formulary book – which explains why the recipients are not named and many proper names are identified only by initials – they are peculiar to the 1394–5 situation and present a remarkable commentary on events. The other source consists of documents delivered to the English exchequer on 25 June 1395. These are the detailed records of thirty-eight Irish chieftains who submitted to Richard and a further thirty-six items, mostly letters to the king.[69] Some of these are requests for safe-conducts; some are excuses for failure to attend court (usually explaining the omission by neighbours' violence, such as 'my enemies took thirty mares from my stud and carried them off' and also, apparently a secondary matter, 'they took my son and hold him hostage');[70] but many of these missives could fairly be described as begging letters and tell us what the Irish chiefs hoped to gain from the king.

This first Irish expedition was the military high point of the reign. The king himself did not fight but members of his army engaged in warfare in the local style – burning property and taking cattle – to such effect that Irish chiefs submitted to the king in great numbers and took an oath of loyalty. Richard's achievement was considerable: the chiefs' submissions should be taken at face value and not regarded as a cynical sham. Irish society saw no shame in submitting to a higher power, since the new vassals acquired higher status and enhanced prestige by so doing; and bringing the chiefs into a legal relationship with the crown for the first time gave the king the prospect of their loyalty, while the chiefs looked to him for justice and protection from the Anglo-Irish. It is true that the only useful Irish account suggests that Richard's

67 Connolly (2002): esp. 9–10, 14–37.

68 Froissart book iv, ch. 64; *Froissart*, ed. Brereton (1978): 409–17.

69 Also indentures and deeds, Curtis (1927b): 57.

70 *Ibid.*, 125–6.

intervention ('The king of England came to Ireland with an immense force, including English and Welsh, and such a fleet did not come to Ireland since the Norse fleets came') brought only a short respite in the feuding which was the writer's staple material;[71] and by 1399 the settlement had been undone by the Anglo-Irish [167].

147. The archbishop of Canterbury orders prayers for the expedition's success, 31 August

Literae Cantuarienses, ed. J Brigstocke Sheppard, III (RS, 1889), 30–1.

William, by divine permission archbishop of Canterbury etc. to his beloved son in Christ the prior of Christ Church Canterbury greeting, grace and blessing. The providence of the Supreme King, wonderful in power, directing the armies of all nations, strengthening souls, training hands for battle and the fingers of the elect for war, manifesting his omnipotence, subjects those whom he wishes to subject and imparts victory to those he favours. Considering these things, therefore, the most excellent prince in Christ and our lord, the Lord Richard, by God's grace illustrious king of England and France and Lord of Ireland, confident more in the assistance of divine strength than in earthly power, has, with a humble and sincere heart entreated us, upon his departure towards the parts of Ireland, that we should deign to pour out before the Most High, on his behalf, prayers in our church of Canterbury through us and our brothers. Therefore, since our lord king holds this church in affection, we enjoin and command you to make solemn processions, with the accustomed singing of the litanies for the God-inspired expedition of the king and his army, on every fourth and sixth working day [*Thursdays and Saturdays*] in our said church; urging also, on behalf of the lord king and ourselves, that each and every monk of this our church should have the lord king and his army especially commended in Masses and other prayers. And, so that we may more readily inspire the minds of the monks of this our church and of the other faithful people of our city of Canterbury to pray for the lord king and company, we grant by these presents – through the immense mercy of the Almighty and of his most Blessed Mother the Virgin Mary, and of the Blessed Apostles Peter and Paul, and of saints Elphege and Thomas the Martyr our patrons, and being confident in the merits and prayers of all the saints – to all and each of those who

71 Miscellaneous Irish Annals, 153–5.

truly repent and confess their sins and who commend the lord king and his army in Masses or other prayers to the Almighty throughout forty days, forty days' indulgence, on the authority of ourselves and others, by our apostolic authority granted to us in this matter.

148. The expedition, and its causes, according to the *St Albans Chronicle*

This, and the next two passages from the St Albans Chronicle [**156, 165**], are not thought to have been written by Walsingham himself, though he continued to supervise the work.

SAC II.6–8.

About the beginning of August, proclamation was made throughout England that all Irishmen should return to their own country before the feast of the Blessed Virgin Mary [*Nativity, 8 September*] to await the king's coming to Ireland, upon pain of death. For it was said that such numbers of Irishmen had come to England, in hope of riches, that their land was almost denuded of people. The result was that the pure-bred Irish,[72] those enemies of the English, devastated that part of the island which was profitable, meeting no resistance. When the illustrious king of England Edward III set up his law court and judges, along with the exchequer, he received £30,000 a year revenue from that land; but now, for lack of people and because of the enemy's unbridled power, nothing comes from there, but each year the king pays out 30,000 marks from his own pocket, to his shame and to the serious detriment of his finances. ...

About that feast the king of England sailed across to Ireland;[73] with him went the duke of Gloucester and the earls of March, Nottingham and Rutland. The Irish were terrified by so great a display of force and did not dare to confront them, but they harried the king's army with many ambushes. Many, however, were compelled, after the English had prevailed, to submit to the king and to the law of that land. Some of them he kept with him, lest they should try any new tricks. ... The king spent Christmas at Dublin, in great state, and remained in Ireland until after Easter.[74]

72 See **72**.

73 He landed at Waterford on 2 October.

74 Richard was at Waterford on 1 May 1395 and is next heard of at Salisbury on 15 May. Easter day was 11 April.

149. Two letters from Richard to a bishop, October

John Waltham of Salisbury, the treasurer, seems the likeliest recipient of these
and **155 b&c.**

(a) Arrival in Ireland

Anglo-Norman Letters and Petitions, ed. M. Dominica Legge (Anglo-Norman
Text Society, III, 1941), 230–1.

We had the most smooth and easy passage, with complete good health,
without any turbulence or disturbance in the air, or any roughness of
the sea, thanks be to God, so much so that our passage lasted no longer
than a day and a night, and we arrived at our city of Waterford in our
land of Ireland, where our citizens there received us most honourably
and very joyfully, and where we found victuals in great plenty and very
cheap, and where every day our faithful lieges come to us to offer their
services, and it is entirely full of others who in summer were our rebels
and adversaries in our absence. ... October 1394.

(b) Progress

Richard's army went up the valley north of Waterford towards Kilkenny. Not
every place indicated in the letter can be certainly identified. Curtis (1927a):
276–303 gives most details of the campaign.

Anglo-Norman Letters and Petitions, ed. M. D. Legge (1941), 222–5.

On Monday 19 October we crossed the river of our city of Waterford
and encamped that night in fields at a place called B., and the following
Tuesday at J[erpoint] where we learnt of the imminent arrival of our
dearest uncle of G[loucester] at Waterford. For this reason we remained
there on Wednesday and Thursday, awaiting our uncle's coming.[75] On
Friday [we waited] in a wood called M., and Saturday in the woods
of L[eighlinbridge] near to the wood of K., where our chief adversary
M[acmurgh][76] has his house and keeps himself secure. In these woods
of Leighlin that same Saturday in the evening our uncle reached us, and
there we remained during Sunday, on which, as you know, we are not
accustomed to ride. Early on Monday morning, planning to occupy that
wood of K. (which is, they say, the greatest fortress which our enemy
Macmurgh has, and which he thought, as was reported to us, to hold by

75 Jerpoint had a large abbey, which provided a comfortable resting-place.

76 Art Macmurrough-Kavanagh, c. 1375–1416, king of Leinster. For his activities, see
　143.

force against us, upon our entry into the lands which Macmurgh claims are his) we ordered our banners to be displayed, and the banners of our other faithful men, namely, of lords Ferrers, Scales, William Arundel and others, and we there knighted many men. Despite all the threat and fortification of that wood, we occupied that strong wood of K., and our enemy was dislodged and his principal house burned in our presence. There, both then and the following night, several skirmishes took place. On the following Tuesday we camped close beside another wood called Leverough, which is the special refuge of our said enemy, and many others of his affinity, where they were, and they did not dare to budge to offer us any resistance. On Wednesday we were encamped three miles from there in the lands of one O'Nolan, then our enemy, who with Shane, his eldest son, came to submit to us, bareheaded, disarmed and ungirdled, with their sword points in their hands, the pommels erect, and they put themselves completely and unconditionally in our grace, though before this act they committed much arson in these lands. The same day, in the same manner, there came to us to render obedience and make submission, Macmurgh, O'Bren, O'Toole and three other captains kneeling and making submission in the same manner, whose oaths we received on the Rood of Dublin to be our faithful and loyal subjects. This done, we left Macmurgh at large for a time, and we have in our company in the city of Dublin O'Bren, O'Toole and Shane, and, moved by pity and compassion, we have received them into [our] grace .... We seem to have conquered and to have imposed peace on the whole of Leinster ... the land and country right up to our city of Dublin, whose woods, meadows, pastures, arable lands and rivers are the most beautiful, plenteous and delectable which man could find anywhere, we believe .... We wish you also to know that on the morrow of the feast of St Andrew next we have summoned our parliament to our city of Dublin, at which we believe we shall have by the grace of the Almighty that which we reasonably desire. *[He was sending one of his knights bachelor with further details.]*

[Postscript.] We beg you also with our whole heart that you will give our dear ones in God the abbot and convent of W*[estminster]* whatever they need, or help them in whatever they have to do in our absence, as best you can, so that we will always be bound to thank you.

150. The king's private muniments put into the care of Westminster Abbey, 25 November

Most of the contents of this strong-box resulted from Princess Joan's colourful marital history. The first five items arose from her first marriage; in 1340 Joan, aged 12, married Sir Thomas Holand; when he later went abroad, she was induced to marry the earl of Salisbury. After Holand returned to England and claimed his wife, Salisbury refused to give her up. During the ensuing litigation at the papal court, Joan was deprived of legal counsel and even her liberty, but in 1349 she and Holand won their case.[77] After Holand's death in 1360, Joan married Prince Edward. The couple were related within the prohibited degrees and did not first obtain a dispensation; hence the many documents subsequently issued to legalise the marriage.

Westminster Abbey Muniments, No. 9584.

This indenture made between the venerable father Thomas [Arundel], archbishop of York, chancellor of England, and the abbot and convent of Westminster testifies that the abbot and convent, on 25 November 1394 in the chapter house at Westminster and in the presence of the venerable father John [Waltham], bishop of Salisbury, treasurer of England, Master Edmund Stafford, keeper of the privy seal, Philip la Vache, knight, John Scarle, keeper of the rolls [of chancery], Laurence Dru and Master John Prophet, received from the lord king certain bulls and public instruments, specified below, given by the said archbishop himself, to the abbot and convent on behalf of the king, in a little chest handed over for keeping, namely an instrument of process and sentence on the side of the lord Thomas Holand against the earl of Salisbury; also the execution of that process under a bull of Pope Clement[78] directed to the bishop of Comacchio[79] and other bishops; also an instrument of execution of that bull under the seal of the bishop of Comacchio; a bull of Pope Clement addressed to the archbishop of Canterbury and others that they should cause the lady Joan, daughter of the earl of Kent, to enjoy her liberty and to appoint a proctor in this case; a bull of Pope Innocent,[80] directed to the archbishop of Canterbury and to the bishop of London and to a certain abbot, to dispense the prince and the said Lady Joan over a contracted marriage; four other bulls on the same subject; another similar bull directed to the archbishop and to

---

77 For background, see Wentersdorf (1979): 203–31; the document printed with comment in McHardy (2000): 11–32.

78 Clement VI (r. 1342–52).

79 The papal nuncio in England.

80 Innocent VI (r. 1352–62).

the bishop of Exeter, of which the record is not contained in this little chest; another bull [*sealed*] close, of the same Innocent which was sent to the said archbishop and to the bishop of London and to the said abbot on the execution of the same matter, to proceed by virtue of another bull sent to them; an instrument under the seal of the archbishop of Canterbury about the dispensation of the marriage contracted between the said prince and Lady Joan and directed to the prince and Lady Joan; another instrument under the seal of the archbishop about the same matter directed 'To all etc.'; another four instruments on the same subject; another bull of Pope Innocent confirming the process ratified by the archbishop in the aforesaid matter of dispensation; another bull on the same sort of matter but not as complete; a bull of Pope Urban[81] supplementing the deficiency of the previous dispensation;[82] another bull in the same vein; an informatory schedule about the things mentioned earlier concerning oaths of allegiance; an obligation of the earl of Arundel;[83] the king's will. In testimony of which the archbishop, abbot and convent affixed their seals to these indentures.

151. Further progress of the Irish campaign

(a) An unknown writer to an unknown recipient

Anglo-Norman Letters and Petitions, ed. M. D. Legge (1941), 207–8.

Most honoured, excellent and gracious lord, may it please you to know the news from these parts, and how our most redoubtable lord the king has most wisely sent certain forces, as it seems to me your poor subject, around the Irish enemies: that is to say, the earl of Rutland and with him the lord de Beaumont, with men-at-arms and archers in one force; the Earl Marshal [*Mowbray*] with men-at-arms and archers in another force, very near the wood of Garrowkill and Leverough where Macmurgh has his dwelling; and Thomas Holand with Lord Percy, well supplied with men-at-arms and archers in the third force. They nobly set about their task and duty of harming those enemies.

The earl of Rutland laboured well and valiantly in this matter, continually spending his time in keeping guard and making *chevauchées* against

---

81 Urban V (*r.* 1362–1370).

82 Obtaining confirmation of such matters was not unusual.

83 Surety of £40,000 for future good behaviour was given by Arundel at Lambeth Palace on 18 August 1394, in the king's presence, *CCR 1392–6*, 368. For discussion of Arundel's wealth, see Given-Wilson (1991): 1–26.

the enemy, and making many good raids, to his great honour. But above all the Earl Marshal, who was stationed nearest the enemy, made several fine raids against them, on one of which he killed many of Macmurgh's men, burned nine villages round about E., and took some 8,000 head of livestock. He launched another raid against Macmurgh and, had he not been detected, would have found Macmurgh and his wife[84] in their beds, but they were forewarned and escaped, though with great difficulty. But so very nearly did they avoid capture that the Marshal seized, among other things, a small coffer belonging to Macmurgh's wife in which were certain feminine objects of no great value; but among other things was found Macmurgh's seal bearing the legend *Sigillum Arthurij Macmurgh dei gracia Regis Lagenie [Seal of Arthur Macmurgh by God's grace king of Leinster].*[85] When the Earl Marshal had failed to take Macmurgh he was very disgruntled and so, to harm him, he burnt his house in Leverough wood, and about fourteen good villages around the wood, and also took 400 beasts.

Also, you should know that the Earl Marshal, with considerable courage and at great personal risk, entered an impregnable and marshy country, called D., where no Englishman usually went, and there killed certain individuals, including one of the greater captains and evildoers of that area, called Tomaltach de Doimasigh,[86] and had him beheaded and sent his head to the king, our most redoubtable lord, at P. Also … you should know that the earl of Cork [*i.e. Rutland*] has organised and gone on many good raids, on one of which he killed upwards of 100 enemies and had his brother made a knight. On another he entered difficult terrain with great boldness against his enemies where S. made his dwelling; and there the earl and his men, with much labour, made a big bridge with trees, cords and branches over the water of P. to harm their enemies. He killed a great number, and he carried off more than 6,000 head of livestock of which he sent 360 to the king. Janico D'Artasso also made a splendid raid on those enemies called O'Neill and took 400 beasts. And so, my most honoured, excellent and gracious lord, you have by the grace of God news that the exploits of our most redoubtable king get better and better.

---

84 Elizabeth de Veel, the Anglo-Norman heiress of the barony of Norragh. In 1403 the couple commissioned a shrine (still surviving) to contain the Book of Mulling, an eighth-century gospel book associated with St Moling.

85 The seal was restored to him when he submitted in January 1395. It no longer survives, but was probably similar to the one illustrated by Curtis (1927a): 280.

86 For a more favourable view of this man, see no. **156**.

(b) Richard to a bishop,[87] January 1395

Anglo-Norman Letters and Petitions, ed. M. D. Legge (1941), 210–11.

Reverend father in God, we salute you with all our heart. ... About our exploits and the present wars in our land of Ireland: be pleased to know also that all our rebels of our land of Leinster have promised us to soon leave the land of Leinster, which among all the others of Ireland is one of the most famous, beautiful and fertile, so that the same land, we believe, will shortly be assured of peace and quiet. The 20th day of the present month of January, there came into our presence at Drogheda, where we were surrounded by our council, the great O'Neill the father, being sufficient proctor and authority for the great O'Neill his son.[88] Kneeling with all humility, he made to us homage, allegiance, subjection and fealty, and swore, both in his own name and in the name of his son, to be our loyal and obedient liege, and to repay, according to his power, all *[in which]* he had offended us or any of our lieges in any time past. And we have also heard today the news that those rebels who call themselves Kings and Captains of Munster and Connaught wish to come with all haste to do and to give us their homage and fealty as humbly and obediently as they can. So we think that by God's grace we shall shortly have complete obedience in all our land, and we believe that with the Lord's help we shall also put it into such good governance that all our loyal lieges, and those who wish to become such, will be very well content.

Dublin, *[late January, or February]* 1395.

(c) Janico Dartasso to Bishop Waltham of Salisbury

This Navarrese (Basque) adventurer was a household squire of Bishop Waltham and later made a considerable career in Ireland.[89] The letter illustrates well Richard's problem of getting outsiders interested in the lordship's future: he could make grants of land, but these were not always profitable to the recipients.

Anglo-Norman Letters and Petitions, ed. M. D. Legge (1941), 132–3.

Know that our lord king is well and in good health for this enterprise, praise God, and it seems that he can conquer the land of Ireland with God's help, but the people are so false that no man can trust them.

87 Probably John Waltham, bishop of Salisbury.
88 The official record of the event is dated 19 January, Curtis (1927b): 105–6.
89 Curtis (1933): 182–205; Walker (1999): 31–51.

And please you to know, my most revered lord, that our lord king has given me a piece of land in the territory of the Irish rebels, which, if it were in the neighbourhood of London, would easily be worth 1,000 marks a year,[90] but by my faith, I have been at such trouble to guard it that I would not wish to lead such a life any longer, for a quarter of the country. On the other hand, most honoured lord, I thank you as warmly as I can for your great lordship which of your excellent goodness you have graciously shown to me up till now, begging you, most reverend lord, for your good continuance.

152. The oath which the Irish chiefs took

(a) Usual preliminaries to the oath

The usual and less melodramatic form of submission, this took place at Drogheda, 16 March 1395.

Edmund Curtis, *Richard II in Ireland* (Oxford, 1927), 58.

Sean MacDonald in person, taking off his girdle, dagger and cap, knelt at the feet of the lord king and, raising his two hands with the palms together and holding them between the king's hands, spoke those words in the Irish tongue, which were translated into English by Thomas Talbot, interpreter of Ardagh diocese, in the presence of many, both clerics and laymen, who understood Irish well.

(b) Unusual preliminaries to the oath

Richard's wish to extend his lordship even to notorious wrongdoers is demonstrated by this ceremony in the Dominican church outside Kilkenny, 21 April 1395.

Edmund Curtis, *Richard II in Ireland* (Oxford, 1927), 62–3.

Art O'Dempsey, with a cord bound round his neck and the palms of his hands joined together, voluntarily fell at the feet of the lord king, striking his body on the ground on account of the wrongs he had unlawfully committed, and, fearful that his guilt could not be purged by his imprisonment, he humbly asked forgiveness. Then the lord king, glowing with mercy and wishing that no right intention of his should be lost, at the instance of ... Robert, archbishop of Dublin, who, kneeling before the king, made many prayers on his behalf about the lawless deeds he [*Art*] had often committed against the English ... granted

90 Grant made 12 Dec. 1394, Legge (1941): 133n.

life and favour to the said Art O'Dempsey, who gratefully spoke these words in Irish, which were rendered in English by John Malachy, interpreter, in the presence of many well understanding the Irish language.

(c) Words of submission to the king

Edmund Curtis, *Richard II in Ireland* (Oxford, 1927), 58–9.

I ... become the liege man of Lord Richard, king of England and France, and lord of Ireland, supreme lord of myself and my nation, and of his heirs, kings of England, from this day forward, in life and limb and worldly honour, so that he and they should have the power of life and death over me; I will be faithful in all things to him and to his heirs forever, and will defend him and his heirs against the whole world, and I will be obedient to the laws, mandates and ordinances of him and of them, as far as I and all my people are able; I will come to the said lord my king and his heirs, the kings of England, to his and their parliament, council or otherwise whenever he or they will send for me, or when, on behalf of him or them or of their lieutenants, I will be required, called or summoned; to the same lord king, his heirs, and lieutenants and any of them, I will come to give counsel, well and faithfully, and I will do in all and everything which a good and faithful liegeman should do and is held to do to his natural liege his lord. So help me God and these holy gospels of God.

153. Agreement with Art Macmurgh, 7 January 1395

Macmurgh long resisted submission, but finally came to this form of agreement.
Edmund Curtis, *Richard II in Ireland* (Oxford, 1927), 80–2.

This indenture was made on Thursday 7 January *[1395]* in the field between Tullow and Newcastle, between Thomas Mowbray, earl of Nottingham and Marshal of England, on the one side, and Art Macmurgh, born liege Irishman of our lord king, for himself and his men on the other, witnesses that at Art's instance and supplication our king received Art into his grace and peace in the following form: Art has sworn ... perpetual fealty to our lord king, his heirs and successors ... and that he will deliver to our lord king, or any of his deputies ... full possession of all lands, tenements, castles, fortresses, woods and pastures with all their appurtenances, which have been recently occupied by Art or his allies, men or adherents within the land of Leinster, without any reservation to himself in any way and without fraud or guile; Art has sworn and promised, for himself and all his people, that all his subjects and tenants of any condition whatsoever in those lands and places shall similarly swear to keep perpetual fealty to the lord king and his successors and deputies … and that they will adhere to and obey the laws, commands and ordinances of the king and his successors; Art has also sworn that by the first Sunday of Lent next *[28 February 1395]*, he will leave the whole country of Leinster to the true obedience, use and disposition of the king, his heirs and successors; *[he promised to deliver a hostage for this agreement]*; and the lord king, after those things are done, shall generously make provision for Art and will grant him and his heirs 80 marks p.a. perpetually, together with the inheritance of Art's wife in the barony of Norragh with its appurtenances; and all the armed men, warriors or fighting men of Art's company, household or nation shall leave the whole land of Leinster and shall go with him and have fitting wages from the king, for the time being, to go and conquer other places occupied by rebels against the king; Art and all his men shall have all lands which they acquire thus, and hold them of the king, his heirs and successors as his true lieges, obedient and subject to his laws ….

1395

This was a year crowded with incident: at the moment of Richard's triumph in Ireland came the resurgence of the 'lollard menace'; the body of Robert de Vere (who had died in 1392) was brought home for burial; a number of prominent people, including several bishops, died; and serious negotiations to end the French war began.

154. The government of England in Richard's absence

(a) The lords in parliament congratulate him and urge his speedy return, 13 February

The Irish expedition was a triumph for Richard, and was acknowledged as such by both politicians and commentators. Identical letters were sent by the lords spiritual and lords temporal, who had been informed, by Gloucester and by the king's squire Lawrence Drew, of Richard's success in pacifying Ireland. Richard returned to England in early May 1395.

Edmund Curtis, *Richard II in Ireland* (Oxford, 1927), 138–9.

... it seems, in our humble opinion, that you have done well, honourably and sufficiently in your noble person, provided that your officers
left behind to govern your land do their utmost diligently to treat your
people there in good and rightful ways of justice, as we truly hope they
will do. We therefore humbly beseech you, sovereign lord, desiring – as
do also your said commons – because the Scots, by what we have heard,
are unwilling to observe or keep the present truces in the nature and
form they have accepted, and because of other great matters concerning
the good and honour of yourself and all your realm, which shall be
shown more fully on your return to this your realm, that it may please
you, once your land of Ireland has been put into good and wise governance against your absence, to hasten your coming to this your realm,
to the great comfort and relief of ourselves and all your subjects ....

(b) The duke of York, Guardian of the Realm, seeks advice on a matter of international diplomacy, 18 March

Six months after Queen Anne's death, Richard was seeking a new bride.
Negotiators, briefed by the king in Ireland, left for Spain in early March 1395,
but were delayed in Paris. In mid-March French emissaries arrived in London
and asked for permission to travel to Ireland to confer urgently and confiden-
tially with the king. Later evidence shows that they wished to offer him an
aristocratic French wife. York, who had been instructed not to bother Richard
in Ireland, was clearly caught out by their arrival and wrote in agitation to the
king. For essential background see Palmer (1971a): 1–16.

J. J. N. Palmer, 'The background to Richard II's marriage to Isabel of France
(1396)', *BIHR* 44 (1971a), 16–17.

May it please you to know that your cousin of France [*Charles VI*] has
asked us that we should have made for Master Guilliam de la Fons,
his secretary, and Hanant de Campbrenart, his usher-at-arms, your
letters of safe-conduct to come to your noble presence to inform you of
various matters on behalf of your said cousin. On this, considering your
cousin's high estate, and presuming that it would certainly displease
your majesty to cause any delay to what your royal cousin had asked
for in this matter, from fear of impeding these matters which perhaps
concern the good and honour of yourself and your realm, and in the
hope of pleasing you in this matter, we have agreed to grant the said
safe-conduct to last until the Nativity of St John Baptist next [*24 June*].
Nevertheless we send to your royal highness with all speed to know
your wish in this matter, so that, if you do not wish them to come to you
at present, by your wise advice we can give them, on this, such a reply

as will be most fitting at this juncture. Most redoubtable and sovereign lord, may the blessed Trinity grant you a very good life of long duration and the very good rule of your people. Written at your palace of Westminster, 18 March. Understanding this, dread lord, we shall delay their coming to your noble presence in the most honourable and suitable manner that we can until we shall be sure of your will in this matter. And in case we are not informed of this during the time when we can honourably delay them longer, we will permit them to cross over to you in the hope that this will be agreeable to you. Your humble and faithful lieges the duke of York and others of your council.

155. Letters from Irish chiefs

The Irish chiefs were not slow to seek the benefits of a link with the English crown; these are two of twenty-three such surviving letters.

(a) From Malachy O'Kelly
Edmund Curtis, *Richard II in Ireland* (Oxford, 1927), 122.

I inform your majesty that I and my father have, for the defence of your kingdom, lordship and your lieges and subjects, suffered infinite damages and wrongs, killings of our men, ruin and plundering, but up to now have received no redress from your officers; but I expect compensation and grace from your highness, and now the time of joy and gladness has arrived ... I have revealed all the secrets of my heart to Lord John, son of the earl of Desmond, to be referred to your majesty, in whom you may have complete faith as speaking on my behalf. From what certain people have told me, however, I understand that the earl of Ormond intends to assert a right to certain lands and possessions which I as your faithful liege and my father also for days and years possessed quietly and peacefully, from time immemorial. I therefore beg your majesty, if it please you, to silence the said earl so that he shall not vex, disturb or in the future molest me in the those possessions, held and peacefully possessed by me and my father .... *[undated]*

(b) From Niall O'Niell, 14 April 1395, near Dundalk
Edmund Curtis, *Richard II in Ireland* (Oxford, 1927), 124–5.

I understand from the information of some, both English and Irish, that your most excellent lordship intends to make his way to England and that, immediately after you leave, the earl of March intends to attack me with his followers; but because I am ignorant of your majesty's planned departure, alas, my enemies would greatly rejoice. I therefore humbly beg your lordship not to leave your lordship of Ireland until I have had speech with you in person, for whenever it shall please you I will gladly come to your majesty whether from far or near. May you please to give no credence to those who would sow distrust between your majesty and me ....

1395

156. The year 1395 according to the *St Albans Chronicle*
SAC II.10–12, 30–4.

After the Octave of Epiphany *[13 January]* a parliament was held at London, convened by the guardian of England, Edmund the king's uncle, duke of York. The duke of Gloucester, who had been sent from Ireland, came to it and before them all he explained the king's necessity; by now he had exhausted the stock of his treasure among the Irish. His mission was so successful that the clergy granted a tenth, and the common people a fifteenth, after first making a protestation that this grant should not be held as arising from strict right but solely from affection for the king. In that parliament the lollards and their supporters, emboldened by the king's absence and maddened with every malice, publicly affixed to the door of St Paul's cathedral and Westminster Abbey abominable accusations against the clergy and hitherto unheard-of Conclusions,[91] on which they relied to destroy ecclesiastical persons and all the sacraments of the church. They were encouraged, it was thought, by the great support of certain nobles and the instigation of chamber knights. Among these commanders were Richard Sturry, Lewis Clifford, Thomas Latimer and John Montagu.[92]

[Then follow the Twelve Conclusions.]

When the king heard this, through the emissaries sent to Ireland, he was greatly moved; he swore that he would have the lollards and their supporters hanged unless they changed their beliefs. He fulfilled this

91 The Twelve Conclusions, which Walsingham includes, are printed in Hudson (1978): 24–9 (original English) and *English Historical Documents* IV, 848–50 (translation).

92 These four were chamber knights, courtiers with successful military and diplomatic careers who made good marriages. McFarlane (1972): pt 2, gives detailed biographies and agrees with Walsingham that they were indeed lollards.

as soon as he landed, because he swore this publicly, and threatened with death the more powerful of their supporters unless they recanted, asserting that they were traitors as much to the king as to the realm, and all who supported them were destroying the faith of their fathers. From Richard Sturry he exacted an oath, upon the gospels, that he would not hold these opinions in future. When he had done this, albeit unwillingly, the king instantly took the book in his own hand and said, 'I swear to you that if you ever violate your oath I will cause you to perish by the most shameful death'.[93] The rest of them, when they heard the voice of the trumpet, drew in their horns and like tortoises withdrew into their shells. By this animosity of the king, peace was soon returned to the English Church, and shortly after this Richard Sturry, chief favourer of those faithless ones died. ...

In September of that year, after the body of his former favourite Robert de Vere, earl of Oxford,[94] had been brought back from Louvain ... the king of England made solemn exequies at Colne Priory in Essex, in his presence, and in every possible way made a magnificent funeral service. He took the trouble to have opened the cypress-wood coffin in which lay the body, embalmed with balsam, to gaze at the face and to touch the fingers, which, it was believed, were bedecked with costly gold rings which were consigned to the earth with the body. He publicly demonstrated his affection for the dead man which earlier he had lavished upon the living. There were present, with the king and the deceased's mother, the archbishop and some other bishops, with abbots, priors and other men of religion, but few nobles attended, because the hatred which they conceived against him had not yet abated. ...

This year John Waltham, bishop of Salisbury, treasurer of the realm, died. The king liked him so much that, despite much grumbling, he was buried at Westminster, among kings, at the king's command.[95] He was succeeded in the office of treasurer by Roger Walden, previously the king's secretary and treasurer of Calais; but as bishop by John [correctly Richard] Mitford, bishop of Chichester, to whose bishopric the archbishop of Dublin [Robert Waldby] was translated because this major see was of minor value. There died also Thomas Brantingham, bishop of Exeter, who was succeeded, at the king's insistence, by Master

93 Richard's epitaph, 160, claimed that he had scotched the menace of heresy.
94 He died 22 November 1392.
95 Waltham's will, dated 2 Sept. 1395, directed burial in Salisbury cathedral, but he was buried, 10 Nov. 1395, in St Edward's chapel, Westminster Abbey, a place of particular honour, *Register of John Waltham*, ed. Timmins, 214/n.

Edmund Stafford, keeper of the privy seal. Henry Wakefield, bishop of Worcester, died; his successor, by provision at the king's entreaty, was a certain Cistercian monk, the king's doctor, called 'Tidman', and the legitimate election of Master John Green was scorned and quashed.[96]

157. The year 1395 according to the *Vita*

The death of the Spanish princess, Constance, duchess of Lancaster, opened the way for Gaunt to marry his long-time mistress, Katherine Swynford.

VR, 134–6.

After the quindene of St Hilary *[27 January]* the duke of York, guardian of England and the king's lieutenant, held a parliament at Westminster. The king sent over from Ireland to this meeting his youngest uncle, Thomas, duke of Gloucester, to seek in his name one tenth from the clergy and one fifteenth from the laity. All these were granted. There came to this parliament Bartholomew de Manera, papal nuncio, seeking the repeal of the frequently-mentioned Statutes of Provisors,[97] but could get no benefit or profit. ... Henry Wakefield, bishop of Worcester, died at Blockley *[Gloucs.]* on *[11]* March while returning home from that parliament. He was succeeded by *[Robert]* Tydeman *[of Winchcombe]*, once a monk of Hailes *[Gloucs.]*, then bishop of Llandaff, who was finally translated to the see of Worcester on the feast of the Conversion of St Paul next following *[25 January]*.[98] The king was present at his installation. This thing was marvellous in our eyes.[99] ... During the summer of that year there died Constance, duchess of Lancaster, and Mary, countess of Derby; they were buried at Leicester. By this countess, Henry, earl of Derby, had four sons, namely Henry, Thomas, John and Humphrey, and two daughters, Blanche and Mary.

96 Robert Tidman of Winchcombe, bishop of Llandaff 1394–5; see Talbot and Hammond (1965): 362. Master John Green was a Benedictine monk, distinguished theologian and prior of Worcester; Emden (1957–9): II.815.

97 Statutes of 1351, 1353, 1365 and 1389 which were designed to curb papal rights of patronage in the English Church.

98 Actually, 15 June 1395.

99 A quotation from Psalm 118:23; clearly the author had a poor opinion of the appointment.

158. Order to demolish Sheen manor house, 9 April 1395

The impression given by chroniclers[100] is that Richard ordered the destruction of Sheen immediately after Anne's death, but this information shows that he waited nearly a year before ordering its demolition. It comes from the accounts of John Gedney, clerk of the king's works from 17 June 1391, who died in office 14 October 1396. His executors presented his accounts during 3 Henry IV: 30 Sept. 1401–29 Sept. 1402.

TNA, Foreign Accounts, E 364/36 rot. H.

£2,708 12s. 5¾d. viz[101] for certain masons, bricklayers, and other craftsmen and labourers 6d., 5d., 4d. and 3d. per day respectively by a writ noted earlier in the roll of this account and also by another writ of that same late king under his privy seal dated 9 April, year 18 [*Richard II, 1395*] directed to the same John Gedney ... by which writ the former king ordered John to cause to be pulled down and razed to the ground all the houses and buildings of the manor of Sheen, both within the court[*yard*] within the moat and within the court outside the moat, also the houses and buildings within *la Neyt*[102] next to that manor, and that he would cause to be sent and stored the glass, tiles, stone, timber, iron and ironwork of that manor for the works of that late king by the advice and according to the orders of the then bishop of Salisbury, treasurer of England [*John Waltham*]. [*A later item in the account mentions six 'pykoys' called 'mattokkes' bought for use at Sheen manor.*]

159. An attempt to have Edward II canonised

This is the most interesting evidence for one of several unsuccessful attempts by Richard to have Edward II canonised; the others were in 1385, July 1392 and June 1397.[103] It was the most cost-effective journey; the other missions were headed by bishops, whose expenses were much higher.

Issues of the Exchequer, trans. Devon, 259; adapted.

24 April 1395: to Peter Merk and James Monald.[104] In money paid to them by the same Peter, in discharge of £6 19s. which the king

100 See above **146a** and Usk (1997): 18.

101 The cost of demolishing Sheen cannot be calculated since it was lumped with other expenses of that year, including the repair of Woodstock manor, Oxon.

102 A manor house in Middlesex.

103 *WC*, 58; Devon (1837), 247–8, 264.

104 Peter Mark and James Monaldi were Italian merchants 'of the Society of Albertini of Florence', *CPR 1391–6*, 688; *CCR 1392–6*, 518–27.

commanded to be paid in reimbursement of their costs incurred in the carriage and transport of a gold cup and a gold ring set with a ruby, also a *Book of the Miracles of Edward late King of England, whose body was buried at the town of Gloucester*, from London to the city of Florence, to make a present of the same to our most holy Father Pope Urban, on behalf of our lord king: £6 19s.

160. Richard's epitaph

The contract for making the tomb and effigies of the king and queen (expensive at £650),[105] was agreed on 24 April 1395. The epitaph was probably composed at about the same time, and shows how Richard wished to be remembered. The Latin is in rhyming couplets.

Royal Commission on Historical Monuments: *London vol. I, Westminster Abbey* (London, 1924), 31.

Prudent and pure, Richard by right the second, vanquished by fate, lies here depicted under marble. Truthful in speech he was, and full of reason. Tall of body, prudent in mind, like Homer. A friend of the church, he subdued the mighty; he cut down anyone who violated royal rights. He struck down heretics and scattered their friends. Oh merciful Christ, to whom he was devoted, oh Baptist, keep safe him who put you first in his prayers. Beside him under stone, Anne now lies entombed. While she lived in the world she was married to Richard the second. Devoted to Christ, she was well known for her deeds: she favoured the poor, always receiving *[thanks]* for her gifts. She settled disputes and relieved the oppressed. She was beautiful in body, fair and mild of face. She proved a comfort to widows, and a tonic to the sick. In the year 1394, in June, the 7th of the month she departed this life.

161. Richard's signed instruction to his ambassadors to France, 8 July 1395

Perhaps his success in Ireland prompted Richard to nurse unrealistic hopes of a diplomatic triumph over France. For comment on these 'breathtaking' demands, see Palmer (1972): 169–71.

J. J. N. Palmer, *England, France and Christendom, 1377–99* (London, 1972): 256–7.

105 Printed in translation in *Chaucer's World*: 416–17.

The instructions given to the revered father in God, the archbishop of Dublin [*Robert Waldby*], the earls of Rutland and Marshal, and to the other messengers sent on behalf of our most redoubtable lord the king to his cousin of France to treat of the marriage between our said lord king and Isabelle, eldest daughter of his said cousin, in the hope of having a better and firmer and more certain peace between the two kingdoms; and to have this agreed plainly in the manner written below; and also to treat of the said peace: that it to say, to conclude by God's grace the said marriage and to report on what will be done concerning the said peace treaty.

First, that touching the said peace the ambassadors should enter into a treaty with the French, making protestation in the most honest fashion that they can.

Also, that the said ambassadors should demand on behalf of our sovereign lord king all the duchy of Guyenne with the fees, lordships, advowsons and all other things as completely as they were earlier granted to King Edward in the last peace and accord which was made at Calais[106] between him and King John of France, to be held by our said lord king and his heirs without doing any homage for that same duchy.

Our lord king should have Calais and the lordship of Mark with the marches of Calais and the county of Guisnes and the lordship of Ponthieu also as completely as they were granted to the said King Edward in that same peace and accord, without doing any homage for them or for any part of them.

The arms which our lord king bears at present should remain with him and his heirs for all time.[107]

Those same ambassadors should demand on our lord king's behalf all the arrears of the ransom of King John of France, together with the damages and costs suffered and endured by the lord king or by any of his progenitors from the start of the war until now.

Our holy father Pope Boniface [*IX*] should be included in the peace treaty.

If it happens by God's grace that from the marriage of our lord king with Isabelle, daughter of his cousin of France, there should be a son, then that son should be duke of Normandy and count of Anjou and of

106 Treaty of Brétigny (Calais), 1361.

107 In 1340 Edward III assumed the title king of France and quartered the fleurs-de-lis of the French royal coat of arms with the leopards of his own.

Maine, and he should have that same duchy and those counties with the fees, lordships, advowsons and all other things so completely and just as any king of England previously had them before this time.

If it happens that from that marriage of our lord king with the said Isabelle there should be another son or daughter, then the eldest son should only have the duchy of Normandy, and the other son or daughter should have the counties of Anjou and Maine.

If God wills that our lord king has several sons from his marriage with the said Isabelle; and if by chance it can be found that the realm of Scotland should be in any manner confiscated, or otherwise that it ought to come to the crown of England; so that the lord king wished to give one of his sons the kingdom of Scotland, then his cousin of France should be bound to find a certain number of men-at-arms and other warriors until that kingdom should be conquered or peacefully enjoyed by that son, or at least for some years.

In testimony of which the great and privy seals and also the signet of our lord king, at his commandment, is put to this instruction. Given at Leeds castle *[Kent]*, 8 July, the 19th year of our reign *[1395]*.

[The king's autograph signature]

162. Agreement for a long truce

The long truce which was finally concluded in 1396 was not seen as remarkable by contemporaries; unlike a peace, a truce was not an occasion for rejoicing. Since the terms of this agreement were ignored by English chroniclers they have to be discovered from official sources, from both parties.

Thomas Rymer, *Foedera, Conventiones, Litterae*, vol. VII (London, 1709), 820–2.

(a) Richard gives authority to his negotiators, 20 December 1395

Richard, by God's grace king of England and France, and lord of Ireland, to all who will see these letters, greeting. Know that, for the honour of God and to avoid the spilling of Christian blood, and the evils and irreparable damage which are caused by wars between us and our adversary of France, which will occur in times to come, just as has happened in times past, and desiring to come to a good peace and agreement with our said adversary, and to bestow peace, quiet and tranquillity upon our subjects: in full confidence in the sense, loyalty, wisdom and discretion of our very dear cousins Edward, earl of Rutland, Thomas, earl marshal and *[earl of]* Nottingham, and William de Scrope, our chamberlain, whom we have ordained and committed, and we ordain and commit, in our place, to meet with the uncles and other deputies of our adversary, having sufficient power from him on the business which follows, in whatever localities and places seem good to them, for making a treaty of peace, And we have given, and we give by these presents, to our said deputies full power, authority and special mandate to convene, negotiate, compose, treat, pacify, and plainly and finally to agree and to come to a good peace and accord on all contentious disputes, questions, wars, riots and discords, and to proceed with all their articles and circumstances, connected, emerging, dependent and linked between us, and our realms ... and to do, execute and expedite all other articles which otherwise appertain to the good completion and accomplishment of the same treaty of peace and accord, of whatever nature it will be .... And we have given, and also give by these presents to our said deputies full power, authority and special mandate to agree and to undertake truces for twenty-eight years, to commence at the end of these present truces, according to the form and condition of these truces. And we promise, loyally in good faith and on the word of a king, to have and always to adhere firmly and agreeably to whatever will be done in our name by our delegates and by our said uncles and brother, three or two of them, on all and each of the matters aforesaid; and to give our letters of confirmation, sealed with our great seal, on all the points which will be thus agreed, to have them executed, upon every point, to the best of our ability, without fraud or bad faith. This we promise, on the pledge and obligations of all our goods, present and future, without ever doing, saying or proposing, in judgment, or out, anything to the contrary. Chiltern Langley, 20 December 1395.

(b) Evidence from France, 11 March 1396

Charles by God's grace king of France, to all those who will see these present letters, greeting. We have seen and caused to be read, word for word, in the presence of our most dear and well-loved uncles and brother, the dukes of Berry, Burgundy, Orleans and Bourbon[108] and of our great council, the letters of our said uncles and brother, about the general truces, by sea and land, by them taken, agreed, passed and sworn by our command, will and order, and by virtue of the power given by us and vested in our said uncles and brother, on behalf of ourselves, our successors kings of France, our kingdom, lands, lordships and subjects, and for

108 The negotiators on the French side. Berry was the king's brother.

our allies, their kingdoms ... and for the king of England our very dear
and well-loved son, his successors, kings of England, his kingdom, lands,
lordship and subjects and for his allies and their realms ..., by sea and
land, this side and across the sea, for twenty-eight years, commencing at
sunrise on Michaelmas day in the forthcoming 1398, when the present
truces lastly agreed at Leulinghen are due to expire, and finishing at
Michaelmas in 1426 following. *[Concluded 11 March 1396.]*

1396

163. The year 1396 according to the *Vita*

This year is seen by historians as a key date in the Anglo-French war, but
to contemporaries it was the year of two noteworthy weddings: Gaunt's to
Katherine Swynford, and Richard's to six-year-old Isabelle of France. The long
truce made less impact upon contemporaries; by 1396 truces were nothing new,
and there had been little fighting against France since 1392.

VR, 135–6.

John of Gaunt, duke of Lancaster, married *[14 January]* Katherine
Swynford, who had been his concubine for a long time while his wife
Constance was alive. By her he had three sons, John Beaufort, earl of
Somerset, Henry Beaufort, bishop of Lincoln,[109] and another Beaufort,[110]
and two daughters, of whom one became countess of Westmorland, the
other countess of Northumberland.[111] They were all legitimised by the
pope. ... On 7 August, the king, proposing to marry the daughter of
the king of France, crossed over to Calais with a large retinue and
impressive household, and stayed there until the feast of St Simon and
St Jude *[28 October]*.[112] So about that feast the two kings, of France and
England, met on a plain near the castle of Guisnes, with a venerable
and distinguished multitude of dukes, earls, barons, and of other lords
of both sides, and held a discussion, and in their tents pitched there
they arranged the marriage between our king and Isabelle, the little
daughter of the French king, who was eight years old. At last, after
much negotiating between the supporters of an agreement, the king of
France handed over his daughter to our king to be his wife and queen
of England. After this our king bade farewell to the king of France

109 Bishop of Lincoln from July 1398; translated to Winchester 1404.

110 Thomas, later duke of Exeter.

111 In fact, Joan, later countess of Westmorland, was their only daughter.

112 Richard was in Calais 7–22 Aug., and 28 Sept. to 11/16 Nov., *HBC*, 40.

and returned with her and all her retinue to Calais, and there, with the
greatest solemnity and in the presence of those lords, he married her
on 10 November. After this they returned safely to England with much
rejoicing. ... On 23 November the queen came to London and was led
through Southwark to Kennington, and many of the citizens came out
over the bridge to see her. But, because of the crowd, some of them were
crushed and trampled to death as they returned.

164. High society opinion of Gaunt's third marriage

The new duchess of Lancaster played an important part in the ceremonies accompanying Richard's second marriage. This prompted Froissart to
comment on the ill-feeling which her own marriage had caused at court.
Froissart, *Chronicles*, II.600.

From affection to these [*Beaufort*] children the duke of Lancaster
married their mother, to the great astonishment of France and England,
for Katherine Swynford was of base extraction in comparison to his two
former duchesses, Blanche and Constance. When this marriage was
announced to the high-ranking ladies in England – like the duchess
of Gloucester, the countess of Derby,[113] the countess of Arundel, and
others connected with the royal family – they were greatly shocked,
and thought the duke much to blame. 'He has sadly disgraced himself
by marrying his concubine', they said, adding that, since it was so,
she would be the second lady in the kingdom, and the queen would be
dishonourably accompanied by her; and they would leave her to do the
honours alone, for they would never enter any place where she was.
They themselves would be disgraced if they suffered such a base-born
duchess, who had been the duke's concubine a long time before and
during his marriages, to take precedence, and their hearts would burst
with grief were it to happen. Those who were the most outraged by
the subject were the duke and duchess of Gloucester; they considered
the duke of Lancaster a doting fool for marrying his concubine, and
declared they would never honour his lady by calling her sister. The
duke of York made light of the matter, for he lived chiefly with the
king and his brother of Lancaster. The duke of Gloucester was of a
different way of thinking; although the youngest of the three brothers,
he yielded to no man's opinion, was naturally proud and overbearing,
and in opposition to the king's ministers, unless he could turn them as

113 In fact she had died in July 1394, *WC*, 520.

he willed. Katherine Roet, however, remained duchess, and the second lady in England, as long as she lived. She was a lady accustomed to honours, for she had been brought up at court during her youth, and the duke fondly loved the children he had by her, as he showed during his life and at his death.

165. Concluding the Anglo-French agreement, autumn 1396

This is the longest English chronicle account of the ceremonies accompanying the conclusion of the long truce, but says nothing about its terms. It is included in full to remind us what contemporaries considered significant.

SAC II.38–48.

In accordance with an agreement made earlier between the ambassadors, the kings of England and France met at a place outside Calais chosen for their meeting, where the magnificent tents of both kings were erected. Before the discussion, each of them, for the security of the peace, publicly took this oath in person:

'We Charles, king of France, swear by our royal word upon the Gospel, on behalf of ourselves and all our subjects, friends, adherents and wellwishers, that we will not do, nor suffer to be committed by us, nor by those named above, damage, interference, trouble, arrest nor disturbance, in any way during the time of our meeting, nor for eight days and nights before the meeting and seven days after, to our son the king of England, nor to any of his subjects, friends, retainers or supporters, before that said time. And if by chance any friction or dispute should arise among our followers – which God forbid – we promise on the word of a king, and by the security aforesaid, that we will cause whatever should be done to resolve this, without delay. On the same security we also swear that if any person or people of whatever rank or condition wishes to contravene that security, we will help our said son, as far as we can, to resist the malice of those wrongdoers, and preserve our said son and his men, by the means we and our people know, and to observe and pursue everything, without fraud or evil intention. To this we swear and promise.' The English king swore the same oath.

On 26 October, the king of England rode from Calais towards his castle of Guisnes, accompanied by the duke of Berry, who had been sent on behalf of the French to Calais to receive the king of England's oath, and *[to receive]* safe-conduct for Frenchmen coming to the meeting of the two kings. While they were riding towards Guisnes, the duke of

Orleans met them, with 500 nobly equipped men. So the dukes of Berry and Orleans dined with the king that night; and after dinner the king gave the duke of Berry a collar worth 500 marks, and to the duke of Orleans a gold goblet (*ciphum*)[114] and ewer worth 200 marks.

Next day, which was Friday, it was proclaimed in the morning that no one should carry a sword, dagger or staff, except 400 noblemen who were specially assigned to assist the kings' discussion and meeting. The king of England, dressed in a long gown of red velvet, wearing on his head a chaplet full of precious stones which he had received as a gift from the French king, and bearing on his breast the hart of his own livery, processed regally with his men, who were all clad in ankle-length red gowns, with a white band of the livery of the lately deceased queen of England. He came with about 100 men to the tent prepared for him. At that moment the king of France came with his men from the castle of Ardres, and arrived at his tent to the sound of loud music. When he had entered the chamber of his pavilion, he immediately sent the count of St Pol to our king to announce his arrival and to enquire at what hour they were to speak together. The king of England sent the earl of Northumberland, for the same reason, to the king of France to know his will on this matter. When this was known, there were sent to our king from the French side, to conduct him to his council pavilion, the dukes of Berry, Burgundy, Orleans and Bourbon [*and four others.*] On our part the dukes of Lancaster and Gloucester, the earls of Derby, Rutland, Marshal [*Mowbray*] and Northumberland were sent to conduct the French king to his Council pavilion.

The French king was dressed in a knee-length gown of red velvet trimmed with a band of black and white, black leggings and spurs, and red-and-white shoes. Around his neck was a collar of his own livery, on his breast the hart of the king of England's livery, and on his head a chaplet of black cloth, covered in jewels. His dukes and counts, whether lords or knights, were clothed in the king's livery, but the squires were wearing cloth of red say,[115] with similar borders, and with black hoods.

At the hour appointed for the meeting, the kings processed, each one from his tent, on foot, so that neither should arrive before the other at the meeting-place, which was between the pavilions. Carrying the sword before the king of England was his [*half*] brother the earl of

---

114 *Ciphum* can mean a cup or bowl, so it is possible that this was a gift of a basin and jug.

115 A fine-quality cloth of mixed silk and wool.

Huntingdon, and with the French king the count de Harecourt. On the kings' arrival and meeting, their people on both sides knelt for a long time. After the meeting, they ate spices and drank wine. Then the king of England gave the French king a large gold goblet (*ciphum*), which King Edward of Windsor had made in the 40th year of his reign, at a cost of 700 marks, and the matching ewer. After this, the kings linked arms and went together to the mill of Ardres, which was not far from the pavilions, so that the people of both sides should see that the kings were in harmony; so in sign of peace, the kings' swords were carried behind them. They returned through the French camp, to inspect the Gallic people and retinue; then they came back through the English camp. Finally, hand in hand, they went together into the pavilion of the English council; there, after wine and spices, our king gave the French king a collar worth 500 marks. Next the kings went together to the place chosen for their meeting and agreed to build there, at their joint expense, a chapel to be called 'Of our Lady of Peace', in perpetual memory of the meeting of the two kings. When this was done, they shook hands, and each returned to his own tent.

On the morning of Saturday, the feast of saints Simon and Jude [28 October], the English king was dressed in a gown of red and white velvet, i.e. motley, which reached his mid-calf; he was preceded and followed by 400 knights and esquires. The knights wore a kind of gold cloth, and esquires wore cloth of say, in the king's livery. The king of France was dressed entirely in yesterday's outfit. The kings met at the French pavilion, where they discussed the articles of the truce, which were put into writing and confirmed by the kings' assent. This done, the kings, with their council, swore on the gospels to observe the pact peacefully and honestly. Then wine and spices were brought. On that occasion the French king gave our king two large golden pouches stuffed with precious stones; then a panel with an image of the Trinity, gold, encrusted with very precious pearls, a panel with an image of St Michael, embellished with most precious pearls, a gold panel with an image of St George, crammed with costly pearls and stones; then a panel with a cross and image of our lord Jesus Christ, kneeling at the foot of the cross, gold, full of precious stones. In return the king of England gave the king of France a torque, made of pearls and precious stones, which Anne the former queen had given him, worth 5,000 marks, which the French king joyfully placed round his neck; and he invited the French king to eat with him on the following Monday, which the French king gladly accepted.

The following Sunday the kings did not meet, but the duke of Berry and the viscount of Melun ate with the English king in his castle of Guisnes. After the meal, the king gave the duke of Berry a collar worth £300. The same day the duke of Orleans dined with the king; after dinner the king gave him a basin and ewer of pure gold, and then the duke gave the king another basin and ewer, which was much more expensive than the king's basin.

Next day, Monday, the king of England, wearing a full-length gown of cloth of gold and blue, rode to the tents with his people. The French king, in his former robe, arrived there shortly after, having on his head a black hood to which was fixed a hart [badge] of the English king's livery. The French king's retinue also came in their previous apparel. The kings met in our king's great tent and there awaited the arrival of the future new queen; and meanwhile wine and spices were brought in. After drinking, the king of England gave the French king a basin, with a gold ewer, and a crystal bottle full of gems, worth 500 marks.

Then the new queen was led to the pavilion of the French council. With her came the duchesses of Lancaster and Gloucester, and the countess of Huntingdon, with their ladies. The dukes of Berry and Burgundy, clad in red velvet, carried the queen to the place chosen for the meeting. She was dressed in a narrow tunic of old-fashioned style, of blue velvet, scattered with fleur-de-lis, and wore on her head a crown of great value. The French king gave her to the English king, with these words: 'Dearest son, I commend to you this creature, the dearest to me over all creatures in the world, except our Dauphin, and our wife'. The English king took her by the hand, and thanked the French king for such an honourable and gracious gift, and promised to accept her on the conditions agreed between them; and, that by this relationship, the subjects of each king could live peacefully, and the kings reach a good conclusion and make perpetual peace between their kingdoms, to end the spilling of Christian blood, which would probably ensue if this relationship were not made at this time. The queen was entrusted to the duchesses of Lancaster and Gloucester, and the countesses of Huntingdon and Stafford, and the other ladies present, who conducted her to Calais with a great entourage of men and horses; she had with her twelve wagons full of lords and ladies.

Afterwards the kings sat down to eat in our king's tent. The French king sat on the right side of the hall, and he was royally served in the manner of his country, that is, from all the food of the first course, all together in a great dish, and from the second course in the same way. The English king was served in the manner of his own country. After the meal, the kings embraced, and mounted their horses. The English king led the French king on his way, and finally, after shaking hands, they separated from each other on horseback. The French king rode to Ardres; the English king turned towards Calais, where he married the French king's daughter, a little girl not eight years old.

166. The duke of Gloucester at these ceremonies, according to Froissart

Gloucester's grumpy attitude to the ceremonial which accompanied the truce-making may be significant in the light of his arrest the following summer.

Froissart, *Chronicles*, II.618.

Every honour and respect that could be imagined was paid to the English lords. The duchess of Burgundy entertained them splendidly at a dinner at which were present the duchess of Lancaster with her son and two daughters. There was an immense variety of different dishes and decorations on the tables, and very rich presents made of gold and silver plate; in short, nothing was spared, so that the English were astonished where such riches could come from, especially the duke of Gloucester, who told his friends that the kingdom of France abounded in wealth and power. To soften the temper of the duke of Gloucester, whom the French lords knew to be proud and their bitter enemy, they paid him the most flattering attentions. Despite this, and the handsome presents they offered, which he accepted, the same rancour remained in his breast and, in spite of everything the French could say or do, whenever the subject of peace was mentioned, his answers were as harsh and severe as ever. The French are very subtle; but, with regard to him, they could never gain his affections; and his conversation was so reserved that it was not possible to discover his real sentiments.

167. Richard's settlement of Ulster destroyed by the earl of March's attack on O'Neill

This short, insignificant-looking item was to have profound consequences for Richard. Unnoticed by English observers, the attack in late 1396 by Roger Mortimer on Armagh, the cathedral city held by O'Neill the elder ('king of

Ulster'), destroyed the king's new-made peace in Ulster, and led to Mortimer's own death in battle on 20 July 1398. Mortimer, earl of March and Ulster, was the grandson of Edward III's son Lionel, so Richard's close kinsman [89], and his killing was a challenge that Richard could not ignore. It was partly to avenge this death that Richard undertook his second Irish expedition in 1399.

Miscellaneous Irish Annals, ed. and trans. Séamus Ó hInnse (Dublin, 1947), 157.

An incursion by the earl of March, and earl of Ormond, the earl of Kildare, the Galls of Ireland and a host of Gaels into the province *[of Ulster]* after the earl of March had made a treacherous raid on O'Neill before that. They went to Armagh, plundered the city, remained a fortnight there and finally burned it, together with the great church of Patrick … and may God restore it! They turned and took sway over Ulster after that.

1397

168. January to June 1397 according to the *Vita*

This was a year of two halves, the second of which is outside the scope of this volume.

VR, 136–7.

On 3 January the queen was again brought to London over the bridge along Bridge Street, through Tower Street, as far as the Tower; and the next day through the midst of Cornhill and Cheap[116] to Westminster. There, on the vigil of Epiphany *[5 January]*, she was solemnly crowned by the archbishop of Canterbury. In February a council was convened at Westminster, to which the duke of Gloucester and the earl of Arundel were summoned by the king, but they refused to come, pleading illness. At this the king was extremely bitter and was moved to very great anger against them.

169. The parliament of 22 January–12 February 1397

This meeting was one of mixed fortunes for the king, who failed to secure a grant for an expedition against Milan, in support of his new French allies.

116 Two wards of the city.

(a) 'Haxey's case'

This episode has prompted considerable speculation.[117] Though unnoticed by chroniclers, it was reported at length in the parliament roll, and Richard's anger at this petition, especially at criticism of the court, seems entirely genuine.[118] Thomas Haxey was a long-serving king's clerk.[119] Was his complaint of 'too many bishops and ladies' at court correct? Richard had made some unusual promotions to bishoprics, advancing several men who had given personal, rather than administrative, service to the crown: three confessors, his surgeon, his physician, a relative and a monk of Westminster [**157–8**]. In the 'general post' of bishops following Archbishop Courtenay's death in 1396 no career administrators were promoted, which may well have provoked resentment among the civil service clerks. The loss of their records means we cannot tell if the new prelates lived in their dioceses or at court. The very masculine character of noble and royal households could explain the complaint about too many ladies. The domestic staff consisted of men and boys [**82a, 92b**], and most visitors were men,[120] but Richard's court always had a strong female element, probably from Princess Joan's influence, which persisted even after her death in 1385 and became strongly politicised; promotions to the ladies' 'Fraternity of St George', which corresponded to the masculine Order of the Garter, allow us to observe this process.[121] The rumpus caused by the petition's perceived insult to the king quickly subsided. On 25 February and 27 May Haxey was restored to good standing in church and realm in terms which indicate a certain grim humour.

RP III.338–9; *PROME* 1397 (1), sections 13–17.

On Friday, the feast of Candlemas [*2 February*], the king summoned before him at Westminster, after dinner, during parliament, the lords spiritual and temporal, and there he told them how he had heard that, on the previous Thursday, they had been with the commons, and that the commons had discussed with them certain matters which seemed to the king to be contrary to his regality and status, and his royal liberty; he ordered the chancellor to describe and inform him about those matters. At this, the chancellor, on the king's command, related these same matters to him, which were on four points:

One was about a statute made concerning sheriffs and escheators, that they should be persons sufficient in land or rent, and that they

117 McHardy (1997): 93–114; Dodd (2000): 78–80.

118 Jones (1968): 73 suggested that Richard himself was behind the petition, in order to demonstrate his power; but opposition, even if fictitious, is not something that authoritarian rulers employ.

119 McHardy (1997): 93–114.

120 Woolgar (2000): 8, 202.

121 Collins (2000): 92–106, 301–2.

should not remain in office for more than a year: on this the commons complained that the statute was not being observed.

Another point was about the Scottish march, and the great oppressions and outrages both committed and attempted by the Scots, in breach of the truces made between the two kingdoms, and to the destruction of the border lands and of the king's subjects: on this they begged that a remedy be ordered, at the good discretion of the king and his lords.

The third point concerned a statute made for the livery of badges, that valets called yeomen of lords, who were neither household nor menial servants, should not wear such liveries of badges, and thereby avoid the maintenance and duress which, by pretext of such liveries, were committed in the land, to the oppression of the people, and in disturbance of the execution of the law. On this the commons begged that the statute should be observed, and that a certain penalty should be set by advice of the lords.

The fourth article was that the great and excessive cost of the king's household should be remedied (*amendez*) and reduced, namely of the multitude of bishops who held lordships and who were advanced by the king, and their hangers-on; and also of many ladies and their hangers-on who stayed in the king's household, at his expense.

In answer to this exposition the king declared his will and intent to the lords: How by the gift of God he was by lineage and right of inheritance the king and inheritor of the kingdom of England, and he wished to possess his regality and the royal liberty of his crown. And he replied to these articles as follows: that some of them greatly infringed regality and his royal estate and liberty. To the first article, about sheriffs and escheators, the king said, that he would be well pleased that those who were sheriffs and escheators should be men of sufficient property and loyalty, as reason demanded; but it seemed to him that it would be more for his profit and for the good execution of those offices, that sufficient persons should remain in their posts for more than a year, subject to their good conduct, than to be removed at the end of one year. This was for several reasons explained by the king …. On the point about the Scottish march, it well pleased the king that the lords should discuss a remedy, that if it were possible to bear the cost it would please the king, and he was ready to do his duty as it appeared reasonable to him. *[There is no record of Richard's answer to the third point but a petition about badges and liveries, which was recorded, resulted in a statute being passed in this parliament whose wording was very similar to that of the petition.]*

At the fourth article, regarding the cost of the king's household, and the presence there of bishops and ladies in his company, the king was greatly aggrieved and offended that the commons who were his subjects should wrongly take or presume on themselves any regulation or management of the king's person, or of his household, or any persons of rank whom he pleased to have in his company; and it seemed to the king that the commons had caused great offence in this matter, in contravention of his regality and that of his royal majesty, and of the liberty of himself and of his honourable progenitors, which he was duty bound to defend and maintain, with God's help. The king therefore commanded that the lords spiritual and temporal should, on Saturday morning, inform and declare fully to the commons the king's will in this matter. And further, the king had heard that the commons had been instigated and incited by a bill presented to them for discussion and to present that last article. He therefore ordered the duke of Guyenne and Lancaster to command Sir John Bussy,[122] speaker of the commons, on his allegiance, to report and reveal to him the name of the person who had presented that bill to the commons.

On the Saturday morning which was the morrow of Candlemas [3 February], the lords spiritual and temporal met with the commons and told them what was the king's wish and command, and the commons handed over that bill to the lords, along with the name of that man who had presented it to them, that is to say the Reverend Thomas Haxey. This bill was then delivered to the clerk of the crown by the clerk of parliament on the king's order, and immediately afterwards the commons came before the king in parliament, at his summons. And there, with all humility and obeisance that they could, they expressed great sorrow, as appeared from their demeanour, that the king should have formed such a bad opinion of them. They humbly begged the king to hear and accept their excuse that it was never their intention or wish to say, show or do anything which would cause offence or displeasure to his royal majesty the king, or against his royal status or liberty; and especially of that business concerning his own person and the management of his household, or of the lords and ladies in his company, or of any other matter which concerned the king himself: they knew and well understood that such things were none of their business, but lay solely within the king's discretion and power. Thus their only intention had been, and was, on account of the great affection which, as his humble subjects, they bore to the king, that the lords should beg the

122 Roskell *et al.* (1992): II.449–54.

king to consider his honourable estate, and in this matter to do as he pleased, though the king had construed it otherwise; but it was never their intention [*to suggest otherwise*], and this weighed heavily upon them. Then the commons humbly submitted themselves to the king's grace and royal will, begging his royal majesty to have them graciously excused; moreover, they said that they were always ready with their power to save his royal estate and liberty, and to put their persons and wealth at his disposal as befitted loyal lieges, to the best of their ability, for the honour and salvation of the king's royal majesty. On this matter the chancellor, at the king's command, told the commons that the king, of his royal goodness and graciousness, entirely excused them, and that he would be a good lord to them as it was always his wish so to be.[123]

(b) The Beauforts legitimised

Richard secured the statutory legitimation of Gaunt's four children by Katherine Swynford: John, Thomas, Henry and Joan Beaufort. Subsequent marriage of parents legitimised children in the eyes of canon law, but not English common law, so this measure was clearly a favour to Gaunt. At this point no bar was put on the Beauforts' descendants inheriting the crown, a provision later imposed by Henry IV.[124] The language of this grant is significant: the king was making it clear that his powers were no less than those of the pope and that he was not being pressured by the papal action.

RP III.343; *PROME* 1397 (1), sections 28–9.

On Tuesday, the fifteenth day of parliament [*4 February*] the chancellor, on the king's order, announced that our holy father the pope, from reverence for the king's most excellent person and for his honourable uncle John, duke of Guyenne and Lancaster, and for his lineage, has enabled and legitimised my Lord John Beaufort,[125] his brothers and his sister. The king, therefore, as complete emperor of his realm of England, for the honour of his lineage, wills, and by the fullness of his royal power,[126] has enabled and made legitimate, by his own authority, the said John, his brothers and sister. He also pronounced and publicised the enabling and legitimisation in the form of a charter granted by the king on that subject [*which follows.*]

123 Haxey's seven ecclesiastical benefices were restored to him on 25 Feb., and on 27 May he was pardoned for his treachery, at the request of 'the bishops and multitude of ladies' at court – surely a grim joke; *CPR 1396–9*, 98, 123.

124 In 1407; Bennett (2008): 23.

125 John Beaufort was created earl of Somerset on Saturday, 10 February 1397.

126 *Sa plenir Roial poiar*. Fullness of power (*plenitudo potestatis*) was claimed by popes.

170. The will of Thomas Holand, earl of Kent, 22 April 1397

This is one of the earliest surviving wills written in English.[127] Its use of English and lack of precise bequests suggest it was made in a hurry. Thomas Holand, the elder and more responsible of Richard's half-brothers, died on 25 April 1397; his will was proved before Arundel at Lambeth, 10 May 1397.

A Collection of all the Wills, now known to be extant, of the Kings and Queens of England, ed. John Nicholas (London, 1780), 118–19.

In the name of God, Amen. In the day of the resurrection of our Lord Jeshu Crist, the yer of hym a thousand thre hondred four score and seventeen, I, Thomas of Holand, erl of Kent and lord Wake, beying in hol memorie, ordeyene and make my testament in this wise. First, I yeve and bytake my soule to our Lord Jeshu Crist, and to hys mercy, and to the help and grace of our Lady, his blisfol moder, and the help of alle seyntes of hevene, and my body to be buried as sone as hit goodlich may, in the abeye of Brune *[Bourne, Lincs.]*. And I yeve and devyse to Alys my wife, and Thomas my sone, al my catyal and godes moebles, praying my wyf for al the love and trust that hath ben bytwyn us, and also praying and chargying my sone, upon my blessyng, that they by good love and on assent governe hem in swych wyse, that at hur power my dettes mowe by quyted, and my old servantes iholpe yn descharge of me. And to execute my will and devys aforesayd, I ordeyne and mak my wyf and sone aforesayd myn executours.

---

127 Haskett (1996): 149–206. Technically it is a testament since it concerns only moveable goods.

V: EPILOGUE

Whether it was the Haxey episode which jolted Richard into actively planning revenge on his old foes, or what effect his half-brother Thomas Holand's death had upon him, we cannot know. Another, possibly significant, event occurred on 3 June when William Montagu, earl of Salisbury, died, for he had been one of the men in Princess Joan's past [150]. By midsummer 1397 Richard should have been on top of the world. He had survived and surmounted both plebeian and aristocratic opposition, he had forged new friendships, pacified Ireland, negotiated peace for his generation, married into Europe's most prestigious family and acquired great wealth;[1] he had also strengthened the bonds of goodwill with his most powerful subject, and shown his mastery of parliament. Had Richard died in the summer of 1397 – or even a year later when he had killed and scattered his enemies in the 'revenge' parliament – he would surely have been regarded as a successful king, for these are all impressive achievements.

171. Richard II's will, 16 April 1399

Composed just before the second Irish expedition, this elaborately regal will was not executed by Richard's usurper. The preamble, in which Richard commended his soul to the Trinity, Virgin Mary, saints John the Baptist and Edward the Confessor, and acknowledged the certainty of death but the uncertainty of its hour, is entirely conventional.

A Collection of all the Wills, now known to be extant, of the Kings and Queens of England, ed. John Nicholas (London, 1780), 191–201.

[1.] First, being in purity and sincerity of the catholic faith, we leave to Almighty God our Creator, our soul which he has redeemed by his precious blood, and we commend it to him with the most intense devotion possible, with all the longing of our heart. But for our body, in whatever place we happen to leave this light, we choose a royal burial in the church of St Peter, Westminster, among our forefathers of famous memory, the kings of England; and we wish to be interred in that monument which we have had raised to our memory and that of

---

1 'the enormous dowry which the French marriage brought provided him with ample private financial resources for perhaps the first time in his reign', Fletcher (2008): 249.

Anne of glorious memory formerly queen of England, our consort, on whose soul may Almighty God have mercy. We wish the exequies of our burial or funeral to be celebrated in the royal manner thus, namely, for those exequies, four excellent hearses, appropriate for our royal funeral, should be honourably prepared in the places named below, agreed by our executors: on two of the hearses five fine and lovely lights, appropriate for royal exequies, should be placed, in two of the more important churches through which our body is carried; the third, with the same number of lights in the same way, should be honourably sited in the church of St Paul, London; the fourth, greater, more impressive and honourable, with brighter lights and in keeping with royal majesty, richly and magnificently adorned, should be placed at Westminster, at the executors' command and discretion.

[2.] Also we wish and ordain that our body should be carried to Westminster from the place where we happen to die, by [stages of] fourteen, fifteen or sixteen miles a day, where suitable lodging can be found. And throughout the whole journey twenty-four torches are to be carried, burning continuously around our bier, until the place where our cortège spends the night, at our executors' decision. There, each evening, as soon as the bier is set down, we wish the exequies for the dead to be solemnly sung, with a Mass the next day before the bier is moved from that place; twenty-four torches, both in the exequies and in this Mass, are always and continually to burn around the bier; and to these twenty-four torches should be added 100 burning torches while our bier is borne through the city of London. If we die within sixteen, fifteen, ten or even five miles, indeed anywhere outside our palace of Westminster, we wish that in twenty-four more important intermediate places (and if there are no intermediate places, in other suitable locations at our executors' discretion) such hearses shall be ordered for four continuous days with the aforementioned solemnities. If we die within our palace of Westminster, we wish that for four days solemn ceremonies shall be made, with one most solemn hearse, but on the last day the exequies are to be more magnificent. We wish further that – if, by unlucky chance, which may God in his mercy prevent – our body is snatched from men's sight by stormy or tempestuous seas or in any other way, and cannot be recovered, or we pay our debt to nature in such parts and regions that our body cannot be brought back to our realm of England because of obvious obstacles, all the aforementioned solemnities around our body, which are described in the present testament should be carried out, and especially on the monument, effigies and all the other works ordered for us and Anne of good memory formerly queen of England and France, our consort; also, the other funeral obsequies and all other observances are to be fully observed, unchanged.

[3.] We will and ordain that our body be clothed in white velvet or satin, in the royal manner, and also that it should be buried with a crown and sceptre regally gilded but, however, without any stones, and also there should be placed on our finger, in the royal manner, a ring with a precious stone worth twenty marks of our English money.

[4.] We will and ordain that each catholic king should have a gold cup or goblet, costing or valued at £45 of our English money; and that all gold crowns, cups, goblets, ewers and vessels, and other gold jewels whatsoever, and also all vestments with all the furnishings belonging to the chapel of our household, and the beds whatsoever, and all cloths of arras should remain for our successor, provided that our successor fully confirms our last will and our executors, and permits this our will to be executed completely and fully; and that he should ratify and confirm all the annuities and fees to household servants who continually served us and our person, who, with our permission, for good reasons such as illness or old age, have withdrawn from our service, and also those granted by us to those who later served us and still serve us, especially about our person, but at the free discretion of our successor and of our executors.

[5.] We will and ordain that the new fabric of the nave of the church of St Peter, Westminster, begun by us, should be completed by means of all our remaining jewels, that is, circlets, brooches and all other jewels whatsoever; and the rest, if any there be, shall remain with our executors to be disposed of according to this our last will. Further, we will and ordain that 6,000 gold marks be specially reserved for our funeral expenses and for carrying our body from the place where we happened to die, to Westminster.

[6.] We wish that lands, rents and tenements, as much as can suffice to support fifteen lepers and one chaplain, to celebrate for us in the church of St Peter at Westminster, be obtained; for doing this we order and bequeath 1,000 marks. We also will that our servants[2] who hitherto have been neither paid by us nor promoted,[3] if such there be, are remunerated first out of our goods up to the sum of 10,000 marks, at our executors' discretion.

2 *Servitores,* lower or menial servants.

3 Clerics who had not been presented to an ecclesiastical benefice by the king.

[7.] We leave to our dear nephew Thomas, duke of Surrey,[4] 10,000
marks, and to our dear brother Edward, duke of Aumâle,[5] 2,000 marks;
and to our dear brother John, duke of Exeter,[6] 3,000 marks; and to our
dear and faithful William Scrope, earl of Wiltshire,[7] 2,000 marks; and we
reserve 5,000 or 6,000 marks to our executors which are to be expended
on the more lavish support of the lepers and chaplains ordained in their
presence to celebrate for us at Westminster and Bermondsey.

[8.] We will and ordain that the rest of our gold – after the true debts
of our household, chamber and wardrobe have been paid, for payment
of which we leave £20,000 – should remain for our successor, provided
that he approves, ratifies and confirms, holds and causes to be held and
firmly observed all the statutes, ordinances, appointments and judgments
enacted, carried and returned in our parliament of 17 September, the
twenty-first year of our reign *[1397]* begun at Westminster, and in
the same parliament continued at Shrewsbury *[1398]*, and held there,
and all ordinances, judgments and appointments of 16 September, the
twenty-second year of our reign at Coventry *[1398]*, and afterwards
enacted, carried and returned at Westminster on 18 March that same
[regnal] year *[1399]*, made by the authority of that parliament, and
also all other ordinances and judgments which by the authority of that
parliament might in future be made, approved, ratified and confirmed,
held and caused to be held and firmly observed: otherwise, if our said
successor does not wish, or refuses, to do the aforesaid (which we do
not believe) we wish that Thomas, Edward, John and William, the said
dukes and earls – after paying the debts of our household, chamber
and wardrobe, 5,000 or 6,000 marks reserved as above for sustaining
and defending these statutes, appointments, ordinances and judgments,
according to their ability, even unto death if necessary – should have
and hold the residue. On these *[matters]* we burden the consciences of
each one of them, as they will wish to answer on the day of judgment.
For implementing all and every of the aforesaid, we ordain and depute
the sum of 91,000 marks, of which 65,000 are in the custody of John
Ikelington and 24,000 marks *[are]* in the hands and custody of our
dear nephew Thomas, duke of Surrey, from which sum we wish our

4 Thomas Holand, son of Richard's half-brother Thomas, so the king's half-nephew.
  Earl of Kent by inheritance, he was created duke of Surrey 29 Sept. 1397.

5 Edward, York's son, so Richard's cousin, created 29 Sept. 1397.

6 Richard's half-brother, John Holand.

7 Created 29 Sept. 1397; builder of Bolton castle, Wensleydale, Yorks., still an impressive fortress.

said nephew to be paid the 10,000 marks bequeathed to him above by us. And 2,000 marks' advance for the expenses of the household for the time when the reverend father Roger [Walden], archbishop of Canterbury, was made treasurer by us[8] are owed to us at present.

[9.] We wish all the jewels which came to us with our dearest consort Isabelle, queen of England and France, to remain entirely with her, if she survives us; that if we survive her, we wish those jewels to remain completely with us and our executors for the execution of this our last will.

[10.] We wish all garments and robes of our body, except pearls and precious stones, to remain with the clerks, valets and grooms who laboured and labour closely around our person, to be distributed amongst them according to our executors' discretion.

We nominate, create and depute as executors of this our testament the venerable fathers in Christ bishops Richard [Medford] of Salisbury, Edmund [Stafford] of Exeter, Tydman [Winchcombe] of Worcester, Thomas [Merks] of Carlisle and Guy [Mone] of St Davids; our dear brother Edward, duke of Aumâle, Thomas [Holand], duke of Surrey, our nephew, John [Holand], duke of Exeter, our brother, and William [Scrope], earl of Wiltshire, to each of whom we leave a gold goblet worth £20, and our dear masters Richard Clifford, keeper of our privy seal, William Ferriby[9] and John Ikelington,[10] clerks, and John Lufwick[11] and William Serle,[12] laymen. We wish each of them to have their expenses and necessary subsistence while they, or any of them, are occupied with the execution of this our testament, but at the discretion of their co-executors. We have charged and we charge all and singular of them that they should cause to be duly executed and fulfilled this our last will, as far as they can, as they will wish to answer before God. We create, ordain, depute and make as supervisors of this our

8 Walden was treasurer 20 Sept. 1395–Jan. 1398.

9 King's chief notary from Nov. 1397, he later supported the 1400 rebellion, Given-Wilson (1986): 179–81, 225.

10 'Clerk of the king's treasure at Holt' (Clwyd), Arundel's former castle, confiscated in 1397. Although implicated in the rebellion of 1400, Ikelyngton was pardoned by Henry IV and entered his service, Given-Wilson (1986): 90, 171–81, 225.

11 Lufwick (Lufwyk, Lowick), a king's esquire who was yeoman of the robes, then keeper of the privy wardrobe from Feb. 1396 and receiver of the chamber from Feb. 1398, Tout (1933): VI.37, 57.

12 A king's esquire, who, after taking part in the 1400 rebellion, escaped to Scotland, from where he plotted against Henry IV. He was recaptured in 1404 and barbarously executed, Given-Wilson (1986): 181–2, 229 and references.

testament the reverend fathers in Christ archbishops Roger [*Walden*] of Canterbury and Richard [*Scrope*] of York, William [*of Wykeham*], bishop of Winchester, and William [*Colchester*], abbot of Westminster Abbey, Edmund, duke of York, our uncle, and Henry [*Percy*], earl of Northumberland, our kinsman. We require and demand all and each of them, inasmuch as it concerns us in the Lord, that they should supervise this our last will and disposition duly and carefully, as will be needful, and cause to be demanded its due execution. The prelates should smite with ecclesiastical censure resisters or contradictors, and, as befits their office, should coerce and restrain them, as they will wish to answer to God. We leave and assign to each of these our supervisors a gold cup and ewer worth 40 marks.

In testimony of all and singular of the above-written last testament of ours we have caused the present page to be put in writing and sealed with our privy seal and signet, and have caused it to be strengthened by the affixing of our great seal and the subscription of our own hand.

The present testament was given, written and ordained in our palace at Westminster 16 April 1399, in the twenty-second year of our reign. Present: the reverend father Robert [*Braybrooke*], bishop of London, and the strong and noble men John [*Beaufort*], marquess of Dorset, Thomas [*Percy*], earl of Worcester, and others.

BIBLIOGRAPHY

Manuscripts

Lambeth Palace Library: Register of William Courtenay (Canterbury) I

Lincolnshire Archives Office: Lincoln Register 12 (Register of John Buckingham: Memoranda)

The National Archives: CP 40/490 (plea roll); E 159/166 (memoranda roll); E 364/36 rot. H (foreign accounts); SC 8/209/10448 (ancient petitions)

Westminster Abbey Muniments, No. 9584

Printed sources

Anglo-Norman Letters and Petitions, ed. M. Dominica Legge (Anglo-Norman Text Society, III, 1941)

Annales Monastici, vol. III: Annales Prioratus de Dunstaplia, Annales Monasterii de Bermundeseia, ed. H. R. Luard (RS, 36, 1866)

The Anonimalle Chronicle, 1331 to 1381, ed. V. H. Galbraith (Manchester, 1927)

Bennett, Michael, 'Edward III's entail and the succession to the crown, 1376–1471', *EHR* 103 (1998), 580–609

The Black Book of the Admiralty, ed. Travers Twiss (RS, 55, 1871)

A Book of London English, 1384–1425, ed. R. W. Chambers and M. Daunt (Oxford, 1931)

Border Ballads: A Selection, ed. James Reed (Manchester, 1991)

Bower, Walter, *Scotichronicon*, 8 vols., ed. D. E. R. Watt (Aberdeen, 1987–96)

The Brut, or the Chronicles of England, ed. F. W. D. Brie (Early English Text Society, original series, 131, 136, 1906, 1908)

A Calendar of the Register of Henry Wakefield Bishop of Worcester, 1375–95, ed. W. P. Marett (Worcestershire Historical Society, new series, 7, 1972)

Calendar of Close Rolls, 1385–9, 1389–92 (HMSO, 1921, 1922)

Calendar of Documents Relating to Scotland, ed. Joseph Bain, vol. IV (Edinburgh, 1888)

Calendar of Letter-Books of the City of London: Letter-Book H, ed. R. R. Sharpe (London, 1907)

Calendar of Entries in the Papal Registers relating to Great Britain and Ireland: Papal Letters IV, 1362–1404 (HMSO, 1902)

Calendar of Patent Rolls, 1374–76, 1377–81, 1385–9, 1391–6 (HMSO, 1916, 1895–1909)

Calendar of Select Pleas and Memoranda of the City of London, A.D. 1381–1412, ed. A. H. Thomas (Cambridge, 1932)

Chaplais, Pierre, *English Medieval Diplomatic Practice*, 2 vols. (London, 1982)

Chaucer's World, selected and trans. Edith Rickert (New York, 1948)

The Chronicle of Louth Park Abbey, ed. Edmund Venables (Horncastle, 1891)

Chronicles of London, ed. Charles Lethbridge Kingsford (Oxford, 1905)

Chronicles of the Revolution, 1397–1400, ed. and trans. Chris Given-Wilson (Manchester, 1993)

Chronicon Angliae, 1328–1388, ed. Edward Maunde Thompson (RS, 64, 1874)

Chronique du Religieux de Saint-Denys, ed. M. L. Bellaguet, repr. with new intro. by Bernard Guenée (Paris, 1994)

The Church in London, 1375–1392, ed. A. K. McHardy (London Record Society, 13, 1977)

Clarke, M. V. and Galbraith, V. H., 'The deposition of Richard II', *Bulletin of the John Rylands Library*, 14 (1930), 125–81

A Collection of all the Wills now known to be extant of the Kings and Queen of England, ed. John Nichols (London, 1780)

Curtis, Edmund, 'Unpublished letters from Richard II in Ireland, 1394–5', *Proceedings of the Royal Irish Academy* 37 (1927a), 276–303

Curtis, Edmund, *Richard II in Ireland* (Oxford, 1927b)

Davies, Richard G., 'Some notes from the register of Henry de Wakefield, bishop of Worcester on the political crisis of 1386–1388', *EHR* 86 (1971), 547–58

The Diplomatic Correspondence of Richard II, ed. Edouard Perroy (Camden Society, 3rd series, 15, 1933)

Dobson, R. B., ed. and trans., *The Peasants' Revolt of 1381*, 2nd edn (London, 1983)

English Gilds, ed. Lucy Toulmin Smith (Early English Text Society, original series, 140, 1870)

English Historical Documents IV: 1327–1485, ed. and trans. A. R. Myers (London, 1969)

Eulogium Historiarum sive Temporis: Continuatio Eulogii, ed. F. S. Haydon, vol. III (RS, 9, 1863)

Favent, Thomas, *Historia sive Narracio de modo et forma mirabilis parliamenti, ccclxxxvi*, ed. May McKisack, Camden Miscellany vol. 14 (Camden Society, 3rd series, 27, 1926), v–viii, 1–27

Flaherty, W. E., 'The Great Rebellion in Kent of 1381 illustrated from the public records', *Archaeologia Cantiana* III, 1860, 64–96

Flete, John, *History of Westminster Abbey*, ed. J. Armitage Robinson (Cambridge, 1909)

Foedera, Conventiones, Litterae, ed. Thomas Rymer, 1st edn, 20 vols. (London, 1704–35), 3rd edn, 10 vols. (The Hague, 1739–45)

Froissart, Jean, *Chronicles of England, France, Spain and the Adjoining Countries*, trans. Thomas Johnes, 2 vols. (London, 1839)

Froissart, Jean, *Chronicles*, selected and trans. Geoffrey Brereton (Harmondsworth, 1978)

Galloway, Andrew, trans. 'History or narration concerning the manner and form of the Miraculous Parliament, declared by Thomas Favent, clerk', in E. Steiner and C. Barrington, eds, *The Letter of the Law* (Ithaca NY, 2002), 231–52

Given-Wilson, C. J., 'Richard II and his grandfather's will', *EHR* 93 (1978), 320–37

Harvey, Barbara, 'Draft letters patent of manumission and pardon for the men of Somerset in 1381', *EHR* 80 (1965), 89–91

Historia et Cartularium Monasterii Sancti Petri Gloucestriae, vol. I, ed. W. H. Hart (RS, 33, 1863)

Historia Vitae et Regni Ricardi Secundi, ed. George B. Stow jr (Pennsylvania, 1977)

Illingworth, William, 'Copy of a libel against archbishop Neville, temp. Richard II', *Archaeologia* 16 (1812), 82–3

Issues of the Exchequer, trans. Frederick Devon (London, 1837)

The Kirkstall Abbey Chronicles, ed. J. Taylor (Thoresby Society, 42, 1952)

'The Kirkstall chronicle, 1355–1400', ed. M. V. Clarke and N. Denholm-Young, *Bulletin of the John Rylands Library*, 15 (1931), 100–37

Knighton, Henry, *Knighton's Chronicle, 1337–1396*, ed. and trans. G. H. Martin (Oxford, 1995)

Literae Cantuarienses, ed. J. Brigstocke Sheppard, III (RS, 1889)

Life of the Black Prince by the Herald of Sir John Chandos, ed. M. K. Pope and E. C. Lodge (Oxford, 1910)

Lopes, Fernão, *The English in Portugal, 1367–87*, ed. and trans. D. W. Lomax and F. J. Oakley (Warminster, 1989)

Maidstone, Richard, *Concordia: The Reconciliation of Richard II with London*, ed. D. R. Carlson, trans. A. G. Rigg (Kalamazoo MI, 2003)

Miscellaneous Irish Annals, ed. and trans. Séamus Ó hInnse (Dublin, 1947)

Pantin, W. A., 'A medieval treatise on letter-writing from Rylands MS 394', *Bulletin of the John Rylands Library* 13 (1929), 326–78

The Parliament Rolls of Medieval England, ed. C. Given-Wilson *et al.* (Leicester, 2005), CD-ROM version

Proceedings and Ordinances of the Privy Council, ed. H. H. Nicolas, 7 vols. (Record Commission, 1827–34)

Recueil des Actes de Jean IV, Duc de Bretagne, ed. Michael Jones, 2 vols. (Paris, 1980–3)

The Register of John Waltham bishop of Salisbury, 1388–1395, ed. T. C. B. Timmins (Canterbury and York Society, 80, 1994)

Riley, H. T., *Memorials of London and London Life in the XIII, XIV, and XV Centuries* (London, 1868)

A Roll of the Proceedings of the King's Council in Ireland for a portion of the sixteenth year of the Reign of Richard the Second A.D. 1392–3, ed. and trans. James Graves (RS, 69, 1877)

Rotuli Parliamentorum, 6 vols. (London, 1767–77)

Royal Commission on Historical Monuments, *London, vol. I, Westminster Abbey* (London, 1924)

The St. Alban's Chronicle, 1376–1422, 2 vols., ed. and trans. J. Taylor, W. F. Childs and L. Watkiss (Oxford, 2003, 2011)

Selections from English Wycliffite Writings, ed. Anne Hudson (Cambridge, 1978)

Somers' Tracts, ed. Walter Scott, 2nd edn, 13 vols. (London, 1809–15)

Statutes and Ordinances and Acts of the Parliament of Ireland, King John to Henry V, ed. Henry F. Berry (Dublin, 1907)

Statutes of the Realm, ed. A. Luders, T. E. Tomlins, J. Raithby *et al.*, 11 vols. (Record Commission, 1810–28)

The Stoneleigh Leger Book, ed. R. H. Hilton (Dugdale Society, 24, 1960)

Stow, John, *A Survey of London*, ed. C. L. Kingsford, 2 vols., repr. (Oxford, 1971)

Suggett, Helen, 'A letter describing Richard II's reconciliation with the City of London, 1392', *EHR* 62 (1947), 209–13

Thorne, William, *Chronica de rebus gestis Abbatum S. Augustini Cantuariae*, ed. Roger Twysden (Historiae Anglicanae Scriptores Decem, London 1652)

The Treaty of Bayonne (1388) with Preliminary Treaties of Trancoso (1387), ed. John Palmer and Brian Powell (Exeter Hispanic Texts, 47, 1988)

Usk, Adam, *The Chronicle of Adam Usk, 1377–1421*, ed. and trans. C. Given-Wilson (Oxford, 1997)

The Westminster Chronicle, 1381–1394, ed. and trans. L. C. Hector and B. F. Harvey (Oxford, 1982)

Walsingham, Thomas, *Gesta Abbatum Monasterii Sancti Albani*, ed. H. T. Riley, 3 vols. (RS, 28, 1867–9)

Wykeham's Register, ed. T. F. Kirby, 2 vols. (Hampshire Record Society, 1896, 1899)

Secondary works

Alexander, Jonathan, and Binski, Paul, eds, *The Age of Chivalry: Art in Planta-genet England, 1200–1400* (London, 1987)

Aston, Margaret, *Thomas Arundel* (Oxford, 1967)

Aston, Margaret, '*Corpus Christi* and *Corpus Regni*: heresy and the Peasants' Revolt', *Past and Present* 143 (1994), 3–47

Baker, John H., *The Order of Serjeants at Law: A chronicle of creations with historical texts and a historic introduction* (Selden Society supplementary series 5, 1984)

Bellamy, J. G., 'The northern rebellions in the later years of Richard II', *Bulletin of the John Rylands Library* 47 (1964–5), 254–74

Bennett, Michael, 'The royal succession and the crisis of 1406', in G. Dodd and D. Biggs, eds, *The Reign of Henry IV: Rebellion and Survival, 1403–13* (York, 2008), 9–27

Biggs, Douglas, '"A wrong whom conscience and kindred bid me right": a reassessment of Edmund Langley, Duke of York, and the usurpation of Henry IV', *Albion* 26 (1994), 253–72

Bird, Ruth, *The Turbulent London of Richard II* (London, 1949)

Boardman, Stephen, *The Early Stuart Kings: Robert II and Robert III, 1371–1406* (East Linton, 1997)

Brown, F. A., Colvin, H. M. and Taylor, A. J., *The History of the King's Works*, 3 vols. (London, 1963)

Catto, J. I., 'An alleged great council of 1374', *EHR* 83 (1967), 764–71

Clanchy, M. T., 'The franchise of return of writs', *TRHS*, 5th series, 17 (1967), 59–82

Clementi, Dione, 'Richard II's ninth question to the judges', *EHR* 86 (1971), 96–115

Cockayne, G. E., *The Complete Peerage of England, Scotland, Ireland*, new edn rev. Vicary Gibbs *et al.*, 12 vols. (London, 1910–59)

Collins, Hugh E. L., *The Order of the Garter, 1348–1461* (Oxford, 2000)

Connolly, Philomena, *Medieval Record Sources* (Maynooth Research Guides for Irish Local History, 4, 2002)

Curtis, Edmund, 'Janico Dartas, Richard the Second's "Gascon Esquire": his career in Ireland', *Journal of the Royal Society of Antiquaries of Ireland*, 73 (1933), 182–205

Davies, R. R., *Conquest, Coexistence and Change: Wales, 1063–1415* (Oxford, 1987)

De Vries, Kelly, 'The reasons for the Bishop of Norwich's attack on Flanders in 1383', *Fourteenth Century England* III (2004), ed. W. M. Ormrod, 155–65

Dodd, Gwilym, 'Patronage, petitions and grace: the "chamberlains' bills" of Henry IV's reign', in G. Dodd and D. Biggs, eds, *The Reign of Henry IV: rebellion and survival, 1403–13* (York, 2008a), 105–35

Dodd, Gwilym, 'Richard II and the fiction of majority rule', in C. Beem, ed., *The Royal Minorities of Medieval and Early Modern England* (New York/Basingstoke, 2008b), 103–59.

Dodd, Gwilym, 'Was Thomas Favent a political pamphleteer? Faction and politics in later fourteenth-century London', *Journal of Medieval History* 30 (2011), 1–22

Du Boulay, F. R. H., *The Lordship of Canterbury: An Essay on Medieval Society* (London, 1966)

Du Boulay, F. R. H. and Barron, C. M., eds, *The Reign of Richard II: Essays in Honour of May McKisack* (London, 1971)

Düll, Siegrid, Luttrell, A. and Keen, M., 'Faithful unto death: the tomb slab of Sir William Neville and Sir John Clanvowe, Constantinople 1391', *The Antiquaries Journal* 71 (1991), 174–90

Emden, A. B., *Biographical Register of the University of Cambridge* (Cambridge, 1963)

Emden, A. B., *Biographical Register of the University of Oxford*, 3 vols. (Oxford, 1957–9)

Fletcher, Christopher, *Richard II: Manhood, Youth and Politics, 1377–99* (Oxford, 2008)

Forrest, Ian, *The Detection of Heresy in late Medieval England* (Oxford, 2005)

Gillespie, James L., 'Thomas Mortimer and Thomas Molineux: Radcot Bridge and the appeal of 1397', *Albion* 7 (1975), 161–73

Given-Wilson, C., *The Royal Household and the King's Affinity: Service, Politics and Finance in England, 1360–1413* (New Haven CT, 1986)

Given-Wilson, C., 'Wealth and credit, public and private: the earls of Arundel, 1306–1397', *EHR* 106 (1991), 1–26

Goodman, Anthony, *The Loyal Conspiracy: The Lords Appellant under Richard II* (London, 1971)

Goodman, Anthony, *Katherine Swynford* (Lincoln, 1994)

Goodman, Anthony, and Tuck, Anthony, eds, *War and Border Societies in the Middle Ages* (London, 1992)

Gordon, Dillian, Monnas, L. and Elam C., eds, *The Regal Image of Richard II and the Wilton Diptych* (London, 1997)

Green, David, *The Black Prince* (Stroud, 2001)

Green, David, 'Masculinity and medicine: Thomas Walsingham and the death of the Black Prince', *Journal of Medieval History* 35 (2009), 34–51

Handbook of British Chronology, ed. E. B. Fryde, D. E. Greenway, S. Porter and I. Roy, 3rd edn (London, 1985)

Harvey, Margaret, *The English in Rome, 1362–1420: Portrait of an Expatriate Community* (Cambridge, 1999)

Haskett, Timothy S., "'I have ordeyned and make my testament and last wylle in this forme": English as a testamentary language, 1387–1450', *Medieval Studies* 58 (1996), 149–206

Hay, Denys, 'The division of the spoils of war in fourteenth-century England', *Transactions of the Royal Historical Society*, 5th ser. 4 (1954), 91–109

Holmes, George, *The Good Parliament* (Oxford, 1975)

Hudson, Anne, *The Premature Reformation: Wycliffite Texts and Lollard History* (Oxford, 1988)

Jones, Michael, *Ducal Brittany, 1364–1399* (Oxford, 1970)

Jones, Richard H., *The Royal Policy of Richard II: Absolutism in the Later Middle Ages* (Oxford, 1968)

Jurkowski, M., Smith, C. L. and Crook, D., *Lay Taxes in England and Wales, 1188–1688* (Kew: Public Record Office Handbook, 31, 1998)

Keen, M. H., 'Treason trials under the law of arms', *TRHS* 5th ser. 12 (1962), 85–103

Kenny, Anthony, ed., *Wyclif in his Times* (Oxford, 1986)

Kipling, Gordon, *Enter the King: Theatre, Liturgy and Ritual in the Medieval Civic Triumph* (Oxford, 1998)

Leach, A. F., 'A clerical strike at Beverley Minster in the fourteenth century', *Archaeologia* 55 (1896–7), 1–20

Lewis, N. B., 'The "continual council" in the early years of Richard II, 1377–80', *EHR* 41 (1926), 246–51

Lewis, N. B., 'Simon Burley and Baldwin of Raddington', *EHR* 52 (1937), 662–9

Lindenbaum, S., 'The Smithfield tournament of 1390', *Journal of Medieval and Renaissance Studies* 20 (1990), 1–20

Logan, F. Donald, *Runaway Religious in Medieval England, c. 1240–1540* (Cambridge, 1996)

Macdonald, Alastair, J., *Border Bloodshed: Scotland, England and France at War, 1369–1403* (East Linton, 2000)

McFarlane, K. B., *Lancastrian Kings and Lollard Knights* (Oxford, 1972)

McHardy, A. K, 'The effects of war on the Church: the case of the alien priories in the fourteenth century', in M. Jones and M. Vale, eds, *England and her Neighbours, 1066–1453: Essays in Honour of Pierre Chaplais* (London, 1989), 277–95

McHardy, A. K., 'Haxey's case, 1397: the petition and its presenter reconsidered', in J. L. Gillespie, ed., *The Age of Richard II* (Stroud, 1997), 93–114

McHardy, A. K., 'Richard II: a personal portrait', in Gwilym Dodd, ed., *The Reign of Richard II* (Stroud, 2000), 11–32

McHardy, A. K., *The Age of War and Wycliffe: Lincoln Diocese and its Bishop in the later Fourteenth Century* (Lincoln, 2001a)

McHardy, A. K., 'Some reflections on Edward III's use of propaganda', in J. S. Bothwell, ed., *The Age of Edward III* (Woodbridge, 2001b), 171–89

McHardy, A. K., 'John Scarle: ambition and politics in the late medieval Church', in L. Clark, M. Jurkowski and C. Richmond, eds, *Image, Text and Church, 1380–1600: Essays for Margaret Aston* (Toronto, 2009), 69–93

McKisack, May, *The Fourteenth Century, 1307–1399* (Oxford, 1959)

Macy, Gary, *The Theologies of the Eucharist in the Early Scholastic Period* (Oxford, 1984)

Mathew, Gervase, *The Court of Richard II* (London, 1968)

Maxfield, David K., 'St. Anthony's Hospital, London: a pardoner-supported alien priory, 1219–1461', in J. L. Gillespie, ed., *The Age of Richard II* (Stroud, 1997), 225–47

Morgan, P., *War and Society in Medieval Cheshire, 1277–1403* (Chetham Society, 3rd ser., 34, 1987)

Mott, R. A. K., 'A study in the distribution of patronage, 1389–99', *Proceedings of the Leeds Philosophical and Literary Society*, Literary and Historical Section, 15 (1974), 113–33

Myers, J. N. L., 'The campaign of Radcot Bridge in December 1387', *EHR* 42 (1927), 20–33

Neville, Cynthia J., *Violence, Custom and Law: The Anglo-Scottish Border Lands in the Later Middle Ages* (Edinburgh, 1998)

Nicholas, David, *Medieval Flanders* (London, 1992)

Nightingale, Pamela, *A Medieval Mercantile Community: The Grocers' Company & the Politics & Trade of London, 1000–1485* (Yale, 1995)

Nijsten, Gerard, *In the Shadow of Burgundy: The Court of Guelders in the Late Middle Ages* (Cambridge, 2004)

Oliver, Clementine C., 'A political pamphleteer in late medieval England: Thomas Fovent, Geoffrey Chaucer, Adam Usk, and the merciless parliament of 1388', *New Medieval Literatures* 6 (2003), 167–98

Oliver, Clementine, *Parliament and Political Pamphleteering in Fourteenth-Century England* (York, 2010)

Ormrod, W. M., 'Government by commission: the continual council of 1386 and English royal administration', *Peritia: Journal of the Medieval Academy of Ireland* 10 (1996), 303–2

Ormrod, W. M., 'In bed with Joan of Kent: the king's mother and the Peasants' Revolt', in J. Wogan Browne *et al.*, eds, *Medieval Women: Texts and Contexts in late Medieval Britain* (Turnhout, 2000), 277–92

Owst, G. R., *Literature and Pulpit in Medieval England*, 2nd edn repr. (Oxford, 1966)

The Oxford Dictionary of National Biography, ed. H. G. C. Matthew and B. Harrison (Oxford, 2004), online at http://oxforddnb.com

The Oxford English Dictionary, 24 vols. (Oxford, 1971)

Palmer, J. J. N., 'Articles for a final peace between England and France, 16 June 1393', *BIHR* 29 (1966), 180–5

Palmer, J. J. N., 'The impeachment of Michael de la Pole in 1386', *BIHR*, 42 (1969), 97–101

Palmer, J. J. N., 'The background to Richard II's marriage to Isabel of France (1396)', *BIHR* 44 (1971a), 1–17

Palmer, J. J. N., 'The parliament of 1385 and the constitutional crisis of 1386', *Speculum* 46 (1971b), 477–90

Palmer, J. J. N., *England, France and Christendom, 1377–99* (London, 1972)

Perroy, E., 'Gras profits et rançons pendant la guerre de cent ans: L'affaire du comte de Denia', in *Mélanges d'Histoire du Moyen Âge dedies á la Memoire de Louis Halphen* (Paris, 1951), 573–80

Phillpotts, Christopher John, 'John of Gaunt and English policy towards France, 1389–1395', *Journal of Medieval History* 19 (1990), 363–87

Powell, Edward, 'Jury trial at gaol delivery in the late middle ages: the midland circuit, 1400–1429', in J. S. Cockburn and T. A. Green, eds, *Twelve Good Men and True: The Criminal Trial Jury in England, 1200–1800* (Princeton NJ, 1988)

Prestwich, Michael, *The Three Edwards: War and State in England, 1272–1377* (London, 1980)

Raban, Sandra, *Mortmain Legislation and the English Church, 1279–1500* (Cambridge, 1982)

Ramsay, Nigel, 'Retained legal counsel, c.1275–c.1475', *TRHS* 5th series 35 (1985), 95–112

Robinson, J. Armitage, 'An unrecognized Westminster chronicler', *Proceedings of the British Academy* iii (1907–8), 61–92

Rogers, A., 'Hoton versus Shakell: A ransom case in the court of chivalry', *Nottingham Medieval Studies* 6 (1962), 74–108; 7 (1963), 53–78

Rogers, James E. Thorold, *A History of Agriculture and Prices in England, 1259–1793*, vol. 2 (Oxford, 1866)

Roskell, J. S., *The Impeachment of Michael de la Pole Earl of Suffolk in 1386 in the context of the reign of Richard II* (Manchester, 1984)

Roskell, J. S., Clarke, L. and Rawcliffe, C., *History of Parliament: The House of Commons, 1386–1421*, 4 vols. (London, 1992)

Russell, P. E., *The English Intervention in Spain and Portugal in the time of Edward III and Richard II* (Oxford, 1955)

Sainty, Sir John, *The Judges of England, 1272–1990* (Selden Society supplementary series 10, 1993)

Sass, Lorna, *To the King's Taste* (London, 1976)

Saul, Nigel, *Richard II* (New Haven CT, 1997)

Saul, Nigel, 'Richard II and chivalric kingship' (Royal Holloway, Egham, 1999)

Scattergood, V. J. and Sherborne, J. W., *English Court Culture in the later Middle Ages* (London, 1983)

Schofield, Roger S. 'The geographical distribution of wealth in England, 1334–1649', *Economic History Review*, 2nd ser. 18 (1965), 483–510

Smith, Charles W., 'A conflict of interest? Chancery clerks in private service', in J. Rosenthal and C. Richmond, eds, *People, Politics and Community in the Later Middle Ages* (Gloucester, 1987), 176–91

Steel, Anthony, *Richard II* (Cambridge, 1941, repr. 1962)

Stow, George B., 'Richard II in Jean Froissart's *Chroniques*', *Journal of Medieval History* 11 (1985), 333–45

Stow, George B., 'The continuation of the *Eulogium Historiarum*: some revisionist perspectives', *EHR* 119 (2004), 667–81

Strohm, Paul, with an appendix by A. J. Prescott, *Hochon's Arrow: The Social Imagination of Fourteenth-Century Texts* (Princeton NJ, 1992)

Talbot, C. H. and Hammond, E. A., *The Medical Practitioners of Medieval England: A Biographical Register* (London, 1965)

Taylor, John, *English Historical Literature in the Fourteenth Century* (Oxford, 1987)

Tout, T. F., *Chapters in the Administrative History of Mediaeval England*, 6 vols. (Manchester, 1920–33)

Tuck, Anthony, 'The Cambridge parliament of 1388', *EHR*, 84 (1969), 225–43

Tuck, Anthony, *Richard II and the English Nobility* (London, 1973)

Vernon Harcourt, L. W., *His Grace the Steward and the Trial of Peers* (London, 1907)

Victoria History of the Counties of England

Walker, David M., *The Oxford Companion to Law* (Oxford, 1980)

Walker, Simon, *The Lancastrian Affinity, 1361–1399* (Oxford, 1990)

Walker, Simon, 'Janico Dartasso: chivalry, nationality and the man-at-arms', *History* 84 (1999), 31–51

Warren, W. L. 'A reappraisal of Simon Sudbury, bishop of London and archbishop of Canterbury', *Journal of Ecclesiastical History* (1959), 139–52

Wentersdorf, K. P., 'The clandestine marriages of the Fair Maid of Kent', *Journal of Medieval History*, 5 (1979), 203–31

Wilks, Michael, ed. Anne Hudson, *Wyclif: Political Ideas and Practice* (Oxbow, Oxford, 2000)

Woolgar, C. M., *The Great Household in Late Medieval England* (New Haven CT, 2000)

Workman, Herbert B., *John Wyclif: A Study of the English Medieval Church*, 2 vols. (Oxford, 1926)

INDEX